THE GREAT DEPRESSION IN LATIN AMERICA

The Great Depression in Latin America

Paulo Drinot and Alan Knight, editors

DUKE UNIVERSITY PRESS *Durham and London* 2014

© 2014 Duke University Press
All rights reserved
Printed in the United States of America on acid-free paper ∞
Typeset in Carter & Cone Galliard
by Tseng Information Systems, Inc.

Library of Congress Cataloging-
in-Publication Data
The Great Depression in Latin America /
Paulo Drinot and Alan Knight, editors.
pages cm
Includes index.
ISBN 978-0-8223-5738-4 (cloth : alk. paper)
ISBN 978-0-8223-5750-6 (pbk. : alk. paper)
1. Depressions—1929—Latin America.
2. Latin America—Economic conditions—
20th century. I. Drinot, Paulo.
II. Knight, Alan, 1946–
HB37171929.G687 2014
330.98′0033—dc23
2014008714

Cover art: Lino Enea Spilimbergo,
Arrabal de Buenos Aires, 1933.
Courtesy of the artist's estate.

CONTENTS

ACKNOWLEDGMENTS

This volume began to take shape at a conference convened by Paulo Drinot at the School of Advanced Study, University of London, in July 2011. The editors gratefully acknowledge the support of Maxine Molyneux, then director of the Institute for the Study of the Americas, and of the School of Advanced Study, which made the event possible. We also would like to thank Peter Fearon and Laurence Brown, who contributed papers to the original conference, and Rory Miller, Colin Lewis, and Rosemary Thorp, among others, who offered helpful critiques of the conference papers. We are particularly grateful to Valerie Millholland and Gisela Fosado at Duke University Press for their interest in and support for this book project. Thanks too to Liz Smith for shepherding the volume to publication, to Heather Hensley for designing the book's cover, and to Gonzalo Romero Sommer for the index. Two anonymous reviewers provided extremely valuable suggestions and helped make the volume a great deal better. Finally, the editors gratefully acknowledge the support of the Latin American Centre at the University of Oxford and the Institute of the Americas at University College London.

Remembering the toxic atmosphere he lived through in his teenage years in Weimar Berlin, Eric Hobsbawm wrote in his autobiography, "The collapse of the world economy was up to a point something young persons of the middle class read about, rather than experienced directly. But the world economic crisis was like a volcano, generating political eruptions. . . . Eruption was in the air we breathed."[1] As is well known, the political eruptions in Europe led, albeit neither directly nor inexorably, to the Nazi seizure of power and the Second World War. In Latin America, the world economic crisis of the 1930s also sparked, or added fuel to, political eruptions from the Rio Grande to Tierra del Fuego. In most countries, governments of the Right and Left fell and were replaced, typically, by governments of the opposite persuasion. In the Southern Cone, for example, the reformist government of Arturo Alessandri in Chile replaced the military regime of Carlos Ibañez. Across the cordillera, the reformist government of Hipolito Yrigoyen in Argentina was replaced by the military dictatorship of General José F. Uriburu. As in Europe, in some cases these political eruptions resulted in military conflicts, such as the Leticia War between Peru and Colombia (1931–32) and, on a far greater scale, the Chaco War (1932–35), which saw Bolivia lose a large proportion of its territory to Paraguay.[2] As in Europe too, these political eruptions also brought about, or accelerated, economic, social, and cultural transformations, including, and perhaps most importantly, a transformation in the role of the state.

This volume explores these transformations as part of a broader examination of the impact of the Great Depression in Latin America. The current global financial crisis, which began in 2007, has produced a new vantage point from which to reassess the history of what remains (although that may change) the deepest economic crisis of the modern era.[3] As one of the key historical processes of the twentieth century, it is no surprise that, time and again since the 1930s, historians as well as economists and policy makers looking to draw lessons and devise policy responses applicable to more recent economic crises (and future crises) have chosen to examine the Great Depression in some detail.[4] Indeed, interpretations of both the causes of the Great Depression and the factors that led to recovery are at the heart of ongoing debates between monetarists and Keynesians, which have acquired fresh currency today in the context of the so-called Great Recession.[5] Since the 1930s, economic historians and historically inclined economists, including key figures in the current economic crisis such as Federal Reserve chairman Ben Bernanke (whose *Essays on the Great Depression* is now in its fifth edition), have fundamentally shaped these debates. As Bernanke notes, "To understand the Great Depression is the Holy Grail of macroeconomics."[6]

Meanwhile, social, political, and even cultural historians, who largely agree on the centrality of the Great Depression to broader global historical processes since the 1930s, have sought to widen the focus beyond the economic collapse itself (or the debates on how recovery was achieved) to examine the ways in which the slump influenced social, political, and cultural processes around the world. In the European context, of course, the Great Depression is at the heart of interpretations of the origins of the Second World War and the making of the postwar welfare state.[7] In the context of U.S. historiography, the Great Depression has prompted countless studies and has been extensively raked over, not least at the regional and local level. By way of contrast, the Latin American historiography is patchier, and despite the importance of the crisis to the economic and sociopolitical history of most countries, few systematic studies of the Great Depression have been published. Indeed, Rosemary Thorp's edited volume on the economic history of the Great Depression, originally published in 1984, remains one of the few book-length studies to explicitly address the slump and to do so in comparative cross-national terms.[8] An earlier collection, edited by Pablo González Casanova, included useful studies of a range of countries that combined economic history perspectives with a broader political angle.[9] However, in the past few decades there has been much new scholarship that examines, albeit often indirectly, both the economic history and the broader social and political consequences of the Great Depression in Latin America.[10]

The chapters in this volume, therefore, build on an extensive literature on the Great Depression but also address processes associated with the slump that have received less systematic attention in previous cross-country studies. There is broad consensus among historians that the Great Depression was a watershed for Latin America. The direct economic impact of the slump varied from country to country. Some Latin American countries, such as Chile, were particularly badly hit, as were many economies in the Caribbean, notably Cuba, but most countries recovered their pre-1929 GDP levels by the mid-1930s.[11] They did so, as Victor Bulmer-Thomas has suggested, at different speeds and in different ways (with different sectors of the economy playing different roles in the recovery of each country).[12] However, arguably, Latin America as a whole weathered the Depression better than its neighbors to the north. In the United States, of course, the slump was catastrophic, with sharp drops in employment, and it brought about a significant shift in economic policy under Franklin D. Roosevelt, characterized by state intervention (the New Deal) and protectionism (with the Smoot-Hawley Act of 1930). Dealt a massive blow by collapsing commodity prices, Canada similarly experienced mass unemployment, perhaps affecting as much as 50 percent of the adult population, and, like its neighbor to the south, adopted New Deal–type reforms to address the impact of the slump. However, as late as 1939, Canada, like the United States, had still not recovered its pre-slump GDP level.[13]

Beyond the direct economic impact, as in Europe and the United States, and indeed as in Africa and Asia, in Latin America too the slump set in motion, or accelerated, a number of broader processes.[14] Of course, establishing the direct causal relation between an economic phenomenon such as the Great Depression and social, political, or indeed cultural processes is far from straightforward.[15] In the case of Africa, historians have debated the extent to which the Great Depression's impact on the continent resulted in a weakening or strengthening of the colonial economic system (particularly in terms of the expansion of commodity production at the expense of a "traditional" agricultural sector) and whether, because of the colonial authorities' attempts to extract further revenue from colonial subjects at a time of economic downturn, the slump stimulated protest and accelerated the process of decolonization that would gain traction after the end of the Second World War.[16] In the case of Asia, similarly, historians have debated the extent to which the slump contributed to the rise of nationalism in India and much of Southeast Asia, where the slump impacted on the colonial economy and, as in Africa, sharpened tensions between colonial authorities and colonial subjects.[17] In the case of Japan, historians argue, the relatively successful proto-Keynesian management of the slump occurred in a context of growing nationalist militarism boosted by the perceived bankruptcy of liberal democracies represented by the Great Depression.[18] Regarding China, there is some debate on the economic impact of the Great Depression, with some authors suggesting that regions that were effectively delinked from the world economy were not greatly affected. By contrast, the impact of the Great Depression was greater in the eastern coastal cities, such as Shanghai and Hong Kong, which were more firmly inserted into the world economy.[19] More generally, historians tend to attribute the major transformations that occurred in China in the post-Depression era to the impact of the 1931 Japanese occupation of Manchuria and the 1937 total war with the nationalist government rather than to the slump itself.

In the United States, historians roughly agree that the Great Depression and its chief legacy, the New Deal, brought about major political and institutional change. The slump engendered what Emily Rosenberg has called a "regulatory state" and extended the reach of federal government while strengthening the executive branch.[20] Moreover, as Maldwyn Jones notes, the Great Depression brought about a major political realignment: "By constructing a coalition that included the South, the big-city Northern machines, organized labor, the intelligentsia, and the underprivileged, it ensured that the Democrats replaced the Republicans as the normal majority party." Finally, though wealth and income were unaffected, Jones contends, "the New Deal redistributed power between capital and labor."[21] In short, the Great Depression and the New Deal reshaped U.S. society profoundly and lastingly. In the late 1980s, Anthony J. Badger noted, "It is not surprising that Americans today cannot escape the memories of the 1930s: they work out their lives in a political economy that still bears the imprint of Franklin D. Roosevelt's New Deal."[22] Such memories were particularly evident in recent debates over President Barack Obama's social policy initiatives, particularly "Obamacare."[23] Most recently, Ira Katznelson has suggested that the New Deal was a pivotal moment not only for modern U.S. history but also for the history of modern liberal democracy. The New Deal, Katznelson argues, addressed the fear that undergirded the dictatorships of the Right and the Left and at the same time demonstrated that liberal democracy had a future despite the collapse of the capitalist economy: "Of the New Deal's many achievements, none was more important than the demonstration that liberal democracy . . . could govern effectively in the face of great danger . . . that not all attempts at nonrevolutionary reform need fail."[24]

General accounts of the impact of the Great Depression on Latin America have similarly tended to view the slump as a point of both economic *and* political inflection characterized by a shift from export-led growth to import substitution industrialization (ISI) in the economic sphere and from oligarchic to populist rule in the political sphere. In his survey of the global impact of the Depression, for example, Dietmar Rothermund views populism as the main political consequence of the slump in the region.[25] This is a view repeated in Robert Findlay and Kevin O'Rourke's recent survey of the world economy: "The result across much of Latin America was populism, with urban workers and capitalists combining to seize power from the traditionally outward oriented landowning elites."[26] In recent decades, historians have revised these accounts, put forward originally if not exclusively by scholars working from a perspective influenced by dependency theory.[27] The Great Depression certainly had a decisive impact on economic thought in Latin America, and the structuralism pioneered in the 1940s at ECLA/CEPAL by Raúl Prebisch was a direct product of how Prebisch and others interpreted the slump.[28] But the slump did not bring about a major shift in the region's economic orientation from export-led growth to ISI. Economic historians have shown that in those few countries where ISI took place it did so usually in conjunction with a resurgence of (not in lieu of) the export sector.[29] Similarly, social and political historians have challenged the idea that the post-1930s political history of the region can be reduced to the emergence of a form of politics characterized by the successful co-option or "incorporation" of popular forces (particularly of urban working- and middle-class sectors) by charismatic populist leaders such as Lázaro Cárdenas in Mexico, Getúlio Vargas in Brazil, and, after a decade-long lag, Juan Domingo Perón in Argentina.[30]

In short, neither ISI nor populism adequately accounts for the range of processes that the Great Depression either set in motion or accelerated. Certainly, the slump created a political and ideological context favorable to change, although the direction of change varied from country to country. Of course, some broad patterns in how contemporaries understood the Great Depression, particularly in relation to what it implied for the status quo, are discernible and help account for the divergent political processes that shaped Latin America in the post-Depression period. For the "outs" of the old order the Great Depression showed that the foundations upon which that order had been built were profoundly shaky and that the moment was ripe for major change, even outright revolution. For the "ins" of the old order, the Great Depression forced a reassessment of the assumptions and hierarchies that had underpinned their privilege, if only to avoid more drastic and uncontrolled change. The social agitation and mobilization of new political forces, particularly of the Left, that either emerged or gained traction in the context of the Great Depression throughout the region often resulted in the establishment of authoritarian regimes (for example, in Argentina, Brazil, Cuba, and Peru), or the further strengthening of military rule (as in much of Central America), or, in a few cases, the development of reformist policies that aimed at both addressing social demands and weakening more radical alternatives. In several countries, repression and (social) reformism were combined with some success.

Indeed, historians tend to agree that one of the key consequences of the Great Depression was a strengthening of the state. But this was not simply a case of creeping protectionism. Throughout the world, in both liberal democratic and authoritarian contexts, the impact of the Great Depression strengthened the idea that the state had a role to play in managing the economy and society.[31] Indeed, several post-Depression governments in Latin America, much as Franklin D. Roosevelt's did in the United States, implemented economic and social policies that, however halting and inadequate, nevertheless signaled a new departure in terms not only of economic policy but more generally of nation building and state formation.[32] A new emphasis on "state action" emerged equally in countries that were governed by the Right and by the Left and included policies developed by progressive governments such as those of Lázaro Cárdenas in Mexico and Arturo Alessandri in Chile and by conservative governments such as those of Getúlio Vargas in Brazil and Oscar Benavides in Peru. Such developments, which Peter Temin refers to as "socialism in many countries," were obviously not exclusive to Latin America or Roosevelt's United States.[33] In many ways, Latin American countries both reacted and in turn contributed to a wave of new "social politics" that swept much of the world during the 1930s. While historians have paid attention to this wave's impact on the North Atlantic economies, they have yet to examine it in similar detail in the case of Latin America, or indeed to pay sufficient attention to the transnational dimensions of the process and to how different countries at once reacted to and inserted themselves into the new social politics of the post-Depression period.[34]

The social politics of the 1930s, in Latin America as elsewhere, were to a significant extent a response to the ways in which the slump appeared, to many national elites, through its effect on employment and, more broadly, on the social welfare of Latin American populations, to sharpen class conflict and create the potential for revolutionary political change by increasing the appeal of radical political movements. In many countries, the Great Depression had a devastating impact on laboring peoples, particularly those that worked in export industries that collapsed, such as nitrate workers in Chile or sugar workers in Cuba, and unemployment soared in such sectors. Even in societies with large subsistence sectors, such as Mexico and Peru, or much of Central America, where in the past economic crises had been weathered by drawing on subsistence agriculture, the slump's impact was noticeable in the countryside. In the cities and export enclaves, a broad-based working class of blue-collar workers in a range of industries from Mexico all the way down to Argentina was particularly affected. But an arguably even more diverse middle class of white-collar workers was equally affected, as jobs were shed, wages were cut, and livelihoods were threatened.[35] In this context, radical political projects of both the Right and the Left, but particularly of the Left, gained considerable traction in most Latin American countries and threatened to challenge severely the status quo. The social politics of the 1930s, which consisted primarily of social programs and social legislation that attempted to alleviate the impact of the slump on working peoples, constituted one element, along with outright repression, that elites drew on to contain popular discontent and undermine the appeal of Communist and other radical movements throughout the region. However, the social politics of the 1930s were not merely reactive. They were also expressive of broader, indeed transnational, shifts in understandings of state–society relations.

As elsewhere in the world, the advent of a new social politics in post-Depression Latin America was a clearly gendered process. Some years ago, Linda Gordon suggested that in the United States the shift in paradigm for social assistance from charity to social security, a shift precipitated by the Great Depression and consolidated through the 1935 U.S. Social Security Act, was accompanied by a rhetorical shift from needs (associated with the private sphere and women's social activism) to rights (associated with the public sphere and male legislative action). The same was true of several Latin American countries, including Argentina, Chile, and Peru, which during the 1930s began to establish the foundations of social welfare systems. In such processes, typically, social assistance and social protection initiatives pioneered in early years by women activists were either co-opted or sidelined by the new state institutions established to protect and "improve" the population. Typically, also, the establishment of such institutions promoted a gendered order in the workplace, since social reformers sought, through the particular ways in which the new institutions operated, to ensure the establishment and well-being of households headed by male breadwinners and female housekeepers. The extent to which the Great Depression brought marked shifts in employment ratios between men and women is difficult to assess given the paucity of data (although some evidence suggests that women were often the first to be laid off) but also because, with some exceptions such as textile manufacturing, it was rare to find men and women employed in the same industries (or, put differently, many industries were gender specific). But what is discernible is the emergence of a new gendered post-Depression discourse, shaped by the new social politics in Latin America, and elsewhere around the world, that sought to place men in the workplace and women in the home.[36]

If both the impact of and the responses to the Great Depression were gendered, they also were racialized. As in the United States, where Depression-era unemployment rates among African Americans were much higher than among whites and where racism often broke down labor solidarity, in much of Latin America too race shaped how the slump was experienced.[37] In the circum-Caribbean black labor migrants from Jamaica, Trinidad, Haiti, and other islands were among the first to be laid off in the sugar and banana industries. In Costa Rica, for example, "anti-black racism pervaded the demands of Hispanic workers and the posturing of Costa Rican planters alike in the 1930s and found direct expression in the 1934 law that forbade the employment of 'colored people' on United Fruit's new Pacific Coast plantations."[38] In Peru, anti-Asian sentiments reached new heights and translated into the introduction of labor laws that implicitly targeted workers of Japanese background.[39] In Mexico, similar laws explicitly targeted the Chinese, and anti-Chinese racism, both bottom-up and top-down, culminated in the expulsions of tens of thousands of Chinese in 1931.[40] In much of the region, anti-Semitism, always present, became more vocal, and fascist movements and parties with overt racist programs were established.[41] But the Depression was also a racialized process in the sense that the social politics that informed post-Depression policies were shaped by racialized, even eugenicist concerns, as indeed they were in Europe and North America, where, for example, the U.S. 1935 Social Security Act was designed in a way that largely excluded African Americans.[42] In Latin America too, race informed the social politics that shaped the post-Depression period, although it did so to different degrees, and with different outcomes, in each country.[43]

In short, although it acknowledges the importance of the economic impact of the slump, this volume widens the focus beyond the economic history of the Great Depression of earlier volumes to consider the broader social, institutional, and political history of the slump while paying attention to the ways in which regional transformations interacted with global processes.[44] Written by scholars with extensive expertise in the history of several Latin American countries, this volume deepens our understanding of this crucial episode in the history of the region and its impact on its societies. To be sure, the authors of the individual chapters approach the impact of the Great Depression on the countries they study in different ways. Moreover, the time period covered in each chapter varies, with some focusing on the early 1930s and others taking a broader perspective. These variations reflect at once the authors' areas of expertise and interest and, in turn, the varied impact of the Great Depression in the region. Regretfully, but perhaps inevitably in a volume of this kind, it has proved impossible to include chapters on all Latin American countries. Notable omissions include Ecuador, Bolivia, Uruguay, and Paraguay, as well as several Central American countries (Panama, Costa Rica, Honduras) and, with the exception of Cuba, the Spanish-speaking Caribbean. As such the discussion of the Great Depression's impact on Latin America offered here is clearly incomplete. Despite these absences and while certainly not the last word on the subject, the chapters that follow offer new and useful perspectives on the slump of the 1930s that will hopefully be of interest to a broad range of scholars and not just to historians of the countries that are discussed. Moreover, it is our hope that this volume will also provide the reader a timely comparative perspective on the current global crisis. In the following paragraphs, I present each chapter briefly.

We begin in Argentina, where Roy Hora addresses the impact of the Great Depression by examining two opposed historiographical perspectives on the slump. An older literature emphasizes the rupture with the export age marked by the Great Depression leading to a period of growing industrialization. According to this view, the slump created conditions for the rise of a fundamental antagonism between conservative forces linked to the authoritarian governments of the Concordancia and urban labor. By contrast, a more recent literature emphasizes continuity between the pre- and post-Depression periods. Hora suggests that rather than being opposed, these two historical narratives are in fact complementary and must be seen as part of a broader historical process marked by the growing homogenization of Argentine society following the end of mass international migration. As Hora shows, different sectors of the Argentine population experienced the Great Depression in different ways. For the middle classes, the slump's impact was short-lived: demographic changes (reductions in family size), access to education, and consumption patterns suggest that social mobility trends that predated the slump were quickly reestablished. By contrast, for the working class, the slump resulted in significant drops in wages and an increase in state repression. Hora argues that this contributed to the growing influence of the Communists among organized labor. Hora concludes by noting that these two developments explain the character of Peronism, which drew on organized labor while at the same time emphasizing middle-class values and aspirations, which organized labor came to see as their own.

In the Chilean case, like Hora, Angela Vergara also focuses on how the Great Depression affected the working class. Vergara stresses the devastating impact that the slump had on workers throughout Chile and particularly in the nitrate fields in the north, where mass unemployment (50,000 nitrate workers were jobless by 1932) was a direct consequence of the collapse of the country's export economy. Emphasizing the agency of workers, Vergara explores the ways in which workers responded to the crisis by demanding that labor laws be observed and by contesting policies aimed at controlling their mobility as they left the nitrate *oficinas* in the north of Chile in search of employment elsewhere. Vergara similarly examines the negotiations that developed between workers and state officials over the state and private programs of social assistance, such as soup kitchens and shelters for unemployed workers. Finally, Vergara addresses worker agency, exemplified by unionization and collective bargaining. In contrast to interpretations that emphasize the ways in which the Great Depression enabled the co-option of labor movements by populist regimes, Vergara uses these case studies to show how, even in a context of economic devastation, mass unemployment, and political repression, Chilean workers were able to influence the formation of a system of labor relations that would characterize Chilean politics for almost half a century.

Like Vergara, Joel Wolfe emphasizes the limits of the capacity of the regime of Getúlio Vargas to co-opt Brazilian labor in the wake of the Great

Depression. Wolfe challenges the widely shared view that Vargas effectively incorporated Brazilian organized labor. Rather, Wolf argues, the Vargas labor initiatives largely failed. Similarly, other state-building initiatives, focused on education and cultural programs, were far less effective than is sometimes suggested. A weak federal state, further weakened by the impact of the Great Depression and confronted by powerful interests in states such as São Paulo and Minas Gerais, could not push through reforms in a vast country hampered by poor transport infrastructure. However, Wolfe suggests that Vargas did succeed in laying the foundations for what would later be called "developmentalism." Policies introduced during the Great Depression, such as a federal price support scheme for coffee and state promotion of new industrial sectors such as steel, automobiles, and later oil, as well as the colonization of the interior, represented a significant shift in ideas about the sources of economic prosperity in Brazil and about the state's role in promoting economic development.

In Peru, as in Brazil, the Great Depression created conditions for innovation in the role the state played in the economic and social spheres, as Paulo Drinot and Carlos Contreras demonstrate. The impact of the Great Depression on Peru was severe but relatively short-lived. The Peruvian economy, quite diverse by regional standards, recovered relatively quickly, thanks to export growth. But the slump created economic dislocations and social tensions that brought about greater state innovation and intervention. In the economic sphere, the governments of the 1930s, lacking international credit, raised taxes in order to fund social assistance programs, created fiat money and a central bank, and set up development banks to extend credit to agriculture, industry, and mining. In the social sphere, institutions such as state eateries, worker housing, and a worker social insurance fund were established in order to address the economic impact of the slump and to undermine the growing appeal of left-wing forces, such as the Peruvian Communist Party and the Alianza Popular Revolucionaria America, among the working class. These policies had a marginal impact and did not result in a radical transformation of either the Peruvian economy or society. In fact, they contributed to strengthening the power of the oligarchy, now in alliance with the military. Nevertheless, as Drinot and Contreras argue, they reflected significant developments in state building, focused exclusively in the "modern" sector, that are expressive of the ways in which Peruvian elites understood national progress as being incommensurable with Peru's indigenous population.

In the case of Colombia, as in Peru, the Great Depression was short-lived and recovery was largely export driven. As Marcelo Bucheli and Luis Felipe Sáenz argue, the Great Depression contributed to a major political shift, as the Liberal Party replaced the Conservatives who had been in power since the beginning of the twentieth century. However, in the economic sphere, the Great Depression did not bring about a major policy shift. Indeed, the policy of "export protectionism," which had been introduced in earlier decades, was continued and strengthened by the new Liberal governments of the 1930s. As in other countries in the region, in Colombia too the state took an active role in managing the economy in the context of the slump. However, as Bucheli and Sáenz show, export protectionism worked in different ways in different export sectors characterized by distinct configurations of local bourgeoisies and foreign capital. In the coffee sector, the state worked closely with, and supported, national planters who controlled the sector by providing credit lines and government-sponsored promotion of exports. In the banana sector, the state had to contend with the United Fruit Company. It worked closely with the company, protecting its interests against those of both local power holders in Magdalena and workers. Finally, in the oil industry, which was largely controlled by Standard Oil, the Depression-era governments shifted away from an earlier antagonism to actively support oil investment and exports.

In Venezuela, again, the economic impact of the slump was slight. As Doug Yarrington shows, significant oil revenues meant that Venezuela was able to ride out the crisis, although the agricultural export economy, particularly the coffee sector, did not fare as well, and many Venezuelans suffered as a result. But it was the death of Venezuela's dictator Juan Vicente Gómez in 1935, rather than the slump itself, that inaugurated a new era in Venezuelan politics, albeit one shaped indirectly by the broader impact of the Great Depression on the world economy. As Yarrington argues, Gómez's successor, Eleazar López Contreras, initiated a number of moderate political and social reforms that sought to shift Venezuela onto a path different from that set during three decades of Gomecista rule. These reforms created a climate in which political forces of the Left, Center, and Right were able to flourish and an opportunity for Venezuela's political leaders to return from exile. In what soon became a highly polarized atmosphere, in which local tensions and the ways in which those tensions refracted international conflicts such as the Spanish Civil War played key roles, López oversaw the establishment of a form of exclusionary democracy, which restricted the participation of the Communist Left and inhibited popular mobilization more broadly. This exclusionary democracy, Yarrington argues, would characterize Venezuelan politics to a greater or lesser degree until the election of Hugo Chávez.

If the Great Depression indirectly led to the establishment of exclusionary democracy in Venezuela, in El Salvador, Guatemala, and Nicaragua it contributed to the establishment of military dictatorships that co-opted indigenous groups, as Jeffrey L. Gould shows. The steep fall in export commodity prices, in particular in coffee prices, hit Central America sharply. However, as elsewhere in the region, recovery from the slump was relatively swift. Nevertheless, the effect of the crisis on the laboring poor was generally devastating. It contributed to indigenous mobilization and support for a nascent Left and led to the establishment of labor and campesino movements. Tracing distinct but related trajectories in each country, Gould shows how, following the initial repression of these movements, the military regimes in all three countries adopted and adapted ideologies of *mestizaje* and *indigenismo* and introduced policies (for example, offering support to indigenous communities in land conflicts with ladinos) that succeeded in breaking nascent alliances between the indigenous communities and the Left. As Gould argues, the establishment of clientelistic relationships between indigenous communities and the military succeeded in co-opting indigenous communities and also gave these communities the capacity to resist ladino encroachment on their lands. These relationships proved to be strong and long-lasting and continued to shape the difficult historical trajectory of Central American democracy in the second half of the twentieth century.

To the north, in Mexico, the impact of the Great Depression was sharp and owed to a significant extent to the Mexican economy's close ties and exposure to the faltering U.S. economy. As elsewhere in the region, as Alan Knight shows, the slump in Mexico was characterized by falling export prices, a sharp drop in government revenue, and rising unemployment, which was compounded by the repatriation of thousands of Mexican workers from the United States. However, again as happened elsewhere in the region, the Mexican economy rebounded relatively quickly, partly because the country's export base was diversified, partly because the country's incipient industrial sector was able to take advantage of opportunities created by the collapse of imports, and partly because a large subsistence sector was able to soak up excess labor. Yet, as Knight argues, government policy also played a role in the recovery, particularly after Alberto Pani took over in the Treasury in 1932 and implemented a series of proto-Keynesian policies. More generally, the recovery from the Depression in Mexico, Knight shows, was shaped by the revolutionary nature of the regime: the major policies implemented under Cárdenas (1934–40), including land reform, a strengthening of labor institutions, and pragmatic economic nationalism (in the shape of nationalizations of key industries such as oil and railways), followed a logic of radical state policy that had its source in the revolution but which was given further traction by the economic dislocations created by the world slump.

With Chile, Cuba was one of the countries in Latin America that most suffered in the Great Depression. Like Mexico, its fortunes were closely linked to those of the United States. The shift to sugar monoculture that accelerated sharply following independence in the late nineteenth century meant that Cuba was particularly exposed to the commodity price shocks that antedated the slump and to the economic devastation that followed the 1929 crash, not least in the context of U.S. protectionism under the Smoot-Hawley Act. As Gillian McGillivray shows, the economic impact of the Depression on Cuba soon translated into labor unrest, which the Machado regime responded to with repression. The 1933 revolution, which deposed Machado and led to the Grau San Martín government, prompted policies that, McGillivray argues, significantly enhanced the role of the state in the economy and went some way toward empowering sectors of the population, including sugar workers, Afro-Cubans, and women, in a bid to channel grassroots mobilization and left-wing activism that was beginning to radically alter the character of Cuban society, including its relation with U.S. capital. Under Batista, these forces were increasingly contained, but, at least until the 1952 coup, and particularly in the period 1937–44, when Batista shifted to the Left in response to both local and global processes, popular forces continued to influence state policy and to gain important concessions. Following Batista's 1952 coup, of course, Cuba's popular forces would again be severely repressed. But, as we all know, they would resurface, with lasting consequences, in 1959.

In the final chapter, Alan Knight undertakes a comparative overview of the processes examined in the previous, country-focused chapters. Knight concludes that the Great Depression was indeed a crucial episode in the history of Latin America. But although it was a single, momentous process, its effects varied considerably from country to country (and, particularly in the larger countries, from region to region, from economic to economic sector, from class to class, and so on). So, while in general, and despite its deep insertion into the global economy that collapsed in the wake of the 1929 crash, Latin America weathered the crisis relatively well and recovered relatively quickly, some countries fared better than others, and most, as argued above, did better than the United States, which took much longer to recover. Moreover, the engine of recovery varied from country to country, with import substitution playing a role in some countries but not in others. In political terms, too, there was considerable variation, although throughout Latin America political instability was characteristic, and in most cases the slump brought about, as I pointed out above, the collapse of the status quo (whether liberal or authoritarian) and its replacement by its antinomy. In structural terms, however, Knight sees the slump as accelerating, rather than starting ab initio, processes of social and political change, such as industrialization, urbanization, internal migration, the expansion of the state, and its role in both the economy and society, which nevertheless had broader consequences for the political configuration of much of the region.

It is therefore interesting to note, in closing, that, in contrast to the Great Depression, the current crisis has not—at least not yet—generated political eruptions, in Latin America or indeed elsewhere, of the sort that Eric Hobsbawm, his contemporaries in Weimar Berlin, and the peoples of Latin America lived through in the 1930s. We can tentatively attribute this to the fact that, in most countries, historically minded policy makers—who, remembering the past, have avoided repeating it—have implemented proactive policies that have stopped the crisis from becoming even deeper, or to the fact that the political (and ideological) elements that fueled the eruptions in the 1930s are largely absent today. Whereas the Great Depression was read as a crisis of capitalism tout court, the Great Recession has tended to be read as a crisis of a particular *variety* of capitalism (characterized by unregulated financial markets and feckless governments). Similarly, whereas the impact of the Great Depression strengthened challenges to liberal democracy from the left and right, there is little to indicate that, for all the calls for "radical rethinking" from the left or despite the emergence or strengthening of neofascist movements in parts of Europe, there is extensive support today for an alternative to liberal democracy, either "straight" or tweaked with participatory elements.[45] This could change if the current crisis spreads further (stalling, or even breaking down, the Chinese motor of the global economy) or deepens (collapsing the Euro and breaking up the European Union). So far, Latin America has weathered the crisis better than other regions. But, as in the 1930s, the fate of the region is firmly tied to that of the rest of the world.

Notes

1 Eric Hobsbawm, *Interesting Times: A Twentieth-Century Life* (London: Abacus, 2012), 47.

2 In turn, defeat in the Chaco War led — again neither directly nor inexorably, but the chain of transmission is clearly discernible — to the "nationalist" revolution of 1952. See Merilee S. Grindle and Pilar Domingo, eds., *Proclaiming Revolution: Bolivia in Comparative Perspective* (London: Institute of Latin American Studies, 2003).

3 Recent examples include Peter Temin, "The Great Recession and the Great Depression," *Daedalus* 139, no. 4 (2010): 115–24; Richhild Moessner and William A. Allen, "Banking Crises and the International Monetary System in the Great Depression and Now," *Financial History Review* 18 (2011): 1–20; Miguel Almunia et al., "From Great Depression to Great Credit Crisis: Similarities, Differences and Lessons," *Economic Policy*, CEPR, CES, MSH, 25 (2010): 219–65; and the special issue of the *Oxford Review of Economic Policy* edited by Nicholas Crafts and Peter Fearon, "Lessons from the 1930s," 23, no. 3 (2010). An earlier (pre-2007) study is Harold James, *The End of Globalization: Lessons from the Great Depression* (Cambridge, MA: Harvard University Press, 2002).

4 See Rick Szostak's useful discussion of shifting macroeconomic explanations of the Great Depression since the 1930s. Rick Szostak, "Evaluating the Historiography of the Great Depression: Explanation or Single-Theory Driven?," *Journal of Economic Methodology* 12, no. 1 (2005): 35–61.

5 See Robert Skidelsky's recent book on Keynes, among others. Robert Skidelsky, *Keynes: The Return of the Master* (London: Penguin, 2010).

6 Ben Bernanke, *Essays on the Great Depression* (Princeton, NJ: Princeton University Press, 2004), 5. The economic history of the Great Depression is the focus of a number of studies. Foremost among them are Charles Poor Kindleberger, *The World in Depression, 1929–1939* (Berkeley: University of California Press, 1973); Peter Temin, *Did Monetary Forces Cause the Great Depression?* (New York: Norton, 1976); Peter Temin, *Lessons from the Great Depression* (Cambridge, MA: MIT Press, 1989); Barry J. Eichengreen, *Golden Fetters: The Gold Standard and the Great Depression, 1919–1939* (New York: Oxford University Press, 1992).

7 As Mark Mazower notes, "Capitalism's great crisis . . . carried with it powerful political implications: was there a democratic alternative to fascism and communism that could face up to the economic challenges of the 1930s." Mark Mazower, *Dark Continent: Europe's Twentieth Century* (London: Penguin, 1998), 117.

8 Rosemary Thorp, ed., *Latin America in the 1930s: The Role of the Periphery in World Crisis* (London: Macmillan, 1984). Dietmar Rothermund's study of the global impact of the slump dedicates one chapter and parts of another to Latin America, in which he largely summarizes the chapters in the Thorp volume. See Dietmar Rothermund, *The Global Impact of the Great Depression, 1929–*

1939 (London: Routledge, 1996), chaps. 10 and 14. For studies that locate the Great Depression in a broader history of financial crises, see Carlos Marichal, *Nueva historia de las Grandes Crisis Financieras: Una perspectiva global, 1873–2008* (Madrid: Editorial Debate, 2010).

9 Pablo González Casanova, ed., *América Latina en los años treinta* (México: Instituto de Investigaciones Sociales, Universidad Nacional Autónoma de México, 1977).

10 A long list of titles is probably unnecessary. Examples of this literature, in English, include, in the case of Brazil and Chile, John D. French, *The Brazilian Workers' ABC: Class Conflict and Alliances in Modern São Paulo* (Chapel Hill: University of North Carolina Press, 1992); Joel Wolfe, *Working Women, Working Men: São Paulo and the Rise of Brazil's Industrial Working Class, 1900–1955* (Durham, NC: Duke University Press, 1993); Barbara Weinstein, *For Social Peace in Brazil: Industrialists and the Remaking of the Working Class in São Paulo, 1920–1964* (Chapel Hill: University of North Carolina Press, 1996); Patrick Barr-Melej, *Reforming Chile: Cultural Politics, Nationalism, and the Rise of the Middle Class* (Chapel Hill: University of North Carolina Press, 2001); Karin Alejandra Rosemblatt, *Gendered Compromises: Political Cultures and the State in Chile, 1920–1950* (Chapel Hill: University of North Carolina Press, 2000); Thomas Miller Klubock, *Contested Communities: Class, Gender, and Politics in Chile's El Teniente Copper Mine, 1904–1951* (Durham, NC: Duke University Press, 1998).

11 As Victor Bulmer-Thomas notes, "The most disastrous combination was a high degree of openness, a large fall in the price of exports, and a steep decline in the volume of exports. It is no surprise therefore that the most seriously affected republics were Chile and Cuba, where the external shock was strongest." Victor Bulmer-Thomas, *The Economic History of Latin America since Independence* (Cambridge: Cambridge University Press, 1994), 201.

12 Bulmer-Thomas, *Economic History of Latin America*, 194–237.

13 Robert Broughton Bryce, *Maturing in Hard Times: Canada's Department of Finance during the Great Depression* (Kingston, ON: McGill-Queen's University Press, 1986), 64; J. M. Bumsted, *A History of the Canadian Peoples* (Don Mills, ON: Oxford University Press, 2007), 334–41.

14 Some of these processes would have a long-lasting impact. As Carlos Marichal notes, the debt defaults in much of Latin America in the early 1930s, following the sharp rise in real interest rates, not only helped to attenuate the impact of the financial and commercial shock but "also reduced financial dependency during more than a decade. This was a historical experience that would bear remembering." Carlos Marichal, *A Century of Debt Crises in Latin America: From Independence to the Great Depression* (Princeton, NJ: Princeton University Press, 1989), 228.

15 See Alan Knight's chapter 10 in this volume.

16 See Bogumil Jewsiewicki, "The Great Depression and the Making of the Colonial Economic System in the Belgian Congo," *African Economic History*

4 (1977): 153–76; Jane I. Guyer, "The Depression and the Administration in South-Central Cameroon," *African Economic History* 10 (1981): 67–79; Moses Ochonu, *Colonial Meltdown: Northern Nigeria in the Great Depression* (Athens: Ohio University Press, 2009).

17 As Dietmar Rothermund notes, "Mahatma Gandhi started his famous Salt March in the Spring of 1930. This was not related to the impact of the depression at all, but once the North Indian peasants were hit by the fall in wheat prices they joined his campaign and gave a new lease of life to it." Dietmar Rothermund, *An Economic History of India: From Pre-Colonial Times to 1991* (London: Routledge, 1993), 98–99. For a revisionist perspective on the impact of the Great Depression on Southeast Asia, see Peter Boomgard and Ian Brown, eds., *Weathering the Storm: The Economies of Southeast Asia in the 1930s Depression* (Leiden: KITLV, 2000).

18 See Myung Soo Cha, "Did Takahashi Korekiyo Rescue Japan from the Great Depression?," *Journal of Economic History* 63, no. 1 (2003): 127–44. See also Mark Metzler, *Lever of Empire: The International Gold Standard and the Crisis of Liberalism in Prewar Japan* (Berkeley: University of California Press, 2006).

19 This point is relevant, of course, to large parts of the Americas. See Tomoko Shiroyama, *China during the Great Depression: Market, State, and the World Economy, 1929–1937* (Cambridge, MA: Harvard University Press, 2009); and Tim Wright, "Distant Thunder: The Regional Economies of Southwest China and the Impact of the Great Depression," *Modern Asian Studies* 34, no. 3 (2000): 697–738.

20 Emily S. Rosenberg, *Spreading the American Dream: American Economic and Cultural Expansion, 1890–1945* (New York: Hill and Wang, 1982), 176–201.

21 Maldwyn A. Jones, *The Limits of Liberty: American History, 1607–1992* (Oxford: Oxford University Press, 1995), 476.

22 Anthony J. Badger, *The New Deal: The Depression Years, 1933–1940* (Houndmills, UK: Macmillan, 1989).

23 According to Paul Krugman, for example, "Mr. Obama took office in a nation marked by huge disparities in income and wealth. But where the New Deal had a revolutionary impact, empowering workers and creating a middle-class society that lasted for 40 years, [Obama's Big Deal—a reference to Joe Biden's reference to the health care reforms as a "big fucking deal"] has been limited to equalizing policies at the margin." Paul Krugman, "The Big Deal," *New York Times*, January 20, 2013.

24 Ira Katznelson, *Fear Itself: The New Deal and the Origins of Our Time* (London: W. W. Norton, 2013), 6.

25 Rothermund, *Global Impact of the Great Depression*, 140–44.

26 Ronald Findlay and Kevin H. O'Rourke, *Power and Plenty: Trade, War, and the World Economy in the Second Millennium* (Princeton, NJ: Princeton University Press, 2007), 468.

27 These scholars, including, most famously, Fernando Henrique Cardoso, Andre

Gunder Frank, and Celso Furtado, were arguably among the first to insist on the importance of the Great Depression in creating the conditions for a more autonomous form of the development based on industrialization. See Andre Gunder Frank, *Capitalism and Underdevelopment in Latin America: Historical Studies of Chile and Brazil* (New York: Monthly Review Press, 1967); Fernando Henrique Cardoso and Enzo Faletto, *Dependencia y desarrollo en América Latina* (Mexico: Siglo XXI editories, 1969); Celso Furtado, *Economic Development in Latin America: Historical Background and Contemporary Problems* (Cambridge: Cambridge University Press, 1970).

28 As Joseph L. Love notes, "Prebisch's interest in industrialization as a solution to Latin America's economic problems originally arose from the desire, shared by many Argentine contemporaries, to make Argentina less economically 'vulnerable,' a vulnerability painfully evident for the whole period 1930–1945." Joseph L. Love, "Economic Ideas and Ideologies in Latin American since 1930," in *Ideas and Ideologies in Twentieth Century Latin America*, ed. Leslie Bethell (Cambridge: Cambridge University Press, 1996), 224. On ECLA and Prebisch, see also Joseph L. Love, *Crafting the Third World: Theorizing Underdevelopment in Rumania and Brazil* (Stanford, CA: Stanford University Press, 1996). See also Valpy Fitzgerald and Rosemary Thorp, eds., *Economic Doctrines in Latin America: Origins, Embedding and Evolution* (Basingstoke, UK: Palgrave Macmillan, 2005).

29 See Thorp, *Latin America in the 1930s*; and Bulmer-Thomas, *Economic History of Latin America*. See also Marcelo de Paiva Abreu, "The External Context," in *The Cambridge Economic History of Latin America*, vol. 2, *The Long Twentieth Century*, ed. Victor Bulmer Thomas, John Coastworth, and Roberto Cortés Conde (Cambridge: Cambridge University Press, 2006), 104–18.

30 See, a fortiori, Daniel James, *Resistance and Integration: Peronism and the Argentine Working Class, 1946–1976* (Cambridge: Cambridge University Press, 1988); and French, *Brazilian Workers' ABC*. For a useful overview of debates on populism in Latin America, see Alan Knight, "Populism and Neo-Populism in Latin America, especially Mexico," *Journal of Latin American Studies* 30, no. 2 (1998): 223–48.

31 For such shifts in the European context, see, for example, Philip Nord, *France's New Deal: From the Thirties to the Postwar Era* (Princeton, NJ: Princeton University Press, 2010).

32 As Victor Bulmer-Thomas notes, many of the changes in the economic sphere were not planned; they did not amount to an "intellectual revolution." Authorities were often forced into implementing reforms by circumstances, but these reforms did pave the way and to some extent amounted to a new paradigm of import substitution, which would come into focus in later decades. Bulmer-Thomas, *Economic History of Latin America*, 234. See also Rosemary Thorp, *Progress, Poverty and Exclusion: An Economic History of Latin America in the 20th Century* (Washington, DC: IDB, 1998), 97–125.

33 See Temin, *Lessons from the Great Depression*.

34 See, in particular, Daniel T. Rodgers, *Atlantic Crossings: Social Politics in a Progressive Age* (Cambridge, MA: Belknap Press of Harvard University Press, 1998).

35 On the middle classes in this period, see, among others, David S. Parker, *The Idea of the Middle Class: White-Collar Workers and Peruvian Society, 1900–1950* (University Park: Penn State University Press, 1998); Brian P. Owensby, *Intimate Ironies: Modernity and the Making of Middle-Class Lives in Brazil* (Stanford, CA: Stanford University Press, 1999); Patrick Barr-Melej, *Reforming Chile: Cultural Politics, Nationalism and the Rise of the Middle Class* (Chapel Hill: University of North Carolina Press, 2001). See also A. Ricardo López and Barbara Weinstein, eds., *The Making of the Middle Class: Toward a Transnational History* (Durham, NC: Duke University Press, 2012).

36 See Linda Gordon, "Social Insurance and Public Assistance: The Influence of Gender in Welfare Thought in the United States, 1890–1935," *American Historical Review* 97, no. 1 (1992): 19–54; Donna J. Guy, *Women Build the Welfare State: Performing Charity and Creating Rights in Argentina, 1880–1955* (Durham, NC: Duke University Press, 2009); Karin Alejandra Rosemblatt, *Gendered Compromises: Political Cultures and the State in Chile, 1920–1950* (Chapel Hill: University of North Carolina Press, 2000); Paulo Drinot, *The Allure of Labor: Workers, Race and the Making of the Peruvian State* (Durham, NC: Duke University Press, 2011).

37 On African Americans during the Great Depression, see Cheryl Lynn Greenberg, *To Ask for an Equal Chance: African Americans in the Great Depression* (New York: Rowman and Littlefield, 2009).

38 Laura Putnam, *The Company They Kept: Migrants and the Politics of Gender in Caribbean Costa Rica, 1870–1960* (Chapel Hill: University of North Carolina Press, 2002), 73. For similar laws and more generally for anti–West Indian racism elsewhere in the circum-Caribbean region, see, among others, Dario Euraque, "The Banana Enclave, Nationalism, and Mestizaje in Honduras, 1910s-1930s," in *Identity and Struggle at the Margins of the Nation-State: The Laboring Peoples of Central America and the Hispanic Caribbean*, ed. Aviva Chomsky and Aldo Lauria-Santiago (Durham, NC: Duke University Press, 1998), 151–68; and Barry Carr, "Identity, Class, and Nation: Black Immigrant Workers, Cuban Communism, and the Sugar Insurgency 1925–1934," *Hispanic American Historical Review* 78, no. 1 (1998): 83–116.

39 See chapter 4 of this volume.

40 Gerardo Rénique, "Race, Region and Nation: Sonora's Anti-Chinese Racism and Mexico's Postrevolutionary Nationalism, 1920s–1930s," in *Race and Nation in Modern Latin America*, ed. Nancy P. Appelbaum, Anne S. Macpherson, and Karin Alejandra Rosemblatt (Chapel Hill: University of North Carolina Press, 2003), 211–36; Robert Chao Romero, *The Chinese in Mexico, 1882–1940* (Tucson: University of Arizona Press, 2011), 155–90; Grace Peña Delgado, *Making the*

Chinese Mexican: Global Migration, Localism and Exclusion in the U.S.-Mexico Borderlands (Stanford, CA: Stanford University Press, 2012), 157–89.

41 On anti-Semitism in the context of the rise of nativism and anti-immigration sentiments, as well as the establishment of anti-Jewish policies, in Brazil in the 1930s, see Jeffrey Lesser, *Welcoming the Undersirables: Brazil and the Jewish Question* (Berkeley: University of California Press, 1995), chaps. 2 and 3. On anti-Semitism in the context of the rise of fascist movements in Argentina, Brazil, and Chile, see part 3 of Sandra McGee Deutsch, *Las Derechas: The Extreme Right in Argentina, Brazil and Chile, 1890–1939* (Stanford, CA: Stanford University Press, 1999).

42 See Robert C. Lieberman, *Shifting the Color Line: Race and the American Welfare State* (Cambridge, MA: Harvard University Press, 2001); and Ira Katznelson, *When Affirmative Action Was White: An Untold History of Racial Inequality in Twentieth-Century America* (New York: W. W. Norton, 2005).

43 In Peru, for example, the 1936 social security law was designed in a way that excluded the indigenous from its coverage. See Drinot, *Allure of Labor*, chap. 6.

44 Thorp, *Latin America in the 1930s*.

45 On the need for "radical rethinking" after the "implosion" of "global free-market capitalism" following the banking crisis and credit crunch of 2007–8, see Stuart Hall, Doreen Massey, and Michael Rustin, "After Neoliberalism: Analysing the Present," accessed April 29, 2013, http://www.lwbooks.co.uk /journals/soundings/pdfs/s53hallmasseyrustin.pdf.

CHAPTER 1

The Impact of the Depression on Argentine Society

Roy Hora

Social and political developments in Argentina during the period that stretches from the beginning of the Great Depression to Colonel Juan Perón's rise to power a decade and a half later have been studied from two points of view. During the 1960s and 1970s, most scholars characterized this period, known as the Década Infame, as one of political reaction and social regression. According to this view, the coup d'état led by General José F. Uriburu on September 6, 1930, that overthrew President Hipólito Yrigoyen and the subsequent systematic use of electoral fraud by the ruling Concordancia (1932–43) allowed the Conservatives and their allies on the right to reverse the reformist politics furthered by the Radical governments (1916–30) after the Sáenz Peña electoral reform democratized the (male) franchise. This interpretation also emphasizes that the Great Depression had a negative impact on popular welfare, in both rural and urban areas, whose effect lasted for more than a decade, and which undid much of the social progress that had been achieved in previous decades, most particularly during the period of Radical rule.

This way of looking at the 1930s holds that this social and political relapse ran parallel to deep economic transformations. As a result of the contraction of the world market for agricultural products, Argentina's export sector lost momentum. When economic recovery began, the inward-looking, labor-intensive manufacturing sector overtook export agriculture as the major engine of growth. Recovery was aided by public policy that, as a result of the change in the political base of the state, became more favorable to business interests than during the democratic era that ended in 1930. After General Uriburu's coup d'état removed Yrigoyen from office, the country fell under the rule of the Concordancia. A sort of united front of those forces of the

Center and the Right that had been ousted from the scene by the rise of the Radicals, the Concordancia controlled politics from 1932 to 1943, and for that matter repeatedly resorted to electoral falsification in various degrees, especially in the province of Buenos Aires. Far more pro-capitalist than its Radical predecessors, the Concordancia served the interests of a business elite made up of large landowners (whose wealth dated back to the agro-export period) and, to a lesser extent, of manufacturing and urban entrepreneurs who benefited from inward-looking growth. Indifference to popular demands on the part of the governing elite, repression of political dissidents and labor militants, and the weakness of the unions explain why there was no social or labor reform in the 1930s, despite mounting discontent. It was only with the accession of Perón to government that social reform became a central aspect of public policy.[1]

According to this narrative, then, the 1930s was a period marked by rupture with the previous export-led era but also with the Peronist years. In fact, much of the persuasive power of this account lies in its capacity to explain the rise of Peronism as the product of the new social forces that emerged in the wake of the economic and social changes brought about by the Depression, and as a response to the reactionary political climate prevalent throughout the Década Infame. Following this interpretation, the critical factor in the emergence of Peronism—the movement that would from that point onward take center stage in Argentinean politics—was the growing tension between this undemocratic, elitist political order and the growing economic and social weight of urban labor.

In the past twenty-five years, this interpretation has been called into question. Major processes of change that have taken place since the 1980s, such as deindustrialization, the erosion of working-class politics, and Peronism's electoral defeats (and changes) during the post-1983 democratic period, have had a strong impact on the way historians regard the 1930s. Also, greater awareness of the importance of manufacturing growth and social betterment during the export-led era has given rise to more balanced, even more sympathetic, views on the oligarchic republic (1880–1916) and the pre-1945 economic and social development of the country. As a result, the rise of industrial society has lost much of its centrality as the dominant theme in the country's mid-twentieth-century history. Understanding of the Década Infame as an era of manufacturing growth and working-class ascent has given way to an alternative view that emphasizes continuity with earlier periods. The 1930s are seen as a period not of rupture but of continuation of the processes of economic growth and diversification and, more importantly, social betterment that wide sectors of society, including the popular classes, had experienced since the turn of the century, and which had gathered pace during the prosperous 1920s. In this way, the Década Infame is located within the context of a broader, interwar period. According to this view, once the worst effects of the Great Depression had subsided, society again became open and mobile, characterized by increasing levels of well-being and renewed opportunities for social advancement, especially in the large littoral cities. It is often noted that, apart from manufacturing, the services sector also experienced significant growth during the 1930s, thus consolidating an economic structure that was not only more industrialized but also more complex and diversified.

According to this view, as social mobility and individual progress became more widespread in the interwar period, the confrontational, class-based popular identities forged during the turn-of-the-century years (when Anarchist influence over the working classes was at its height) lost salience. Thus, while adherents to the first interpretation outlined above suggest that the formation of labor institutions and a stronger (albeit repressed) worker culture gained momentum during the 1930s, this second interpretation emphasizes a gradual erosion in class-based identities. Instead, it points to the making of a wider "popular sectors" identity, in part shaped by middle-class values, and defined less by class than by determinants such as culture, consumption, and residential patterns. In sum, where the first narrative emphasizes the social and political alienation of the new urban laborers created by industrialization, the second highlights the identification of large sections of the urban population with aspirations for social or family betterment compatible with the existing order and, as a result, a strong popular identification with the moderate, reformist political agenda articulated by the Radicals and the Socialists.[2]

Finally, this second perspective sees the political developments that put an end to the Década Infame under a different light. Explanations of the rise of Peronism downplay the analytical weight of labor activism and of popular demands that could not be accommodated within a reformed version of the political order of the Década Infame. In the more integrated and harmonious society portrayed by proponents of this argument, the economic and social transformations brought about by the growth of manufacturing play a minor part in the emergence of Peronism. Politics and ideology, rather than social and economic change, are the most important explanatory variables. According to this view, the authoritarian, nationalist ideas dominant in the armed forces and the Catholic Church, the political and ideological impact of World War II, the mobilization of the center and left political parties and the middle classes against the military that took power in June 1943, and the besieged military regime's struggle for survival in 1944–45 were developments even more important than the upsurge of working-class activism in shaping the political scenario that brought Colonel Perón to power.[3]

Because of their emphasis on either change or continuity, exclusion or integration, these two interpretations of the Great Depression years are often regarded as alternative narratives. However, important divergences stem from the fact that they focus on two distinct groups: the industrial workers in the first case, and the urban middle classes and the more integrated and prosperous segments of the urban popular classes in the second. In fact, this chapter argues that these interpretations actually explore two parallel and (to some extent) complementary realities, both of equal importance for understanding how Argentina developed during the 1930s and what was the political legacy of the Great Depression. In order to achieve a better understanding of the 1930s, therefore, these two narratives need to be brought together.

The first section of this chapter briefly describes the impact of the Great Depression. Then, the chapter looks into how the slump affected the middle classes and the most integrated and prosperous sectors of the urban workers. I contend that long-established forces of integration were at play during this period, promoting social mobility and increased levels of welfare. However, this experience was less widespread and less potent than in earlier decades. The next section shifts attention to the word of labor, exploring how the rise of industry and new forms of labor organization affected the workforce. It states that deteriorating living conditions and greater hostility toward the established order contributed to the emergence of the first industry-wide trade unions in the manufacturing sector, and it assesses the long-term significance of the changes in the workers' political consciousness associated with this process. Finally, the concluding section summarizes the central themes of this article and offers some indications on integrating the two narratives outlined above into a more complex view of how Argentinean society was transformed as a result of the Depression.

Argentina into the Depression

The Argentine economy, highly integrated into international trade and finance flows, was strongly affected by the world slump. Between 1928 and 1932, exports fell from $1 billion to $335 million. GDP contracted by 14 percent between 1929 and 1932. Public finances also suffered, the consequence not only of decreasing revenues (still highly dependent on international trade taxes) but also of the drying up of external credit. To balance the trade deficit, the government restricted external purchases and remittances (devaluation of the peso, exchange controls). Duties on imported goods were increased, and quantitative restrictions on imports were imposed.

These measures created incentives for the development of domestic production through import substitution industrialization, and by 1933 the manufacturing sector began to revive. Argentina's industrial structure, the most advanced in Latin America, developed in new directions. A modest increase in export values contributed to growth, but economic recovery was largely the result of increased production for the domestic market, led by new sectors such as textiles, chemistry, and metals. Between 1933 and 1945, GDP expanded by almost 4 percent per year on average, barely a point below the 1920–29 pace of growth.[4] Despite the weak performance of the export sector throughout the decade, the impact of the Great Depression was less intense in Argentina than in Chile, Canada, or the United States, all countries where GDP fell by over 20 percent and recovery was slower and more laborious.[5] However, recovery was not as fast as in Brazil or Mexico, probably because strong links with Britain and a rather timid, orthodox economic policy prevented Argentina from channeling more resources into the most dynamic sectors of the economy. The much-criticized Roca-Runciman bilateral agreement, designed to protect beef exports to Britain and which forced Argentine producers and consumers to buy British goods rather than cheaper and more useful U.S. and German products, was probably inevitable in a world that was moving toward bilateralism. Even if less contentious, servicing the debt proved less beneficial, largely because, despite Argentina's good behavior, the influx of foreign loans and investment was never resumed. To a certain extent, then, Argentina paid a higher price for its financial policy than for its commercial policy.[6]

Economic recovery was largely an urban phenomenon, spurred by the development of manufacturing and the expansion of the services sector.[7] One of the most important consequences of the shift from export agriculture to inward-looking development was that it reshaped the economic elite, which had up to that point been dominated by large landowners. The fall in exports brought with it a dramatic decrease in the value of both the assets and the income of this group. Large *estancieros* suffered heavy losses. Over the course of the 1930s, rural wealth was silently displaced from the top echelons of the wealthy elite by the more dynamic and prosperous urban capitalists. By the early 1940s, less than one out of every six among the largest one hundred taxpayers derived their income from rural business. However, newly amassed wealth remained detached from high society. Very few of these urban nouveaux riches came from upper-class circles, and even fewer of them harbored aspirations to marry into or intermingle with the landed establishment. Thus, the renovation of the top echelons of the business community was deeper and more abrupt than the social decline of the turn-of-the-century rural elite. In the popular mind, wealthy landowners remained as the country's most powerful group. In a period of greater popular hardship, this came at a price. During the 1930s, the public image of Argentina's most exclusive group turned increasingly negative. Widely perceived as reactionary, exploitative of the laborers who worked the land, and harmful to the national interest, the *oligarquía terrateniente* became the object of much criticism.[8]

Public hostility toward this landed oligarchy was closely tied to the problems faced by the rural population. We lack a clear picture of the impact of the Depression in the interior provinces. The available evidence, however, suggests that the gap in living standards between the littoral and the interior provinces deepened further.[9] This was also what most contemporaries believed. In a well-known study of social conditions in the northwestern provinces published in 1938, Alfredo Palacios denounced "the lack of any future for innumerable Argentinean children," the consequence of all those "illnesses fostered by misery."[10]

The Great Depression had a profound and negative impact on popular welfare in the pampean countryside, the heart of the agrarian export economy. Agricultural mechanization in the 1920s and the collapse of grain and livestock prices during the Depression led to a twin, long-lasting contraction in labor demand and income. Large landowners saw their assets and incomes shrink, but their superior market power allowed them to transfer much of this fall to tenants and wage laborers. A number of important labor conflicts and tenant strikes erupted between 1930 and 1933. Lacking a strong organization and further weakened by the economic downturn, workers and tenants were always defeated. Thereafter, migration became a more viable option than speaking out.[11]

Migration, one of the most important consequences of the Depression, had a profound demographic impact. Between 1930 and 1947, Argentina grew from eleven to sixteen million inhabitants. However, during the 1930s, for the first time in the country's history, the rural population (those residing in settlements of less than two thousand inhabitants) declined, reaching a similar level to that of 1914. People leaving the countryside went primarily to the large littoral cities, especially Buenos Aires and its surrounding area. Between 1936 and 1943, this metropolis absorbed some 72,000 internal migrants each year; between 1943 and 1947, that average rose to 117,000.[12] In little over a decade, one million *provincianos* settled in Buenos Aires. This sustained increase in urban population meant that by the mid-1940s, one in every four Argentines resided in the federal capital and its urban periphery. The growing demographic weight of this large metropolis did not go unnoticed. By the 1940s, views like those of Alejandro Bunge and Ezequiel Martínez Estrada, who argued that Argentina was a country with a large head and a withered body, had become quite common.[13]

Migration from the pampean provinces dominated during the first half of the 1930s (when the impact of the crisis in export agriculture was at its height), accounting for some two-thirds of total migrants. In the latter part of the decade, however, migration from the interior provinces increased markedly. For residents of places such as Santiago del Estero, Catamarca, or La Rioja, leaving their land was not a new experience: migration from the poor interior provinces to the labor-hungry pampean region stretched back to colonial times. For much of the nineteenth century and until 1930, however, the sheer size of the European migration made internal migration rather invisible. Furthermore, much of the internal migration that took place before 1930 was directed toward the more developed and labor-demanding areas of the interior, such as Mendoza or Tucumán. As a result of the Depression, this pattern was dramatically altered. European migration stopped (with the exception of a brief resumption in the immediate postwar period) at the same time that an increasing number of dark-skinned provincianos were moving toward the large littoral conurbations. Between 1914 and 1947, foreign-born inhabitants in Buenos Aires fell from 49.3 to 27.5 percent of the total population. In that same period, provincianos rose from 18 to 44 percent of the total native population in the federal capital, and most likely to over 55 percent in Greater Buenos Aires.

This demographic transformation coincided with, and reinforced, cultural change. In the 1930s, the coastal cities lost some of their cosmopolitan character, acquiring instead a more native flavor. New forms of imagining the nation, which rediscovered and idealized pre-immigration Argentina and were hostile to the Europeanized ideas that had captivated the imagination of the country's ruling elite for much of the previous half century, gained ground. This nativism was often accompanied by a new appreciation of the Spanish cultural roots and legacy, which in some cases included a critique of democracy and political liberalism. Anti-imperialist rhetoric also became more apparent. British economic and political interests became the subject of open attack, starting with the publication in 1934 of *La Argentina y el imperialismo británico* by Julio and Rodolfo Irazusta.[14]

It was not only in elite circles that these visions of a less cosmopolitan Argentine culture gained ground. They also appealed to the middle and popular classes, to both recently arrived and long-established urban residents. In the large cities that set the tone of the country's political and cultural life, the growing demographic weight of *provincianos* contributed to the emergence of a more nationalistic, inward-looking cultural climate. First- and second-generation Argentine descendants of European immigrants turned their backs on their forebears and became open critics of recently arrived Europeans.[15] The development of musical genres such as tango and folklore, together with the growth of the radio and of a local film industry, offered powerful channels for the exploration of new themes relating to this *Argentina criolla*.[16]

The Quest for Social Mobility and the Middle Classes

It is important not to exaggerate the disruptive power of the new ways of imagining the nation. In the 1930s, new social and cultural tensions that divided white, European Argentina from its *criollo* counterpart contributed to the spread of views that praised the virtues of the land and demonized the big, artificial, cosmopolitan city that only looked toward Europe. However, this trend rarely implied a rejection of urban modernity or condemnation of the urban experience as such: for most people, migrants included, the superiority of the city lay not only in the dynamism of its labor market but also in its greater opportunities for leisure, consumption, access to education, and improved medical care (all of which were praised in the popular press, on the radio, and in the cinema). The example of the young Eva Duarte, who moved from the provincial village of Los Toldos to Buenos Aires to start a career in the entertainment industry, speaks of the appeal of urban life for the popular classes of the interior. In this context, it is unsurprising that even among internal migrants of criollo stock—the group most castigated by the modernizing project of the nineteenth-century liberal elites, and the ones who suffered most acutely the discrimination of urban residents of European origin—the desire for incorporation was paramount.[17] Provincianos moved not only to escape poverty but also to take advantage of the wider social opportunities offered by the prosperous metropolis of the littoral. In contrast with the 1850s–1930 transatlantic cycle of immigration, which saw almost half of all those who arrived at Argentina's ports ultimately returning to Europe, very few of the internal migrants of the 1930s and 1940s eventually headed back. The rhetoric that exhorted provincianos to return to their roots, such as that of the shrill, plaintive song of Atahualpa Yupanqui ("si tu puedes, vuélvete / me dijo el río llorando / los cerros que tanto quieres / me dijo / allí te están esperando"), perhaps succeeded in reminding migrants of the natural beauty and superior moral values of their homelands, but it could not change the minds of those who sought to establish new lives in the large littoral cities.[18]

Demography and familial structures offer an eloquent insight into the aspirations for integration and the appeal of the idea of social mobility that predominated during the interwar decades. The national censuses of 1914 and 1947 (the only countrywide censuses from the period) reveal a significant transformation in the reproductive patterns of the population, the result of a simultaneous reduction in death rates and birthrates. The former can be explained by an increase in welfare, developments in sanitary infrastructure (from access to running water to improved sewer systems), greater awareness of hygiene, and better access to public health. The declining birthrate, in turn, reflects the importance of birth control. As a result of family planning, the average number of children per female fell from 5.3 to 3.2 between 1914 and 1947. This trend was more notable and widespread in the provinces of the littoral than in those of the interior, and it was most prevalent in the large cities. In Buenos Aires, for example, the average number of children per female fell from 3.5 to just 1.5.

This sharp reduction in family size, which took place over a short period of time, points to the wide diffusion of new ideas about the family, closely linked with aspirations for respectability, social mobility, and greater material comfort. Smaller families were perhaps seen as good per se, but also as a necessary precondition for attaining improved levels of welfare and education. In fact, during this period female participation in the labor market reached its lowest level in the entire twentieth century, probably because greater numbers of young women from relatively affluent households were attending school or staying at home rather than going to the factory or the shop.[19] It is important to note that, in the large cities, reduction in family size was dominant throughout the entire social scale, with the exceptions of the traditional upper classes and the most marginalized poor.[20] Between these two extremes, the type of family most frequently associated with the middle class—one with few offspring, which valued saving and moderation, hard work, and education—spread far beyond the imprecise frontiers of that group. The strident rhetoric of the defenders of "tradition," chief among them the Catholic Church, could do little to alter the growing influence of these new ideas about the "modern" family.[21]

Patterns of reproductive behavior and attitudes toward the family indicate the extent to which upward social mobility continued to be a key goal for much of the population after the Depression. Scant statistical information, however, makes it difficult to determine how strong the impact of the slump on welfare and social betterment was. In some areas, its negative effects seem to have been modest. Life expectancy shows continued improvements in welfare: in the capital, average life expectancy rose from forty-nine years in 1914 to sixty in 1936 and sixty-five in 1947. Assessing how much of this increase depended on family income (and thus better nutrition, clothing, heating, etc.) and how much on the development of infrastructure and public health is not easy. However, it seems reasonable to conclude that, albeit at a slower pace, some advance in the quality of life of urban inhabitants was made once the worst years of the Depression were over.[22]

Access to education points in the same direction. By 1930, two-thirds of the school-age population attended primary schools. This percentage increased through the 1930s, contributing to reducing illiteracy from 48.5 percent in 1914 to 13.6 percent in 1947 (for comparison, 56 percent of the Brazilian population was illiterate in 1940).[23] By 1947, illiteracy was concentrated in peripheral regions of the country and in the older generations that had not benefited from the major expansion the education system had experienced since the turn of the century. The most significant advances in education, therefore, were attained in the secondary level. Between 1930 and 1945, enrollment in high school increased at an annual rate of 8.8 percent, well above the population growth rate (just under 2 percent per year). The number of secondary schools rose from 421 in 1930 to 762 in 1939.

Increase in enrollment was due in part to the massive incorporation of girls from relatively comfortable households for the first time. Largely absent from formal politics and public debate until the 1947 women suffrage law, women made inroads into public life through the educational system. The great majority of these girls chose the *magisterio* schools, where they trained as teachers. But the fact that enrollment in commercial and technical schools grew two times faster than in the more traditional Colegios Nacionales (which were the path to the universities and liberal professions) or the *magisterio* suggests that expansion of education toward lower rungs of society was taking place.[24] This set the stage for a further, and more rapid, increase during the Peronist decade, when enrollment in secondary education reached an average annual rate of 11.4 percent. University enrollment also increased between 1930 and 1945, rising from 19,800 to 33,500, at an annual rate of 5.5 percent.[25]

Albeit at a slower pace than in the 1920s and after 1945, gains in education were a key element in the long process of social betterment and improved welfare that characterized the broader period between the end of the nineteenth century and the 1970s. An exploration of other indicators highlights another aspect of this process. Following a contraction during the worst of the Depression, consumption of products such as pasteurized milk, alcoholic drinks, clothing, and footwear began to rise again.[26] In the second half of the 1930s, the Argentines were eating on average more meat (over 100 kg per person per year), more sugar, and far more cheese and butter than before the slump.[27] The leisure industry also grew. In 1929, there were 972 cinemas in Argentina; by 1936, that figure had risen to 1,424. In 1942, the average Argentinean went to the cinema seven or eight times per year, watching mainly American films (unlike in trade and financial policy, in this sphere the U.S. influence was paramount).[28] Telephone lines more than doubled (from 200,000 in 1928 to 460,000 in 1941 and 510,000 in 1945). The increase in the more democratic radio was more notable: between the end of the 1920s and 1947, the number of radios more than tripled (from 520,000 to 1.8 million), and the corresponding figure of number of inhabitants per radio fell from twenty to nine.[29] By 1947, half of all households had a radio. Although there were some regional differences, the distribution of radios was more or less equal across the country. In this period, two-thirds of all radio receivers in South America were in Argentina.[30]

In sum, although there is a lack of statistical information that would help us analyze more closely the period between 1930 and 1945, an examination of factors such as family structures, demographic changes, educational attainment, and consumption patterns suggests that following the slump, the gradual improvement in welfare that had characterized earlier periods was resumed. The emergence of an increasingly visible and populous middle class, whose values and way of life served as a reference point for broad sectors of the working class, was one of the most significant consequences of this process. The growth of the services economy, the increase in public sector and administrative employment, the expansion of the education system, and the development of larger manufacturing firms meant that the middle classes not only increased their numbers but also were present in increasingly diverse areas of activity.

These middle sectors were generally made up of European immigrant families and their descendants, but also of migrants from the interior who had successfully joined the league of better-paid urban workers, benefited from state employment, or ran their own businesses, taking advantage of the growing demand for skilled labor and more sophisticated services. Defining the contours of this amorphous and protean group is not easy, in part because the newly arrived were constantly joining its ranks. Gino Germani estimated that in Buenos Aires, the middle class rose from 38 percent of the population in 1914 to 46 percent in 1936 and 48 percent in 1947.[31] Even if there are doubts regarding the accuracy of these statistics, they nevertheless underscore the extent to which this group continued to grow during this period—although at a slower pace than in previous decades. It is perhaps more useful to point out the growing cultural and social weight of the middle class, rather than seek to determine its exact size. The middle classes and the ideology of self-improvement and social mobility that this group embodied became a visible and increasingly important element of the post-Depression society, spread through the cinema, the popular press, and the radio.[32]

The social impact of the slump on the middle classes, however, should not be overlooked. As Lila Caimari has recently noted, the anxieties associated with the dire experience of the economic downturn made the members of this group more cautious, in both social and political terms, thus giving a wider popular base to the conservative and in some cases antiliberal reaction of the period.[33] The rise in vagrancy, unemployment, and job insecurity and the spectacle of larger numbers of families struggling against deteriorating income made middle-class people more insecure of their place in society. Greater awareness of the fragility of individual and family betterment, and of the dangers of urban society, was therefore a new experience, as well as an important theme in the political discourse geared toward mobilizing the conservative feelings of these groups. This feeling of discomfort contributed to the conservative political climate so typical of the 1930s and was also exploited a few years later by Colonel Perón when seeking to capture the support of this group.[34]

The Transformations of the World of the Working Classes

Even if many of its members were dominated by a sense of uneasiness, the growth of the middle classes, although slower than in the 1920s, points to a pattern of social change characterized by strong continuities between the pre- and post-Depression period. When we turn our attention to the world of labor, however, change becomes more apparent. After the Depression, the industrial working class became more central to the economic life of the country, and also more politically articulated. A full understanding of this development needs to be put in a broader perspective.

Since the late nineteenth century, manufacturing grew at a rapid pace.[35] For several decades, however, transport workers (mainly in the railways and ports) stood among the most powerful, well-organized sectors of the workforce. In most other areas, only skilled, male laborers were organized in small craft unions (*sindicatos por oficio*). Manufacturing lacked any significant organization until the 1930s, as did many other sectors that were largely made up of unskilled workers. On the eve of the First World War, probably less than one out of ten urban workers were unionized. Trade unions, though much stronger than in any other Latin American country, were modest by the standards of industrialized Western Europe, where union density was around three times higher than in Argentina.[36]

Historians have exaggerated the problems that labor organization experienced as a result of the ideological and political disputes of this period (Anarchists vs. Socialists vs. Syndicalists). Rather, the limitations of the pre-1930s labor movement had a more structural origin. To a large extent, they resulted from the problems associated with organizing an uprooted labor force largely unwilling to invest much energy in the forging of unions. It is important to remember that, like the middle classes, the vast majority of workers in the large littoral cities were foreigners (in 1914, three-quarters of all adult males in places like Rosario and Buenos Aires were foreign-born). European migrants had come to Argentina because they were attracted by the prospect of high salaries and social and economic mobility, and as such they sought to escape, rather than reinforce, their proletarian status. They were for the most part more individualistic, more ambitious, and more educated than their countrymen who had remained on the other side of the Atlantic, and indeed than the native popular classes.[37] Even among those immigrants with left-wing sympathies, either of a Socialist or Anarchist nature (fewer indeed than those loyal to the Catholic Church), the idea of "hacer la América" was powerfully alluring. And for those who failed to improve their condition, or could not envision succeeding in the near future, it was often the case that returning to Europe, or moving on to another place, was an option that held an equal or greater appeal than collective action (as mentioned before, half of all immigrants in the 1852–1930 period ultimately left). Furthermore, the class-based loyalties that labor activists sought to promote often clashed with other powerful influences. In many workshops and factories, for example, hiring often took place on the basis of ethnic origin, which encouraged collaboration and paternalistic relations between workers, overseers, and employers. As in the United States, immigrants created a powerful network of ethnic institutions that diverted immigrant workers' energies from unions and radical politics.[38] Class solidarity and class identity, thus, were difficult to build. When activists succeeded in overcoming these obstacles, capitalists—always reluctant to tolerate any form of labor organization—set about sabotaging nascent unions.[39]

Broadly speaking, this context gave rise to two different types of labor organization and two different patterns of collective action. A negotiating style of trade unionism—which emphasized responsible dialogue with bosses and managers—emerged at quite an early stage within the most powerful and permanent organizations, often made up of skilled workers, such as in the railways. A quite different picture can be found in sectors where unskilled and casual workers predominated, especially where laborers had very little control over working conditions and hiring and firing. Weak unions in those sectors meant that protests were more sporadic, less able to secure the support of large sectors of the workforce, and (in part, as a consequence) often more violent. Up to the 1910s, the organization of protests for groups in this second category mostly depended on the initiative of small but hardened militant groups, among which the Anarchists were paramount. This minority caused increasing concern to both businessmen and governing elites and was subjected to persistent repression.[40]

The 1920s brought a rise in the importance of trade unionism, as well as a growing predominance of moderate and reformist voices within the workers' movement. Two factors contributed to these developments: the growing weight of Argentine-born laborers within the workforce and the democratization of the political system following the 1912–16 electoral reform. The period began with a strong wave of labor unrest, which reached its highest point in 1917, as the Great War came to an end. But once the dust of those years of popular impoverishment, social violence, and revolutionary aspirations began to settle, most workers increasingly adopted a moderate and pragmatic stance, turning their backs on the confrontational politics advocated first by Anarchists and later by Communists. The growing dynamism of the moderate Syndicalist current exemplified the extent of this shift. The *sindicalistas* focused their energy on the strengthening of unions and the improvement of labor conditions. They engaged in dialogue and negotiations with managers and actively sought, and increasingly secured, the approval and support of the government. The combination of a deeper democracy (the consequence of the 1912 reform) and an increasingly native (and thus enfranchised) working class provided a powerful incentive for those in government to pay heed to workers' demands. Finally, improvement in popular welfare following the postwar crisis made political extremism less attractive—a change that proved favorable to those sectors of the workers' movement more respectful of the social and political order.

Elected in broad and free elections, the Radical governments were supportive of this negotiating style of trade unionism. They favored *sindicalismo* not only because it helped them to secure allies, but also because it worked against the Anarchist organizations and challenged the unions influenced by the Socialist Party. The fortune of the Socialist Party had risen with democratization, and like the Radicals, it devoted resources to the worker movement, forging close links with skilled laborers in the service industries and public sector workers. Its influence, however, was largely restricted to the city of Buenos Aires. At the end of the 1920s, then, the railway unions, united since 1922 in the Unión Ferroviaria, continued to make up the backbone of the worker movement. But the combination of a more favorable political climate and the changing composition of the laboring population (in favor of more native Argentineans) triggered the growth of new unions. Chief among these organizations were the public sector and skilled service industries, such as telephone and shop employees. In the manufacturing sector, in contrast, unions made no gains. Overall, the worker movement was characterized by its moderate and reformist approach. After the demise of the Anarchists, the only exception to this rule was the small group tied to the Communist Party, still a very marginal player in the world of labor.[41]

In the 1930s, this panorama changed. Apart from deteriorated living standards, the Depression caused the highest levels of unemployment that the country had ever seen. Argentina, previously an importer of European labor, was suddenly faced with an unemployment rate of over 20 percent. Labor demand recovered in 1933, spurred by manufacturing growth. However, salaries remained low throughout the 1930s, particularly in manufacturing. In 1936, some three years into the recovery, the Departamento Nacional del Trabajo (National Department for Work, DNT) estimated that the average monthly salary of a working head of family could cover just 77 percent of the household basic needs (food representing some 57 percent of total expenditure).[42] The DNT also found that real salaries did not rise at all between 1932 and 1943.[43] Information on income distribution, available from 1935 on, confirms this bleak picture. Despite steady economic growth, labor's share of national income shrunk between 1935 and 1942.[44] As the Década Infame went by, inequality became more acute, with more wealth concentrating at the top. Between 1932 and 1943, the top 1 percent increased their share of national income from 17 to 25 percent. By 1943, the level of income concentration in Argentina was very high by international standards.[45] The 1930s was a good period for the rich, especially for the rich that derived their income from urban and industrial concerns.

Most probably, greater economic inequality affected workers more than any other group in urban society. It is important to break down this broad category in order to identify which types of laborers were particularly deprived. Existing evidence suggests that manufacturing workers were among the most afflicted. From the middle of the decade, manufacturing became the principal generator of new jobs (the factory labor force more than doubled during this period, from 400,000 in 1936 to 900,000 in 1946).[46] However, the majority of these jobs were characterized by low salaries and poor working conditions. This was the result of the peculiar circumstances in which industry became the leading sector in the post-Depression economy. Scarcity of up-to-date technology and a contraction in financing meant that manufacturing growth depended on cheap labor rather than on technical innovation and productivity gains (in fact, despite significant manufacturing growth, in the 1930s imports of capital goods declined in comparison with the previous decade from 20 to 15 percent of total imports). This pattern played a central role in the creation of a large factory proletariat that was more disadvantaged than other urban subaltern groups.

Official surveys indicate that wages in the manufacturing sector were among the lowest in the urban labor market. Between the end of World War I and the late 1920s, real salaries almost doubled. Thereafter, they stagnated below the 1928–29 levels for more than a decade. Some estimates suggest that real wages for industrial workers were 10–15 percent lower than average salaries.[47] In 1938, the DNT estimated that a sum of $165 was necessary to cover the basic needs of a worker's family. This was equivalent to the average salary of public sector and electrical workers. For laborers in other sectors, however, this amount remained far from reach: average salaries ranged from $113 in the food processing and wood industries to $111 in construction, $108 in chemicals, $93 in clothing, and just $84 in the textile industry.[48] In the textile industry, the fastest-growing manufacturing sector throughout the 1930s, salaries were some 30 percent lower by the end of the decade than in 1928/29.[49] It is important to note that these were the average wages in some of the most dynamic industries at a time when the worst of the Depression had been left behind. Thus, Miguel Murmis and Juan Carlos Portantiero seem to have got it right when they argued in a pioneering study that one of the most significant consequences of manufacturing growth during the post-Depression years was the formation of a large and deprived industrial workforce.[50] For many newly arrived to the world of the factory in the 1930s, the old belief that Argentina always offered a future that was brighter than the present or the past no longer held true.

An examination of labor conflicts offers further evidence of the degree of deprivation experienced by workers in the manufacturing sector, as well as some indirect insight into how workers perceived their circumstances. During General Uriburu's dictatorship (1930–32), union activists were criminalized and persecuted, and protests were banned. The repression, which included firing squads and deportations, was particularly targeted at Communists and Anarchists. Managers took advantage of state repression to lower salaries, alter working conditions, and fire workers. In the Unión Telefónica, a North American company, the firings began the same day Uriburu seized power. Repression and restrictions on union activity were relaxed when the dictatorship came to an end.[51] In the first months of Agustin P. Justo's presidency (1932–38), there was a wave of strikes, as workers sought to recover the ground they had lost. The fact that the early 1932 strikes took place at the height of the Depression, and that they lacked state support, largely doomed them to failure. Virtually all were defeated: official data indicate that more than 70 percent failed to achieve their aims.[52]

Workers became more cautious following this bitter experience. In the three years that followed, the number of strikes fell dramatically. Weakened by the economic downturn, union leaders sought new ways to press their demands. As Joel Horowitz has shown, the most successful were those who garnered support from within the political system, particularly through their links with the Socialist Party. The Radical withdrawal from elections between 1931 and 1935 made the victory of the Concordancia possible, but it also gave disproportionate weight to the Left in Parliament. With forty-three deputies—27 percent of the lower chamber, and seven or eight times more benches than during the 1920s—the Socialist Party became an active articulator of union demands. Socialist support was crucial in passing legislation in favor of shop assistants, including shorter working days, greater regulation of working conditions, and protection from redundancy. The principal spokesman of the shop workers was Ángel Borlenghi, who had strong links with the Socialist Party. Municipal workers—also led by a figure close to the Socialist Party—secured similar rights during this period. In contrast, unions that were more closely affiliated with *sindicalismo* suffered with the decline of the Radicals. The Federación Obrera Marítima (Maritime Workers Federation), which had already suffered important defeats in the late 1920s, continued to decline. To avoid a similar fate, the Unión Ferroviaria, still the only truly important national union (with 70,000 members, almost half of all unionized workers in the country belonged to this organization), shifted from a *sindicalista* leadership to one more closely affiliated with Socialism in 1934. Unsurprisingly, the following year the Confederación General del Trabajo (General Confederation of Labor, CGT) fell under Socialist control.

The achievements of the Socialist Party in the world of labor must be placed in context. They only benefited a minority of the workforce, largely composed of skilled workers in the most prosperous and long-established service sectors who enjoyed good salaries and had also been unionized for some time. For that reason, the rising influence of this type of trade union and their leaders within the party did little to alter the profile of Socialism as a party of the middle classes—white-collar, skilled, and politically moderate workers.[53] Hence, the task of organizing the new swathes of workers who were entering the industrial labor force remained largely undone. It was here, in the fast-growing but little-organized manufacturing sector, that the Communists won their most important battles.

The Communist Party was founded in 1920 as a breakaway group from the left wing of Socialism. Created at a time when liberalism and thus political reformism were powerful forces in Argentinean public life, Communism's appeal was very limited in both intellectual circles and the student movement.[54] From the mid-1920s onward, the party emphasized its worker profile; it adopted a cell structure and eagerly sought to increase its presence in workshops and factories.[55] Once the harshest years of the Uriburu government were over, the Reds made important gains. The rising influence of the small Communist Party within the working class coincided with the post-1933 tightening of the labor market. In a context that offered workers greater incentives and means to protest, the Communist militants contributed decisively to the organization of labor in the manufacturing sector. Between 1936 and 1941, the membership of organized labor as a whole increased by approximately 18 percent, but members of industrial unions doubled. This was largely the product of the Reds' efforts. In this five-year period, the growth of the four most significant unions led by Communists made up 95 percent of the total increase in unionization. As a result, between 1936 and 1941 unionized workers grew from 15 to 20 percent of the industrial workforce.[56]

In the food sector, the Reds overcame the resistance of the large companies (the meat-packing plants were particularly tough) and organized the powerful Federación Obrera de la Alimentación (Federation of Food Workers), which boasted 20,000 members by 1940. The union was headed by José Peter, a native of Entre Ríos and one of the most popular Communist leaders.[57] In the textile industry, where female, low-paid laborers made up a considerable portion of the workforce, Communist militants also established the basis of a strong union. These newcomers to the world of organized labor achieved their most notable success in the construction industry, which had hitherto been divided into numerous profession-based unions (brick layers, plasterers, painters, plumbers, etc.). In 1935 and 1936, the Communists initiated a series of strikes that laid the foundations for the powerful Federación Obrera Nacional de la Construcción (Federation of Construction Workers, FONC), an organization that "with close to 58,000 members (of which some 40,000 regularly paid dues) became the second largest organization in the country, second only to the Unión Ferroviaria in terms of numbers."[58] The FONC—which succeeded in recruiting almost half of its total potential membership in the large cities—was very much an organizational miracle in a procyclical industry, also characterized by size diversity and the geographical dispersion of the companies.[59] As a result of their success in the manufacturing unions, by the end of the decade the Reds had emerged as a potent force in the world of labor and shared the leadership of the CGT with the Socialists.

The Reds had a more ambitious and clear vision of the organizational challenges faced by the manufacturing workers than their Socialist and Syndicalist counterparts, as well as greater incentives to overcome them. They concentrated their energy not on the formation of factory or profession-based unions (*sindicatos por oficio*), but rather on industry-wide, large unions and federations: organizations that were made up of all workers in a particular sector, regardless of gender, rank, or skill level.[60] These new types of unions played a key role in improving the bargaining power of the weakest sectors of the labor force, where organization was largely absent. Establishing unions of this nature required much energy, tactical flexibility, and resources. One example of this flexibility was the Communists' attitude toward female workers, a group of increasing importance in the manufacturing sector. The Red activists promoted an agenda that centered on securing rights for this underpaid and overexploited group, demanding maternity legislation and a guarantee of equal pay with male workers. Even though they were operating in sectors with little or no experience of organization, Communists benefited from the resources of a small but highly disciplined party machine that (in contrast with the Socialists) was focused on the manufacturing working class. Finally, it is important to note that the party achieved its greatest successes when it abandoned the "class against class" rhetoric of the Third Period and agitated in favor of a center-left Popular Front against Fascism (1936–39). During those years, Communist militants presented themselves not as class warriors but as responsible leaders, always willing to improve the conditions of the workers and to institutionalize negotiations between labor and capital.

In spite of their moderation, however, the Communists never entirely renounced their revolutionary goals and remained staunch critics not only of Fascism but also of the Argentinean social and political order. The founding charter of the FONC, for example, stated that "the private property of the means of production and change is the permanent cause of the hunger and misery of the working classes . . . foreign-owned monopolies and the Argentine dominant classes they control keep the working class in an in-human condition of work and life, trying to sink the popular masses into the Fascist terror in order to perpetuate the actual state of things and to prevent the independent organization of the proletariat."[61] All the Communist-led unions promoted this view. Time and again, in workshops, on street corners, and in meetings, their militants and party propaganda emphasized the need to build class power and to destroy the capitalist order. When we consider that in the previous 20 years most laborers had embraced reformist tendencies, the success of the Communist Party in attracting wide support among workers is notable. This, of course, was not because in the 1930s the Communists enjoyed more freedom to organize. On the contrary, during this period, fears of the "Red danger" meant that Communist activists were persecuted even more systematically than in the past (in 1937, for example, Guido Fioravanti, the secretary-general of the FONC, and several other Communist militants were deported to Italy, where they were imprisoned by the Fascist government). Also, it is important to note that among workers the appeal of Communism did not lie in the power of its vision of a classless society or (as was often the case in some intellectual circles) in admiration for the Soviet Union's achievements. Some historians, therefore, have argued that the success of Communist unionism lay instead in the organizational capabilities and the commitment of its activists, which transformed Communism into a powerful promoter of higher salaries and better working conditions.[62]

However, emphasizing this pragmatic, instrumental dimension of the relationship between Communist activists and rank-and-file workers runs the risk of an overly narrow, pre-Thompsonian approach. The rise of Communists was not just the product of their dedication and self-sacrifice, nor of the success of a new type of bread-and-butter unionism. A better understanding of the link between militants and workers needs to take into account those elements of the people's experience that, in the 1930s, made Communism far more attractive than before. In the wake of the Depression, the Reds' criticism of Argentina as an unequal and unjust society coincided—more than at any other moment in the past—with the inner feelings and perceptions of a significant number of workers. Rather than the intellectual or ideological appeal of the idea of revolution or of a classless society, commitment to Communist unionism indicates the considerable degree of political alienation and hopelessness felt by some of the most deprived sectors of the urban workforce. The Communists' success in the world of labor speaks less of a thorough rejection of middle-class values and the ideal of social mobility than of the feeling that, in the present circumstances, those ideals were simply unattainable.

How did the Great Depression affect Argentinean society, and what were its broader consequences? A number of works published since the 1980s have argued that, as the world slump receded, Argentina returned to the path of greater social mobility and increased welfare that had characterized its development during the first three decades of the twentieth century. Throughout the Década Infame, the middle classes continued to expand and played an increasingly important role in the social and cultural realm. In those years, the large estancieros saw their wealth diminished and their cultural influence eroded. As a result of the move toward inward-looking development forced by the Depression, there emerged a new wealthy elite, largely autonomous, in values and outlook, from the traditional landed families. In the 1930s, the growing influence of the middle classes was felt throughout much of the social scale. Amid much criticism of the traditional upper class, patterns of consumption, attitudes toward the family, and ways of life associated with the middle classes became more prominent, providing an inspirational model for a growing number of members of the popular classes. This process ran parallel to the formation of a more culturally integrated and homogenous national society, the product of the expansion of primary and secondary education; the growth of the popular press, the cinema, and the radio; and the development of consumerism and professional sport.

The end of transatlantic migration and the rise in internal migration — the latter a consequence not only of rural decline during the Depression but also of the allure of urban life — also contributed to fostering the cultural homogeneity of the population. Internal migration brought about new social tensions. However, by the end of this period, when two-thirds of the country's inhabitants lived in the littoral region (and almost one-quarter of the total population in Buenos Aires alone), descendants of European immigrants and first-generation migrants from the interior had increased their symbolic and physical integration into the nation. By 1945, Argentinean society had lost much of its deference to its traditional elites and was both more homogeneous and better articulated.

Narratives that emphasize the continuity of the 1930s with previous decades, however, often fail to acknowledge the limitations of these twin processes of social change and cultural integration. The early 1930s economic downturn had a lasting impact on the middle classes. Greater awareness of the fragility of upward social mobility made this group more insecure and more conservative. Also, for the most part, progress did not extend to the poorest regions in the interior, especially in the northwestern provinces: any serious change in the lives of the inhabitants of those marginal areas was the result of emigration. Similarly, the large littoral cities also experienced conflicts and tensions, which would have more serious political implications.

Accounts focused on the working class have noted that the growth in manufacturing during the 1930s contributed to the swelling of an industrial workforce that lacked many of the benefits of urban life that more prosperous and integrated sectors of society enjoyed. Neither the governing elites nor the main opposition forces—the principal actors in the fraudulent political scenario of the Década Infame—paid much attention to this group, and both remained unwilling to set up a program of social reform capable of incorporating their demands. Eager to reverse the economic downturn, the ruling coalition expended much energy to ensure recovery of tax collection and to instill new life into the exporting sector and the domestic market. When the worst of the Depression was over, the Concordancia's most ambitious projects were geared toward the renovation and expansion of infrastructure, primarily through the construction of roads and buildings. More concerned with economic recovery than with social reform, they abandoned many of the welfare initiatives that their Radical predecessors had begun in the 1920s, for example, in housing (where a program of freezing urban rents was discontinued).[63] Furthermore, little was done to supply better medical care, regulate working conditions, or further worker rights. Growing conservatism in large sectors of the urban population meant that there was less pressure from below to move in a reformist direction. Unlike Chile or Mexico, which shifted to the left as a result of the Depression, Argentina turned to the right not only because of Uriburu's coup d'état and the Concordancia's fraudulent regime, but also because this program of order could count on a social base that included not only elite groups but also large sectors of the middle classes.

Lacking representation not only within the Concordancia and the state elite but also within the established world of Radicals, Socialists, and moderate, reformist trade unionists, the most vulnerable and unprotected sectors of the urban working classes became the target of more radical interpellations. Communism was the main beneficiary of this situation. During the 1930s, this force made important inroads into the expanding world of industrial labor. It is ironic that precisely at the same time when the nationalization of the masses was gaining ground (in 1936, the national anthem was sung at the celebration of Workers' Day for the first time), the most dynamic labor activists felt the allure of international revolutionary Communism. In the manufacturing sector, the advance of the Reds was both rapid and deep. Brutal state repression failed to stem it. Communist success did not transform organized labor overnight. But by the beginning of the 1940s, several large industrial unions were consolidated, and unionized workers represented around 20 percent of the nonagricultural workers in the country. This figure, while only half the rates of unionization in Europe's industrial core, was surely the highest in Latin America.

Seen from the point of view of class formation, however, the forward march of Communist unionism after the Great Depression proved fragile. The class rhetoric of the Reds ultimately failed to alter in any lasting sense the inner feelings of the workers on the shape of a desirable social order, which had its roots not only in traditional notions of the good order but also in the growing appeal of middle-class lifestyles and the persistent power of the ideology of social mobility. The making of a culturally more homogeneous society meant that the popular classes felt with increased force the embrace of integration. To a certain extent, thus, the formation of a more articulate proletarian politics and stronger unions in the aftermath of the Depression coincided, rather than with a critique of the world of the middle classes in the name of proletarian or popular values, with a certain degree of frustration at being unable to take advantage of opportunities for social advancement that extended to the middle classes. In fact, those who described the rise of Communism as the result of a worker consciousness hostile to the existing order were proved wrong just a few years later. This explains why the Peronist regime's implementation of a program that broadened worker rights and gave greater importance to labor organization, while at the same time seeking to cast the workers in an anti-Communist, middle-class mold, received massive popular support, not least from the workers of the very unions in which the Reds' influence had been most powerful.

Notes

I would like to acknowledge comments by Lila Caimari and the participants in the Great Depression in the Americas and Its Legacies Conference, Institute for the Study of the Americas, London, June 20, 2011.

1   The classic account is Miguel Murmis and Juan Carlos Portantiero, *Estudios sobre los orígenes del peronismo* (Buenos Aires: Siglo XXI, 1971). See also David

Tamarin, *The Argentine Labor Movement, 1930–1945: A Study in the Origins of Peronism* (Albuquerque: University of New Mexico Press, 1985).

2 Leandro Gutiérrez and Luis Alberto Romero, *Sectores populares, cultura y política: Buenos Aires en la entreguerra* (Buenos Aires: Sudamericana), 1995. See also Francis Korn and Luis Alberto Romero, "Introducción," in *Buenos Aires/ Entreguerras: La callada transformación*, ed. Francis Korn and Luis Alberto Romero (Buenos Aires: Alianza, 2006), 9–33. Critical assessments of this approach can be found in Matthew B. Karush, "The Melodramatic Nation: Integration and Polarization in the Argentine Cinema of the 1930s," *Hispanic American Historical Review* 87, no. 2 (2007): 293–326; and Hernán Camarero, "Consideraciones sobre la historia social de la Argentina urbana en las décadas de 1920 y 1930: Clase obrera y sectores populares," *Nuevo Topo: Revista de historia y pensamiento crítico* 4 (2007): 35–60.

3 See, for example, Loris Zanatta, *Perón y el mito de la nación católica: Iglesia y Ejército en los orígenes del peronismo (1943–1946)* (Buenos Aires: Sudamericana, 1999).

4 Pablo Gerchunoff and Lucas Llach, *El ciclo de la ilusión y el desencanto: Un siglo de políticas económicas argentinas* (Buenos Aires: Ariel, 1998), 463–64.

5 Angus Maddison, *Monitoring the World Economy, 1820–1992* (Paris: OECD Development Centre, 1995); Victor Bulmer-Thomas, *An Economic History of Latin America since Independence* (Cambridge: Cambridge University Press, 1994), 218–22.

6 Rosemary Thorp, *Progress, Poverty and Exclusion: An Economic History of Latin America in the 20th Century* (Washington, DC: Inter-American Development Bank, 1998), 116.

7 Arturo O'Connell, "Argentina into the Depression: Problems of an Open Economy," in *Latin America in the 1930s: The Role of the Periphery in World Crisis*, ed. Rosemary Thorp (London: Macmillan, 1984).

8 Roy Hora, *Los terratenientes de la pampa argentina: Una historia social y política, 1860–1945* (Buenos Aires: Siglo Veintiuno de Argentina Editores, 2005), 279–351; Gerchunoff and Llach, *El ciclo de la ilusión*, 140; Roy Hora and Leandro Losada, "Clases altas y clases medias en la Argentina, 1880–1930: Notas para la definición de una agenda de investigación," *Desarrollo Económico* 50, no. 200 (2011): 611–30.

9 Ricardo D. Salvatore, "Stature, Nutrition, and Regional Convergence: The Argentine Northwest in the First Half of the Twentieth Century," *Social Science History* 28, no. 2 (2004): 297–324.

10 Alfredo Palacios, *El dolor argentino* (Buenos Aires: Claridad, 1938).

11 Hora, *Los terratenientes de la pampa argentina*, 325–33.

12 Gino Germani, *Estructura social de la Argentina* (Buenos Aires: Raigal, 1955), 75–76; David Rock, "Argentina, 1930–46," in *Argentina since Independence*, ed. Leslie Bethell (Cambridge: Cambridge University Press, 1993), 198.

13 For a recent assessment of these changes, see Lila Caimari, "Población y sociedad," in *Argentina: Mirando hacia dentro (1930–1960)*, ed. Alejandro Catta-

ruzza (Madrid: Mapfre-Taurus, 2012), 191–244. Intellectual debates on the growth of Buenos Aires are explored in Anahí Ballent and Adrián Gorelik, "País urbano y país rural: La modernización territorial y su crisis," in *Crisis económica, avance del Estado e incertidumbre política*, ed. Alejandro Cattaruzza (Buenos Aires: Sudamericana, 2001), 180–84.

14 See, among others, Tulio Halperin Donghi, *La Republica Imposible (1930–1945)* (Buenos Aires: Emece, 2007); David Rock, *Authoritarian Argentina: The Nationalist Movement, Its History and Its Impact* (Berkeley: University of California Press, 1992); Beatriz Sarlo, *Una modernidad periférica: Buenos Aires 1920 y 1930* (Buenos Aires: Nueva Visión, 1998).

15 See Fernando Devoto, *Historia de la inmigración en la Argentina* (Buenos Aires: Sudamericana, 2001).

16 Elina Tranchini, "El cine argentino y la construcción de un imaginario criollista, 1915–1945," *Entrepasados* 9, nos. 18/19 (2000): 113–43; Karush, "Melodramatic Nation," 293–326; Andrea Matallana, *"Locos por la radio": Una historia social de la radiofonía en la Argentina, 1923–1947* (Buenos Aires: Prometeo, 2006).

17 On racial discourses discriminating dark-skinned people, see Enrique Garguin, "'Los argentinos descendemos de los barcos': The Racial Articulation of Middle-Class Identity in Argentina (1920–1960)," *Latin American and Caribbean Ethnic Studies* 2, no. 2 (2007): 161–84.

18 On Atahualpa Yupanqui, see Sergio Pujol, *En nombre del folclore: Biografía de Atahualpa Yupanqui* (Buenos Aires: Emecé, 2008), 177–78.

19 Catalina Wainerman, "Mujeres que trabajan: Hechos e ideas," in *Población y bienestar*, ed. Susana Torrado (Buenos Aires: Edhasa, 2007), vol. 2, 333.

20 Susana Torrado, *Historia de la familia en la Argentina moderna (1870–2000)* (Buenos Aires: Ediciones de la Flor, 2003), 323–69.

21 These changes are analyzed in Caimari, "Población y sociedad."

22 An exploration of access to housing, however, presents us with a less encouraging picture. The 1947 census shows that only 17.5 percent of the dwellings in Buenos Aires and 43.3 percent in Greater Buenos Aires were owner occupied. On the eve of Perón's accession to government, access to a home of one's own—which had since the beginning of the century been a key milestone in the path to social betterment—remained far from reach for the majority of urban dwellers. It is unclear, however, whether the situation worsened during the 1930s. In fact, housing in the major cities had been a problem since the nineteenth century, as an ever-increasing population always put pressure on the available housing stock. Anahí Ballent, "La casa para todos: Grandeza y miseria de la vivienda masiva," in *Historia de la vida privada en la Argentina*, vol. 3, ed. Fernando Devoto and Marta Madero (Buenos Aires: Taurus, 1999).

23 Fernando Devoto and Boris Fausto, *Argentina-Brasil, 1850–2000: Un ensayo de historia comparada* (Buenos Aires: Sudamericana, 2008), 244.

24 Juan Carlos Tedesco, "La crisis de la hegemonía oligárquica y el sistema educativo argentino, 1930–1945," in *Educación y sociedad en la Argentina (1880–1945)*,

ed. Juan Carlos Tedesco (Buenos Aires: Siglo XXI, 2008), 236; Ministerio de Educación y Justicia, Departamento Estadístico, Enseñanza Media, *Enseñanza Media, Tomos I y II, 1914–1963* (Buenos Aires, 1964), 58–59 and 283, cited in Juan Carlos Torre and Elisa Pastoriza, "La democratización del bienestar," in *Los años peronistas (1946–1955)*, ed. Juan Carlos Torre (Buenos Aires: Sudamericana, 2002), 298.

25 Juan Carlos Tedesco and Alejandra Cardini, "Educación y sociedad: Proyectos educativos y perspectivas futuras," in Torrado, *Población y bienestar*, 2:465. See also Pablo Buchbinder, *Historia de las universidades argentinas* (Buenos Aires: Sudamericana, 2005).

26 Fernando Rocchi, "La americanización del consumo: Las batallas por el mercado argentino, 1920–1945," in *Americanización: Estados Unidos y América Latina en el Siglo XX: Transferencias económicas, tecnológicas y culturales*, ed. María Inés Barbero and Andrés Regalsky (Buenos Aires: Eduntref, 2003).

27 Consumption of imported food (such as coffee and tea) remained stagnant or fell, suggesting that there was import substitution in this area too. See *Revista de Economía Argentina* 24, no. 286 (April 1942): 98, and 24, no. 287 (May 1942): 128.

28 Karush, "Melodramatic Nation," 299.

29 Matallana, *"Locos por la radio,"* appendixes 1 and 2.

30 Matallana, *"Locos por la radio,"* 36.

31 Germani, *Estructura social de la Argentina*, 139–225.

32 Caimari, "Población y sociedad."

33 Lila Caimari, *Mientas la ciudad duerme: Pistoleros, policías y periodistas en Buenos Aires, 1920–1945* (Buenos Aires: Siglo XXI, 2012).

34 Ezequiel Adamosvky, *Historia de la clase media argentina: Apogeo y decadencia de una ilusión, 1919–2003* (Buenos Aires: Planeta, 2009), 245–50.

35 Fernando Rocchi, *Chimneys in the Desert: Industrialization in Argentina during the Export Boom Years, 1870–1930* (Stanford, CA: Stanford University Press, 2006).

36 For useful comparisons in unionization levels in other large Latin American countries, see Brian Loveman, *Chile: The Legacy of Hispanic Capitalism* (Oxford: Oxford University Press, 2011), 205; Joel Wolfe, *Working Women, Working Men: São Paulo and the Rise of Brazil's Industrial Working Class, 1900–1955* (Durham, NC: Duke University Press, 1993), 78–83. For unionization levels in Europe, see Geoff Eley, *Forging Democracy: The History of the Left in Europe, 1850–2000* (New York: Oxford University Press, 2002), 70.

37 Roy Hora, *Historia económica del siglo XIX en Argentina* (Buenos Aires: Siglo XXI, 2010), 174–82.

38 John Laslett, *Reluctant Proletarians: A Short Comparative History of American Socialism* (Westport, CT: Greenwood, 1984).

39 The development of labor politics in this period is analyzed in Ricardo Falcón, "Izquierdas, régimen político, cuestión étnica y cuestión social en Argentina,

1890–1912," *Anuario* (Rosario: Universidad Nacional del Litoral, 1986/87), 365–89; Roberto Korzeniewicz, "The Labour Movement and the State in Argentina, 1887–1907," *Bulletin of Latin American Research* 8, no. 1 (1989): 25–45; Jeremy Adelman, "Socialism and Democracy in Argentina in the Age of the Second International," *Hispanic American Historical Review* 72, no. 2 (1992): 211–38; Hernán Camarero and Carlos Miguel Herrera, "El Partido Socialista en Argentina: nudos históricos y perspectivas historiográficas," in *El Partido Socialista en Argentina: Sociedad, política e ideas a través de un siglo*, ed. Hernan Camarero and Carlos Miguel Herrera (Buenos Aires: Prometeo, 2005), 9–73.

40 On the relationship between Anarchists, the labor movement, and the state, see Ruth Thompson, "The Limitations of Ideology in the Early Argentine Labour Movement: Anarchism in the Trade Unions," *Journal of Latin American Studies* 16 (1984): 81–99; Korzeniewicz, "Labour Movement"; Juan Suriano, "Trabajadores, anarquismo y Estado represor: De la Ley de Residencia a la Ley de Defensa Social (1902–1910)," in *Conflictos y Procesos de la Historia Argentina Contemporánea* (Buenos Aires: Centro Editor de América Latina, 1988); Eduardo Zimmermann, *Los liberales reformistas: La cuestión social en la Argentina 1890–1916* (Buenos Aires: Sudamericana–Universidad de San Andrés, 1995).

41 For a comprehensive study of labor politics during the Radical period, see Joel Horowitz, *Argentina's Radical Party and Popular Mobilization, 1916–1930* (University Park: Penn State University Press, 2008). See also David Rock, *El radicalismo argentino, 1890–1930* (Buenos Aires: Amorrortu, 1975), 146–56; Tulio Halperin Donghi, *Vida y muerte de la República verdadera (1910–1930)* (Buenos Aires: Emecé, 2000), 131–42; Juan Carlos Torre, "¿Por qué no existió un fuerte movimiento obrero socialista en la Argentina?," in *El político y el científico: Ensayos en homenaje a Juan Carlos Portantiero*, ed. Claudia Hilb (Buenos Aires: Siglo XXI/UB, 2009), 33–49; Ricardo Falcón and Alejandra Montserrat, "Estado, empresas, trabajadores y sindicatos," in *Democracia, conflicto social y renovación de ideas (1916–1930)*, ed. Ricardo Falcón (Buenos Aires: Sudamericana, 2003), 151–94.

42 Departamento Nacional del Trabajo, División de Estadística, *Condiciones de vida de la familia obrera* (Buenos Aires, 1937), 28.

43 Joel Horowitz, *Los sindicatos, el Estado y el surgimiento de Perón, 1930–1946* (Buenos Aires: Eduntref, 2004), 55.

44 Secretaría de Asuntos Económicos, *Producto e ingreso de la República Argentina en el período 1935–54* (Buenos Aires: G. Kraft, 1955), 63, 120–21; Sebastián Galiani and Pablo Gerchunoff, "The Labor Market," in *A New Economic History of Argentina*, ed. Gerardo Della Paolera and Alan M. Taylor (Cambridge: Cambridge University Press, 2004), 152.

45 Facundo Alvaredo, "The Rich in Argentina over the Twentieth Century," *mimeo*, 2008, 14.

46 *Censo Nacional de 1947*, vol. 3, 26–27.

47 Tamarin, *Argentine Labor Movement*, 32.

48 Departamento Nacional del Trabajo, División de Estadística, *Investigaciones sociales, 1938* (Buenos Aires, 1939), 19.

49 Roberto Cortés Conde, "Los comienzos de la industrialización argentina," in *La economía argentina en el largo plazo: Ensayos de historia económica de los siglo XIX y XX*, ed. R. Cortés Conde (Buenos Aires: Editorial Sudamericana, 1997), 220.

50 Murmis and Portantiero, *Estudios sobre los orígenes del peronismo*, 76.

51 Tamarin, *Argentine Labor Movement*, 84–85.

52 Departamento Nacional del Trabajo, División de Estadística, *Estadística de las Huelgas* (Buenos Aires, 1940), 20; Horowitz, *Los sindicatos*, 111. See also Roberto Korzeniewicz, "Las vísperas del peronismo: Los conflictos laborales entre 1930 y 1943," *Desarrollo Económico* 33, no. 131 (1993): 324–25.

53 Juan Carlos Portantiero, "Imágenes de la crisis: El socialismo en la década de 1930," *Prismas* 6 (2002): 231–41.

54 Andrés Bisso, "De *Acción Democrática* a la *Unión Democrática*: El civismo antifascista como prédica política y estrategia partidaria del Socialismo Argentino (1940–1946)," *Prismas* 6 (2002): 257–64; Ricardo Pasolini, "El nacimiento de una sensibilidad política: Cultura antifascista, comunismo y nación en la Argentina: entre la AIAPE y el Congreso Argentino de la Cultura, 1935–1955," *Desarrollo Económico* 45, no. 179 (2005): 403–33.

55 On the Communists, see José M. Arico, "Los comunistas y el movimiento obrero," *La Ciudad Futura* 4 (1987): 15–17; Jorge Cernadas, Roberto Pittaluga, and Horacio Tarcus, "La historiografía sobre el Partido Comunista de la Argentina: Un estado de la cuestión," *El Rodaballo* 4, no. 8 (1998): 30–39; and Hernán Camarero, *A la conquista de la clase obrera: Los comunistas y el mundo del trabajo en la Argentina, 1920–1935* (Buenos Aires: Siglo XXI, 2008).

56 Tamarin, *Argentine Labor Movement*, 149.

57 On Peter, see his autobiography, *Crónicas Proletarias* (Buenos Aires: Esfera, 1968).

58 Hugo del Campo, *Sindicalismo y peronismo: Los comienzos de un vínculo perdurable* (Buenos Aires: CLACSO, 1983), 96.

59 Celia Durruty, *Clase obrera y peronismo* (Córdoba: Cuadernos de Pasado y Presente, 1969); Korzeniewicz, "Las vísperas del peronismo," 333–34.

60 Tamarin, *Argentine Labor Movement*, 148; Korzeniewicz, "Las vísperas del peronismo."

61 Departamento Nacional del Trabajo, División de Estadística, *Organización Sindical: Asociaciones obreras y patronales* (Buenos Aires, 1941), 31.

62 Tamarin, *Argentine Labor Movement*, 152; Korzeniewicz, "Las vísperas del peronismo," 335.

63 Anahi Ballent, "Políticas de la vivienda, arquitectura doméstica y cultura del habitar," in Torrado, *Población y bienestar*, 2:420.

CHAPTER 2

Chilean Workers and the Great Depression, 1930–1938

Angela Vergara

In November 1930, Jacinto Vera asked the governor of Mataquito for a railway ticket to travel to Talca or Santiago. After losing his job as a cook in the Oficina Alianza, a nitrate complex located about sixty miles southeast of Iquique, Vera had arrived in the small southern town of Curepto, in the Valley of Mataquito, in October 1930. He had traveled more than a thousand miles and, like many nitrate workers, boarded a steamship in the port of Iquique, traveling as a third-class passenger on the deck, took a train from Valparaíso to Santiago, and waited in the Alameda Station for a train to the south. Since he had probably arrived in the north as an *enganchado*, the Association of Nitrate Producers had covered his travel expenses from Iquique to Curepto, and national authorities had carefully recorded his movements. However, Vera was unable to find a job in his native town, and he decided to move again and try his luck in Talca (the provincial capital) or Santiago.[1] Like Vera, Berta Campos and her two-year-old son were also hoping to travel. After being abandoned by her husband in Iquique, Campos was living in one of the many emergency shelters opened by the Ministry of Social Welfare (Ministerio de Bienestar Social) in that impoverished city. She had no formal employment history and no hope to find work in Iquique, and she decided to ask local authorities for economic assistance to move to Valparaíso, where she expected to live with some relatives.[2]

Vera's and Campos's stories, as well as their uncertain futures, reflect both the devastating impact of the Great Depression on the Chilean economy and working people and some of their personal strategies to cope with this crisis. Since the end of 1929, Chileans like Vera and Campos had been suffering the dramatic consequences of the collapse of the international market, which hit first and with special intensity the nitrate and mining industries located in the far north. Following the fall of international prices and the export sector, the country was unable to pay for imports or access foreign loans, and the crisis quickly expanded to other economic sectors. Price deflation and a growing state deficit characterized the first years of the crisis (1929–31), and by July 1931, the Chilean state was unable to continue making payments on its foreign debt, support public works, or pay the salaries of public employees. Facing the imminent collapse of the national economy and widespread protests, President Carlos Ibáñez del Campo, an authoritarian populist general who had assumed power in 1927, was forced to resign.[3]

Throughout 1932, growing political instability, erratic economic policies, changes in monetary policies, and increasing state expenditures in unemployment relief and public works turned deflation into uncontrollable inflation.[4] This year was also marked by the radicalization of politics, and the leaders of the Socialist Republic (from June to September 1932) promised Chileans a "republic of workers not of slaves, of dignified, free and committed workers."[5] Public demonstrations, protests, and rallies and the growing visibility of the poor in the public space of Chile's main cities added to the effervescence of those months, creating fear and anxiety among the elite. Although unable to resolve the crisis or consolidate its power, the symbolic one hundred Socialist days left a deep imprint on the Chilean Left.[6] Elected in 1932 and supported by a broad center-right political coalition, President Arturo Alessandri Palma enforced strict stabilization measures, supported the ongoing process of unionization, but heavily repressed social movements that stepped outside the law. By 1933, the Chilean economy started recovering, but international prices for mining exports only improved in 1935, employment in the mining sector never recovered to the pre-Depression era, and working people's wages remained low.[7]

This chapter looks at the impact of the Great Depression on working people and the ways in which state agencies responded to the social and economic crisis, focusing on the period between 1930 and the victory of the Popular Front in 1938. As in other parts of the Western world, the social and economic consequences of the crisis created a wider consensus on the need for a strong and interventionist state, a state that could sponsor and promote social programs, enforce and supervise labor rights, regulate the national economy, and promote the industrialization of the country.[8] In doing so, the state responded to the drama of impoverished Chilean working families and incorporated the political and social sensibilities of a new generation of students and young professionals (e.g., medical doctors, social workers, lawyers), men and women, who eagerly joined the ranks of public officers and contributed to the construction—and eventual transformation—of welfare and social services and the state.[9] To understand the impact of the Great Depression and the relationship between state agencies and working people, this chapter focuses on three main issues: unemployment and public work, social assistance, and union rights and struggles during these critical years.

Challenging the traditional image that has depicted the 1930s as a time when social and labor laws co-opted a radical and militant labor movement, this chapter demonstrates that working people were able to resist, negotiate, and adapt to the changing economic and political conditions.[10] Chilean workers were far from being passive, and they actively participated in political rallies and protests, negotiated better working conditions and salaries, protected the few jobs available, organized in the numerous shelters, and started joining the recently formed legal trade unions. But above all, they were on the move, leaving the regions more struck by the crisis to find work in the countryside; in the construction of roads, railways, and dams; in gold mining; and even in the Bolivian tin mines and Argentine southern *estancias*. In doing so, they brought along their own political, organizing, and labor experiences, spreading fear among landowners and political authorities from smaller towns and cities.

The relationship between the unemployed and the state agencies in charge of their well-being was complex. The years of the Great Depression illustrate the tensions between a state that attempted to use public services, relief programs, and labor laws to control and co-opt working people and working families' efforts to interpret and use those services and laws to improve conditions in their own ways.[11] In the following years, as scholars of Chile's Popular Front and Latin American populism have clearly demonstrated, workers and labor organizations navigated a complex reality, finding ways to negotiate, adapt, and transform the meanings of social assistance and labor laws, redefining the meanings of the welfare state.[12] In this context, the deep transformations that took place in the early 1930s established the rules that determined the future struggles for the political and economic empowerment of Chilean working people.

Unemployment and Geographical Mobility

The ways in which the Great Depression impacted the Chilean economy and working people and the enormous difficulties in recovering were a result of the characteristics of the country's most important commodity: the nitrate industry. Chile's strong dependency on the external market and nitrate production, economic historians argued, explained the devastating impact of the crisis on the country. Since the end of the War of the Pacific (1879–83), nitrate, found throughout the Atacama Desert, had become the engine of the Chilean economy, generating considerable revenues to the national state, funding public investment in infrastructure, and providing a market for cheap consumer and industrial goods and agricultural products. Through the traditional *enganche* system, thousands of Chilean workers had migrated to the north, where they faced harsh working conditions, employment insecurity, and precarious living arrangements.[13] By the late nineteenth century, the nitrate fields were home to a proletarian labor culture and identity, and nitrate workers had started leading local and general strikes that became the foundation of a national and radical labor movement that brought the labor question to the forefront of national politics.[14]

As with many other commodities, the nitrate market was very unstable, and the Chilean state and the national economy had become particularly sensitive to these international cycles. Following the outbreak of World War I, nitrate had suffered its most severe crisis, representing, for many, the beginning of the end of the nitrate era.[15] At this time, most nitrate *oficinas* (nitrate complexes) closed down, and thousands of nitrate workers migrated back to Santiago, Valparaíso, and the Central Valley, forcing the national state and private institutions to organize a few relief programs. The Servicio de Colocaciones, for example, opened in 1914 under the supervision of the Labor Department. "In face of the extraordinary severity of the general work crisis," the government stated, "superior considerations of public interest and social welfare motivate the Government to adopt . . . all those useful measures to regularize the distribution and placement of unemployed blue-collar workers."[16] A sort of placement office, the Servicio de Colocaciones registered and placed unemployed workers in jobs in agriculture, public works, and industries throughout the country. In addition, local authorities, private charity institutions, and Catholic parishes organized soup kitchens and shelters for migrant and unemployed workers.[17] Many of these programs became the basis of the public response to the Great Depression in the early 1930s.

In the late 1920s, a short economic prosperity brought new waves of migrants to the north, and enganches started, once again, arriving regularly in the ports of Antofagasta and Iquique. The recently opened large-scale and foreign-owned copper mines of Potrerillos (Atacama) and Chuquicamata (Calama) also offered plenty of job opportunities for mine and construction workers, motivating the arrival of not only Chilean peons but also Bolivian and Peruvian nationals. The economic prosperity was short-lived, and by December 1929, local authorities in the northern nitrate ports of Iquique and Antofagasta were reporting that oficinas were shutting down, and many workers once again faced the threat of unemployment.

Although the crisis turned out to be much more severe, more extensive, and longer than previous economic downturns, workers in the Great Depression era had more rights, political resources, and experience to survive and negotiate with both employers and local and national authorities. In the first decades of the twentieth century, increasing levels of social and labor mobilization, as well as awareness or fear of the dangers of the so-called social and labor questions, had inspired the enactment of the first social laws.[18] The movement for social laws had advanced slowly, and only after military pressures (the well-known "rattling of sabers / *ruido de sables*") led by General Carlos Ibáñez del Campo in 1924 did the National Congress approve a large package of laws that included the right to unionize, work contracts, arbitration boards, accident compensation, and social security.[19] In the following years, and especially during the Ibáñez administration (1927–31), the state carefully enforced the new laws as efforts to control and co-opt workers and a skeptical and radicalized labor movement represented by the Federación Obrera de Chile (FOCH).[20]

Despite its limited enforcement until the late 1930s, labor laws provided workers with some rights when facing layoffs and offered public officers a way to manage and regulate unemployment during the Depression. As a result, the Labor Department, with its offices located throughout the country, would play an important role in organizing a local reaction to the crisis, responding to workers' complaints of unpaid salaries or social benefits and massive layoffs. In fact, when nitrate oficinas started shutting down in early 1930, the Labor Department assigned three extra employees to Tarapacá to make sure that employers "let go blue-collar workers from their work in a proper way."[21] Similarly, government officials strongly believed that their ability to both relocate workers throughout different economic sectors and regions and prevent social turmoil was based on having control over when and how workers were being fired and on being able to negotiate with employers the terms and pace of the shutdowns. The minister of social welfare, then, instructed all local officers to prevent "surprise layoffs," requiring all employers to provide a twenty-day notice of any layoff involving more than fifty workers.[22] While many authors have looked at the years of the Great Depression as a time of regression in labor laws, the rich documentation from the Office of Labor showed very active public administrators who, despite the economic and institutional constraints, struggled to enforce the law.[23]

As labor authorities made efforts to control the labor market in a time of crisis, the question of workers' mobility and migration became especially complicated. The Great Depression had put, once again, nitrate workers and their families on the move, both demonstrating the fragility of the Chilean export economy and the importance of geographical mobility as a survival strategy for workers and bringing the reality of poverty and unemployment to the streets of Chile's main cities.[24] Between September 1930 and February 1931, 46,459 people (22,415 men, 9,072 women, and 14,972 children) had left the nitrate fields, boarded steamships in Antofagasta or Iquique, and arrived in Santiago and other smaller provincial cities.[25] Public authorities attempted to control and supervise the return-migration process, making sure that workers were distributed evenly throughout the country and avoiding the dangerous concentration of the unemployed in larger cities such as Santiago and Valparaíso. According to the instructions of the Labor Department, unemployed nitrate workers were to be sent either to their place of origin (where they could confirm that they had relatives who could support them) or where there were available employment opportunities.

The demands of unemployed nitrate workers in the province of Tarapacá in 1930 illuminate some of the debates regarding workers' migration, as well as the state's effort to control it. In the first months of 1930, when there was not a clear understanding of the dimension and extension of the economic crisis, nitrate employers in Tarapacá attempted to reallocate workers within the nitrate industry, moving them from the oficinas that were closing down to the ones that were still operating. However, according to the Intendente of Tarapacá, workers were arriving on a daily basis to his office demanding to be sent back to the south, where, according to them, there were better living and working opportunities. The ambiguity of the situation led to several interpretations of the rights and obligations of nitrate employers.[26] The Labor Department and the Intendencia of Tarapacá agreed that while companies probably had the legal right to relocate workers within the nitrate districts, since they were unable to guarantee basic living and working conditions, especially for workers with families, the contract should be considered terminated and employers had to pay workers' travel expenses.[27]

Despite state control and lack of economic resources, Chilean workers continued moving throughout the early 1930s, contesting the state's policies. Mobility, then, exemplified both the state effort to relocate and distribute people and working people's own personal strategies of survival. As the intendente of the province of Cautín denounced in November of 1930, many of the unemployed who were arriving in this southern province had no or only a very distant connection to the region and no means of survival.[28] The arrival of these *forasteros* (outsiders) in small provincial cities inspired both fear and frustration among regional authorities and members of the elite, many of whom believed that it was not their responsibility to care for them. "There are one thousand unemployed people," explained the intendente of Coquimbo, "who are wandering through towns and homes in search of food, producing great alarm among residents."[29] In these small regional cities and towns, the fear produced by the arrival of masses of unemployed men was aggravated by the lack of employment opportunities or a public infrastructure to assist unemployed migrants.

The extension and intensity of the crisis made the movement of unemployed workers and their families much more difficult and controversial, and public authorities struggled to control workers' geographical mobility despite their legal rights and personal choices. When the intendente of Magallanes announced that at the end of the 1930 sheep-shearing season Magallanes would face the challenge of relocating about five thousand unemployed workers, the minister of social welfare commanded him to send workers only to Puerto Montt and Talcahuano and avoid sending people to Santiago. Given the desperate situation in Magallanes, the intendente of Puerto Montt suspended all future enganches to that region, attempting to dissuade workers from his province from moving there. Since workers, especially from the island of Chiloé, insisted on moving to Magallanes, and given the fact that there were no legal mechanisms to prevent people from moving, public officers forced any worker going to the province of Magallanes to sign a document renouncing their right to seek public assistance.[30] In other words, workers could move to Magallanes at their own risk.

As the crisis expanded throughout the entire country and people were on the move, registering and supervising unemployed men, women, and

Table 2.1. Labor Market: Monthly Report

MONTH AND YEAR	NUMBER OF PEOPLE SEEKING A JOB	NUMBER OF PEOPLE PLACED	DIFFERENCE
December 1929	5734	1679	4055
January 1930	1414	1051	363
February 1930	1507	852	655
March 1930	1666	1147	519
April 1930	1332	830	502
May 1930	927	280	647
June 1930	885	321	564
September 1930	1730	180	1550
October 1930	4300	2749	1551
November 1930	4339	1375	2964

Source: Oficina de Colocaciones, ARNAD, Dirección General del Trabajo, volumes 213, 214, 215, 216, 220, and 222.

children and finding local employment opportunities for them became especially challenging. The minister of social welfare relied on local *carabineros* to register people at the regional offices of the Labor Department, where they would receive a registration card that confirmed their status as unemployed.[31] Throughout the first two years of the crisis, the Oficina de Colocaciones carefully registered the number of unemployed workers and made serious efforts to distribute workers in agriculture, mining, and public construction works (e.g., city improvement projects, railroads, roads, dams, canals). However, as table 2.1 suggests, the number of workers placed by this agency was always lower than the number of registered workers seeking a job, who were probably also a small percentage of the total of unemployed people in the country.

Job opportunities were limited to agriculture, public works, and gold mining, but they became even scarcer as the crisis affected almost every sector of the Chilean economy by 1932.[32] In the summer of 1930, there was a still a high labor demand in agricultural fields, but it was seasonal and short-term work, and labor officials recognized that conditions and salaries were below workers' expectations, and thus many refused to go. In San Felipe, in the Valley of Aconcagua, there were three hundred unemployed men (most of whom had come from the nitrate fields). While a few of them were working in the construction of a new hospital in the town of Putaendo, most were working in agriculture (hemp plantations and grape vineyards).[33] In April 1930, at the end of the summer season, not only were many facing unemployment again, but the 110 people who had being working for one of the local wineries, Viña Errázuriz Panquehue, complained to the Labor Department that they had not been paid.[34] The following year, a mix of weather conditions, bad prices, and lack of credit reduced agricultural production by about 20 percent, and unemployment rates in agricultural provinces such as Chillán, Los Angeles, and Cautín soared.[35]

As during the World War I nitrate crisis, state officials resorted to placing unemployed workers in construction work. Public works included a wide range of construction jobs from railroads, country roads, canals, port infrastructure, and public buildings. Throughout 1930 and early 1931, they offered one of the most important sources of employment, and the Labor Department in tandem with regional authorities attempted to control the placement of workers, negotiate with private construction firms and contractors, and regulate working conditions. In March 1931, for example, the city of Rancagua announced that it would start paving the city streets and planned to hire about two hundred people. For this purpose, the Municipal Government and the Labor Department opened an office in town to register workers, but since local authorities expected to fill up all job openings with local unemployed men, regional officers especially feared that a large number of "outsiders" would come to Rancagua looking for a job.[36] In general, while work in urban construction projects was relatively attractive, building isolated railroads, roads, and canals was very hard and unappealing for the majority of unemployed men.

As the state deficit increased and the country's ability to import dropped throughout 1931, many important public construction works were suspended or slowed down.[37] In April 1931, the firm Fernández, Vallejos y Cía slowed down the construction of the road between Valdivia and La Unión and laid off three hundred workers, and Dyckerhoff and Widmann suspended work in the port of Puerto Montt and fired 110 workers.[38] In May, road construction projects were interrupted in the province of Aysén, and the same happened to the railroad Corte Alto-Maullín in Valdivia.[39] In the works that remained opened, salaries and working conditions deteriorated. The general director of public works and the Ministry of Social Welfare allowed contractors to pay salaries only every two months and advance part of the salary in tokens for the company store.[40] In many cases, construction firms would not pay workers on time, as was the case of the five hundred workers employed in road construction in the province of Aysén. Without their salaries, some of them had decided to wait in the small city of Puerto Aysén, where they had spent all their money on lodging and food, while others had gone back to the island of Chiloé only with a receipt. And despite the fact that the contractor had made the mandatory social security deductions, none of these construction workers had received or seen their *libretas* (social security payment books).[41]

Gold mining was one of the few remaining mining activities in a country that had based its economic prosperity on the extraction of minerals and nitrate and, thus, attracted a large number of former mine workers from the north. In an effort to increase the country's gold supply and create jobs, the Ibáñez administration had promoted gold panning, offering credit, supplies, and assistance to small mining entrepreneurs. In return, these contractors had to sell their entire production to the state.[42] Throughout 1932, gold mining appeared in government discourses as an effective solution against unemployment and the general crisis. "The so-called Gold Campaign," explained Víctor Navarrete (minister of Fomento during the Socialist Republic), was a response to "people starving because of lack of work."[43] Despite the government's promises that gold mining would employ about 40,000 workers, gold production had a limited impact on reducing unemployment or recovering the economy. In addition, working conditions, the Labor Department recognized, were very "*sui generis*." The Dirección General de Cesantía was responsible for bringing workers to gold-panning sites — assuming the costs of transportation — but people were employed by a private contractor. There were no work contracts, and the Labor Department only required contractors to provide some documentation defining working arrangements, method of payment, and food and housing conditions. The contractor was also responsible for providing health care in case of work accidents and making regular payments for the workers' social security fund, but there was no effort to build permanent labor camps since work was considered transitory.[44]

As public authorities struggled to place unemployed men in the few still-available jobs in agriculture, gold mining, and public construction works, they became increasingly concerned about the consequences of unemployment. The ability to work was at the core of the social and labor reforms of the first three decades of the twentieth century, and as work had become increasingly regulated and formalized, it also guaranteed people access to basic social services (health care, social security, and protection). Massive and long-term unemployment, then, seriously threatened the viability of this model, and even the survival of basic institutions such as the Caja de Seguro Obrero (Social Security Fund).[45] Already in 1924, Carlos Contreras Labarca, a prominent politician and member of the Communist Party, had argued that forced unemployment was the greatest danger to "social collectivities" and made an urgent call to national authorities and labor organizations to design effective programs to prevent and ameliorate its impact.[46]

More conservative sectors were especially concerned about masses of unemployed people who could not support themselves or could become socially and politically dangerous individuals. If women and children needed to be protected and fed, men needed to work and be productive in order to prevent their social degradation. Putting healthy men to work was also necessary to reactivate the economy, and it quickly became evident that for the state the amount of the salary was less important than the experience (and discipline) of regular work. Because of this, most public officials were eager to get men out of the shelters, believing that these places would only make them lazier and accustomed to charitable aid.

When the Prefectura of Cautín decided to place some unemployed men on road construction work in 1931, they believed that by "paying salaries low enough [two to four pesos] to cover individuals' food expenses, they would provide economic help and prevent them both from losing their work habits or having time to develop subversive activities."[47] Alarmed by workers' refusal to work, police officers took their names out of the unemployment list, making them ineligible for future benefits or jobs. In Linares, public officials faced a similar situation. When a local landowner, Miguel Bustamantes, offered to hire forty men, paying them eighty cents per day and providing daily meals, unemployed men who were staying in the local shelter refused to go. In response to what was considered an unreasonable reaction, an angry representative of the Ministry of Labor ordered suspension of all food rations to these men.[48]

As these examples suggest, despite widespread poverty and state coercion, public officials faced many difficulties in trying to convince unemployed workers to accept low salaries or bad working conditions, and many unemployed men preferred to keep moving and work only occasionally. Labor inspectors, regional authorities, employers, and police officers continuously complained about workers abandoning the job after a few days or refusing to accept work. In some cases, unemployed men and women made serious efforts to negotiate better working and salary conditions, suggesting the existence of a militant labor tradition. In the coal town of Coronel, for example, unemployed workers decided to organize and form a committee to negotiate with the Labor Department. Assisted—according to a police report—by the FOCH, workers agreed to the following:

> (1) To not accept a $4 pesos salary, but $5 pesos—working per day and to reject piece work; (2) That the weekly salary would be paid in cash and not in food . . . ; (3) Agreed on asking a cash advance of a minimum $.20, to leave to each family, with the purpose they would not be abandoned without resources; (4) That when needing workers the Labor Department must deal directly with the Committee to be able to control which are the ones who have more need to work; (5) Not to accept any kind of work, before these demands have been accepted.[49]

Despite these instances of worker resistance, by 1932 more than 50,000 nitrate workers had lost their jobs, most of whom moved to other parts of the country in search of better opportunities. But factories, agricultural fields, and public and construction works were also feeling the impact of the Depression. In 1931, according to the Ministry of Labor, there were 56,000 blue-collar workers (*obreros*) and 11,300 white-collar workers (*empleados particulares*) unemployed. By late 1932, the numbers had increased to 98,000 obreros and 25,200 empleados.[50] The labor laws enacted during the first decades of the twentieth century on the one hand, and Chilean workers' increasing politicization and militancy, and their traditional mobility, on the other, shaped the ways in which Chilean workers initially responded to the economic crisis. However, given the enormous difficulties in finding work and daily survival, most unemployed families would have to rely on some form of public and/or private aid.

Occupying Public Spaces: Shelters and Soup Kitchens

As in many other countries hit by the Depression, the image of "poverty" and the impact that poverty had on working men and their families raised public and private concerns. Children and women needed food, migrant workers did not have a place to sleep or bathe, and masses of unemployed presented a threat to public order, public health, and political stability. While the programs did not differ much from previous responses to economic and unemployment crisis, the extension of the Great Depression quickly demonstrated the need both to expand assistance and to design a national response.[51] As during previous economic crises, a mix of public, private charity, and religious institutions organized soup kitchens and food distribution programs and opened the first shelters in most cities. The desire to assist the needy also intertwined with social apprehension, and most programs of social assistance attempted to both assist and control the unemployed.

The ways in which the state and private institutions responded to the needs of the unemployed were clearly a product of the deep changes that social assistance had experienced. Since the late nineteenth century, both private and public institutions had made efforts to define the "poor" and provide aid only to those who were really in need (e.g., children, the elderly, the disabled, abandoned women). Consistent with this perception, institutions made efforts to record, evaluate, and measure the "needs" of the poor, building the bases of the professionalization of social work in the first decades of the twentieth century. At the same time, aid became increasingly rationalized, and social workers, medical doctors, and nurses developed notions of what was the "right" meal, shelter, or attention that the poor in need should receive. Women, especially social workers and nurses, were at the forefront of social services, showing not only the incorporation of women into the state but also the increasing professionalization of traditional women's roles and jobs.[52]

Conditions in the northern port of Coquimbo were characteristic of the ways in which local authorities outside Santiago struggled to help unemployed families. In the first months of 1931, Coquimbo had recorded 509 families in need of some form of aid. In February, with the support of local businesses and rural estate owners (*hacendados*), the city was able to deliver only 350 food rations. In March, the food delivery increased to 1,194 rations, local bakers provided twenty daily bread rations, and the Alcaldía had organized the delivery of ninety rations of milk every day. In addition, about thirty local households were receiving unemployed families for either lunch or dinner in their homes. In April, however, private donations had radically plunged, and although the delivery of bread and milk continued, food rations for the first two weeks of the months had been reduced to two hundred. In two months, the Alcaldía had spent 1,369.70 pesos in assisting the unemployed, 441.50 of which had come from private donations.[53] Since Coquimbo had no shelter, most of the people in need were local or former nitrate and mine workers who had relatives in the city.

The difficulties faced by authorities in Coquimbo were also emblematic of how the Ibáñez administration's response to the crisis lacked a coherent centralized structure and mostly relied on local institutions and resources. On the eve of Ibáñez's downfall, most cities were unable to continue supporting shelters and soup kitchens, and the government encouraged the organization of regional committees that could organize a quick response to the crisis and make use of available local resources. The so-called Comités Pro-Auxilio de Cesantes included representatives of different local groups and institutions, and they worked along with the regional government. In Iquique, for example, the committee was integrated by the intendente, the bishop, one representative of industry (general manager of the railway), president of the Cámara de Comercio (business organization), a representative of unemployed white-collar employees, a representative of the blue-collar workers, and the regional head of the Ministry of Social Welfare. In this northern port, the committee was in charge of administering resources, providing 24,000 daily food rations (buying, cooking, and distributing them), and maintained three shelters that housed a total of 563 people.[54]

Building on its historical tradition in assisting the poor, the Catholic Church played an important role in organizing soup kitchens, providing services, and collaborating with the state. In 1931, archbishop of Santiago Horacio Campillo recommended all parishes to open soup kitchens, making a special call to rich families to protect "at least one poor person, a brother, and to contribute with money to redress the hunger and cold of those who are suffering."[55] Other Catholic groups such as the Sociedad de San Vicente de Paul organized the distribution of daily meals and clothes, and many Catholic women quickly signed up as volunteers in many shelters.[56] While some of these actions responded to traditional Christian values (charity), in other cases they represented a larger transformation of Catholic social thought. Especially significant was the influence of Catholic intellectuals such as Juan Enrique Concha and Francisco Vives. Vives, a Jesuit priest, returned to Chile in 1931 after more than a decade in Europe. In the midst of the economic and political crisis, Vives mentored student groups and Catholic labor unions, disseminating the Vatican's encyclicals *Rerum Novarum* (1891) and *Quadragessimo Anno* (1931) and denouncing the dangers of both capitalism and Communism.[57]

The motivations of public and private aid were complex, shaped by an effort to help, control, and transform poor communities. To save the unemployed from the social, physical, and moral decay into which they had been pushed by the Depression, social workers, Catholic volunteers, and police officers offered shelter, healthy food, and safe spaces for recreation. As in the question of migration and job placement, working people's expectations and demands clashed with public authorities' discourse of control and intervention. In many cases, social assistance and intervention intertwined with discourses and practices of social control, and the line between the needy unemployed and the dangerous one was blurred. In the shelters and soup kitchens, for example, public workers and volunteers sought not only to provide assistance but also to inculcate notions of hygiene, nutrition, and a work ethic. For these same reasons, public authorities opposed workers' own efforts to organize and control assistance, which challenged top-down solutions. In the working-class neighborhood of San Miguel in Santiago, for example, the municipal government immediately rejected the petitions of the "Comité de obreros cesantes de la Población La Legua" to collect food and money, arguing that it was not safe to authorize unknown people to replace the state.[58]

For some, as the following case from Valparaíso clearly suggests, institutionalized assistance was an effective way to prevent what was perceived as the radicalization of unemployed men. In this port, for example, city authorities were especially concerned with the large number of unemployed workers who were arriving on a daily basis from the nitrate fields. Unemployed workers had formed a Comité de Cesantes, local authorities explained, that was supported by a local labor union of "anarchical ideas," which had also offered them shelter in the union hall. The committee had attempted to negotiate better working conditions in public works and other places where unemployed men had been placed, to the point, according to the city report, that employers and contractors were refusing to receive unemployed workers from the port. The city responded by exerting more control over unemployed workers, and as an effort to break down the solidarity between unemployed nitrate workers and local port workers and political activists, the Intendencia opened a special shelter that was under the strict supervision of the regional office of the Ministry of Social Welfare and police officers.[59]

As the Depression deepened, concerns grew about the impact of unemployment and poverty on the country's social fabric and stability. The shelters became especially problematic, identified as sites of moral and physical decline. Adriana Izquierdo, a Catholic social worker, explained in 1932 that shelters were no more than places of "disorder, organized resistance, subversion, committees with communist ties, and political weapons against the government."[60] The shelters, then, were always under strict police surveillance. In Puerto Montt, the shelter was established in an old police building, and police officers controlled and supervised all its operations. In Santiago, for example, while the Red Cross and its committed female volunteers administered the three shelters (Santa María, Bascuñán, and El Salto) that were operating in the city by late 1931, police officers were in charge of safety and security. Given the strict police control, it was not uncommon for men to be expelled from a shelter or to be refused admittance, and they were constantly accused of heavy drinking, committing crimes, or misbehaving in public spaces.

In the El Salto shelter, located in a working-class neighborhood north of downtown Santiago, police officers reported that unemployed men were constantly consuming alcohol and committing "excesses" in the neighborhood. Police officers ordered residents from El Salto shelter to find a job, and they announced that "under no circumstances they would accept that they [unemployed] are swarming around the city streets or around the mentioned shelter [El Salto]."[61] Similarly, in the Calle Bacuñán shelter, located in Santiago's Estación Central neighborhood, six workers were expelled and accused of arriving drunk (three men) and robbery (three men) in July 1931. But the expelled men quickly responded to what they perceived as an arbitrary decision, and the president of the shelter committee went to a meeting in La Casa del Pueblo; with the support of those assembled, they were able to denounce police brutality and receive the support of three members of the National Congress.[62] The leaders of the Bascuñán shelter also denounced delays in the daily delivery of milk, which usually arrived around lunchtime, leaving children without breakfast.[63]

Whether the shelters were too strict or there was not enough room, a large number of destitute people preferred to occupy public spaces, confronting Chileans with the daily image of homeless, dirty, and hungry men, women, and children. More than five hundred people were living informally in Cerro Blanco, a small hill with many caves located near the National Cemetery, north of Santiago. Journalists described bad and precarious conditions, labeling the new tenants as an overt threat to public health and public order.[64] As the number of squatters increased, the Labor Department ordered their immediate removal, sending them to the Casa de Limpieza, "where they were subjected to a special cleaning, bathed, shaved, and had a haircut." Their clothes were also washed and disinfected, and social workers provided them with additional clothes. Following this severe "disinfection" that reminds us of the methods used during the epidemics of the turn of the century, the men were taken on a truck and sent to do public work, and the few women in the group were diagnosed as being mentally or physically sick and sent to a public hospital.[65] The different fate faced by women and men also suggested how notions of gender influenced public views of unemployment and assistance.

In 1932, the worst year of the Depression, unemployment, poverty, and hunger expanded throughout the entire country, forcing political authorities to expand public aid. The widespread political instability that had followed the downfall of Ibáñez in July 1931 and the rise of the Socialist Republic had also created the political conditions to introduce changes in monetary policies and increase public expenditures. As the 1932 annual report of the Central Bank recognized, "the fact that the Government considered it impossible to adopt strong actions to reduce its expenses" forced the Central Bank to increase the money supply to finance "the needs of the State."[66] For example, in April 1932, the National Congress authorized President Juan Antonio Montero to spend an additional 152 million pesos to pay for government expenses, public works, and public aid for the unemployed. To do so, the government was authorized to print money and "vales de Tesoro."[67] This new source of funding made it possible to increase public assistance. By July 1932, popular restaurants were delivering about 100,000 meals a day throughout the country; in Santiago alone, there were twenty-seven soup kitchens providing more than 60,000 meals a day.[68] In the case of Santiago, where housing had become a real challenge, the government authorized unemployed families to occupy vacant houses and lots in the Población San Eugenio Nuevo.[69]

Following the electoral victory of President Arturo Alessandri in October 1932, the Labor Department made a new effort to centralize public assistance, and the many committees and *servicios de cesantías* were placed under its jurisdiction. This reorganization coincided with the effort to exert more control over who was receiving help and what was being done with public resources, as well as to start closing some of the shelters. In their many visits throughout the country, labor inspectors complained of people who were able but did not want to work and were receiving public aid. In Huasco, the inspector denounced "the enormous abuses that existed in giving food rations to people who were neither unemployed blue-collar workers nor white-collar employees, but only destitute people who have never worked in their life. Adding to this, there was a substantial number of women who before the soup kitchen used to work doing laundry, in agriculture, or as domestics."[70] He found a similar situation in La Serena, where he believed that many of the men who were receiving food rations "did not want to go to work."[71]

By 1933, most of the shelters and soup kitchens were closed down and unemployment rates were declining, but workers were confronted with the strict economic measures of the Arturo Alessandri administration (1932–38) and his so-called minister of hunger, Gustavo Ross. High rates of inflation continued to threaten workers' income, and since the nitrate industry never really recovered to the precrisis levels, many stayed in Santiago and larger cities, struggling to find permanent work and housing and dealing with the high costs of living. Many of them had made enormous sacrifices during the worst years of the Depression, and through the recently formed labor unions they demanded a legitimate share for their work.

Negotiating Working Conditions amid the Crisis and Inflation

As discussed earlier, following the enactment of the most important pieces of labor legislation in Chile in 1924, workers and labor authorities made serious efforts to enforce the law, unionize, and engage in collective bargaining.[72] How workers were able to organize, file grievances, and defend their jobs in a time of severe economic crisis and political instability and repression is a compelling story that demonstrates the influence of the Chilean labor movement, their long tradition of struggle, and their strong capacity to understand and use the labor legislation and build political alliances. In the midst of the most severe economic crisis of the twentieth century, the Chilean workplace was a contested space, and the many small and local struggles over wages, benefits, and work hours eventually empowered the labor movement and gave them an important presence not only in workers' everyday life but also in the political history of Chile.

On the eve of the Depression, as most labor authorities throughout the country pointed out, the offices were overwhelmed with the amount of grievances presented by both urban and rural workers, and lack of funding made it increasingly difficult to offer enough assistance or carry out careful inspections of work sites. In the late 1920s, labor inspectors strived to enforce the social security and work accident laws and encouraged employers to provide written work contracts to all their employees and to have clear internal regulations (*reglamentos internos*). Similarly, inspectors paid special emphasis to bakeries in an effort to control abuses in a trade that usually required night shifts and long hours of work. An important part of the grievances also came from rural workers and *inquilinos* (agricultural tenement workers), who, despite landowners' opposition, brought to light the many abuses that were being committed in the countryside.[73] Many times, officials recognized, their work mostly consisted of teaching how the new laws worked, answering the many questions from both employers and employees.

As scholars of the Chilean countryside have pointed out, to enforce the labor legislation in rural communities was especially challenging; long distances, isolation, and employers' opposition quickly limited the impact of labor laws. Rural employers made constant efforts to hinder the enforcement of labor laws. In Victoria, the governor recognized in 1930, for example, that "there are rebel rural employers who do not forget the time when they were owners of lives and haciendas, and when authorities did not dare to judge their acts. Now, when they receive a summons to respond to a complaint, either they do not show up at the Gobernación or, if they do, it is to say that they will not accept any agreement."[74] Similarly, in Los Angeles, for example, landowners demanded the suspension of Law 4054 (the social security law that required employers to contribute to workers' social fund) in the countryside, arguing that it made it too costly to hire workers and that without the "burden" of this law, they would be able to offer them some form of small and odd jobs.[75]

Under the Ibáñez administration (1927–31), it became clear that the new laws could be used as powerful tools to control workers, prevent the radicalization of the labor movement, and marginalize older activists linked to leftist and anarchist groups.[76] In 1930, for example, the governor of El Loa, Carlos Vegas, carefully supervised the organization and election of a labor union in the copper mine of Chuquicamata, hoping to "clean up" the organization, prevent the empowerment of "caudillos," and only allow the "good worker" to be included.[77] Similarly, in Valparaíso, the Secretario de Bienestar Social recognized that some of the local union leaders had been involved in "subversive" and politically inspired actions, but they were quickly removed from their positions.[78] Near Santiago, in La Calera, labor inspectors and police officers feared Communist influence on cement workers from the El Melón plant, who were planning to walk out in November 1931. In response, the Labor Department sent a new inspector to "calm down" the workers.[79] Despite the repression, Chilean historian Jorge Barría explains, about eighty-five legal labor unions were formed under the Ibáñez administration, representing nearly 25,000 members.[80]

As the Depression worsened, labor inspectors and workers focused on unpaid salaries and layoffs, and the question of unionization was temporarily postponed. Many of the situations were particularly extreme, and most of the time Labor Department officials were not dealing with unionized workers or with formal workers' organizations. In the southern province of Magallanes, for example, the labor inspector and the intendente had to intervene to provide some form of solution to the forty mine workers who had been employed in Isla Diego de Almagro and had been unpaid and abandoned for more than eleven months.[81] When there were labor unions, workers mostly negotiated with employers and the Labor Department to maintain their job, or at least part of it. While sometimes these conversations were part of the regular process of collective bargaining and employers' efforts to redefine the work contract, most of the time they were temporary agreements between workers and employers mediated by local labor inspectors. More importantly, these initiatives were important in establishing a relationship between workers and officers from the Labor Department, which became the basis for the enforcement of labor laws at the local level.

Despite the efforts of labor inspectors to mediate and prevent unemployment, new conditions, whether a shorter work schedule or changes in pay, were not always accepted. This seems to be especially the case when the measures were imposed by employers and not a result of a conversation with workers' representatives. In the Anaconda-owned mine of Potrerillos, for example, the company imposed, in December 1931, two measures to cope with the economic crisis: a 10 percent reduction in wages and salaries, and a four-day workweek. In January 1932, more than four hundred workers rejected the new labor arrangements, and a crowd of 806 people — 410 workers and 396 women and children — left Potrerillos. A special wagon train, paid for by Andes Copper, brought workers and their families to Copiapó, increasing the "list of unemployed; it especially affects their families because of the lack of food."[82] In Chuquicamata, copper workers faced similar problems. In 1932, Burr Wheeler, general manager of Chuquicamata, also announced a 10 percent wage reduction for all workers.[83] These rejections also suggest how workers and their families were probably weighing different choices and opportunities, making careful decisions about their future.

With the recovery of the national economy, labor inspectors undertook again the challenge of unionization. During his first government tenure,

Arturo Alessandri (1920–24) had made enormous efforts to pass labor reforms, but he had faced strong opposition from the National Congress and the laws were only approved under military pressures. Although the Alessandri who returned to power in 1932 had clearly left behind the popular style that had characterized his first government and his conservative fiscal policies affected working families, his government showed a commitment to institutionalizing labor relations, conceiving labor unions and collective bargaining as efficient tools to incorporate and control the labor movement. Indeed, between 1932 and 1938, union membership rose from about 54,000 members to more than 125,000.[84] The records of the Department of Labor also show a large diversity of unions, cases, and grievances, suggesting the large impact that labor legislation had on the entire country. More importantly, the process of unionization was especially relevant in cities, where industries were recovering at a faster pace than the mining industry and where workers had access to labor inspectors and support from both the state and the increasingly organized leftist political parties.

But if the process of unionization expanded, workers' material gains were less clear. In many factories, mines, and construction sites, workers had made enormous sacrifices during the Depression to maintain production, accepting wage and benefit reductions. As the economy started recovering but inflation still eroded workers' income, working people felt entitled to demand wage increases. Whether they faced legal difficulties in calling a strike (the number of legal strikes and the percentage of workers involved in a strike remained low), found little support from Labor Department officials, or faced enormous opposition from employers, advancing workers' economic demands was especially difficult.[85] The setbacks were even more evident in the countryside, where landowners were successfully preventing the enforcement of the Labor Code. The legal rights of rural workers, then, remained ambiguous, and without the support of the state, unionization in the countryside was severely compromised for the next thirty years. In June 1934, a violent repression against the land demands of a rural community in Ranquil (Alto Bío-Bío) confirmed that the Alessandri administration would side with landowners and protect their traditional power.[86]

Throughout 1935 and 1936, the Alessandri administration repressed a national railroad strike, teachers, and solidarity strikes in Santiago, showing how the government was ready to use special powers to control the labor movement. Workers' growing sense of frustration consolidated their commitment to radical political change, an alliance between local labor unions and leftist political parties, and, eventually, their support for the Popular Front.[87] In 1936, unionized workers came together in the Confederación de Trabajadores de Chile (CTCH), which played a critical role in the campaign and victory of the Popular Front, as well as bringing local and dispersed labor unions into a national organization. As the CTCH bylaws clearly stated, "To defeat fascism and carry on the economic and social progress of the country, the working class must establish alliances with other sectors and head the struggle of all democratic forces."[88] More importantly, the experiences of the Great Depression and the setbacks under Alessandri confirmed workers' commitment to both local economic struggles (collective bargaining) and larger political changes.

Conclusions

The Great Depression had a devastating impact on the Chilean economy and, especially, on working families. Severe unemployment, economic instability, falling wages, and—after 1932—uncontrolled inflation deteriorated living and working conditions. For many, the only possibility of survival was to access public and private aid, and public works, shelters, and food distribution programs became an important resource for the thousands of people who had lost their jobs and were forced to move and migrate throughout the country. But, as this chapter has demonstrated, while public assistance was inspired by the belief that the state had to intervene and prevent the social debacle, it was also a tool to exert control over working people and, as many public officers argued, prevent their eminent radicalization. The history of unemployment relief, shelters, and unionization in the 1930s shows, then, the tensions between a state welfare project and workers' demands and expectations. In addition, the history of the Depression in Chile clearly suggests the many ways in which workers and their families resisted and accommodated to the crisis, challenging the traditional image of the passive unemployed.

In the midst of this devastating economic crisis and political instability, Chileans built a system of labor relations that would define workers' rights for almost half a century. In the early 1930s, workers and labor inspectors used the laws to protect jobs and salaries, demonstrating the critical importance of having and learning to use these rights. In the following years, industrial and mine workers organized labor unions, engaged in collective bargaining, and filed countless grievances against their employers. However, working people quickly understood that the effectiveness of the law was hindered by the lack of commitment from the state, and that improving economic conditions required larger political reforms. In 1938, the recently formed labor confederation CTCH joined the Popular Front, and workers across the nation demanded "bread, roof, and shelter."

Notes

1 Curepto, November 26, 1930. Archivo Nacional de la Administración del Estado (hereafter ARNAD), Fondo Dirección del Trabajo (hereafter DT), vol. 218.

2 Iquique, May 20, 1931. ARNAD, DT, vol. 242.

3 For an overview of the political and general history of this period, see Brian Loveman, *Chile: The Legacy of Spanish Capitalism* (New York: Oxford University Press, 2001).

4 The economic history of the Great Depression in Chile has been well studied. Carmen Cariola and Osvaldo Sunkel, *La historia económica de Chile, 1830–1930: Dos ensayos y una bibliografía* (Madrid: Ediciones Cultura Hispánica del Instituto de Cooperación Iberoamericana, 1982); J. Gabriel Palma, "Chile 1914–1935: De economía exportadora a sustitutiva de importaciones," *Colección Estudios CIEPLAN* 12 (1984): 61–88; Manuel Marfán, "Políticas reactivadoras y recesión externa: Chile 1929–1938," *Colección Estudios CIEPLAN* 12 (1984): 89–119; Michael Monteón, *Chile and the Great Depression: The Politics of Underdevelopment, 1927–1948* (Tempe: Arizona State University Press, 1998); Oscar Muñoz Gomá, *Chile y su industrialización: Pasado, crisis y opciones* (Santiago: CIEPLAN, 1986); Luis Riveros, *La Gran Depresión (1929–1932) en Chile*, documento de trabajo (Santiago: Facultad de Economía y Negocios Universidad de Chile, 2009).

5 Eugenio Matte Hurtado, "La República Socialista de Chile (1932)," accessed January 26, 2014, www.memoriachilena.cl.

6 The "Socialist Republic" was especially influential on the foundation of the Socialist Party (1933) and on crafting a series of law (e.g., price controls) that were later used by the Popular Front governments. On the Socialist Party and the influence of the Socialist Republic and its emblematic leader Marmaduke Grove, see Paul W. Drake, *Socialism and Populism in Chile* (Urbana-Champaign: University of Illinois Press, 1978).

7 Riveros, *La gran depresión en Chile.*

8 During the years of the Popular Front (1938–42) and the Radical Party–led governments (1942–52), Chile embarked on an ambitious project of industrialization. Created in 1939, the Corporación de Fomento Fabril (CORFO) — a state developmental agency that supervised, provided technical assistance to, and funded industrialization projects — became the symbol of the import substitution effort of the next two decades. Some of the most emblematic ac-

complishments were the steel mill of Huachipato in Concepción, an oil refinery in Con-Con, and a copper smelter in Paipote, Copiapó. CORFO also lent money to important private industries such as the Manufactura de Metales (MADEMSA) and Manufactura de Cobre (MADECO). Muñoz Gomá, *Chile y su industrialización*.

9 For a discussion on this generation and the role of women, see the work of Karin A. Rosemblatt, *Gendered Compromises: Political Cultures and the State in Chile, 1920–1950* (Chapel Hill: University of North Carolina Press, 2000). On the middle class and intellectuals at the time, see Patrick Barr-Melej, *Reforming Chile: Cultural Politics, Nationalism and the Rise of the Middle Class* (Chapel Hill: University of North Carolina Press, 2001). Salvador Allende was representative of this generation. He graduated from medical school in 1926, participated in the foundation of the Socialist Party in 1933, and became minister of public health under the Popular Front in 1938. His work on public health is representative of this sensibility. Salvador Allende, *La realidad médico-social chilena* (Santiago: Ministerio de Salubridad, Previsión y Asistencia Social, 1939).

10 New studies on Chilean labor history have demonstrated the agency of Chilean workers in the 1930s and during the Popular Front. The most recent work on this line is Jody Pavilack, *Mining for the Nation: The Politics of Chile's Coal Mining Communities from the Popular Front to the Cold War* (College Park: Penn State University Press, 2011).

11 Silvia M. Arrom, *Containing the Poor: The Mexico City Poor House, 1774–1871* (Durham, NC: Duke University Press, 2000), provides a long-term historical perspective in the case of Mexico.

12 On Chile's Popular Front, see Pavilack, *Mining for the Nation*; and Rosemblatt, *Gendered Compromises*. On the relationship between Latin American populism and labor, see Paulo Drinot, *The Allure of Labor: Workers, Race, and the Making of the Peruvian State* (Durham, NC: Duke University Press, 2011); John French, *The Brazilian Workers' ABC: Class Conflict and Alliances in Modern São Paulo* (Chapel Hill: University of North Carolina Press, 1992), and *Drowning in Laws: Labor Law and Brazilian Political Culture* (Chapel Hill: University of North Carolina Press, 2004); Daniel James, *Resistance and Integration: Peronism and the Argentine Working Class, 1946–1976* (New York: Cambridge University Press, 1993); Matthew Karush and Oscar Chamosa, *The New Cultural History of Peronism: Power and Identity in Mid-Twentieth Century Argentina* (Durham, NC: Duke University Press, 2010). For a general view on populism, see the classic work Michael Conniff et al., *Populism in Latin America* (Tuscaloosa: University of Alabama Press, 1999).

13 Since the 1880s the enganche had provided mining employers with workers, making possible a labor migration that for generations had moved workers from the southern agricultural valleys to the north. The enganche, however, had been tainted by constant accusations of abuses and exploitation and, along with other mechanisms of social and labor control, had inspired a strong and

militant labor movement. As a result, in the 1920s social and labor laws regulated and institutionalized enganche, providing workers with some rights and guarantees. Michael Monteón, "The *Enganche* in the Chilean Nitrate Sector, 1880–1930," *Latin American Perspectives* 6, no. 3 (1979): 66–79.

14 The historiography on the nitrate industry is very extensive and rich. Some of the most relevant scholarly works are Harold Blakemore, *British Nitrates and Chilean Politics, 1886–1896: Balmaceda and North* (London: Athlone Press, 1974); Sergio González, *Hombres y mujeres de la pampa: Tarapacá en el ciclo del salitre* (Santiago: LOM, 2002); Michael Monteón, *Chile in the Nitrate Era: The Evolution of Economic Dependence, 1880–1930* (Madison: University of Wisconsin Press, 1983); Thomas O'Brien, *The Nitrate Industry and Chile's Crucial Transition, 1870–1891* (New York: New York University Press, 1982); Julio Pinto, *Trabajos y rebeldías en la pampa salitrera: El ciclo del salitre y la reconfiguración de las identidades populares (1850–1900)* (Santiago: Universidad de Santiago, 1998).

15 Luis Riveros argues that the postwar crisis had considerably debilitated the Chilean economy, aggravating the state deficit, the foreign debt, and the inflationary pressures. In 1930, the crisis hit an economy that was only slowly recovering from a serious downturn. Riveros, *La Gran Depresión (1929–1932) en Chile.*

16 Ministerio de Industria y Obras Públicas, "Servicio de Colocación," August 18, 1914, in Moisés Poblete Troncoso, *Legislación social obrera chilena (Recopilación de leyes vigentes sobre el trabajo y la previsión social)* (Santiago: Imprenta Santiago, 1924), 182–83. Another response to the World War I crisis (which was also used during the Great Depression) was the state effort to create agricultural cooperatives by placing unemployed white-collar employees and blue-collar workers in public lands and offering them credit. Decreto, May 23, 1916, in Poblete Troncoso, *Legislación social obrera chilena*, 214–17.

17 For a discussion of some of these early public and private initiatives, see Juan Carlos Yáñez Andrade, *La intervención social en Chile, 1907–1932* (Santiago: Ril Editores, 2008).

18 Chilean labor history for this period is especially rich. See, for example, Peter DeShazo, *Urban Workers and Labor Unions in Chile, 1902–1927* (Madison: University of Wisconsin Press, 1984); Elizabeth Q. Hutchison, *Labors Appropriate to Their Sex: Gender, Labor, and Politics in Urban Chile, 1900–1930* (Durham, NC: Duke University Press, 2001); Thomas Miller Klubock, *Contested Communities: Class, Gender, and Politics in Chile's El Teniente Copper Mine, 1904–1951* (Durham, NC: Duke University Press, 1998); Julio Pinto, *Trabajos y rebeldías en la pampa salitrera: El ciclo del salitre y la reconfiguración de las identidades populares (1850–1900)* (Santiago: Universidad de Santiago, 1998); Julio Pinto and Verónica Valdivia. *¿Revolución proletaria o querida chusma? Socialismo y Alessandrismo en la pugna de la politización pampina (1911–1932)* (Santiago: LOM, 2001); Jorge Rojas, *La dictadura de Ibáñez y los sindicatos (1927–1931)* (Santiago: Centro de Investigaciones Barros Arana, 1993).

19 For a comprehensive list of the social and labor legislation enacted before 1924, see Moisés Poblete Troncoso, *Legislación obrera chilena (recopilación de leyes y disposiciones vigentes sobre el trabajo y la previsión social)* (Santiago: Imprenta Santiago, 1924). For an overview of the social laws approved during this period, see Yáñez Andrade, *La intervención social en Chile*.

20 Jorge Rojas has carefully studied this period and the relationship between the labor movement and General Ibáñez. Rojas, *La dictadura de Ibáñez*.

21 Intendencia de Tarapacá, n.d., ARNAD, DT, vol. 215

22 Santiago, August 19, 1929, ARNAD, DT, vol. 214.

23 See, for example, José Pablo Arellano, *Políticas sociales y desarrollo en Chile, 1924–1984* (Santiago: CIEPLAN, 1985).

24 Chilean workers had been moving since the mid-nineteenth century, and geographical mobility had become an important survival strategy. For Sergio González, for instance, the ability to move had characterized the identity of nitrate workers. "In the *pampa*, the *enganche* along with independent migration," González explains, "produced a sort of mentality based on mobility and freedom which defined the character of the *pampino* and his labor organizations." Similarly, Juan Carlos Yáñez argues that the ability to move "was the natural mechanism to adapt to the seasonal character of productive activities." González, *Hombres y mujeres de la pampa*, 151; Yáñez Andrade, *La intervención social en Chile*, 193.

25 "Resumen estadístico de la paralización, movilización y ocupación de los obreros de la región salitrera," ARNAD, DT, Informes Varios of 1932.

26 At the center of the discussion on the future and rights of unemployed workers in Chilean mines and nitrate fields was the work contract that, among other things, also regulated and limited the enganche system. According to the law that regulated labor contracts, employers were required to pay workers "the reasonable costs of a round-trip ticket" if they had been asked to move in order to work. *Ley 4053 sobre contrato del trabajo* (Santiago: Imprenta Nacional, 1924).

27 Iquique, January 23, 1930, ARNAD, DT, vol. 215.

28 Temuco, November 15, 1930, ARNAD, DT, vol. 222.

29 La Serena, February 9, 1931, ARNAD, DT, vol. 238,

30 Puerto Montt, March 18, 1931, ARNAD, DT, vol. 239.

31 Carabineros are the national police force. Considered one of the four branches of the armed forces, they are heavily militarized. Santiago, February 16, 1931, ARNAD, DT, vol. 238. Given their extensive presence throughout the country, police officers played a central role in the state response to the crisis. Employers would usually inform the nearest police station of any significant layoff.

32 The data on unemployment or the size of the labor force are, according to most economists, extremely unreliable, providing only a glimpse of the magnitude of the problem. According to Luis Riveros, in the mining sector, the sector most affected by the Depression, employment had fallen about 60 percent by 1931–32, but mine workers were and remained a very small percentage of the

Chilean workforce. In contrast, unemployment in agriculture and industry was only severe between 1931 and 1932. Because of this, Riveros argues, qualitative descriptions of social and work conditions at the time are essential to understand the problem. Riveros, *La gran depresión en Chile*.

33 San Felipe, April 31, 1931, ARNAD, DT, vol. 241.
34 Telegram, Valparaíso, April 17, 1931, ARNAD, DT, vol. 242.
35 Marfán, "Políticas reactivadoras y recesión externa."
36 Rancagua, March 13, 1931,,ARNAD, DT, vol. 239.
37 For an overview of public work projects at the time, see Teodoro Schmidt, *Los trabajos públicos y la cesantía 1931–1934* (Santiago: Imprenta Nascimento, 1934).
38 Valdivia, April 21, 1931, ARNAD, DT, vol. 241; Puerto Montt, April 24, 1931, ARNAD, DT, vol. 243.
39 Aysén, May 13, 1931, and Valdivia, May 25, 1931, ARNAD, DT, vol. 243.
40 Santiago, May 2, 1931, ARNAD, DT, vol. 243.
41 Puerto Aysén, June 11, 1931, ARNAD, DT, vol. 245.
42 Banco Central de Chile, *Sépitma memoria anual: Año 1932* (Santiago: Imprenta Dirección General de Prisiones, 1933), 37.
43 *Oro*, August 1932, 1.
44 Santiago, September 15, 1932, ARNAD, DT, vol. 309.
45 The Caja's funding and social security benefits came from the contributions of workers, employers, and the state. High rates of unemployment threated the economic viability of this system, and many argued that the Caja started and remained broken.
46 Carlos Contreras Labarca, *La defensa del proletariado contra el riesgo profesional de la desocupación* (Santiago: Imprenta del Inst. de Sordomudo y ciegos, 1924). This discussion remained very central, especially since Chile did not develop unemployment insurance or benefits.
47 Santiago, July 14, 1931, ARNAD, DT, vol. 248.
48 Telegram, Linares, December 21, 1931, ARNAD, DT, vol. 293.
49 Santiago, December 5, 1931, ARNAD, DT, vol. 258.
50 Banco Central de Chile, *Séptima memoria anual: Año 1932*. Numbers are especially problematic for this period since there are no consistent data on the size of the labor force.
51 Contreras Labarca explained that during the 1914 and 1921 nitrate crises, the government focused on relocation and transportation of unemployed workers, organization of public workers, distribution of food, and opening of shelters. The same responses were implemented in 1930–32. Contreras Labarca, *La defensa del proletariado*.
52 On the history of this transition and the increasing professionalization of social aid in Chile, see María Angélica Illanes, *Cuerpo y sangre de la política: La construcción histórica de las visitadoras sociales, Chile 1887–1940* (Santiago: LOM, 2006); and Macarena Ponce de León Atria, *Gobernar la pobreza: Prácticas de caridad y beneficencia en la ciudad de Santiago, 1830–1890* (Santiago: Editorial Uni-

versitaria, 2012). For a general perspective on this issue, see Robert Castel, *Les métamorphoses de la question sociale* (Paris: Librairie Arthème Fayard, 1995).

53 Coquimbo, April 22, 1931, ARNAD, DT, vol. 242.

54 Santiago, December 24, 1931, ARNAD, DT, vol. 305.

55 Adriana Izquierdo Izquierdo Phillips, *Como se organizó la ayuda a los cesantes y la participación que en ella correspondió a la Escuela de Servicio Social Elvira Matte de Cruchaga* (tesis, Escuela de Servicio Social Elvira Matte Cruchaga, 1932).

56 *Memoria de la Sociedad de San Vicente de Paul año 1931* (Santiago: Dirección General de Prisiones, 1932).

57 Father Vives is considered one of the precursors of social Catholicism in Chile, and he had a strong influence on students and workers. He became the mentor of people like Father Alberto Hurtado, also a Jesuit, and many of the Catholic youth of the Conservative Party who would later create the Falange Nacional and the Christian Democratic Party. Rafael Sagredo, *Escritos del Padre Fernando Vives Solar* (Santiago: DIBAM, 1993).

58 San Miguel, September 16, 1931, ARNAD, DT, vol. 251.

59 Valparaíso, April 25, 1931, ARNAD, DT, vol. 242.

60 Adriana Izquierdo, "Como se organizó la ayuda a los cesantes y la participación que en ella correspondió a la Escuela de Servicio Social Elvira Matte de Cruchaga" (thesis, Santiago, 1932).

61 Santiago, September 28, 1931, ARNAD, DT, vol. 251.

62 Santiago, July 20, 1931, ARNAD, DT, vol. 246.

63 Santiago, October 31, 1931, ARNAD, DT, vol. 254.

64 "Reminiscencias de la edad primitiva: Los desheredados del Cerro Blanco," *Zig-Zag*, May 7, 1932, 24–25.

65 "Higienización de los cesantes," *Zig-Zag*, May 7, 1932, 42–43.

66 Banco Central de Chile, *Séptima memoria anual presentada a la Superintendencia de Bancos año 1932* (Santiago: Dirección General de Prisiones, 1933), 13.

67 Ley 5105, April 18, 1932, in Banco Central de Chile, *Séptima memoria*, 63–74.

68 "Organización de la mendicidad," *Zig-Zag*, April 30, 1932, 43–44.

69 "Ollas comunes para alimentar cesantes," *Zig-Zag*, July 2, 1932, 29–30.

70 "Informe de los servicios de Cesantía del Departamento del Huasco (Vallenar)," Santiago, November 22, 1932, ARNAD, DT, vol. 365.

71 "Informe de los servicios de Cesantía del Departamento de La Serena," Santiago, November 22, 1932, ARNAD, DT, vol. 365.

72 Although the Ibáñez administration did not survive the Great Depression, he was able to enact the first Labor Code (May 1931, Decreto Fuerza de Ley 178), shaping the future of Chilean workers and the labor movement. The Labor Code gave workers the right to unionize, engage in collective bargaining, and strike. Like most Latin American labor codes, it divided blue-collar workers and white-collar workers into two labor unions: the *sindicato industrial* (plant or industrial union) and the *sindicato profesional* (professional or craft union). Workers in industrial plants with more than twenty-five blue-collar workers

were given the right to unionize. After 55 percent of the labor force on the local shop floor approved the formation of a union, all workers were automatically considered members. White-collar workers organized along craft lines, also with a minimum of twenty-five members. All unionized workers democratically elected the board, regularly participated in assemblies, and paid monthly fees. The Code stated the procedures for collective bargaining and enforced arbitration through tripartite conciliation boards (*juntas de conciliación*) integrated by workers, employers, and state authorities. A nationwide system of labor courts and regional offices of the Labor Department (*Dirección del Trabajo*) supervised the enforcement of labor and social laws at the local level. Alfredo Gaete Berrios, *Código del Trabajo (concordado y anotado)* (Santiago: Ediciones Ercilla, 1945); Moisés Poblete Troncoso, *El Derecho del trabajo y la seguridad social en Chile* (Santiago: Editorial Jurídica, 1945).

73 For a history of Chilean rural workers and the impact of labor legislation on the countryside, see Brian Loveman, *Struggle in the Countryside: Politics and Rural Labor in Chile, 1919–1973* (Bloomington: Indiana University Press, 1976).

74 Victoria, November 1, 1930, ARNAD, DT, vol. 221.

75 *Las Noticias* (Los Angeles), July 6, 1931, in ARNAD, DT, vol. 246.

76 For a discussion of the effects of the Ibáñez dictatorship on the labor movement, see DeShazo, *Urban Workers*; Rojas, *La dictadura de Ibáñez*.

77 Carlos Vega to *intendente* of Antofagasta, Calama, October 18, 1930, Archivo Nacional, Fondo Intendencia de Antofagasta, vol. 80.

78 Valparaíso, July 11, 1931, ARNAD, DT, vol. 248.

79 Calera, November 11, 1931, ARNAD, DT, vol. 255.

80 Jorge Barría, *El movimiento obrero en Chile* (Santiago: Universidad Técnica del Estado, 1971).

81 Santiago, October 16, 1930, ARNAD, DT, vol. 221.

82 "410 obreros se les dio sus pases en Potrerillos," *El Progreso* (Chañaral), January 2, 1932.

83 Calama, April 30, 1930, Archivo Nacional, Fondo Intendencia de Antofagasta, vol. 115.

84 Loveman, *Chile*, 205.

85 Mario Garcés, *Movimiento obrero en la década del treinta y el Frente Popular* (tesis, Pontificia Universidad Católica de Chile, Santiago, 1985); Hernán Venegas Valdebenito, "Crisis económica y conflictos sociales y políticos en la zona carbonífera. 1918–1931," *Contribuciones Científicas y Tecnológicas, Área Ciencias Sociales y Humanidades*, no. 16 (1997): 124–52.

86 Thomas M. Klubock, "Ranquil: Violence and Peasant Politics on Chile's Southern Frontier," in *A Century of Revolution: Insurgent and Counterinsurgent Violence during Latin America's Long Cold War*, ed. Greg Grandin and Gilbert Joseph (Durham, NC: Duke University Press, 2010).

87 Formed in 1936, the Chilean Popular Front was inspired by the international effort to create a broader coalition against the advance of Fascism, and initially

it included the Communist and the Radical Parties. In face of the presidential election of 1938, the front expanded to incorporate the Socialist Party, organized labor represented in the CTCH, and the student movement. Led by Pedro Aguirre Cerda, the Popular Front won the elections in 1938, governing until 1941. Pedro Milos, *Frente Popular en Chile. Su configuración: 1935–1938* (Santiago: LOM Ediciones, 2008). For a history of how workers understood and became involved in the Popular Front, see Pavilack, *Mining for the Nation*.

88 CTCH, *Declaración de principios y estatutos de la Confederación de Trabajadores de Chile* (Santiago: Imprenta Yungay, 1943), 1.

CHAPTER 3

Change with Continuity:

Brazil from 1930 to 1945

Joel Wolfe

A political crisis unrelated to the onset of the Great Depression brought on Brazil's so-called Revolution of 1930. President Washington Luís, the consummate Paulista politician, overreached by choosing as his successor Julio Prestes, the sitting governor of São Paulo. Minas Gerais, São Paulo's rival in the politics of "coffee with milk" (*café com leite*) that defined the politics of the governors during the Old Republic, sought to reclaim presidential power by backing Getúlio Vargas, the governor of Rio Grande do Sul, in the 1930 election.[1] When Prestes won, São Paulo's opponents seized power through military means. After more saber rattling than shots fired, Vargas took power with the backing of much of the army. He at first became Brazil's provisional president from 1930 to 1937, but then scrapped any democratic pretense during the 1937–45 Estado Novo dictatorship. He was also elected president in 1950 and served from 1951 until his August 1954 suicide.[2]

Before 1930, disagreements between Paulista and Mineiro politicians led to a brief interregnum, with the governor from some other state taking charge until São Paulo's and Minas Gerais's leaders agreed again to the terms of how to proceed with the presidential rotation. Vargas's assumption of power changed that and ushered in a new style of national elections for presidents, which eventually broke down and then ended with the 1964 military seizure of power and its more than two decades of rule.[3]

The textbook understanding of the Vargas years emphasizes his regime's success in transforming Brazil's economy, social structure, and politics. His flashiest and most obvious success is said to be the structuring of individual workers into organized labor under state control in a corporatist system.[4] Associated with Vargas's populist mobilization of labor is the perceived success he had in centralizing power in the national capital, Rio de Janeiro. This challenge to Brazil's long tradition of extreme federalism is also said to have brought national education and cultural programs that expanded national state power and further centralized authority in Rio. While it is unquestionably the case that the Vargas years represented a major rupture with the past and that he ended the politics of the governors in national elections, the standard view of his rule overestimates his successes, particularly with labor and political centralization.[5]

The economy of the 1930s, with the sharp decline in international trade and concomitant drop in demand for Brazilian coffee, limited federal revenue but also offered Vargas a unique opportunity to focus on internal development. Despite this opportunity, Vargas's ability to transform Brazil was circumscribed by weak state capacity, which he hoped to overcome through that transformation, and by the opposition of the Paulista elite, who went so far as to launch a civil war in 1932. He did have a powerful ally in the military, but even Brazil's single most powerful institution could not act nationally and so was severely limited itself.[6] With weak institutional support and an assertive opposition, Vargas adroitly altered course in the early and mid-1930s. He did not, however, centralize political and economic power in Rio, bring labor into a robust corporatist system, or integrate the nation's disparate population through education and cultural programs. In changing course, he did manage to lay the groundwork for a developmentalist program that would fundamentally alter Brazil and make it a much more physically, economically, and culturally integrated nation in the long term. Late in the 1930s, Vargas also took the very first, tentative steps to alter the practice of politics by addressing what he saw as the actual interests of the majority of Brazilians. By paying more attention to popular demands, which were often articulated directly to him through various means, Vargas began to embrace an inchoate form of mass politics. These changes, which provided the institutional infrastructure and political vocabulary of developmentalism and the first stirrings of mass politics, are the signature accomplishments of Vargas in the 1930s and beyond.[7] Moreover, it was the Great Depression that provided the necessary context for such fundamental change.

In many ways, the dominant narrative on Vargas and labor is the clearest example of how the historiography has perverted our understanding of the impact of the Great Depression on Brazil. The central debate in the literature focuses on how workers became empowered. Some see Vargas as having granted workers new rights and powers with the establishment of a corporatist labor system in the 1930s, which he then codified in the Consolidated Labor Laws (CLT) in 1943. This is the so-called *outorga*, for Vargas gave (from *outorgar*, to grant or sanction) workers their rights.[8] Others argue that workers, particularly clever labor leaders, seized the day and took control of the fledgling structure Vargas had created.[9] Both interpretations assume that Vargas used the emergency conditions of the Great Depression to preside over an activist and powerful central state. Whether or not the "father of the poor," as Vargas's propaganda machine referred to him, had given workers these rights or the people had claimed them, there is the assumption in the literature that these rights existed, a labor bureaucracy functioned, and the national government succeeded in penetrating Brazil's urban industrial areas beyond the national capital.

The historical record challenges these assumptions. Vargas's labor policies largely failed with rank-and-file workers. This was most obvious in the macropolitical arena. When the military ousted him in 1945, there were no popular protests supporting Vargas. Workers did, however, show up en masse to demand higher wages in vast wildcat strikes in urban areas in 1945 and 1946. Hundreds of thousands of workers took to the streets of Rio de Janeiro, São Paulo, Belo Horizonte, Porto Alegre, and elsewhere, demanding raises after years of wartime inflation and flat wages that Vargas's labor bureaucracy had not rectified.[10] These strikes were in direct violation of labor law—all wage disputes were to be settled by tripartite labor courts housed in the Ministry of Labor—and were an obvious critique of the state-sponsored unions that had worked closely with both industrialists and the state to maintain labor peace during the 1930s and throughout World War II.[11]

Once the repression or threat of repression of the Estado Novo years had passed, workers took to the streets. Fear of the state had not translated into quiescence. Throughout Vargas's first period of rule, Brazil's workers simply shunned the new labor bureaucracy. Unionization was a two-step process. First, all workers paid a mandatory union tax (*imposto sindical*), which funded both the national Ministry of Labor and local unions. Next, to join a union, workers had to go through the process of becoming *sindicalizado/a*, which involved a cursory Ministry check for fealty to the regime or at least ideological neutrality and then the payment of dues beyond the imposto sindical. São Paulo, Brazil's largest city and industrial hub, had a formal union structure tied to the Ministry of Labor, but only tiny numbers of workers bothered to join them. Union density (the percentage of workers who paid the imposto sindical and also paid additional dues to become sindicalizado/a) was extremely low: at most 2.58 percent of textile workers, the largest group of industrial laborers in the city, joined the union at this time, and the high point of unionization for metalworkers was 5.10 percent in 1936, with that number declining during the Estado Novo.[12]

São Paulo was Vargas's most egregious failure with labor. Throughout Brazil, the new national Ministry of Labor sanctioned unions and organized labor courts where it could, but it had very little impact on either industry or its workers beyond keeping wages depressed during an era of rising prices. Without effective unions or an effective labor bureaucracy they trusted, workers instead expressed their dissatisfaction with bosses, local politicians, and even the national government by communicating directly to Vargas. Letters and petitions, couched in the regime's rhetoric, called on the dictator to fulfill his promises to act as the "father of the poor." In response, the government would occasionally make an individual financial grant to a worker or provide some other form of relief, but the regime did not promote workers' collective interests with increased wages or improvements in factory conditions. Vargas's first, clumsy attempts to fashion a sort of populist alliance with workers beginning in 1943 was, in part, in response to these worker letters. It was also his first response to the probability of elections with the end of World War II.[13]

Brazil's economy during the Vargas era circumscribed what the regime could accomplish. Despite its great size and geographical diversity, Brazil was economically, and thus politically, dependent on coffee when the Depression began. In 1931, coffee prices were less than half their average in the mid-1920s. Export revenue fell from U.S. $445.9 million in 1929 to U.S. $180.6 million in 1932. Moreover, the collapse of world trade and concomitant price deflation all but ended the entry of foreign capital into Brazil.[14] Early on, the Vargas government was therefore forced to devalue the currency and attempt to renegotiate its foreign debt. It also quickly moved to support the coffee sector, which had provided more than 70 percent of export revenues before the crash. National intervention in agriculture was unprecedented. Indeed, Paulista planters had sought federal government support for a price valorization scheme in 1906, but were quickly rebuffed. São Paulo's coffee interests were able to finance that program on their own, but they were in no shape financially to prop up prices in the 1930s. Vargas therefore created the National Coffee Council (Conselho Nacional do Café or CNC) in May 1931. This federal intervention in agriculture broke new ground, and the CNC quickly displaced the poorly financed state price support programs.[15]

As Vargas moved to increase commodity prices with the operation of the CNC, he also sought to expand demand for goods through the establishment of Brazil's first minimum wage. Although the 1934 constitution called for a minimum wage, Vargas did not implement it until 1943 to coincide with the promulgation of his CLT. The CNC and minimum wage highlight the political limitations Vargas faced in the 1930s. He had come to power by displacing a representative of the Paulista oligarchy. Although they distrusted the exercise of national power, the state's planters were willing to tolerate the CNC because it put federal money in their pockets. Paulista industrialists, on the other hand, had no interest in politicians and bureaucrats in Rio dictating what they would have to pay their workers. When Vargas finally implemented the minimum wage in 1943, it was too little too late for Brazil's working people, who never had embraced Vargas's attempts to bring them into a populist coalition. As the strikes of 1945 and 1946 demonstrated, Vargas's policies had failed to provide Brazil's workers with direct support (e.g., wage increases) or indirect aid (through union-based social services) during an era of sustained increases in the cost of living.

These failures during the Estado Novo had their origins in Vargas's first years in office. As early as 1931, Vargas had attempted to mediate industrial relations and increase workers' wages. The creation of the Ministry of Labor and early interventions in strikes seemed to suggest a pro-worker orientation, but sustained pushback from Paulista industrialists brought an abrupt halt to these policies and revealed the structural limits to Vargas's plans.[16]

Vargas's interventions in what locals saw as internal Paulista politics in the early 1930s were a driving force in that state's decision to launch a civil war in July 1932. As part of his initial centralizing, Vargas had replaced most states' governors with appointed "interventors" who reported to Rio rather than representing the interests of a state's elites. João Alberto Lins de Barros, the Pernambucano interventor in São Paulo, quickly put himself in the middle of the state's complex labor politics. In the midst of the economic depression of 1930, he ordered the state's factory owners to provide their workers with a full forty-hour workweek (many factories were operating less than half-time in 1930) and to provide all workers with a 5 percent pay raise. João Alberto followed this unprecedented governmental action by attempting to settle wage disputes between São Paulo's textile workers and industrialists. This infuriated Paulista elites, who claimed that their workers were not in fact on strike, when in reality they were. Paulista industrialists then simply closed their factories rather than subject themselves to state-mandated and state-run mediation.

Interference in how they ran their businesses and treated their workers was just the latest and most egregious insult to Paulista pride. The very presence of Vargas in the Catete Palace was an affront to São Paulo's elites, who had assumed that Júlio Prestes would continue their state's dominance of national politics. In the name of state autonomy in the face of Rio's meddling in their affairs, Paulistas launched a surprisingly effective civil war against the Vargas government beginning on July 9, 1932, and ending October 2 of that same year. The 10,000-man Força Pública Paulista fought the Brazilian army well but missed several opportunities to score major victories.[17] In the end, Paulistas lost the war but won a major political victory, for in the aftermath of 1932 Vargas largely left São Paulo alone and permitted that state's elites to run their own affairs with little interference from Rio. The civil war effectively ruined Vargas's push to centralize power in Rio and ended his flirtation with Brazil's single largest group of workers. After 1932, all national labor legislation would be managed in São Paulo by the State Department of Labor, which was run by the Paulista textile magnate Jorge Street. No other state was given such autonomy, and no other state had as many factories and workers.

The civil war, like the world economic depression, severely limited Vargas's room to maneuver during much of the 1930s. He was in many ways helpless to do much more than simply support the coffee economy through the CNC. Doing so, however, turned out to be much more heterodox than either Vargas or his critics could have imagined. The most obvious innovation was the actual intervention of the federal government in local agriculture. The less obvious aspect of this innovation was the inadvertently Keynesian nature of the price support program. Vargas effectively increased demand throughout the economy not only by pumping money into the coffee sector but also through massive government borrowing. Without planning to, Vargas used deficit spending to create demand, which in turn led to the expansion of domestic manufacture.[18]

From the establishment of the CNC in 1931 until 1937, industrial output grew, but it did so primarily through the expanded use of existing capacity. The industrial expansion of the 1920s provided that capacity, so the consumption of inputs such as steel and cement did not surpass 1920s levels until 1937.[19] In other words, Vargas's single most effective policy instrument for the revival of the Brazilian economy up until 1937 was the debt-financed support of the coffee economy. None of his elaborate plans for the centralization of political authority or the regulation of industrial labor had any real impact on the economy. And, politically, they did little more than alienate the Paulista elite.

In the mid-1930s, before the formal declaration of the Estado Novo dictatorship in November 1937, Vargas retooled his program. With political centralization beyond his reach, Vargas instead attempted to bolster the idea of Brazil as a unified nation through educational and cultural programs. The administration in Rio had some success stimulating national patrimony in both Rio and Ouro Preto, the colonial mining center in Minas Gerais. The government in Rio promoted a unique interpretation of life in Ouro Preto and stressed what it said were the proto-nationalist components of 1789's Inconfidência Mineira uprising.[20] Through museums and tourism, Vargas sought to use a type of soft power to encourage Brazilians to think in highly nationalistic terms and, in turn, to abandon the chauvinism they held for their states.[21] This program was about as successful as it could be. It introduced a new historical narrative of Brazil that no doubt appealed to those intellectuals who had long sought national unification and a broad sense of nationalism. Given the weak transportation links available for the bulk of the population to travel to Ouro Preto or Rio, and given the poverty in which the vast majority of Brazilians lived, promoting nationalism through tourism had little broad impact.

Vargas had one more set of policies that could potentially promote both cultural nationalism and the physical and economic integration of the nation. A set of nationwide education policies could potentially bridge Brazil's great cultural gaps, elevate the vast majority of the population, and put the federal government in individual municipalities. Education reform under Vargas, however, was just as freighted with the weaknesses of the central state and extant race and class ideologies as all Brazilian public policy. The Ministry of Education had little impact outside of Rio, and its policies reproduced dominant narratives of race despite the Vargas regime's nationalist focus, which at times promoted the interests of Afro-Brazilians much more than in any previous era.[22] Like his flirtation with labor, Vargas's education policies suffered most from the extremely limited capacity of the national government, particularly its inability to levy taxes. Individual states could more easily and efficiently tax their citizens than the government in Rio, and so states controlled their own education budgets. Schools, like the vast majority of governmental institutions with which Brazilians outside of Rio interacted, were tied to their local and state governments.[23]

The historical record demonstrates that the onset of economic depression and the Revolution of 1930 were not enough to break the stranglehold of the states over the national government, and so Brazil remained highly federated. Given this political and economic framework, Vargas moved to implement policies that both his main institutional supporters (the military) and detractors (the Paulista and other regional elites) would either support or, at the very least, not oppose. He chose what would come to be termed in the post-1945 period "developmentalism."[24]

Strategic governmental intervention in the economy to break bottlenecks or nurture new industries had been a central if contested component of Brazilian national identity since the late nineteenth century.[25] The Republic was founded in 1889 by positivist military men, many of whom were trained engineers, under the banner of "Order and Progress." They had a near-religious belief—that religion being positivism—in the transformative power of the state.[26] Their ability to use state power to foster development was limited by the presence of a weak national government and Brazilian states that maintained strong regional identities, as well as powerful militias. In retrospect, then, it was not surprising that Prudente José de Moraes Barros, a lawyer and leader of the São Paulo Republican Party, was elected president in 1894 after the administrations of two generals, Deodoro da Fonseca (1889–91) and Floriano Peixoto (1891–94), had stoked regional resentments and uprisings.

Although the ethos of economic liberalism dominated during the Old Republic (1889–1930), both the national and individual state governments did intervene to support targeted businesses. An 1890 tariff attempted to stimulate national industries by taxing imported products but lowering the cost of factory equipment. The 1901 tariff specifically targeted cotton textiles and played a key role in the rapid growth of that industry.[27] One of the most spectacular interventions in trade was rejected by the federal government as being too activist, but was implemented in a single state. Paulista planters borrowed directly from foreign bankers to fund the 1906 Coffee Valorization, which did result in higher prices for their principal export.[28] These governmental interventions in the market were all ultimately tied to coffee, which dominated the Brazilian economy from the 1840s until at least the outbreak of World War II. Indeed, even cotton factories produced jute sacks for coffee, and later cotton cloth became a staple of *colono* clothing. The valorization was directly about coffee prices. And so, Brazil's most illiberal economic policies were responses to its extraordinary success in the liberal economic order—the country produced 75 percent of the world's coffee in 1900–1901.

Success as a commodity exporter increasingly strained Brazil's attachment to laissez-faire economics and extreme political federalism. Lines of communication served the export sector at the expense of national integration. Unlike the experience of the United States, in which railroads were often built to spur the settlement and development of new regions, Brazilian rails and roads tended to connect coffee counties to ports to facilitate exports.[29] Elites began to note that this was a problem when they adopted the new European fashion of automobile ownership. They could drive within Rio and São Paulo, but could not drive between the two cities.[30] The military took note of these poor lines of communications as early as the 1893–97 Canudos uprising.[31] They had trouble enough getting the army to Salvador; the march inland to Canudos overtaxed the military's logistical skills. This problem repeated itself in the 1910s in the nation's supposedly developed center-south. The Contestado rebellion (1912–16) again demonstrated how little the nation had penetrated even the close-in interior of the border of Santa Catarina and Paraná. Even military expeditions to improve internal communications, such as Cândido Mariano da Silva Rondon's attempts to build telegraph stations in a portion of the Amazon, proved too challenging to complete.[32]

The military's forays into Brazil's interior involved much more than frustrating attempts to gain control over vast, seemingly empty spaces. The army soon discovered the social component of Brazil's profoundly uneven development, which military thinkers quickly identified with the nation's liberal export economy. The impoverished *nordestinos* at Canudos and the seemingly fanatical millenarians in the Contestado region were completely disconnected from Brazilian society and often had turned their backs on the Brazilian economy. The indigenous peoples Rondon encountered were even more culturally, socially, and economically remote. It is within this connect that Brazilian military journals embraced a series of policies in the early 1900s that would later be described as developmentalist.[33]

The army's interest in national integration and development makes a lot of sense, especially in the Brazilian context. There simply were no other significant national institutions after the fall of the empire in 1889. What is perhaps more significant was the Paulista elite's embrace of similar ideas. São

Paulo's planters had the advantage of following coffee producers from the state of Rio de Janeiro, and this made them particularly forward looking. The Cariocas had planted coffee literally everywhere they could and so destroyed the productive capacity of their land. Moreover, they had relied exclusively on slave labor.[34] São Paulo, which was blessed with seemingly endless farmland, managed the environment well and moved toward free wage labor. The state government established agricultural extension services and funded agricultural research. And, in the aftermath of abolition in 1888, it was the São Paulo state government that financed the transportation to interior settlement of the millions of immigrants who became coffee *colonos*.[35] This state activism helps put São Paulo's role in the 1906 Coffee Valorization into its proper context and explains why Paulistas went through with the project after the governments of Minas Gerais and Rio de Janeiro bowed out when the national government refused to support it.

Paulistas supported state-based interventions in the economy. Their distrust of the national government, even when they controlled it, stemmed from a fear that they would end up financing development projects, particularly in Brazil's impoverished Northeast. Export revenues based in the state's coffee in fact paid for the extensive federal drought relief efforts in the Northeast during the administration of Epitácio Pessoa (1919–22).[36] Paulistas did not want to continue to be the figurative locomotive pulling the empty boxcars of Brazil's other states, and so they opposed spending their wealth elevating those states. São Paulo's elites wanted other states' elites to emulate them and develop their own regions.[37]

So, when Vargas turned to developmentalism in the aftermath of his initial setbacks, he not only invoked deeply held beliefs about the need for a powerful, central force to create the order necessary for progress, but also spoke to the long-held aims of both his supporters in the army and his opponents in São Paulo. Given the complex political environment after the 1932 Civil War, Vargas had to craft a program that would appeal to both the generals and the Paulista elite without infringing on their cherished sense of autonomy. The simplest way for Vargas to do that was to use the federal government to produce something that those groups wanted, but with no real costs to them.

Growth in the industrial sector of the economy had largely been spurred by the price support of coffee and by the dramatic drop in world trade and industrial production in the United States and Western Europe. As industry gained momentum in the mid-1930s, it faced significant bottlenecks in inputs and transportation. These were the sorts of problems that the market either could not or would not address. Moreover, the largely rural orientation of the São Paulo state government, despite that state's status as Brazil's industrial center, meant that only the federal government could act to spur even greater industrial output. The issue of developmentalism as it emerged over the course of the 1930s was tailor-made for Vargas.

The National Steel Company (Companhia Siderúrgica Nacional or CSN), which Vargas founded in 1941 on a defunct coffee plantation in the interior of the state of Rio de Janeiro, was a nearly perfect developmentalist project. With no private sector sacrifice, the federal government established a national steel industry that would supply needed inputs for everything from urban construction to advanced machine manufacture. The presence of a national steel industry also spoke directly to the army's strategic concerns about armaments. The steel complex was put in Rio near the Minas border specifically to protect it from an enemy, presumably the Argentine army.[38] Paulista industrialists and real estate developers benefited from a national supply of steel for manufacture and construction. São Paulo's growing auto parts sector was particularly well served by nationally made steel. The presence and growth of the steel industry would not only provide raw materials for Paulista industry but also make more likely the establishment of a national automobile industry, which São Paulo so vigorously backed.[39] And, by locating the CSN in Volta Redonda, Vargas also satisfied the interests of the nearby Mineiro elites. For after São Paulo, Minas Gerais was Brazil's second most economically and politically powerful state. Minas also produced a great deal of iron ore for Volta Redonda.

The creation of a state-sponsored aircraft engine factory during World War II was a logical and significant forward linkage for the CSN. U.S. military officials aided the Brazilians in opening the National Motors Factory (Fábrica Nacional de Motores or FNM) as an additional source of engines for fighters and bombers during the war. The Rio plant, which was 99 percent owned by the Brazilian government, did not manage to aid the war effort. After the armistice, it quickly made the transition to manufacturing trucks designed by Italy's Isotta-Fraschini.[40] Although not as culturally or personally inspiring as producing automobiles for individual consumption, producing trucks in Brazil complemented another component of the regime's developmentalism: the "March to the West" (*Marcha para o Oeste*). At the beginning of 1937, Vargas announced government support for the settlement of vast interior sections of the nation. The goal was to transform the center-west (the states of Goiás, Mato Grosso, Mato Grosso do Sul, and Toantins) and the north or Amazon region (including the current states of Acre, Amazonas, Amapá, Pará, Rondônia, and Roraima) into economically developed areas on par with the center-south (Minas Gerais, Rio de Janeiro, and São Paulo). Trucks and crude roads would be the key to the March to the West. They would move people in and goods out.[41]

Volta Redonda and the March to the West were big, splashy projects with deep roots in the Brazilian psyche. Moving off the coast and into the interior had long fascinated Brazilians and was even a central component of the Inconfidência Mineira in the late eighteenth century, which had explicitly called for moving the national capital off the coast. And, during the nationalist ferment and modernist ascent in the 1920s, the barbarous slave hunters of the colonial and early national periods, the *bandeirantes*, were recast as nationalist pioneers who brought civilization to Brazil's seemingly empty interior spaces. Like the national steel industry, this colonization scheme addressed the increasing interest of nationalists and modernist intellectuals in diversifying Brazil's largely agricultural economy, but it did so without costs to the nation's powerful planters and commercial interests.

Vargas's developmentalism included less heralded initiatives as well. The seemingly insignificant Decreto-Lei 3651 of September 25, 1941, established the National Traffic Code, one of the first laws promulgated in Rio that affected everyday life in every corner of Brazil, and began the process of the national government addressing transportation as a national issue. It was a seventy-page set of detailed driving regulations that would also shape street and highway design. Although mundane, the National Traffic Code explicitly overrode all state and local driving rules. No state or municipality was given the sort of exemption São Paulo had received to implement the nation's labor laws.[42] Moreover, unlike Vargas's other attempts to assert control from Rio, this one worked.

No group surrendered political or economic power by accepting a standardized driving code, so the immediate impact of this assertion of national power was limited. Indeed, the long-term impact was limited as well. The significance of the National Traffic Code was that it was Vargas's most successful assertion of federal power over state authority. A much more heralded component of Vargas's developmentalism had almost no immediate impact during his era, but like the national steel industry, the March to the West, and even the traffic code, it provided the governmental and intellectual infrastructure for the deepening of Brazilian industrial development.

The 1943 CLT codified the corporatist labor structure, even though it was at best sporadically implemented for more than twenty years.

Various administrations used components of the CLT, but the corporatist system was not fully implemented until the 1964 military coup. Particularly at the beginning of the dictatorship, but also in the aftermath of strikes in 1968, the military used all the aspects of the labor code that increased centralized control and limited worker autonomy. Unions either were neutered or became true instruments of the state. The military used the CLT in order to prevent unions from becoming oppositional institutions and to keep wages low as Brazilian industry concentrated on exports over expanding domestic markets. Successive military presidents rejected the state Fordism imagined by Vargas and implemented by Juscelino Kubitschek (1956–61) and instead used the state to keep wages low and workers in their factories.[43]

Another Estado Novo–era initiative that reverberated long after the end of the dictatorship was the National Petroleum Council, which set out to study what role the government should play in oil exploration and refining. Valuable import duties on petroleum and the absence of obvious oil deposits limited the council's activities, but nationalist critiques of foreign companies, a deteriorating balance of payments, and the steady growth of automobility changed the political calculus around state intervention. In the face of the popular "The Oil Is Ours" campaign, Vargas vowed to create a national oil monopoly. Petrobras came into existence in October 1953.[44] The national oil company did little in its early years beyond satisfying popular demands for action. Even without major oil discoveries, though, Petrobras played an increasingly important role in coordinating national energy policy during the military dictatorship and was front and center in the development of the military regime's ethanol program in the 1970s.

In retrospect, then, Vargas's developmentalism did not reflect some sort of master plan for either his preservation of political power or the Brazilian economy. Over his fifteen years of rule in the 1930s and 1940s, Vargas faced considerable financial and political constraints. The one constant of this era was his desire to hold on to power, first as Brazil's provisional president and then as its dictator. During the Estado Novo, Vargas mixed authoritarianism with a proto-populist outreach to workers and the poor. He did not, however, understand that his attempts to manipulate the popular classes led to the first initial shifts in national politics. Vargas came to power in 1930 in a coup that sought to set right the politics of the governors. Political leaders in Minas Gerais, Rio Grande do Sul, and other states reacted against Paulista overreach by launching the Revolution of 1930. After Vargas's 1945 ouster, Brazil took its first tentative steps toward national elections that no longer reflected the power of individual states. Indeed, Vargas himself was elected to the Brazilian Senate in 1946 from both Rio de Janeiro (the state he had become associated with as the nation's leader from 1930 to 1945) and Rio Grande do Sul (his home state where he had served as governor). He chose to serve from Rio Grande do Sul, in part to prepare for the 1950 presidential election.

Vargas inadvertently accelerated the move toward mass politics in Brazil. His broad use of radio and newsreels to promote himself and the regime, along with a narrative of unifying Brazil, encouraged the population to look beyond parochial politics around local bosses. Brazil's working people increasingly corresponded directly with Vargas to seek redress for their specific demands.[45] National developmentalist programs, nationwide radio and newsreel campaigns, and no shortage of rhetoric on the physical, social, and economic unification of Brazil over the course of the Great Depression and World War II succeeded in ending the politics of the governors. Middle-class and working-class voters, beginning with the December 1945 elections, chose candidates from newly formed political parties. From 1945 to 1962, the three major parties, the PSD (Partido Social Democrático), UDN (União Democrática Nacional), and PTB (Partido Trabalhista Brasileiro), accounted for about three-quarters of the members of the Chamber of Deputies.[46] Although this inchoate form of mass politics Vargas initiated remained highly circumscribed by restrictions on the franchise, it did bring to an end the patronage-based politics of the governors that had privileged large agriculture interests, especially in São Paulo and Minas Gerais.

Vargas, the former governor of a powerful state, had not originally sought to transform Brazilian elections, but the conditions he encountered during the Great Depression led him to a series of policies that fundamentally altered politics in Brazil. So often the story of Latin America during the Great Depression is of experiments with populism and new forms of state intervention in the economy.[47] From Cárdenas in Mexico to the Popular Front governments in Chile, liberal-left solutions to land tenure questions, foreign ownership of strategic enterprises, and the overall issue of social justice took center stage. Some major policy innovations, such as the founding of Pemex in Mexico, had long-lasting consequences for ongoing development. In Chile, the initial political alliances of the 1930s and 1940s would continue to shape electoral politics until the 1973 military seizure of power. Argentina in the early to mid-1940s in some ways witnessed the most spectacular example of seemingly radical change, which affected the nation's economy and polity throughout the twentieth century and beyond. In all these cases, the changes wrought in this era maintain a deep hold on the national psyche and continue to be invoked directly and indirectly in national elections, even though the reforms and policy shifts were either limited by future administrations or abruptly halted by vicious military dictatorships.

In Brazil, the Vargas of textbooks, who all but created the modern labor movement and was the first leader since Pedro II (1841–89) to centralize power in the national capital, is more fiction than fact. Vargas attempted to do those things, but the power of the Paulista elite and the weak state capacity he inherited circumscribed his most ambitious plans. Where Vargas did succeed, it was in less conspicuous ways. He succeeded in creating the bureaucratic infrastructure and economic, political, and social vocabularies of developmentalism and mass politics that in their more democratic and consumerist forms would later be associated with Kubitschek and in their more authoritarian and basic industries orientation would resonate with the generals who governed Brazil, particularly Ernesto Geisel (1974–79).

A great irony of Vargas's rule is that he may have been his epoch's most successful Latin American leader, but not for the reasons so many have been taught over the years. He failed in much of what he initially set out to do. Moreover, he failed to hold onto power as a proto-populist in 1945, and although he was a successful candidate for the presidency in open elections in 1950, he failed so miserably in office then that he chose suicide as his only way out. It is Vargas's developmentalist legacy that is impossible to ignore from the vantage point of the twenty-first century. More than the significant enterprises such as Volta Redonda and Petrobras, Vargas left Brazil with a mind-set of national development, economic diversification, and an activist state. Throughout the Great Depression, he altered the national conversation from a fulsome embrace of economic liberalism with its laissez-faire market orientation to a much more variegated and nuanced relationship between the state and markets.[48] His record with political liberalism (in terms of democracy and open government) is, at best, mixed. Vargas addressed the long legacy of political exclusion in Brazil through his initial attempts to incorporate workers into his government. This had the potential to alter politics, as did his populist gestures in 1945, but Vargas's failures with labor ended up deepening Brazil's antidemocratic traditions.[49] Still, the political system that followed provided Brazil's first experiments with electoral mass politics.

A final irony of how Vargas navigated the complex politics of the Great Depression is that his developmentalism created the economic and social spaces for the creation of arguably Brazil's first true discourses of democracy in the 1970s and 1980s. Although not often thought about as part of the legacy of the Great Depression, the transformations wrought by the deepening of industrialization, the physical integration of the nation, and the slow centralization of power that finally came to fruition with the opening of Brasília in 1960 and then was dramatically accelerated by the 1964–85 military dictatorship changed the ways Brazilians thought about their country and their place in it. The developmentalism rooted in Vargas's policies altered the ways people thought about themselves. They became more Brazilian and less of their states or regions. And people began to consider themselves more citizens than subjects. Vargas, without necessarily intending to do so, brought down the liberal economic order he had inherited, which he had initially tried to bolster by propping up the coffee sector. In doing so, he laid the groundwork for the eventual establishment of political liberalism. Although not part of the ways Brazilians remember Vargas, this may be the ultimate legacy of the changes he brought to the nation during the Great Depression.

Notes

1 Mineiros believed that it was their turn to have the presidency as the chief executive was supposed to rotate between the governor of São Paulo (the greatest coffee producer) and Minas (the dairy state).

2 Boris Fausto's *A Revolução de 1930: Historiografia e História* (São Paulo: Brasiliense, 1970) remains one of the best interpretations of the political meaning of Vargas's ascent to power. See also Maria Celina Soares d'Araújo, *A Era Vargas*, 2nd ed. (São Paulo: Editora Moderna, 2004).

3 Thomas E. Skidmore's *Politics in Brazil, 1930–1964: An Experiment in Democracy* (New York: Oxford University Press, 1967) still provides the best context for the politics of this era. The basics of politics during the Old Republic are well analyzed in José Maria Bello's classic *A History of the Republic, 1889–1964* (Stanford, CA: Stanford University Press, 1966).

4 Luiz Carlos Bresser Pereira's *Desenvolvimento e Crise no Brasil: História, Economia e Política de Getúlio Vargas a Lula*, 5th ed. (São Paulo: Editora 34, 2003) is

one of the most recent examples of this analysis. See also Boris Fausto, *História do Brasil* (São Paulo: EDUSP, 1994). Even Thomas E. Skidmore in his *Brazil: Five Centuries of Change*, 2nd ed. (New York: Oxford University Press, 2010), 114–118, hedges his bets on the question of Vargas's effectiveness in transforming social relations during the Estado Novo.

5 There is no shortage of works on Vargas's labor legislation. One of the best on his program's intentions is Angela Maria de Castro Gomes, *A Invenção do Trabalhismo* (São Paulo: Vértice, 1988). A classic study that puts this legislation into a coherent framework is Luiz Werneck Vianna, *Liberalismo e Sindicato no Brasil* (Rio: Paz e Terra, 1976).

6 It was precisely during this era that the military began to question how it could in fact become a more powerful national institution. See Frank D. McCann, *Soldiers of the Patria: A History of the Brazilian Army, 1889–1937* (Stanford, CA: Stanford University Press, 2004); and Cláudio Moreira Bento, "Getúlio Vargas e a evolução da doutrina do exército, 1930–1945," *Revista do Instituto Histórico e Geográfico Brasileiro* 339 (1983): 63–71.

7 I develop this argument in terms of Vargas speaking to the long-held dreams of modernist intellectuals in *Autos and Progress: The Brazilian Search for Modernity* (New York: Oxford University Press, 2010). For Vargas's developmentalism in historical and regional context, see Joel Wolfe, "Populism and Developmentalism," in *A Companion to Latin American History*, ed. Thomas H. Holloway (Malden, MA: Blackwell, 2008), 347–64.

8 A classic example of this school of thought is Ricardo Antunes, *Classe Operária, Sindicatos e Partido no Brasil: Da Revolução de 30 até a Aliança Nacional Libertadora* (São Paulo: Cortez, 1982).

9 An excellent example of this perspective is John D. French, *The Brazilian Workers' ABC: Class Conflict and Alliances in Modern São Paulo* (Chapel Hill: University of North Carolina Press, 1992).

10 The broad failure of Vargas's attempted intervention in industrial relations is detailed in Joel Wolfe, "The Faustian Bargain Not Made: Getúlio Vargas and Brazil's Industrial Workers, 1930–1945," *Luso-Brazilian Review* 31, no. 2 (winter 1994): 77–96. An excellent analysis of the decline in working-class living conditions under Vargas can be found in John J. Crocitti, "Vargas Era Social Policies: An Inquiry into Brazilian Malnutrition during the Estado Novo (1937–45)," in *Vargas and Brazil: New Perspectives*, ed. Jens R. Hentschke (New York: Palgrave Macmillan, 2006).

11 For a clear explication on how the corporatist labor system was supposed to obviate the need for strikes, see Kenneth S. Mericle, "Conflict Resolution and the Brazilian Industrial Relations System" (PhD diss., University of Wisconsin–Madison, 1974).

12 Joel Wolfe, *Working Women, Working Men: São Paulo and the Rise of Brazil's Industrial Working Class, 1900–1955* (Durham, NC: Duke University Press, 1993), 78, 83.

13 Joel Wolfe, "'Father of the Poor' or 'Mother of the Rich'? Getúlio Vargas, Industrial Workers, and Constructions of Class, Gender, and Populism in São Paulo, 1930–1954," *Radical History Review* 58 (winter 1994): 80–111.

14 Werner Baer, *The Brazilian Economy: Growth and Development*, 2nd ed. (New York: Praeger, 1983), 43–44.

15 Departamento Nacional do Café, *Relatório apresentado ao Consehlo consultivo pelo seu president Jaime Fernandes Guedes* (Rio: Departamento Nacional do Café, 1941).

16 Wolfe, *Working Women, Working Men*, 49–58.

17 For a fascinating and thorough justification of the civil war written thirty years after the uprising, see Aureliano Leite, "Causes e Objetivos da Revolução de 1932," *Revista da História* 25, no. 51 (julho–setembro 1962): 139–44. For a critical analysis of Paulista motives, see Barbara Weinstein, "Racializing Regional Difference: São Paulo versus Brazil, 1932," in *Race and Nation in Modern Latin America*, ed. Nancy P. Applebaum (Chapel Hill: University of North Carolina Press, 2003), 237–62.

18 Celso Furtado made this argument in his now-classic *Formação Econômica do Brasil* (Rio de Janeiro: Editôra Funda de Cultura, 1959). A more formal economic proof of this is provided in Simão Silber's "Análise da Politica Econômica," in *Formação Econômica do Brasil: A Eperiência da Industrilização*, ed. Flávio R. Versiani and José Roberto Mendonça de Barros (São Paulo: Ed. Saraiva, 1977).

19 Baer, *Brazilian Economy*, 45. See also Tamás Szmrecsányi and Ruis Guilherme Granziera, *Getúlio Vargas e a economia contemporânea*, 2nd ed. (Campinas: Hucitec, 2004).

20 Daryle Williams, *Culture Wars in Brazil: The First Vargas Regime, 1930–1945* (Durham, NC: Duke University Press, 2001), 123–24, 130–32. The *Inconfidênica Mineira* is widely considered to be the first, incomplete attempt at independence from Portugal.

21 For a fascinating contemporary view of Vargas's cultural offensive, written from a learned and critical perspective, see Karl Loewenstein, *Brazil under Vargas* (New York: Macmillan, 1942), 285–314.

22 On Vargas's complex relationship with the Afro-Brazilian community in São Paulo, see George Reid Andrews, *Blacks and Whites in São Paulo, 1888–1988* (Madison: University of Wisconsin Press, 1991), 147–56. On how Vargas altered state politics in the northeast state of Bahia and also created new cultural and political opportunities for Afro-Brazilians in Salvador, see Scott A. Ickes, "Adorned with the Mix of Faith and Profanity That Intoxicates the People: The Festival of the Senhor do Bonfim in Salvador, Bahia, Brazil, 1930–1954," *Bulletin of Latin American Research* 24, no. 1 (April 2005): 181–200.

23 Two outstanding studies of education and attempts at educational reform under Vargas are Jens R. Hentschke, *Reconstructing the Brazilian Nation: Public Schooling in the Vargas Era* (Baden-Baden: Nomos, 2007); and Jerry Dávila,

Diploma of Whiteness: Race and Social Policy in Brazil, 1917–1945 (Durham, NC: Duke University Press, 2003).

24 The most ambitious critique of developmentalism, which locates its origins in the Cold War era, is Arturo Escobar, *Encountering Development: The Making and Unmaking of the Third World* (Princeton, NJ: Princeton University Press, 1995).

25 Steve Topik's *The Political Economy of the Brazilian State, 1889–1930* (Austin: University of Texas Press, 1987) remains one of the best works challenging the conventional wisdom on the extreme laissez-faire nature of economics during the Old Republic.

26 On positivism and its religious implications for many of the engineers in the army, see Todd A. Diacon, *Stringing Together a Nation: Cândido Mariano da Silva Rondon and the Construction of a Modern Brazil, 1906–1930* (Durham, NC: Duke University Press, 2004), 79–99.

27 See Stanley J. Stein, *The Brazilian Cotton Manufacture: Textile Enterprise in an Undeveloped Area, 1850–1950* (Cambridge, MA: Harvard University Press, 1957); and Wilson Suzigan, *Indústria Brasileira: Origem e Desenvolvimento* (São Paulo: Brasiliense, 1986).

28 Thomas H. Holloway, *The Brazilian Coffee Valorization of 1906: Regional Politics and Economic Dependence* (Madison, WI: State Historical Society, 1975).

29 For a somewhat more sanguine analysis of the impact of railroads on internal development, see William R. Summerhill, *Order against Progress: Government, Foreign Investments, and Railroads in Brazil, 1854–1913* (Stanford, CA: Stanford University Press, 2003).

30 Wolfe, *Autos and Progress*, 13–32.

31 Understanding Canudos in this context helps explain Euclides da Cunha's nearly neurotic description of the physical condition of the area in and around Canudos. See Euclides da Cunha, *Rebellion in the Backland* (1903), trans. Samuel Putnam (Chicago: University of Chicago Press, 1944).

32 Todd A. Diacon, *Millenarian Vision, Capitalist Reality: Brazil's Contestado Rebellion, 1912–1916* (Durham, NC: Duke University Press, 1991); and Diacon, *Stringing Together a Nation*.

33 On the military's frustrations with the interior, see Todd A. Diacon, "Bringing the Countryside Back In: A Case Study of Military Intervention as State-Building in the Brazilian Old Republic," *Journal of Latin American Studies* 27, no. 3 (October 1995): 569–92, and "Searching for a Lost Army: Recovering the History of the Federal Army's Pursuit of the Prestes Column in Brazil, 1924–1927," *Americas: A Quarterly Review of Inter-American Cultural History* 54, no. 3 (January 1998): 409–36. See also Frank D. McCann, "The Formative Period of Twentieth-Century Brazilian Army Thought: 1900–1922," *Hispanic American Historical Review* 64, no. 4 (November 1984): 737–65, and *A Nação Armada: Ensaios sobre a História do Exército Brasileiro*, trans. Sílvio Rolim (Recife: Editôra Guararapes, 1982).

34 Stanley J. Stein's *Vassouras: A Brazilian Coffee County, 1850–1900* (Cambridge, MA: Harvard University Press, 1957) remains the single best work on the environmental destruction of this area.

35 Warren Dean, "The Green Wave of Coffee: Beginnings of Tropical Agricultural Research in Brazil, 1885–1900," *HAHR* 69, no. 1 (February 1989): 91–115; and Thomas H. Holloway, *Immigrants on the Land: Coffee and Society in São Paulo, 1886–1934* (Chapel Hill: University of North Carolina Press, 1980).

36 Linda Lewin, *Politics and Parentel in Paraíba: A Case Study of Family Based Oligarchy in Brazil* (Princeton, NJ: Princeton University Press, 1987), 91–92.

37 Joseph Love, *A Locomotiva: São Paulo na federação brasileira, 1889–1937* (Rio: Paz e Terra, 1982).

38 John D. Wirth, *The Politics of Brazilian Development* (Stanford, CA: Stanford University Press, 1970), 71–129. See also Oliver J. Dinius, *Brazil's Steel City: Developmentalism, Strategic Power, and Industrial Relations in Volta Redonda, 1941–1964* (Stanford, CA: Stanford University Press, 2011), 14–38.

39 Caren Addis, *Taking the Wheel: Auto Parts Firms and the Political Economy of Industrialization in Brazil* (University Park: Penn State University Press, 1999).

40 José Ricardo Ramalho, *Estado-Patrão e Luta Operaria: O Caso FNM* (Rio: Paz e Terra, 1989), 31–57; and Helen Shapiro, *Engines of Growth: The State and Transnational Auto Companies in Brazil* (Cambridge: Cambridge University Press, 1994), 62–63.

41 Getúlio Vargas, *A Nova Política do Brasil* (Rio: José Olympio, 1938), 5:124–26. See also Wolfe, *Autos and Progress*, 104–5.

42 República dos Estados Unidos do Brasil, *Coleção das Leis de 1941*, vol. 5, *Atos do Poder Executivo, DecretosLeis de Julho a Setembro* (Rio: Imprensa Nacional, 1941), 335–405. Until the military coup of 1964, local authorities were responsible for the implementation of the traffic code. After the coup, military police took over primary responsibility for even these laws.

43 An analysis of the transition in labor relations from a loose relationship with federal laws in the 1950s and early 1960s to their stringent implementation after the coup can be found in António Luigi Negro, *Linhas de Montagem: O Industrialismo Nacional-Desenvolimentista e a Sindicalização dos Trabalhadores* (São Paulo: Boitempo, 2004).

44 Maria Augusta Tibiriça Miranda, *O Petroleo É Nosso: A Luta contra o "Entreguismo" pelo Monopolio Estatal, 1947–1953* (Petrópolis: Vozes, 1983); Laura Randall, *The Political Economy of Brazilian Oil* (Westport, CT: Praeger, 1993), 9–12; Wirth, *Politics of Brazilian Development*, 160–83.

45 Specific worker petitions to Vargas are detailed in Wolfe, "'Father of the Poor.'"

46 E. Bradford Burns, *A History of Brazil*, 2nd ed. (New York: Columbia University Press, 1980), 440.

47 I summarize these trends for Argentina, Brazil, Chile, and Mexico in Wolfe, "Populism and Developmentalism."

48 Indeed, the one moment of unfettered liberal economic policy making in the

post-Vargas years came during the first few years after the 1964 coup. The extremely unpopular reaction to these policies led the military to quickly change course and insert itself in planning and the economy overall. Peter Evans's *Dependent Development: The Alliance of Multinational, State, and Local Capital in Brazil* (Princeton, NJ: Princeton University Press, 1979) remains the best single analysis of this process.

49 Ruth Berins Collier first suggested this in a comparative analysis with Mexico in the 1920s and 1930s. She argues that the gains made by labor through incorporation in Mexico weakened labor over the long term, while Brazilian workers did not benefit from the state but gained politically in the long term by not being tied to either the government or a particular political party. See her "Popular Sector Incorporation and Political Supremacy: Regime Evolution in Brazil and Mexico," in *Brazil and Mexico: Patterns in Late Development*, ed. Sylvia Ann Hewlitt and Richard S. Weinert (Philadelphia: ISHI, 1982).

CHAPTER 4

The Great Depression in Peru

Paulo Drinot and Carlos Contreras

Relatively severe but brief—this is how the historiography has described the impact of the Great Depression in Peru.[1] As a result, and given that in contrast to other countries in Latin America Peru did not experience a major transformation in its economic structure (from being a primarily mineral and agricultural economy to becoming an industrial economy) or in its economic policy (from export-led growth to import substitution industrialization), the dominant view on the Peruvian experience of the Great Depression remains that at least as far as the economy is concerned, there was a great deal of continuity between the period that preceded the Depression and the period that followed it. Peru is thus perceived as an outlier in relation to other medium to large economies, characterized by a diverse export quantum in the region and, implicitly, as conforming to historical processes associated with the small mono-export economies of Central America, or, in Carlos Diaz Alejandro's useful formulation, as having been more passive than reactive in relation to the slump.[2] In turn, the absence of a major rupture in the economic orientation of the country as a consequence of the Great Depression is typically understood as expressive of the economic, and by extension political, power of elites. Drawing their power from their control of the dynamic export sectors, these elites were able to absorb the economic and political shocks of the crisis and would go on to benefit in terms of economic and political supremacy from the continuation of the export-led character of the Peruvian economy until the military coup of 1968.

By contrast, historians who have focused on the political sphere broadly agree that the late 1920s and early 1930s were pivotal years for Peruvian history: the emergence of political parties of the Left, namely, the Peruvian Communist Party (PCP) and, more importantly, the Alianza Popular Revolucionaria America (APRA), radically redefined the Peruvian political arena.[3] Neither of these parties was able to achieve power in the arguably favorable political crisis that followed the end of Augusto B. Leguía's eleven-year rule in 1930. But the governments of both Sánchez Cerro (who led the military insurrection that deposed Leguía and, in the 1931 elections, defeated the APRA leader, Víctor Raúl Haya de la Torre) and Oscar Benavides (who established a dictatorship—1933–39—after Sánchez Cerro was assassinated by an APRA sympathizer) became preoccupied with, indeed primarily focused on, containing the social forces (urban labor, workers in the export industries, and sectors of the emerging middle sectors) that the PCP and APRA jostled with each other to represent and to lead. As several scholars have argued, the containment of APRA (and to a lesser extent the PCP) by an alliance of military officers and the "oligarchy" continued to shape, and arguably came to define, Peruvian politics until the 1968 military coup of General Juan Velasco Alvarado (1968–75). In this chapter, we do not challenge these broad narratives. However, we do attempt to highlight a dimension of these broad processes that has not received the attention it deserves: the developments in the state's management of the economy and society in the context of the Great Depression.[4]

We argue that the slump created conditions favorable to the establishment of institutions whose function was to manage the economy while not radically altering its primary orientation and to manage "the social" without challenging the dominant structures of social domination. These developments in the economic and social spheres had clear antecedents, not least in the 1920s during the authoritarian regime of Leguía. But the slump accelerated transformations both in understandings of the state (indeed of the idea of the state as a form of power) and in the capacities of the state to act upon both the economy and society. Peru would emerge from the slump with a number of economic institutions, such as an autonomous central bank, paper currency, and development banks focused on establishing credit lines to agriculture, industry, and mining, that consolidated the economic power of elites. Similarly, the elites' political power was strengthened through the deployment of a number of social institutions such as worker housing, state-run restaurants, and a workers' social insurance fund aimed at neutralizing the appeal of radical political alternatives to urban workers and workers in the export industries. Importantly, such institutions not only reflected the belief among the elite that the state should discipline unruly social actors, but also worked to "improve" the population, or, rather, specific sectors of the population. Implicitly, and sometimes explicitly, as we discuss briefly at the end of this chapter, such developments helped to further entrench racialized understandings of the sources of "progress" and "backwardness" in Peru.

The Economic Impact of the Great Depression

The economic effect of the Great Depression on Peru needs to be read against developments in the previous decades, particularly the 1920s.[5] The reconstruction period that followed the War of the Pacific (1879–84), and particularly the 1895 civil war, was marked by the creation of an open economy that specialized in exports of primary commodities. In contrast to most Latin American countries, Peru's exports were highly diversified, including sugar, cotton, rubber, wool, oil, and metals (particularly copper but also silver and gold), as well as other products such as coffee and cocaine. These export sectors, which fed a sustained economic expansion in the first few decades of the twentieth century, tended to be linked to particular regional economies: sugar and cotton were found on the coast, wool primarily in the southern highlands, rubber in the Amazon, oil in the northern tip of the country, and metals in the central highlands. Until the 1910s, the returned value of export-led growth was relatively high.[6] Thanks in part to the growing availability of new sources of credit (composed in large part of merchant—particularly British, U.S., and German—capital), an economic elite made up of Peruvian and recent (particularly Italian) migrant entrepreneurs open to, and capable of, diversification began to invest the gains from the export trade in new sectors, including a financial and banking sector and a fledgling industrial sector, with textile and food processing industries leading the way.[7]

In the following decades, as Rosemary Thorp and Geoffrey Bertram have convincingly shown, relative factor prices and the denationalization of the mineral and oil export sectors reduced the returned value of export growth to the economy and slowed down and even reversed the industrialization process of the previous period. Agricultural exports, such as cotton, sugar, and wool, which had dominated the export quantum and were largely in Peruvian hands, were overtaken by mineral exports, particularly copper and oil, but also lead and zinc, largely in foreign (primarily U.S.) hands (although cotton maintained a key role in the economy given the large number of producers). This process was accompanied by the increasing influence of the

United States as a source of capital, both portfolio and direct, and as a trading partner, as well as by the declining influence of other core trading economies, particularly Britain.[8] During the authoritarian regime of Augusto B. Leguía (1919–30), in particular, the sharp reduction in the returned value of the export sector was matched by an equally sharp increase in government borrowing in international financial markets. Between 1920 and 1928, foreign funded debt was U.S. $105 million. Much of this was invested in large infrastructural projects, such as road building, irrigation projects, and urban modernization, typically undertaken by U.S. companies, so that in some ways, as Paul Drake puts it, "US loans were used to pay US companies."[9] But a significant amount was siphoned off through widespread corruption networks that centered on Leguía and his family, while the infrastructure projects were typically ill-conceived and rarely completed.[10] Moreover, in the latter half of the 1920s a large proportion of foreign loans were used to service the foreign debt.[11]

Leguía claimed that his objective, no less, was to reestablish the nation and to construct a "Patria Nueva" (New Fatherland). The ideology of this Patria Nueva shared many of the assumptions and prescriptions of other projects of "authoritarian modernization" in Latin America (such as the Porfiriato in Mexico).[12] Like those other projects, the Patria Nueva was characterized by a nominal expansion of state capacity (in both cognitive and coercive terms, as reflected, among other things, in the number of public employees, which increased exponentially between 1920 and 1930, and in the establishment of a "modern" police force) but also of the very idea of the state: concretely, of the fields—economic, administrative, social, cultural, etc.—deemed amenable to state action and design.[13] For example, one of the Leguía regime's key characteristics was the growing centralization of political and economic power in Lima as levels of representation at local and regional levels were eliminated. Another was a complex relationship between the executive and subaltern sectors such as the indigenous and organized labor, characterized by a combination of institutionalization—through the establishment of state agencies such as the Sección del Trabajo (Labour Office) and the Sección de Asuntos Indígenas (Indian Affairs Office) in the Ministerio de Fomento (Ministry of Development) that were supposed to promote the interests of the subaltern and a constitution (1920) that recognized and guaranteed a number of social and economic rights specific to workers and Indians—and repression, which was selective but systematic (with a few notable exceptions, such as in the context of peasant uprisings in the south of the country in the early 1920s) and entrusted to a new police force.[14] Although Leguía directed numerous resources to the armed forces, which, like so much else, he sought to "modernize," he also alienated the military by pursuing the settlement of a territorial dispute over the southern provinces of Tacna and Arica with Chile left over from the War of the Pacific.[15]

As this suggests, the expansion of the state apparatus under Leguía reflected the growing number of economic and social agents that state actors had to contend with. As Drake suggests, under Leguía's authoritarian rule, "state articulation responded to the increasing need to deal with foreign capital, economic growth, urbanization, and emergent middle and working classes."[16] But such developments in statecraft had a longer, and more complex, genealogy and corresponded to transnational developments that connected Peru in the early twentieth century with broader ideological currents and processes of state formation in much of the world. As Daniel T. Rodgers has shown in his magisterial *Atlantic Crossings*, the process whereby the contradictions of capitalism were seen to create a growing role for state intervention in the economy and society was an inherently transnational process that intimately linked the North Atlantic economies of the late nineteenth and early twentieth centuries.[17] Of course, this process was not restricted to the North Atlantic economies. In Latin America too, throughout this period, new ideas about the state and society emerged, shaped by particular ideological currents, including social Catholicism and positivism, which challenged some of the dominant liberal ideas of the nineteenth century and created new areas of intervention for the state.[18] Such developments are clearly discernible in the Peruvian case from as early as the 1880s, when political economists such as Luis Esteves, as Paul Gootenberg has shown, began to argue in favor of a greater state involvement in the economy and for the promotion of industry as an alternative to the country's dependence on guano exports.[19] In short, the "expansion" of the state under Leguía is best understood as, at once, a consolidation of a particular idea of the state and of its role in managing the economy and the social with a long and broad genealogy and, in turn, as a reaction to growing demands from various economic and social agents.

Historians disagree about the extent to which the policies pursued by Leguía effectively transformed Peruvian society during the 1920s. But most agree that his sins of commission and omission created antagonisms on several fronts. His opponents momentarily came together in late 1930 to oust him. The "revolution" that toppled the regime, led by a young army major (commandant), Luis M. Sánchez Cerro, originated in Arequipa, was backed by provincial elites and gained immediate widespread popular support. It was a bloodless coup. No one attempted to defend the old regime. The manifesto issued by the revolutionaries attacked the Leguía regime for its corruption and "tyranny," its centralism, and its economic policies, which compromised the country's economic independence. The new leader, a mestizo, became a popular hero almost immediately. He was quick to consolidate his popularity through a series of measures. He set up a special court, the Tribunal de Sanción Nacional (Court of National Sanction), to organize trials of known Leguía cronies and allegedly corrupt civil servants.[20] Three weeks after assuming power, he ordered the distribution of food rations to the city's poor in the police stations. The abolition of the Ley de Conscripción Vial (Law of Road-Building Conscription) further contributed to Sánchez Cerro's popularity, particularly in the provinces. The Leguía regime created this law in order to provide cheap labor for construction projects, especially road building. Many opposed the law on the grounds that it amounted to a system of forced labor. Although this was not always the case, its abolition was welcomed broadly.[21]

The slump was only one factor in Leguía's downfall, as the above suggests. It was transmitted to Peru through the sharp fall in the dollar value of its exports, from U.S. $132 million in 1929 to U.S. $38 million in 1932. Mineral exports, in volume and value, were particularly affected as a consequence of sharp drops in international prices: the price of copper, lead, and zinc more than halved between 1929 and 1933. Agricultural exports, such as sugar and cotton, did not fare much better.[22] As such, the economic impact of the slump was felt primarily in those sectors of the economy that had grown considerably in the previous thirty years, spurred by demand for export commodities and which successfully if gradually established stable workforces (largely from migrants who moved from the highlands to the coast), as was most evident in coastal sugar plantations, central highland mines, and northern oil fields. Cayaltí, a sugar plantation in Lambayeque, "was transformed from a work camp into a community of households larger than most towns in the department," and its workforce rose from 900 in 1896 to 1,421 in 1932.[23] Employment at the U.S.-owned Cerro de Pasco mine doubled from 7,840 in 1920 to 13,000 in 1929. These were not mere work camps: workers employed by the companies were a relatively small percentage of the total population. A 1932 census of the Talara and Negritos oil camps reveals that out of a total population of almost 19,000 inhabitants, workers represented a mere 17 percent. Their families accounted for almost half the camps' population. Merchants and a number of "gente ajena" (outsiders) represented another 22 percent.[24] At Cayaltí in 1923 the number of nonworkers (mostly women and children) stood at around 57 percent of the total population.[25] The growth of these new population centers altered settlement patterns that dated back to the colonial period, characterized by primarily "white" cities and primarily indigenous haciendas and villages, which were still evident in the 1876 census.[26]

Like the export "enclaves" (which, in some ways, were nothing of the sort) of the northern coast and central highlands, Lima, and to a lesser extent some provincial cities, underwent a rapid expansion and demographic growth, driven by the export economy.[27] By the 1930s, the capital had acquired the feel of a modern metropolis, boasting new boulevards, factories, and wide avenues crisscrossed by trams, taxis, and buses. Among the city's most distinguishing features was a nascent urban workforce, distinct from both the elite and a growing middle class of state and commercial employees.[28] Internal migration, spurred by Leguía's road-building policies in the 1920s, was largely responsible for the bulk of demographic growth in the cities, and most spectacularly for Lima's growth. Between 1919 and 1931, 65,000 *provincianos* moved to the capital city. Though provincial cities also grew in this period as a consequence of migration from their hinterlands, they were at the same time sources of migration to Lima. Between 1876 and 1916, Arequipa's population, for example, grew from 33,000 to 48,000 inhabitants. However, in the 1920s Arequipa, along with Junín, Ayacucho, and Ancash departments, was the source of 80 percent of all migrants to Lima. Though this figure applies to the department of Arequipa, not the city, it is nevertheless suggestive. Migration was not strictly a rural-urban phenomenon: provincial city dwellers were largely responsible for the migration to Lima in the 1920s.[29]

As the cities grew, workers came to represent an increasingly large proportion of the total urban population. In 1931 there were approximately 110,000 persons with blue-collar jobs in Lima, compared to only 66,000 in 1920. While those with blue-collar jobs had accounted in 1920 for 58 percent of the city's total employed population, by 1931 they represented 68 percent.[30] Though similar figures are not available for the major provincial cities, it is clear that while neither Cuzco nor Arequipa nor Trujillo experienced the same degree of growth as the capital, they were also affected by those processes and acquired a sizable urban workforce. Although an increasingly important number of the urban workforce found employment in new factories (particularly textile) and in transport sectors (railways, trams, taxis, and buses), by the early 1930s the majority of Peru's urban population continued to be employed in essentially nonindustrial occupations such as domestic service (14 percent of Lima's urban workforce in 1931), or as tailors and seamstresses (11 percent), and in construction (8 percent). Lima also had some 1,314 market food vendors and 253 lottery sellers, two examples of low-skill jobs that formed the backbone of the urban economy. The typical urban workplace was therefore not the factory but rather the artisan workshop, or even more commonly, the home and the street.[31]

Workers both in the export sectors and in the cities were hit hard by the slump, as employers dismissed part of their workforce and attempted to cut wages. But so were Peru's middle classes, for whom the economic crisis represented not only a decline in living standards but also, as David Parker has argued, a decline in social status, as it became increasingly difficult for clerks or doctors to sustain the sort of class performance, dependent on consumption of both material and cultural goods, that formed the basis of differentiation with the working class.[32] In contrast to previous crises, when workers in the sugar or mining sector shed by struggling businesses could be reabsorbed into subsistence agriculture, in the 1930s this was no longer such an easy option. It is estimated that the population in 1930 was twice the size it had been at the previous national census in 1876. In the 1930s, population growth was deemed to be around 1.5 to 2 percent per year, a growth rate that corresponds to the beginning of the country's demographic transition. The population as a whole had reached five million, equivalent, according to some estimates, to the maximum population levels reached prior to the demographic catastrophe that followed the Spanish conquest.[33] Two-thirds of the population was concentrated in the highlands, where over the first few decades of the twentieth century land became an increasingly scarce resource while labor became abundant as a consequence not only of demographic change but also of conflict, sometimes violent, over land between elites seeking to produce for the export market and the indigenous peasantry. This explains why the ability of highlanders to combine work in areas of export production with subsistence agriculture that had characterized prior decades and much of the nineteenth century had become increasingly difficult.[34]

Consequently, unemployment in the cities and in the export sectors emerged as a major social, and political, problem for the first time in the context of the 1930s crisis. No "national" unemployment figures are available for this period, but available data suggest a drop in field laborers in the sugar sector from circa 26,000 in 1928 to 20,000 in 1932 (in Peru, employment in the sugar sector was less seasonal than elsewhere in the Americas). Blue-collar and white-collar employment in the mining sector fell from 25,000 to 13,000 and from 3,000 to 1,000, respectively, in the same period.[35] The figures collected by the Junta Pro-Desocupados de Lima (the Lima Unemployment Office), a state agency set up in 1931 to initiate public work that would provide employment for unemployed workers, are suggestive at best, as they merely indicate the number of workers registered with the Junta. According to the Junta, between 1931 and 1934 some 22,151 workers registered. Of these, 9,230 were from Lima, another 1,380 from Junín, 1,881 from Arequipa, 1,540 from Ancash, and 355 from Cuzco.[36] The 1931 Lima census's unemployment figures have been shown to be unreliable. According to the census, some 31,139 men between the ages of 14 and 69, or 25 percent of the working population, were unemployed. Construction workers, 70 percent of whom were unemployed, fared particularly badly. Significantly, workers in highly unionized industries, such as textiles, appear to have fared considerably better than those in nonunionized industries. Unemployment in the heavily unionized textile industry, for example, stood at 12 percent.[37]

Anecdotal evidence provides a more detailed picture of unemployment in the early 1930s. Some firms, like the International Petroleum Company (IPC) at Talara, began to shed labor relatively early. The number of blue-collar workers employed by the IPC fell from almost 4,000 in 1928 to 1,740 in 1932. Contrary to what contemporary observers such as Edwin Kemmerer, appointed as head of a U.S. "mission" of economic experts to stabilize the Peruvian economy, and some historians argue, there is evidence that wages were cut drastically in some sectors, falling in the case of the IPC, according to one estimate, from an average of 3.04 soles to 1.34 between 1928 and 1931.[38] Most mining firms and several sugar plantations simply closed down to await better times. The closure of the Cerro de Pasco mines in November 1930 had negative consequences for both related industries and the regional economy. The same month, the Central Railway, which transported mineral produced by the Cerro de Pasco mining company to the port of Callao, reduced its workweek to four days, or thirty-two hours, and warned of further cuts if the situation did not improve.[39] When Cerro de Pasco reinitiated operations in late 1931, it did so with a new wage scale.

Some wages were reduced by as much as 40 percent. The *enmaderadores*, for example, saw their wages cut from 5.50 soles to 4.00. Safety, workers complained, was being compromised. The company refused to issue waterproof clothing to workers working in humid and cold areas of the mine. Moreover, as one worker pointed out, Cerro de Pasco was now hiring "Indios" who would work for whatever wage they were offered and in the worst conditions.[40] Workers unwilling to take the new wages or accept the working conditions were fired.[41]

As this suggests, the crisis created conditions favorable to the emergence of political parties, such as the PCP and APRA, which claimed to represent and sought to guide the very sectors of the population most affected by the economic downturn. In absolute terms urban workers and workers in the export sectors represented a small proportion of the laboring peoples of Peru; the vast majority were subsistence farmers who typically supplemented the income they derived from small-scale agriculture with handicraft production and petty trade. But urban workers and workers in the export sectors (overall no more than 200,000 in a country of five million people in 1930) gained a prominence in politics and state policy disproportionate to their numbers. This owed in part to the fact that such workers, key to strategic export industries or urban industrial production, were thrust to the foreground of politics by the rise of political parties of the Left in the 1930s.[42] It also owed to the fact that elites sought to contain and manage the challenge to the status quo that these parties represented by co-opting or incorporating such workers and thus neutralizing the appeal of the parties. But it owed too to the fact that such workers were identified, both by the elite and by the new political forces, as agents of national progress. This responded to a highly racialized identification of "the worker" as a category distinct from other types of laboring peoples and, often implicitly but sometimes explicitly, from the indigenous.[43] As we discuss below, this prominence helps explain the particular focus that state management of society took in the 1930s.

The Rise of Mass Politics

The months that followed the collapse of the Leguía regime saw an unprecedented degree of political freedom gradually evolve into an unprecedented degree of social unrest, as both urban workers and workers in the export sectors began to turn to the strike in order to resist the growing attempts by employers to transfer the impact of the slump to their workforce. Under the leadership of Eudocio Ravines, the PCP pursued a highly confrontational strategy in relation to the Sánchez Cerro regime, which it branded a Fascist dictatorship, and sought to transfer that confrontation to evolving labor disputes. Thanks to its control of the CGTP (Central General de Trabajadores del Perú), to the labor confederation, and to the work of its cadres among organized labor, the PCP played an important role in the radicalization of several strikes, most notably in the mining camps of the central highlands in November 1930 and during the general strike of May 1931. Despite effective repression of labor unrest by the government, these strikes contributed to a general sense of social chaos.[44] In this context, the sectors of the elite that had backed Sánchez Cerro's insurrection against Leguía began to waver in their support (this was particularly true of elites in the provinces, whose interest in reversing the centralization of the previous decade went largely unheeded by Sánchez Cerro), while the popular sectors too began to voice growing dissatisfaction with the failure of the new government to address the effects of the slump.

In March 1931 Sánchez Cerro stepped down and was replaced by a transitional government junta led by David Samanez Ocampo. In addition to overseeing much of the economic and financial restructuring that contributed to Peru's rapid emergence from the slump, the Samanez Ocampo junta played a decisive role in organizing Peru's first "popular" elections. In contrast to previous elections in the century, which had been disputed between political parties that primarily represented the interests of sectors of the elite or of military caudillos, the October 1931 elections pitted two political movements against each other, Haya de la Torre's APRA and Sánchez Cerro's Unión Revolucionaria, which both drew their support from a "mass" electorate composed primarily of the urban working and middle sectors.[45] True, this was still an election that excluded both women and the bulk of the indigenous population. But as the demonstrations and rallies for one or the other party prior to the elections demonstrated, the 1931 electoral process inaugurated a new era of mass popular politics in Peru.[46] Sánchez Cerro won the relatively free and fair elections, but APRA refused to accept the result. The tensions between the two parties escalated following the elections, as APRA was driven underground, from where it sought to unseat the president through a series of plots and rebellions. Sánchez Cerro's repression of APRA reached a climax in the northern city of Trujillo in 1932, when, following a rebellion led by APRA supporters, the armed forces first bombed and later assassinated a large number of militants.[47] In 1933, in the context of a border conflict over the river port of Leticia with Colombia that Peru would lose, an APRA militant assassinated Sánchez Cerro. His replacement, Oscar Benavides, also a military man, initially pursued a policy of rapprochement toward APRA, but by 1934, and particularly following his decision to annul the 1936 elections, in which the APRA-backed candidate stood to claim victory, his "peace and concordance" policy gave way to repression.

Not surprisingly, historians have tended to view this period as the moment when the character of twentieth-century Peruvian "politics" was established, certainly until the 1960s and in some ways until as late as the 1980s: that is, a politics dominated by the conflict between APRA on the one hand and the "oligarchy" in alliance with the military on the other. It was a politics characterized by the systematic if selective repression of political opposition (often resulting in exile) in combination with attempts to neutralize the popular sectors that had emerged in the course of the 1920s and demonstrated their political power in the 1931 election through policies that "co-opted" or "incorporated" them. Put differently, historians have tended to see the social policies implemented by the governments of the 1930s, discussed in the following section, as political devices to undermine political opposition, namely, APRA. There is little doubt that this was the purpose of these policies. But the policies in themselves, irrespective of their purpose, point to something that historians have for the most part paid little attention to: the fact that the Great Depression contributed to a significant change in conceptions of the state's role vis-à-vis the social, and, more specifically, in ideas of the social fields amenable to state management. Of course, as we have already noted, such ideas had been present prior to the 1930s. They are evident in the 1920s and earlier. But in the 1930s, as we discuss below, they became increasingly dominant: they were integral to APRA's ideology and to its political program, but also to the project of government of Sánchez Cerro and, particularly, Benavides.

State Management of the Economy

Before discussing how the Depression contributed to such changes in the state management of the social, it is worth examining similar, if arguably more discreet, changes in the economic sphere. As noted above, the world depression was transmitted to economies such as Peru's, specialized in primary exports and whose public finances depended on these exports and on loans from U.S. banks, through a balance of payments crisis. The reduction in foreign exchange inflows as a consequence of the fall in exports and the dearth of new loans was compounded by capital outflows (as foreign investors repatriated their capital) and pressures from foreign banks for the prompt payment of Peru's foreign debt. In March 1931, like several other countries in the region, the Peruvian government suspended the payment of its foreign debt, as an emergency measure to address the balance of payments crisis. This decision was taken while the Kemmerer mission, which had recommended that debt payments be continued, was in Peru, and can therefore be seen as a clear demonstration of, or at the very least as an attempt to assert, autonomy vis-à-vis both international creditors and, arguably, the United States (although as Carlos Díaz Alejandro pointed out some years ago in examining policies in the context of the Great Depression, there is a risk in attributing autonomy to "a series of improvisations more or less forced by circumstances, and whose logic may be clearer *ex post* than at the time of their adoption").[48] Peru would not resume payment of its international debt obligations until after World War II. This situation forced the Peruvian governments of the 1930s to develop internal credit facilities and new sources of fiscal income that would replace the funds that had previously been obtained in international credit markets.

Overall, Peru, like Colombia, did not attempt to spend its way out of the crisis, as other countries in the region, and beyond, did. Government expenditure fell significantly following the Wall Street Crash, and even in 1937 it remained below the 1928 level in monetary terms.[49] Isolated increases in expenditure, such as when Sánchez Cerro drew on the country's reserves to pay the bureaucracy and the military, or during the Leticia border conflict with Colombia, were not envisioned as proactive policies to kick-start Peru's economic recovery.[50] Instead, Peru's recovery, achieved in GDP terms by 1934, was due primarily to the export sector, particularly cotton, but also to minerals such as lead and zinc and especially gold, which faced favorable prices after 1932 as countries, including Peru, were forced off the gold standard. As we indicated in the introduction to this chapter, Peru was more passive than reactive in terms of policy, and the country's economic structure at the end of the 1930s was not much changed from the early 1920s. But the Peruvian governments of the 1930s did introduce some economic and, as we discuss below, social policy measures that reflected a broader, transnational move toward increasing state management of the economy and society, a move common to divergent—indeed, opposed—political systems, including Roosevelt's New Deal, Mussolini's Fascist Italy, and Stalin's Soviet Union. Some of these measures were the product of the recommendations of the economic mission led by Edwin Kemmerer, which had as its goal the maintenance, or reassertion, of economic orthodoxy in the Andean region.[51] But others departed in interesting ways from the Kemmerer recommendations.

For much of the nineteenth century and the early twentieth century, Peru was "exceptionally under-taxed," as Thorp and Bertram have suggested.[52] Peruvian governments in the early twentieth century timidly expanded taxation and came to rely on it for revenue at times when other sources of fiscal income were limited or when, as during Leguía's Patria Nueva, expenditure ballooned. Under Leguía, revenues from direct and indirect taxes increased by 129 percent between 1919 and 1929, as the debt-financing strategy proved unable to generate sufficient funds to cover the growth of the state bureaucracy and the debt service and public works expenditure.[53] In the context of the world crisis, the Samanez Ocampo junta introduced a new temporary "unemployment" (pro-desocupados) tax. It was established on the basis of small increases of one or two percentage points to taxes that already existed, such as export and import taxes, taxes on business profits, and taxes on movable capital, and more significant increases of between ten and twenty-five percentage points on taxes on tobacco consumption and automobile registrations. It also was funded through new levies on gambling and on salaries that exceeded 200 soles per month.[54] This temporary tax, which generated substantial new income for the state, was supposed to end on December 31, 1931, but it was prolonged until after the end of World War II. When it was finally abolished, some of its levies were in effect retained as elements in income tax.[55]

In order to legitimate the new levy, the funds raised by the unemployment tax were to be managed not by the government but by unemployment juntas (Juntas Pro-Desocupados) created in each territorial administrative unit or *departamento* (briefly discussed above). They were to be composed of local worthies (the head of the Lima Junta was the historian and conservative politician José de la Riva Agüero), recruited by the government as allies following the collapse of the Leguía regime. These juntas were to undertake a number of public works, including the building of schools, prisons, roads, bridges, water and sewage works, worker housing, markets, and small-scale irrigation projects. A central entity, the Comisión Distribuidora (Distribution Commission), assigned monies to each departmental junta. Some of these juntas had substantial sums at their disposal. The Lima junta's resources between 1931 and 1934 totaled some 7 million soles, of which 2 million was spent on roads and bridges, 1.11 million on hospitals and worker housing, 1.6 million on paving and sanitation, and 1.22 million on school buildings.[56] The juntas also provided work to the unemployed. Between 1931 and 1943, a total of 32,018 workers registered with the Lima junta and received some support in the form of employment in public works.[57] The juntas also provided more immediate forms of relief. As late as April 1933, the Lima junta's soup kitchen fed some five hundred persons a day.[58] The Lima junta, moreover, helped a fair number of those provincianos unable to find employment in Lima to return to their place of origin: some 8,060 between 1931 and 1934, 1,957 between 1935 and 1936, 615 between 1937 and 1938, and 836 between 1939 and 1941.[59]

These unemployment juntas were part of a broader strategy to placate and to some extent co-opt labor in a context in which, as we discuss below, radical parties of the Left claiming to represent the interests of the urban working class and workers in the export industries appeared to be in the ascendant.[60] They also reflected broader transnational trends shaped by nationalism and xenophobia in the wake of the Depression. A number of laws benefiting workers were passed at the expense of foreigners and foreign companies. Law 7704 obliged mining companies, which were largely foreign owned, to deposit the wages and salaries that had not been paid to workers in the last ten years into a special account in the Caja de Depositos y Consignaciones. These monies were to be used in the establishment of social assistance for miners. Another law, 7519, obliged the oil companies, again almost exclusively foreign owned, to provide free education to the population in their camps and to employ qualified teachers who were granted public employee status.[61] Law 7505 stands out among the laws passed in this period. It included two major provisions. Industrial and commercial establishments were bound to employ a workforce composed 80 percent of Peruvian citizens. These workers, moreover, were to receive 80 percent of total wages and salaries. In addition, the law established a fifteen-day holiday for blue-collar workers. The law was decreed in April 1932, but subsequently amended on several occasions. The first part was aimed almost exclusively at Chinese and Japanese businesses and was intended to draw support from artisans and small retailers most affected by what was increasingly perceived as disloyal Asian competition in a context marked by rising anti-Asian xenophobia and racism. As the British minister noted, "the legislation was really designed to prevent Japanese infiltration into Peru."[62] In May 1935, a press report indicated that the majority of employers fined for failing to comply with the law were either Japanese or Chinese.[63]

Besides increasing taxation, a second mechanism employed by the Depression-era governments to address the loss of access to foreign sources of credit was the establishment of a monetary system based on fiat money. From the time of independence, Peru had been reluctant to use paper money, particularly following the disastrous experience in the years 1873–88, which bankrupted a number of people. The adoption of the gold standard in 1897 was done on the basis of gold and silver coins. During World War I, "cheques circulares" (bankers' cheques) issued by private banks began to circulate. These were replaced after 1922 by paper currency issued by the state-backed Banco de Reserva (Reserve Bank) created that same year. From that point onward, paper money began to be accepted, which gave the Depression-era governments some room for maneuver during the slump. Indeed, early in the crisis, the government suspended the convertibility of its emitted notes into gold. The Kemmerer mission's recommendations regarding servicing the debt were ignored. But the Peruvian government did adopt its recommendations regarding the creation of a Central Reserve Bank with greater autonomy and a Superintendency of Banks (Superintendencia de Bancos). Both of these institutions gave the post-Depression governments the ability to determine the quantity of money in circulation in the economy.[64]

Finally, the Depression-era governments innovated with regard to credit finance. The bankruptcy of the Banco del Perú y Londres in the depths of the Depression and the collapse of international trade had left Peru's agro-exporters with limited access to credit.[65] In August 1931, the Samanez Ocampo junta approved the creation of the Agricultural Bank of Peru (Banco Agrícola del Perú), whose function was to provide credit, based on funds made available by the Central Reserve Bank, to Peru's agro-exporters. The creation of this state development bank was an emergency response to the absence of credit in a context in which there was a real risk of losing the 1932 cotton harvest. But its creation had longer-term implications for coastal agriculture.[66] Five years later, the Benavides government established the Industrial Bank of Peru (Banco Industrial del Perú), with the aim of promoting industrial production. A few years later, a Mining Bank (Banco Minero) was also established. These development banks served to channel low-interest loans, usually below the inflation rate, to sectors of the oligarchy. The Central Reserve Bank, the Superintendency of Banks, and the state development banks were three of the most important legacies of the Great Depression in the economic sphere. The latter of the three survived until the 1990s, when they were finally swept away by the neoliberal reforms of Alberto Fujimori. Their establishment did not represent a major departure in terms of economic policy. They did not correspond to, nor were they even minor elements in, a policy shift toward import substitution industrialization as occurred in other Latin American countries. But they did reflect a departure in terms of state management of the economy, expanding in important ways the sectors of the economy deemed amenable to state intervention and promotion, as well as the mechanisms through which the state could exercise its influence over those sectors.

State Management of the Social

The Depression-era governments also implemented a series of social policies that similarly signaled a departure in terms of statecraft. These measures, which echoed developments in Latin America and, indeed, in Europe and the United States, included work creation schemes for the unemployed (as already discussed), housing projects for workers, and state-run eateries that provided cheap food to workers, as well as new labor legislation. Most importantly, in 1936 the Benavides government created a social insurance system for blue-collar workers. As the historiography has suggested, and as contemporary critics of the measures argued, both the Sánchez Cerro and Benavides governments created social policy with a clear political intent. Both APRA and the PCP claimed that the governments' social policies were a thinly veiled strategy to weaken their political appeal to organized labor. APRA, in particular, claimed (with some justification) that many of the policies implemented by the Benavides government had been lifted from its 1931 electoral program.[67] Arguably, the government's "borrowing" of APRA's project was evidence of the relative strength of APRA and the relative weakness of the government: the government had little choice but to offer what the opposition was offering. But the ideas included in the APRA project were far more widely shared than APRA's critique of the government would suggest.

A speech given in March 1939 by Benavides may help illustrate some of the ideas that underpinned his regime's social policy. Benavides began by noting that Peru was undergoing a process of change that went beyond the material sphere: a veritable change in the moral climate had occurred.

Thanks to his intervention, pessimism, "our most incurable disease," had given way to an optimism based on "our wealth, our capacity to exploit it, in the profound and true faith that leads Peruvians towards the great reality of Destiny."[68] One of the cornerstones of this new optimism was a new approach to social problems. Those who believed that the just aspirations of well-being and improvement of the working class could be postponed indefinitely or only partially satisfied, Benavides suggested, were blind accomplices of sectarianism (that is, of APRA). Social problems, he now realized, were intimately tied to questions of security and progress. Although he made sure to stress that those who manipulated the legitimate aspirations of the working class for personal ambition deserved nothing but condemnation, Benavides declared,

> I once said: "I do not know, nor do I want to know, whether I am or not, a socialist. I am, above all, human." Though this should not be interpreted as a rectification of my own thinking, I want to say that if socialism is heightened, compassionate and ample social justice, [in tune with] the Supreme interest of the Nation and the untouchable authority of the state, I not only share these principles, I have put them into practice, with deep faith, in these five years of government. And not with empty words and easy promises. With laws that function and that are now an inseparable part of our collective existence, which harmonize the legitimate interests of all classes; with useful and long lasting public works, whose existence cannot be denied or disfigured.[69]

Had "la secta" (APRA) taken power when he did, Benavides stressed, none of the social deeds he had undertaken would exist and Peru would have been plunged into chaos.

Although Benavides attributed the successes of his regime to his personal actions, he also emphasized the importance of the state in achieving what he called "social equilibrium." He suggested that the increase of wealth at the expense of human capital represented a threat to the nation. Similarly, if labor became too expensive, a drop in entrepreneurship would result, while capital would flee the country, economic depression would ensue, and unemployment would increase. Because of its vast natural resources, Peru could look forward to many centuries of prosperity and increased collective well-being. However, Benavides implied, this prosperity would only result from the abandonment of class struggle in favor of class cooperation. New sources of capital would bring about the development of industry and commerce and create new sources of employment. However, the key to national greatness resided in the protection of human capital: "With a laboring class that is fed deficiently, forced to live in unhygienic housing, incapable of providing education to their children, condemned to live in misery by disease, and in the utmost helplessness by disability and old age, it was impossible to create that state of confidence, of faith, of permanent security that is necessary for the progress of nations."[70] These social problems, Benavides claimed, had been addressed by the social action of the state through the creation of the "Restaurantes Populares" (state-run eateries), the "Barrios Obreros" (worker housing), and the 1936 social security law, among other measures.[71] More generally, the state had initiated "an era of solidarity between classes and . . . instilled in them a consciousness of their responsibilities and duties to the Nation."[72]

As this confirms, the purpose of these policies was to combat APRA by addressing the problems faced by urban labor in the wake of the Great Depression. But, just as importantly, the policies themselves expressed a new idea of "the social" and of the state. This idea is evident in the 1933 constitution, particularly in the articles that relate to labor, which reprised and developed the main points of the 1920 constitution.[73] Thus, article 46 established the state's power to legislate on the organization and "general security" of industrial work, the length of the working day, and a minimum wage. Articles 48, 49, and 50 pointed to the state's role as guarantor of public health and provider of, in effect, social security, establishing that "the law will create a social security system (régimen de previsión) to address the economic consequences of unemployment, old age, sickness, disability and death and will develop social solidarity institutions, savings and insurance establishments and cooperatives," and gave the state the power to "cheapen" subsistence goods. Although the 1933 constitution made no mention of compulsory arbitration in labor disputes (an aspect of the 1920 constitution), it nevertheless included a number of innovations. Article 43, possibly inspired by the Italian corporatist Carta del Lavoro of 1927, established that the state would legislate on the collective labor contract, although article 44 prohibited the inclusion in collective contracts of any restrictions to civil, political, and social rights. Finally, article 45, possibly drawing on article 123 of the 1917 Mexican constitution, established that the state would favor a profit-sharing regime for workers.[74]

Although APRA and the Depression-era governments of Sánchez Cerro and Benavides were clearly on opposite ends of the political spectrum, they shared to a significant extent a common understanding of the role of "the so-cial" and of the state. The 1933 constitution, partly drafted by APRA congress-men, contained and reflected the ideas that were expressed by Benavides in his speech: the need to protect "human capital," as the president termed it, in order to bring about "the progress of nations" expressed a new concep-tion of "the social" and of the state's role in relation to it, which was increas-ingly understood as self-evident. Of course, these ideas predated the Great Depression: they are to be found in the 1920 constitution, in the ideological substance underpinning a number of policies pursued by Leguía, and in a series of treatises and theses dealing with the social question that began to appear in Peru in the late nineteenth century. But the Great Depression, in Peru as elsewhere, contributed to establishing a growing consensus regard-ing the role that the state would need to play henceforth in managing and regulating "the social." In so doing, it also entrenched a particular under-standing of those sectors of the population deemed amenable to state regu-lation and management, since "the social" was conceived in narrow terms as being limited to the "modern" sectors of Peruvian society, such as the urban working class, workers in the export industries, and the emerging middle sectors, and exclusive of Peru's majority indigenous population.[75]

Conclusion

In sum, in this chapter we have not challenged the views dominant in the historiography regarding the economic continuity and political change that characterized the impact of the Great Depression on Peru. We have argued, however, that the crisis contributed in important and clearly discernible ways to the consolidation of developments in statecraft that reflected, at once, broader ideological transnational processes that linked Peru to other coun-tries in the region and beyond and, in turn, responses to particularly Peru-vian economic and political circumstances (such as the need to develop new sources of credit for the export sector, or the need to address the challenge to the social order posed by the new political forces of the Left). Such devel-opments in state formation, in both the economic and social spheres, served, at once, to strengthen elites who drew their economic and political power from the Peruvian economy's export orientation and, in turn, to further ce-ment the export orientation of the Peruvian economy. In so doing, they also served to strengthen the notion, which formed the basis of the postcolonial project of nation formation, that the sources of Peru's "progress," and indeed

Peru's dominant "national" character, were to be found not in the highlands and within the country's majority indigenous population, but rather on the coast (and its mining annexes) and within the white and mestizo minorities. Although this notion was continuously challenged throughout the twentieth century by a number of social actors, indigenous and otherwise, and by *indigenista* intellectuals, it proved resilient and in many ways continues to inform projects of nation formation in Peru today.

Notes

The authors are grateful to two anonymous readers and to Rory Miller for comments on an earlier version of this chapter.

1 Rosemary Thorp and Carlos Londoño, "The Effect of the Great Depression on the Economies of Peru and Colombia," in *Latin America in the 1930s: The Role of the Periphery in the World Crisis*, ed. Rosemary Thorp (London: Macmillan, 1984). See also Heraclio Bonilla, ed., *Las crisis económicas en la historia del Perú* (Lima: Centro Latinoamericano de Historia Económica y Social / Fundación Friedrich Ebert, 1986).

2 Carlos Diaz Alejandro, "Latin America in the 1930s," in Thorp, *Latin America in the 1930s*, 23–25.

3 Aníbal Quijano, "El Perú en la crisis de los años treinta," in *América Latina en los años treinta*, ed. Pablo González Casanova (Mexico: Universidad Nacional Autonoma de Mexico, 1977); Julio Cotler, *Clases, estado y nación en el Perú* (1978; repr., Lima: Instituto de Estudios Peruanos, 1992); Steve Stein, *Populism in Peru: The Emergence of the Masses and the Politics of Social Control* (Madison: University of Wisconsin Press, 1980).

4 In invoking the idea of state "management" of the economy and society, we are mobilizing a very large literature that deals with state formation, with two broad strands: institutionalist (which can trace its origins to Weber) and culturalist (influenced by the work on state power, or sovereignty and governmentality, of Foucault). The general argument is that in contrast to an earlier period, in which the state focused primarily on its public order functions and intervened only marginally in either the economy or society, by the 1920s the Peruvian state had begun to expand its functions and to play a more direct role in shaping both the economy and society. To be sure, the "state," in the shape of a bureaucracy or state-directed infrastructure projects, had experienced earlier phases of expansion, such as during the Castilla (1840s–1860s), Pardo (1870s), or Piérola (1890s) governments. But in the 1920s state growth was both quantitatively and qualitatively different, reflecting a new *idea* of the state as the key actor in the management of the economy and "the social." This was a transnational process, but it was inflected in particular ways in the Peruvian case, as

we show in this chapter. For discussion of this literature, see Paulo Drinot, *The Allure of Labor: Workers, Race and the Making of the Peruvian State* (Durham, NC: Duke University Press, 2011), 7–11.

5 Some parts of this chapter draw on Paulo Drinot, "O advento do social: Política, Estado e a Grande Depressão no Peru," in *A Grande Depressão: Política e economia na década de 1930- Europa, Américas e Asia*, ed. Flavio Limoncic and Francisco Palomanes Martinho (Rio de Janeiro: Civilizacao Brasileira, 2009), 143–70.

6 Rosemary Thorp and Geoffrey Bertram, *Peru 1890-1977: Growth and Policy in an Open Economy* (London: MacMillan, 1978). See also Paulo Drinot, "Peru, 1884–1930: A Beggar Sitting on a Bench of Gold?," in *An Economic History of Twentieth-Century Latin America*, vol. 1, *The Export Age: The Latin American Economies in the Late Nineteenth and Early Twentieth Centuries*, ed. Enrique Cardenas, José Antonio Ocampo, and Rosemary Thorp (Basingstoke, UK: Palgrave, 2000), 152–87.

7 Thorp and Bertram, *Peru 1890-1977*; Alfonso W. Quiroz, *Banqueros en conflicto: Estructura financiera y economía peruana, 1884-1930* (Lima: Universidad del Pacífico, 1989).

8 Thorp and Bertram, *Peru 1890-1977*. See also several chapters in Rory Miller, *Empresas británicas, economía y política en el Perú* (Lima: Banco Central de Reserva / Instituto de Estudios Peruanos, 2011).

9 Paul W. Drake, *The Money Doctor in the Andes: The Kemmerer Missions 1923-1933* (Durham, NC: Duke University Press, 1989), 216. On U.S. investment in the Leguía period and in the 1930s, see Thomas F. O'Brien, *The Revolutionary Mission: American Enterprise in Latin America, 1900-1945* (Cambridge: Cambridge University Press, 1996), 109–59. See also Baltazar Caravedo Molinari, *Clases, lucha política y gobierno en el Perú (1919-1933)* (Lima: Retama Editorial, 1977).

10 Thorp and Bertram, *Peru 1890-1977*, 115. See also Alfonso W. Quiroz, *Corrupt Circles: A History of Unbound Graft in Peru* (Baltimore: Johns Hopkins University Press, 2008), 229–44.

11 Roxanne Cheesman, "La crisis de 1929 y la reactivación," in Bonilla, *Las crisis económicas*, 267.

12 The intellectual architect of the "Patria Nueva" was the philosopher Mariano Cornejo, a member of a generation of scholars influenced by positivism and particularly by the teachings of Javier Prado at San Marcos University. The term "Patria Nueva" indicated a break with the so-called Aristocratic Republic, 1895–1919, which had been characterized by the rule of the Partido Civil. It reflected the rise of new social sectors, particularly the middle and working classes, but also a growing number of professionals, to positions of influence within society and the state and the idea that such sectors would lead Peru in a different direction. On these processes, see, among others, Manuel Burga and Alberto Flores Galindo, *Apogeo y crisis de la República Aristocrática: Oligarquía, Aprismo y comunismo en el Perú, 1895-1932* (Lima: Ediciones Rikchay Perú, 1980).

13 Drake, *Money Doctor in the Andes*, 221.

14 On peasant uprisings, see Alberto Flores Galindo, *In Search of an Inca: Identity and Utopia in the Andes* (Cambridge: Cambridge University Press, 2010), chap. 8.

15 On the military, see Víctor Villanueva, *Ejercito peruano: Del caudillaje anarquico al militarismo reformista* (Lima: Editorial Juan Mejía Baca, 1973).

16 Drake, *Money Doctor in the Andes*, 220.

17 Daniel T. Rodgers, *Atlantic Crossings: Social Politics in a Progressive Age* (Cambridge, MA: Harvard University Press, 1998).

18 The influence of social Catholicism on state formation, and particularly on the ways in which states such as the Peruvian sought to address the social question in early twentieth century, remains little understood. European social Catholic thought, which developed in light of Leo XIII's *Rerum Novarum* of 1891, was influential among a number of intellectuals in Peru, most notably Víctor Andrés Belaúnde. As in Europe and other parts of Latin America, where the social question had become the key issue of the day, Belaúnde and others argued in favor of a third way between capitalism and Marxism (although in Peru social Catholic thought focused not only on urban workers, as it did in, say, Argentina, but also on indigenous populations), which would address the excesses of capitalism while helping to prevent social revolution; in so doing they argued in favor of an expanded social role for the state. Such arguments, as we show below, are clearly discernible in the discursive justifications for the social policies implemented by the governments of the 1930s, particularly by Benavides (1933–39), although the extent to which Benavides and his advisors were directly influenced by social Catholic thought remains to be studied. On social Catholicism, see Ricardo Cubas Ramaciotti, "The Politics of Religion and the Rise of Social Catholicism in Peru (1884–1935)" (PhD diss., Cambridge University, 2011). See also Drinot, *Allure of Labor*, 22–24.

19 Paul Gootenberg, *Imagining Development: Economic Ideas in Peru's "Fictitious Prosperity" of Guano* (Berkeley: University of California Press, 1993).

20 Felipe Portocarrero Suárez and Luis Camacho, "Impulsos moralizadores: El caso del Tribunal de Sanción Nacional 1930–1931," in *El pacto infame: Estudios sobre la corrupción en el Perú*, ed. Felipe Portocarrero Suárez (Lima: Red de Ciencias Sociales, 2005), 35–73; and Quiroz, *Corrupt Circles*, 238–46.

21 Stein, *Populism in Peru*. The Ley de Conscripción Vial (1920) required all males age 18–60 to provide labor for road building in their provinces. They were required to work one week a year if they were 18–21 or 50–60 years old, and two weeks a year if they were 21–49. It was possible to be exempted from these labors if one paid the wages one would have otherwise received. In effect, this made the law a tax on urban and mestizo workers and a form of tribute for Indians. Labor shortages, which plagued much of Peru in the early twentieth century, explain why the law was introduced. In 1930, it became easy to repeal the law, since with the crisis the labor shortages disappeared. See Nelson

Pereyra Chávez, "Los campesinos y la conscripción víal," in *Estado y mercado en la historia del Perú*, ed. Carlos Contreras and Manuel Glave (Lima: Pontificia Universidad Católica del Perú, 2002), 334–50.

22 Carlos Contreras, "La crisis mundial de 1929 y la economía peruana," in *Crisis Internacional: Impactos y respuestas de política económica en el Perú*, ed. Oscar Dancourt and Felix Jimenez (Lima: PUCP, 2009), 30–35.

23 Michael Gonzales, *Plantation Agriculture and Social Control in Northern Peru, 1875–1933* (Austin: University of Texas Press, 1985), 147.

24 AGN/MI/325/Fomento, Prefectura de Piura, Censo de los campamentos, June 30, 1932.

25 Gonzales, *Plantation Agriculture and Social Control*, 148.

26 In fact, historians have shown that the idea of "white" cities is largely a myth expressive of the ways in which nonwhite urban groups have been made invisible by representations of the city. See, among others, Jesús Cosamalón Aguílar, *Indios detrás de la muralla* (Lima: Fondo Editorial PUCP, 1999).

27 The idea of agro-export or mineral-producing units, such as the sugar estates on the north coast of Peru or the mines of Cerro de Pasco, disconnected from local, regional, or even national economies was influential in the context of dependency theory–inspired approaches to the economic history of Latin America, but research undertaken by a number of scholars demonstrated that these units developed significant linkages and stimulated economic activity both locally and more broadly. See, among others, Peter Klarén, *Modernization, Dislocation and Aprismo: Origins of the Peruvian Aprista Party, 1870–1932* (Austin: University of Texas Press, 1973); Gonzales, *Plantation Agriculture and Social Control*.

28 On urban growth in Lima in this period, see Augusto Ruiz Zevallos, *La multitud, las subsistencias y el trabajo: Lima: 1890–1920* (Lima: Pontificia Universidad Católica del Perú, 2001); and Juan Carlos Callirgos, "Reinventing the City of Kings: Postcolonial Modernizations of Lima, 1845–1930" (PhD diss., University of Florida, 2005).

29 Stein, *Populism in Peru*, 65.

30 Stein, *Populism in Peru*, 70.

31 Wilma Derpich, José Luis Huiza, and Cecilia Israel, *Lima años 30, salarios y costo de vida de la clase trabajadora* (Lima: Fundación Friedrich Ebert, 1985), 14–15.

32 David S. Parker, *The Idea of the Middle Class: White-Collar Workers and Peruvian Society, 1900–1950* (University Park: Penn State University Press, 1998).

33 Noble David Cook, *Demographic Collapse: Indian Peru 1520–1620* (Cambridge: Cambridge University Press, 1981).

34 This was a process subject to regional variation. In the southern altiplano, as Nils Jacobsen has shown, the crisis of the wool export sector in the early 1920s stopped hacienda expansion with a consequent shift in the balance of power between landowners and the indigenous peasantry. By contrast, in the central and northern highlands, and on the coast to which peasants migrated to look

for work, there is evidence of a process of proletarianization accelerating in the 1930s as peasants became increasingly dependent on the mining and sugar export sectors for their livelihoods. See, among others, Nils Jacobsen, *Mirages of Transition: The Peruvian Altiplano, 1780–1930* (Berkeley: University of California Press, 1993); Florencia Mallon, *The Defense of Community in Peru's Central Highlands, 1860–1940* (Princeton, NJ: Princeton University Press, 1983); Gavin Smith, *Livelihood and Resistance: Peasants and the Politics of Land in Peru* (Berkeley: University of California Press, 1989); Gonzales, *Plantation Agriculture and Social Control*; Carmen Diana Deere, *Household and Class Relations: Peasant and Landlords in Northern Peru* (Berkeley: University of California Press, 1992); Vincent Peloso, *Peasants on Plantations: Subaltern Strategies of Labor and Resistance in the Pisco Valley, Peru* (Durham, NC: Duke University Press, 1999).

35 Contreras, "La crisis mundial," 36.

36 Peru, Ministerio de Salud Publica, Trabajo y Previsión Social, *Boletín de Trabajo y Previsión Social*, Año 1, No 1 (Lima, 1935), n.p.

37 Stein, *Populism in Peru*, 80. As Derpich, Huiza, and Israel have argued, the accounting used by the census takers was particularly poor, women were not considered, and, as the census takers admitted, many who declared themselves unemployed, such as white-collar workers employed by the state or in the private sector, had found employment in other areas, as salesmen or manual laborers. In addition, many workers considered by the census as unemployed worked in industries where work was irregular or seasonal, such as construction. Derpich, Huiza, and Israel, *Lima años 30*, 32–35.

38 Diana Davila Apolo, "Talara, los petroleros, y la huelga de 1931" (BA thesis, Pontificia Universidad Católica del Perú, 1976), 158; Humberto Nuñez Borja, *Legislación social peruana* (Arequipa: Tipografía Cuadros, 1934), 300–301. On wages, see Thorp and Londoño, "Effect of the Great Depression," 102; and Contreras, "La crisis mundial," 38.

39 PC/B4/19A, Peruvian Corporation (Lima) to Director de Obras Públicas y Vías de Comunicación, November 26, 1930.

40 As Drinot has suggested, "workers" and "Indians" were incommensurable categories in early twentieth-century Peru. Although his phenotype may not have been greatly different from that of the Indians hired to replace him, the worker viewed himself, and was viewed by his employers, as non-Indian by virtue of his status as a worker. See Drinot, *Allure of Labor*, chap. 1.

41 *La Tribuna*, December 8 and 13, 1931.

42 Charles Bergquist has examined this development in detail for four South American cases. See Charles Bergquist, *Labor in Latin America: Comparative Essays on Chile, Argentina, Venezuela and Colombia* (Stanford, CA: Stanford University Press, 1986).

43 Drinot, *Allure of Labor*.

44 On strikes in central highlands, see Alberto Flores Galindo, *Los mineros de Cerro de Pasco, 1900–1930*, in *Obras completas*, vol. 1 (Lima: SUR, 1993); Mallon,

Defense of Community. On strikes in Lima, see Alan Dawson, "Politics and the Labour Movement in Lima, 1919–1931" (PhD diss., University of Cambridge, 1981).

45 It is worth noting, however, a growing literature that emphasizes popular participation in pre-1930s politics. See, among others, Carmen McEvoy, *La utopía republicana: Ideales y realidades en la formación de la culture política peruana (1871–1919)* (Lima: Fondo PUCP, 1997); and Iñigo García-Bryce, *Crafting the Republic: Lima's Artisans and Nation Building in Peru, 1821–1879* (Albuquerque: University of New Mexico Press, 2004).

46 Stein, *Populism in Peru*.

47 Margarita Giesecke, *La Insurrección de Trujillo: Jueves 7 de Julio de 1932* (Lima: Fondo Editorial del Congreso del Perú, 2010). See also Iñigo García-Bryce, "A Revolution Remembered, a Revolution Forgotten: The 1932 Aprista Insurrection in Trujillo, Peru," *A Contracorriente* 7, no. 3 (2010): 277–322.

48 Diaz Alejandro, "Latin America in the 1930s," 23.

49 Thorp and Londoño, "Effect of the Great Depression."

50 Drake, *Money Doctor in the Andes*, 245.

51 Drake, *Money Doctor in the Andes*.

52 Thorp and Bertram, *Peru 1890–1977*, 127

53 Cheesman, "La crisis de 1929," 267.

54 Decreto Ley 7103 del 10 de abril de 1931, *Anuario de la Legislación Peruana*, tomo XXV, 1930–31.

55 On fiscal policy in the late nineteenth and early twentieth centuries, see Carlos Contreras, *La economía pública en el Perú despues del guano y del salitre: Crisis fiscal y élites económicas durante su primer siglo independiente* (Lima: Banco Central de Reserva / Instituto de Estudios Peruanos, 2012).

56 FO 371/18720, Forbes to Simon, April 25, 1935.

57 *Memoria de la Junta Departamental de Lima Pro-Desocupados, 1942, 1943 y 1944* (Lima: Tipografía Peruana, 1946), n.p.

58 *El Comercio*, April 5, 1933.

59 *Memoria al 31 de diciembre de 1934 de la Junta Departamental de Lima Pro-Desocupados* (Lima: Imprenta Torres Aguirre, 1935), xxv; *Memoria de la Junta Departamental de Lima Pro-Desocupados, 1935–1936* (Lima: Imprenta Torres Aguirre, 1937), xix; *Memoria de la Junta Departamental de Lima Pro-Desocupados, 1937–1938* (Lima: Sanmartí, 1939), xxiv; *Memoria de la Junta Departamental de Lima Pro-Desocupados, 1939, 1940, y 1941* (Lima: Empresa Gráfica T. Scheuch, 1943), 23.

60 Beyond Lima, however, the juntas operated in somewhat different ways, as David Nugent shows for Chachapoyas. See *Modernity at the Edge of Empire: State, Individual, and Nation in the Northern Peruvian Andes, 1885–1935* (Stanford, CA: Stanford University Press, 1997), 284–85.

61 Pedro Ugarteche, *Sánchez Cerro: Papeles y recuerdos de un Presidente del Perú*, vol. 4 (Lima: Editorial Universitaria, 1969), 58–59, 62–64. The impact of this

last measure is unclear and depends on whether one believes accounts that depict the schools in the camps as far superior to those in the rest of the country or those that portray the schools as little more than pigsties, as claimed by the APRA newspaper *La Tribuna* and other opposition papers.

62 FO 371/17819, The Commercial Negotiations with Peru, Summary of the United Kingdom Case, 249.

63 FO 371/18724, Forbes to Simon, March 18, 1935. The subsequent alterations to the law were largely aimed at stifling protests from foreign, non-Asian, business interests, and in July 1934, an article was introduced to exempt "specialised experts" from the provisions of the law. It is clear from the documents of the Peruvian Corporation that foreign (typically U.S. and British) firms banded together to press the government to modify the original wording of the law, which, if applied as it stood, would, they believed, have seriously undermined their interests. Japanese diplomats also brought substantial pressure to bear against the 80 percent law, and the modifications to the law were designed also to accommodate Japanese interests. See PC/B3/43, Draft of letter to be signed by "British merchants and representatives of British interests established in Peru" to British Minister in Lima, January 31, 1933; Balfour to Cecil, May 28, 1932.

64 See Antonio Zapata, "Control, tributos y supervisión bancaria: Historia económica e institucional," in *Guerra, finanzas y regiones en la historia económica del Perú*, ed. Carlos Contreras, Cristina Mazzeo, and Francisco Quiroz (Lima: Banco Central de Reserva / Instituto de Estudios Peruanos, 2010), 373–410.

65 On the Banco del Perú y Londres, see Alfonso W. Quiroz, *Banqueros en conflicto: Estructura financiera y economía peruana, 1884–1930* (Lima: Universidad del Pacífico, 1989).

66 We are grateful to Rory Miller for raising this point.

67 On APRA's proposals, see Robert J. Alexander, *Aprismo: The Ideas and Doctrine of Víctor Raúl Haya de la Torre* (Kent, OH: Kent State University Press, 1973); Stein, *Populism in Peru*; and Heraclio Bonilla and Paul W. Drake, eds., *El APRA de la ideología a la praxis* (Lima: Editorial Nuevo Mundo, 1989).

68 *El General Benavides a la Nación, Mensaje del 25 de Marzo de 1939* (Lima: Oficina de Informaciones del Perú, 1939), 4.

69 *El General Benavides*, 55.

70 *El General Benavides*, 56–57.

71 These measures are discussed in detail in Drinot, *Allure of Labor*.

72 *El General Benavides*, 57.

73 The 1933 constitution and the constituent congress that created it are the subject of Carmen Rosa Balbi and Laura Madalengoitia, *Parlamento y lucha política: Perú 1932* (Lima: DESCO, 1980).

74 "Constitución Política del Perú (29 de Marzo de 1933)," http://www.congreso.gob.pe/ntley/Imagenes/Constitu/Cons1933.pdf.

75 This point is discussed extensively in Drinot, *Allure of Labor*.

CHAPTER 5

Export Protectionism and the

Great Depression: Multinational

Corporations, Domestic Elite, and

Export Policies in Colombia

Marcelo Bucheli and Luis Felipe Sáenz

Scholars studying globalization in the twentieth century have pointed to World War I and the Great Depression as the events marking the end of a laissez-faire economics system and its gradual replacement with a state-led inward-looking protectionism.[1] In the political sphere, it has been argued that the effects of the Great Depression opened the door to nationalist populist governments that sought their countries' economic and political independence from the uncertainties of international markets and the decisions of the world powers.[2] Traditional interpretations of the Latin American case have not differed much. The long-accepted paradigm developed by researchers at the Economic Commission for Latin America (ECLA) in the 1960s stated that the Great Depression abruptly ended laissez-faire economics in the continent, opening the door to a protectionist system that permitted economic recovery through a process of state-promoted import substitution industrialization.[3] Similarly, many authors have maintained that the Great Depression galvanized existing social and political forces that led to the rise of a nationalist populism in most of the continent that manifested itself (among other things) in policies increasing domestic control of the economy and reducing the power of foreign multinational corporations.[4] Several economic historians have challenged ECLA's interpretation, arguing that Latin American governments already started developing protectionist mechanisms years before the Great Depression, in particular after the export crisis generated by World War I.[5] In fact, they maintain, the 1930s recovery and subsequent industrialization were a result of the strength and rebound of the export sector.[6]

This chapter aims to contribute to the existing debates on the effects of the Great Depression in national economies by developing the concept of "export protectionism." We define this term as the set of policies established by a government to actively intervene in the economy in order to protect its country's main export industries. Export protectionist policies can result from lobbying activities by a particular export industry or a group of them, through pressures on the government from domestic or foreign actors involved in the export industry, or as part of a political program led by a government or ruler who wants to favor a particular constituency whose jobs, welfare, or wealth depend on the fate of a particular export sector. We consider export protectionism to be a nationalist model that does not conflict with import protectionism. In fact, both policies can go hand in hand and benefit from each other. For instance, a policy designed to devalue national currency benefits both producers oriented to international markets and those orienting their activities to the domestic market.

This chapter studies the evolution of the policies toward the export sector in Colombia between 1922 and 1934. We study Colombia because, contrary to what happened in other Latin American countries, the Great Depression did not give birth there to populist governments that engaged in expropriation of foreign property.[7] During most of the twentieth century, Colombia kept a solid civilian bipartisan system that left no space for other political forces or alternative economic ideologies.[8] After the end of the Thousand Days' War (1899–1902) between the laissez-faire federalist Liberals and the protectionist centralist Conservatives, with the eventual triumph of the latter, Colombia consolidated itself as a highly centralized country with strong government economic interventionism.[9]

We find that the Colombian government maintained a continuous export protectionist policy before and after the Great Depression started. The main effect of the Great Depression was to deepen and institutionalize the existing export protectionist model. During this period, coffee, oil, and bananas constituted the majority of Colombian exports, with coffee dominating over the other two. Similar to what happened in other Latin American countries, exports played an important role in making the effects of the Great Depression in Colombia relatively brief and mild.[10] While in the 1920s exports were considered the main engine of growth, after 1929 the government considered them the main engine for recovery and oriented its policy accordingly. This explains the government's consistency at keeping the export protectionist model before and after the Great Depression started.

A consistent export protectionist policy did not mean that the government behaved the same way toward each one of the export sectors. We find that in the coffee sector the policy translated into the creation of an increasingly symbiotic relationship between the Colombian state and the coffee growers, in the oil sector it went from having a hostile attitude toward foreign capital to gradually shifting into a friendly relationship, and in the banana sector it manifested itself in a policy of constant support to foreign investors.

We argue that the different approach taken by the Colombian government toward coffee, oil, and banana exports was a response to a combination of two factors: (1) the technological entry barriers that the Colombian bourgeoisie faced in each one of these industries, and (2) the capacity of each one of these industries to develop mechanisms of collective action to defend their interests. The coffee industry had very low entry barriers that permitted the national bourgeoisie to control production. In addition, the coffee bourgeoisie developed a very efficient organization to defend their interests, the Federación Nacional de Cafeteros de Colombia (Colombian National Coffee Growers' Association, FNCC), with a leadership composed of highly influential individuals with close links to the government and other industries. Entry barriers in the banana industry were higher than in the coffee industry. Domestic planters did not have the capability to invest in plantations and transportation infrastructure, something that was solved by the U.S. corporation United Fruit Company (UFC).[11] Once these investments were made, however, UFC could rely on domestic producers as providers. During the period we study, the Colombian planters made attempts to develop mechanisms of collective action to decrease UFC's enormous power, but their relative economic and political weakness at the national level led them to fail in their efforts to influence national policy. Finally, the oil industry had the highest entry barriers of all. Before the 1960s, the only actors with the capability and means to make the investments necessary in oil exploration and production were multinational corporations.[12] In 1920s Colombia, the national bourgeoisie or the state clearly lacked these capabilities and had no choice but to invite foreign firms in, so contrary to the coffee and banana industries, domestic participation in the industry was minimal. By that decade the main oil multinational operating in Colombia was the Standard Oil Company of New Jersey (SONJ).[13] Under those circumstances the only role the local elite could aspire to in this industry was that of land speculators, skilled laborers, or lobbyists at the level of local government.[14] The main mechanism that U.S. oil corporations developed to influence policy was to utilize the support of the U.S. Department of State and use its strong influence in international financial circles. Although this

Table 5.1. General Overview of Ownership, Entry Barriers, Collective Action Mechanisms, and State Policies in the Coffee, Banana, and Oil Industries in Colombia (1910–34)

INDUSTRY	TYPE OF OWNERSHIP	ENTRY BARRIERS	COLLECTIVE ACTION MECHANISM	EXPORT PROTECTIONISM
Coffee	Domestic	Low	National association	Symbiotic relationship
Bananas	Foreign with domestic providers	Medium	Regional association	Support to foreign capital
Oil	Foreign	High	Diplomacy; financial pressure	Hostility toward foreign investors (1919–29); support to foreign capital (1930–34)

strategy bore fruits, it was a risky one because it inflamed nationalist feelings, putting in danger the oil companies' property rights. The limited presence of the domestic bourgeoisie in the sector and the strategies used by the oil firms explain why in the 1920s the government constantly attempted to decrease the oil companies' economic control of the sector. The shift by the Colombian government and bourgeoisie toward a more friendly relationship after 1930 was a result of an interest in keeping the oil sector running. The new industrial elite were also interested in cheap energy sources, regardless of who produced them.

In sum, even though the policies toward each one of the main Colombian export sectors differed, they were all consistent with a general policy of export protectionism, in which the government actively intervened to maximize output regardless of ownership. Table 5.1 shows the general points analyzed in this chapter.

Colombia's political characteristics make of this country an interesting case. Contrary to what happened in other Latin American countries, Colombia did not experience a serious rise in populism before or after the Great Depression.[15] This has been explained as a result of the solid power of the two main traditional parties (Liberal and Conservative) and their success in using clientelistic methods of holding power. During most of the twentieth century (and particularly during the period we analyze), there were no major ideological differences between Liberals and Conservatives in terms of political economy, and as a result both parties shared a consensual view in economic policy.[16]

Our study makes the following contributions to scholarship. First, by introducing the concept of "export protectionism," we hope to provide studies on political economy with a new approach to understanding economic policy. As this chapter shows, economic policy during the Great Depression went beyond the dichotomy between laissez-faire economics and import substitution protectionism. Second, to our knowledge no historian has made a systematic comparison of these three sectors in Colombia. The need for comparison has been dismissed with the argument that the simple fact that coffee was domestically owned and so much more important than the other two explains why economic policy was so focused on that sector.[17] We agree that it makes sense that the relative weight of coffee in the economy made it more important for the government, but this does not explain the different strategies followed by each sector to influence economic policy, nor does it explain why even though bananas and oil were foreign owned, the government followed two different approaches toward each of them. Moreover, even though bananas and oil exports were less important than coffee, they still represented a nonnegligible 20 percent of the total in a country that was basing its economic development on exports of primary goods. Several studies have also shown that during the period we study there was a heated political and intellectual debate around the policies to follow in each of those two sectors, and this debate played a central role in the crucial 1930 presidential elections.[18] Third, our comparison makes a contribution to the studies on mechanisms of collective action in Latin America.[19] Previous studies have analyzed the FNCC using the theoretical framework developed by Mancur Olson.[20] In fact, Olson himself pointed to the FNCC as a test case for his own theory of collective action.[21] A comparison of the coffee industry initiatives of collective action with those of the oil and banana sectors provides us with a counterpoint to understand industries without that type of organization.

Export Protectionism and External Shocks in Colombia

Economic historians argue that Colombian state economic interventionism did not start with the Great Depression, but had a long history that goes back to colonial times.[22] The post-Independence legitimization and consolidation of state economic interventionism as an accepted paradigm, however, came after the shock generated by the Thousand Days' War. In this bloody conflict, the protectionist, centralist, Catholic-oriented Conservatives defeated the free-market, federalist, secular Liberals in a war that left the country's economy and infrastructure in ruins.[23] Eager to rapidly revive the economy, the Conservative government put its efforts into promoting coffee exports and opening the door to foreign corporations to invest in other export sectors (such as oil and bananas) and transportation and communication infrastructure, while simultaneously imposing some tariffs to protect Colombia's incipient industry.[24] After the war, coffee, oil, and bananas constituted the main Colombian exports (table 5.2).

The country suffered a second shock with World War I, when the increasingly important coffee industry faced a crisis while at the same time the war-generated fall in imports led to an unexpected industrial boom in the city of Medellín. The war also increased awareness by the country's elite of the international strategic importance of the oil industry and generated concerns about the country's dependence on a single export and the underdevelopment of economic institutions.[25] During the 1920s, the government increased dramatically its investment in infrastructure and modernization of the economy by the establishment of the country's first Central Bank in 1923.[26] This was possible thanks to a bonanza of cheap credit in international markets that increased foreign lending to Colombia from $24 million in 1923 to $200 million a year in 1928, plus the U.S. compensation payment for the loss of Panama of $25 million.[27] The Central Bank followed an orthodox monetary policy and firmly adopted the gold standard.[28] The 1920s also witnessed increased labor organization and organization of the bourgeoisie by the establishment of the FNCC in 1927.

The third shock coming with the Great Depression started what has been defined as "modern government interventionism" in Colombia.[29] During the 1930s, the country adopted new intervention mechanisms that included the establishment of instruments to regulate macroeconomic variables, the creation of institutions for the promotion of manufacture industrialization, and the strengthening and modernization of the financial and public service sectors.[30] In 1931, the country abandoned the gold standard, which allowed for a more independent and less restrictive monetary policy.

The effects of the Great Depression on the Colombian economy were relatively mild and brief compared to other countries, but in the short term it was a serious matter.[31] In 1930 Colombia suffered a negative GDP growth

Table 5.2. Colombian Exports of Coffee, Oil, and Bananas in Tons, Pesos, and Percentages, 1920–45

	COFFEE			OIL			BANANAS		
YEAR	GROSS TONNAGE	VALUE (THOUSANDS OF CURRENT PESOS)	SHARE OF TOTAL EXPORTS (%)	GROSS TONNAGE	VALUE (THOUSANDS OF CURRENT PESOS)	SHARE OF TOTAL EXPORTS (%)	GROSS TONNAGE	VALUE (THOUSANDS OF CURRENT PESOS)	SHARE OF TOTAL EXPORTS
1922	105.869	36,292	68.8				162.273	3,572	6.8
1923	123.697	45,089	74.8				170.395	3,704	6.1
1924	132.950	68,793	79.8				202.488	4,459	5.2
1925	116.808	66,524	78.4				221.369	5,563	6.6
1926	147.257	85,884	76.9	643.682	9,437	8.4	238.820	5,302	4.7
1927	141.391	70,916	65.1	1,874.96	22,343	20.5	186.952	5,475	5.0
1928	159.575	88,171	66.0	2,488.173	25,809	19.3	223.684	8,636	6.5
1929	170.147	76,886	60.6	2,577.203	27,016	21.3	230.322	8,850	7.0
1930	190.381	61,654	54.4	2,656.193	26,292	23.2	226.078	8,741	7.7
1931	182.015	55,180	56.1	2,375.601	15,863	16.1	97.203	4,858	4.9
1932	191.135	42,910	61.1	2,211.339	16,329	23.3	133.552	6,007	8.6
1933	199.610	49,276	67.1	1,695.363	9,924	13.5	136.905	4,908	6.7
1934	185.053	82,459	54.1	2,350.608	28,162	18.5	144.030	6,124	4.0
1935	226.134	79,222	55.5	2,278.647	29,099	20.4	155.541	8,939	6.3
1936	236.531	91,968	58.3	2,356.390	28,269	17.9	159.684	8,207	5.2
1937	250.670	99,172	53.8	2,546.437	35,079	19.0	153.172	6,983	3.8
1938	256.417	88,775	54.4	2,650.871	37,206	22.8	195.241	8,864	5.4

Source: Armando Samper, Importancia del café en el comercio exterior de Colombia (Bogotá: FNCC, 1928).

Table 5.3. Growth Rates for Aggregate and Sectoral Economic Indicators of Colombia, 1923–36

YEAR	GROSS DOMESTIC PRODUCT (%)	PRIVATE CONSUMPTION (%)	INVESTMENT (%)	AGRICULTURE AND MINING (%)	INDUSTRY AND MANUFACTURING (%)	CONSTRUCTION (%)
1925	5.3					
1926	10.0	6.0	24.0	13.0	10.0	100.0
1927	8.2	3.8	18.5	1.8	−1.8	1.0
1928	7.6	0.0	22.4	9.6	0.9	60.9
1929	3.9	8.2	−15.6	1.6	3.7	−24.3
1930	−0.8	−8.4	−34.9	4.7	−5.3	−33.7
1931	−1.5	3.7	−18.2	−5.2	−1.9	−14.7
1932	6.2	−2.7	42.0	4.7	14.3	2.9
1933	5.8	20.0	−17.4	4.5	16.7	23.8
1934	6.2	15.9	0.0	3.6	6.4	−10.2
1935	2.6	−3.3	18.9	1.4	10.1	27.0
1936	5.0	4.1	8.0	6.2	9.1	6.9

Source: Calculation made with data from Andrés Fernández, "Essays on Business Cycles in Emerging Economies" (PhD diss., Rutgers University, 2010), 41.

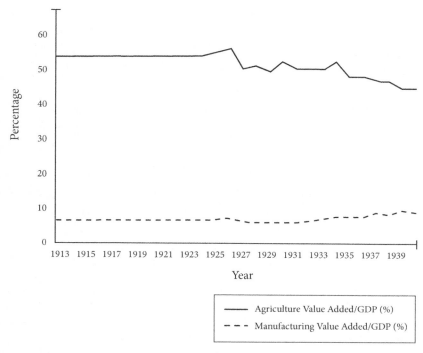

Figure 5.1. Colombia, Percentage Share of Agricultural and Manufacturing Value to GDP, 1913–40. *Source*: The Montevideo-Oxford Latin American Economic History Database (http://oxlad.qeh.ox.ac.uk, accessed November 9, 2011).

of 0.9 percent, followed by another contraction of 1.6 percent in 1931. Investment fell by half, with construction suffering the most and significant falls also in private consumption, agriculture, and industry. After 1931, however, the trend reversed, with the economy achieving a rate of growth of 6.2 percent in 1932 and good performance in the subsequent years (table 5.3). While some studies argue that the recovery was a result of expansionary policies through government spending, subsidized credit, and industrial protectionism,[32] others maintain that the recovery and the capacity for expansionary policies resulted from the good performance of exports, especially coffee.[33] In figure 5.1 we show that although after 1931 the country's economic structure changed, with industrial production becoming increasingly important in terms of its contribution to the value added of GDP, agriculture was always above 44 percent in the 1913–39 period. This shows how export protectionism of the primary sector was also consistent with a policy of industrialization.

The post-1931 expansionary policies were also possible thanks to Colombia's abandonment of the gold standard, which gave the Central Bank greater freedom to print more currency when needed and also gave the government more leeway to promote exports (and eventually import substitution) through exchange rate mechanisms and emission of currency and not simply through import tariffs.[34] As we show in the next section, these policies were related to the capability of the coffee sector to influence economic policy.

The Coffee Industry: Low Entry Barriers, Strong Collective Action

Before coffee, Colombia went through a series of booms and busts of different export commodities. Coffee was the first product that had a long-term stable growth, providing decades-long stability sought by the Colombian elite.[35] This commodity has played a prominent role in Colombian politics since the end of the nineteenth century. The Thousand Days' War began partly as a conflict around coffee exports. While the Liberals wanted this sector to be left free of any government interventionism, the Conservatives wanted to tax it and reinvest this revenue in other areas.[36] By the end of the war, coffee exports represented around half of Colombian exports, and the country's new rulers put their recovery hopes in the fate of the coffee industry.[37] According to Marco Palacios, however, the real coffee export–led growth only started in the early 1910s.[38]

LOW ENTRY BARRIERS AND SMALL-SCALE PRODUCTION

In areas where the climate and soil are suitable enough, coffee production does not require high technology or enormous initial investments. During the first two decades of the twentieth century, production was made in some areas by small farms and in others by large landholdings. Scholars studying the industry after the 1970s went against a romanticized interpretation of small farm production that promoted the idea of the small coffee grower as a representative of a prosperous rural middle class. On the contrary, authors such as Marco Palacios and Absalón Machado maintain that the fact that there were small family farms did not mean that these peasants were not exploited. In areas where rural property was divided among a large number of families, these peasants had no choice but to sell their coffee beans to a small group of urban *trilladores*, who cleaned the skin from the coffee beans, selected those to be exported, and packed them ready to sell to the export houses.[39] In areas where property was highly concentrated, the same large landowners also controlled the *trilladoras* and often exported the coffee themselves until 1923, when a financial crisis at home and problems in the international coffee market led many to bankruptcy and to be replaced by American export companies.[40]

The tight control the small number of urban commercial companies and large landowners had on the trilladoras and trade allowed them to pay the coffee growers relatively low prices. These intermediaries also benefited from the fact that most coffee growers combined coffee trees with subsistence agriculture, which allowed them to survive independent of their coffee activities. In fact, Palacios has argued that the coffee expansion of the 1920s was based on the existence of extensive and low-technology traditional crops that kept production costs very low given that most coffee growers lived at the subsistence level.[41] These characteristics permitted an accumulation of capital among large landowners and the intermediaries that allowed for the creation of the powerful coffee bourgeoisie that eventually created and led the FNCC.[42]

AN INDISSOLUBLE MARRIAGE: THE COFFEE BOURGEOISIE AND THE COLOMBIAN STATE

Most scholars agree with historian Marco Palacios's comparison of the relationship between the FNCC and the Colombian state with that of a "Catholic indissoluble marriage."[43] After 1931, these scholars argue, the FNCC had a strong say in agrarian, labor, monetary, fiscal, and foreign trade policies.[44] Even the more FNCC-sympathetic studies that highlight the fact that in some instances there were disagreements between the FNCC and the government acknowledge that this was the most influential and powerful organization in the country for decades.[45]

Government intervention in the coffee sector started before the creation of the FNCC. World War I led to a fall in the international coffee prices that provoked a crisis in the sector, allowing some U.S. firms to take over control of export activities. This generated concern among the members of the coffee bourgeoisie, who met in the First Coffee Congress (1920) to discuss solutions and to appeal for government support.[46] In 1923 and 1924, the government took its first initiatives to protect the Colombian coffee quality, its main competitive advantage in the international markets, by prohibiting the import of foreign coffee seeds.[47] In 1923 the national government also endorsed and funded the First International Meeting of Mild Coffee Producers and approved funding for tax-exempted warehouses.[48]

The type of government interventionism in the coffee sector changed after 1927, gradually going from tariff protectionism and funding of some organizational activities to a symbiotic relationship between the government and the coffee industry. The process started when a drop in the international coffee prices in 1927 created a sense of urgency, leading the government to call a new meeting with the representatives of the coffee growers and create the FNCC.[49] The goals of this new organization were to be the main organization defending the sector, oversee application of legal provisions affecting the industry, promote cost-reducing measures, improve transportation, and promote and market Colombian coffee abroad.[50] In 1928, after a series of negotiations, the FNCC agreed to accept a new export tax to finance the association, and the government committed itself not to use this tax for any other purpose.[51] The government had a presence in the association by having a delegate on its board.[52] In following decades, the FNCC also had its own delegates in the main government bodies of economic policy.

COLLECTIVE ACTION AND THE GREAT DEPRESSION
IN THE COFFEE INDUSTRY

Between 1928 and 1930, the coffee sector suffered two external shocks that accelerated the growing influence of the FNCC. The first one came from a fall in the international coffee prices resulting from exceptionally large Brazilian production, and the second and hardest one was the Great Depression.[53] These two events led the FNCC to advocate for changes in Colombia's monetary policy. Despite the fact that the coffee bourgeoisie (or *cafeteros*) were involved in exports, they did not oppose the Colombian peso overvaluation because most of their debts were in foreign currency and they had very low production costs.[54] Besides, the country's pre-1931 adherence to the gold standard made it impossible for the government to devalue anyway. When the Great Depression started and many industrialized countries abandoned the gold standard, the Colombian government made big efforts to keep the existing value of the peso through exchange controls. The critical state of the coffee sector, however, led the FNCC to make dramatic calls for a devaluation of the peso as the only way to survive the crisis.[55] In September 1931, unable to keep the value of the peso owing to continuous losses in foreign exchange and with ever-growing pressure from the FNCC, Colombia abandoned the gold standard. Shortly afterward, in March 1932, the government finally devalued the peso 10 percent, and the trend continued the

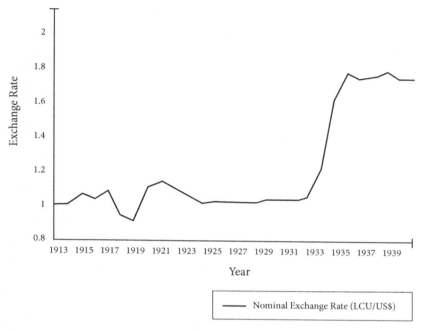

Figure 5.2. Colombia, Nominal Exchange Rate Pesos vis-à-vis U.S. Dollars, 1913–40.
Source: The Montevideo-Oxford Latin American Economic History Database (http://oxlad.qeh.ox.ac.uk, accessed November 9, 2011).

following years (figure 5.2), something the FNCC reported as highly beneficial.[56]

Besides influencing monetary policy, the FNCC also played an important role in the creation of new financial institutions. In 1931, after a campaign led by the FNCC, the Colombian government established a bank designed to provide loans to the agrarian sector (the Caja Agraria) in favorable conditions. The FNCC contributed with 4 percent of the capital for the creation of the Caja Agraria, and the coffee growers were the main beneficiaries.[57] In addition, the government subsidized 40 percent of the debt the coffee growers had with Banco Agrícola Hipotecario, a government-owned agrarian mortgage bank. As a result of these policies, the coffee sector went through the 1930s with very low levels of debt, while the Caja Agraria survived through emission of cash by the Central Bank until the 1940s.[58]

A major concern of the FNCC from the time of its creation was the control foreign corporations had over Colombian coffee exports. During the 1930s and 1940s, the FNCC in concerted action with the Colombian government successfully decreased foreign participation in exports from 47.30 percent in 1933 to 27.75 percent in 1944.[59] The government also participated actively in promoting Colombian coffee as a particular brand in consumer markets and provided funding for the creation of a fleet to transport coffee and the building of warehouses, increasing Colombian control of the coffee value chain.[60] At the same time, the FNCC invested in some areas outside of the strictly defined coffee business, such as transportation infrastructure and housing in the producing areas.[61]

Government attempts to decrease the FNCC's power in the 1930s did not succeed. During the Colombia-Peru War of 1932–33, Colombian president Enrique Olaya Herrera (Liberal) attempted to increase taxation to the coffee sector, something the FNCC successfully opposed.[62] In fact, for the rest of the twentieth century the cafeteros enjoyed minimal taxation.[63] In 1933, Olaya Herrera also attempted to increase the number of government delegates in the FNCC so that this association would have tighter government control, but he faced the federation's resistance. A new attempt for stronger government control came with President Alfonso López Pumarejo (Liberal, 1934–38), so that he could reach an agreement on coffee production with Brazil. Even before he took power, as president-elect in 1933 López Pumarejo approached the FNCC in his quest to reach an agreement with Brazil. The cafeteros opposed any agreement to control production, because they preferred to free ride the fate of the much larger Brazilian production.[64] According to most authors (those both critical of and sympathetic to FNCC), the FNCC's success at opposing López Pumarejo before and after he took power marks the consolidation of the Great Depression–induced symbiotic relationship between the government and the association that continued for the following decades.[65]

The Banana Industry: Medium Entry Barriers, Weak Collective Action

The UFC had dominated the Colombian industry since 1899 by combining production in its own plantations and subcontracting from domestic planters. Production was concentrated in a few *municipios* of Magdalena and transportation provided and coordinated by UFC's railway, telegraph, and steamship fleet. The company also had similar major investments in Central America (where it was more economically and politically important than in Colombia) and had distribution channels in the United States.[66]

The dramatic increase in U.S. banana demand after the 1880s led many Magdalena entrepreneurs to see a promising business in that sector.[67] These pioneers' dreams were shattered by a succession of failures to bring the fruit on time to the U.S. market. The domestic growers lacked a good transportation and marketing infrastructure, something crucial when trading a fruit that rots rapidly. It was only after the arrival of UFC with its steamship fleet, telecommunications infrastructure, and railway investments that the Magdalena banana export finally took off.[68] In the beginning UFC produced most of the fruit it exported, but local participation in the total of the fruit exported by the multinational rapidly climbed from 20 percent in 1910 to 80 percent by 1930.[69] In short, once the initial entry barrier represented by the need of transportation and marketing infrastructure was overcome by UFC, the local planters could have a serious participation in the international banana business.

FAILED COLLECTIVE ACTION INITIATIVES
IN THE BANANA INDUSTRY

As long as the domestic planters' participation in production increased, some of them sought to become independent of UFC's monopsonistic power by looking for other buyers. In order to avoid planters becoming independent, UFC designed a contractual mechanism that made it very hard for the locals to develop their own business. The contracts with the local planters established that the fruit belonged to UFC as soon as it was cut from the tree. However, if the fruit happened to have any defect, the ownership reverted to the planter. Moreover, even if the company approved the fruit and shipped it, but U.S. customs officials rejected the bananas in the U.S. port, again the fruit ownership reverted to the planter, who received no payment. The contract also said that the fruit the company rejected could not be sold to anyone else. In addition, if a planter decided to sell his land, he had to transfer the purchase contract he had with UFC to the new landowner.

Some local planters disliked their dependence on UFC and attempted to develop their own business. However, these attempts failed because of UFC's mechanisms to enforce the existing contracts. The company calculated the termination of all contracts at different dates, avoiding having too many planters "free" to join forces and create their own export firms. When some planters succeeded at exporting the fruit, they used the courts in the destination ports and expropriated the fruit. Finally, UFC was the main financial institution in the *municipios* where it operated and tied the loans to long-term purchase contracts.[70]

The strategies followed by UFC led some local planters to develop mechanisms of collective action to decrease the company's power. In 1927, some local planters created the Sociedad de Productores de Ciénaga y Santa Marta (SPCSM), linked to the opposition Liberal Party, to lobby at the national government to open a branch of the Banco Agrícola Hipotecario to break UFC's monopoly in financial services. The first calls to break UFC's power as the only lender in the region had started in 1924, but once the Banco Agrícola Hipotecario opened a branch in the banana zone, the members of the SPCSM were disappointed. The bank's loan requirements were even harder to fulfill than those demanded by UFC, and its interests were higher. UFC also defeated the purpose of the new bank by rewarding the planters that did not want to join the pressure group represented by the SPCSM by issuing unprecedented numbers of cheap loans. The recipients of these UFC loans created their own society (linked to the ruling Conservative Party), competing with and weakening the SPCSM.[71]

Since the arrival of UFC to the Colombian Caribbean, several local Liberal politicians had disliked the generous tax exemptions the multinational enjoyed. UFC, however, maintained strong support from the government. During the 1920s, Colombian authorities (including the Supreme Court) declared illegal every single attempt made by the local authorities to tax banana exports or UFC railway operations. The opposition to taxation came not only from the national government but also from UFC's domestic providers, who feared that the multinational would pass the extra cost of a new tax to them, weakening local efforts to decrease the company's power.[72]

THE GREAT DEPRESSION AND POLICY CONTINUITY
IN THE BANANA SECTOR

The Great Depression did not translate into nationalist populist policies in the banana sector. As shown for the case of oil, in the banana sector the Liberal government taking power in 1930 sought to assure UFC that their operations were not under threat. With the concession on the UFC-owned railway in the banana region of Magdalena ending in 1930, domestic politicians expected their region to benefit from the operations of this railway once ownership reverted to the local government. To their disappointment, President Olaya Herrera extended the concession for thirty years despite local opposition. The local government was also disappointed when Olaya Herrera decided to end UFC's tax exemption, but instead of having the new (and relatively low) tax go to the Magdalena coffers, he decided that the proceeds should go to the national government. The Magdalena departmental assembly had supported the abolition of the exemption and the creation of an export tax to finance the local banana industry because the Banco Agrícola Hipotecario had proven useless, so Olaya Herrera's decision came as a great boon for them.[73] It is worth highlighting that Olaya Herrera was adopting these measures after the infamous "banana massacre" of December 1928, in which the Colombian army repressed striking banana workers, an action that contributed to the rise of the Liberal Party left wing represented by Jorge Eliécer Gaitán.[74]

The main changes toward UFC did not come from local initiatives in the banana-producing regions, but from above. After his election in 1934, López Pumarejo supported the banana workers (an important component of his constituency) and forced UFC to agree with the workers' demands. Nevertheless, López Pumarejo did not do anything to improve the local planters' bargaining power, nor did he challenge UFC's property rights.[75]

The Oil Industry: High Entry Barriers, Diplomatic Political Strategy

Oil multinational corporations were some of the main targets of populist governments in the 1930s. Their very presence had been the source of nationalist feelings in the host countries, and their operations were considered part of an imperial scheme to exploit the oil-rich countries.[76] The Colombian case shows a different story: after facing nationalism from the Conservative government in the 1920s, the oil companies enjoyed a better environment after the Great Depression. Similar to what happened in other cases, however, U.S. diplomatic power was one of SONJ's main competitive advantages.

HIGH ENTRY BARRIERS IN THE OIL INDUSTRY

During the first two decades of the twentieth century, the extremely high costs, complex technology, and high levels of uncertainty in setting up a production oil company left Colombian entrepreneurs no other choice but to look for business in three stages of the value chain: exploration, refining, and distribution. The exploration efforts were closely linked to land speculation. Oil explorers such as novelist Jorge Isaacs investigated lands with potential for oil production in order to sign concession contracts with the government and then sell these contracts to foreign multinationals. Conducting a technical study showing the oil potential of a particular territory was not an easy task, and once the study was done, getting the concession depended more on political connections than on technical merits.[77] In 1916, one of these domestic concessionaires, Roberto De Mares, partnered with the U.S. firm Tropical Oil Company to exploit a territory he had obtained a concession for. The concession was completely transferred to Tropical in 1919, and Tropical was eventually acquired by SONJ in 1920.[78]

The entrepreneurs who tried to enter the refining sector succeeded in their early attempts. In 1905, Diego Martínez signed a contract with the Colombian government to build a plant to refine imported oil in Cartagena. The plant was built in 1909, and the firm (the Cartagena Oil Refining Company) enjoyed a monopoly until 1922, when SONJ started producing domestic oil, leading to a fall in prices that bankrupted Martínez. For several years Colombia's main refining plant was the SONJ-owned plant in the city of Barrancabermeja.[79] No Colombian firm would try or be able to compete with the multinationals in the following decades.

OIL COMPANIES, FOREIGN POLICY,
AND NEGOTIATION STRATEGIES

During the 1910s and 1920s, the U.S. oil multinationals' main bargaining power vis-à-vis the Colombian government relied on the support they received from the U.S. government. This advantage, however, was a double-edged sword. The problematic historical relations between Colombia and the United States and the fact that there was very little participation of the national bourgeoisie in the industry often turned the mentioned U.S. support into a liability that translated into hostile government actions against the foreign firms. With the Great Depression, the relationship between the oil multinationals and the government changed because both the government and the national bourgeoisie considered that a good relationship with the United States and the foreign firms was good for the economy. Those involved in the incipient industrial sector were more interested in having cheap energy sources than in alienating foreign capital.[80]

The U.S. government supported U.S. corporations in Colombia not just because of their corporate citizenship. The story of this support is closely linked to the events surrounding the separation of the province of Panama from Colombia in 1903. Right after the destructive Thousand Days' War,

Colombians suffered the demoralizing and humiliating dismemberment of their territory when the U.S. government supported a secessionist movement in the province of Panama, where an interoceanic canal was to be built. This act tainted U.S.-Colombia relations for several years and legitimized the Conservative rulers' argument for the benefits of a tightly centralized political system.[81] Making a pragmatic decision and eager to normalize relations with the United States in 1909, Colombian president Rafael Reyes signed a treaty recognizing the independence of Panama and accepting a $2.5 million payment from the U.S. government. This initiative, however, was considered treasonous by many; the Colombian Congress rejected the agreement, and Reyes was forced to resign and go into exile.[82] In 1910, the United States offered $10 million for the recognition of the independence of Panama plus privileges for Colombian ships crossing the canal, but the Colombian Congress also rejected this proposal.[83]

The affair concerning the recognition of Panama as an independent state affected the oil industry after 1913. In that year, the British firm Pearson and Son started negotiations with the Colombian government for oil exploration concessions. Just when the British investors and the Colombian government were about to reach an agreement, SONJ torpedoed the negotiations by telling the U.S. government that Pearson and Son's real goal was to build a canal to compete with the one to be built in Panama. To make things worse, the U.S. government disliked the British firm because of its alleged involvement in the Mexican Revolution. Worried about the possibility of a strong influence of Pearson and Son in Colombia, the U.S. government warned Colombia that an agreement with Pearson would harm a payment of reparations for the loss of Panama. Under these circumstances, Pearson withdrew from the negotiations, leaving the field free for U.S. investors, and the following year the U.S. and Colombia governments signed the Urrutia-Thompson Treaty, by which the United States committed to pay $25 million in exchange for the recognition of Panama. The treaty, however, still needed to be approved by the U.S. Congress.[84]

The U.S. companies used the ratification of the Urrutia-Thompson Treaty as a bargaining chip. Tropical Oil purchased the promising De Mares concession in 1916, started drilling in 1918, and made its first discovery in 1919.[85] As soon as Tropical started pumping oil, the government changed the existing legislation for a more nationalist one, by which it declared the country's subsoil property of the state.[86] The American investors considered this new law a potential threat, and the U.S. government responded by postponing the ratification of the Urrutia-Thompson Treaty until Colombia revised the legislation.[87] Eventually, in December 1919 the Colombian Supreme Court cleared the way by declaring the subsoil legislation unconstitutional.[88] The next year, SONJ acquired Tropical Oil and started lobbying the U.S. Congress for the ratification of the Urrutia-Thompson Treaty.[89] SONJ's interest in having the treaty ratified was to also have a concession over a pipeline approved by the Colombian government. SONJ succeeded in its lobbying activities, and in 1922 the U.S. Congress ratified the treaty, promising a $25 million payment.[90]

THE GREAT DEPRESSION AND THE ESTABLISHMENT OF FRIENDLY POLICIES TOWARD THE OIL SECTOR

The relations between oil multinationals and the government changed after 1926. Colombian oil exports (mostly in the hands of SONJ) jumped from 4,642,249 barrels in 1926 to 13,679,199 in 1927, bringing oil exports from 8.4 percent of total exports to 20 percent (see table 5.2).[91] Until that year, the company had reported friendly relations with the government.[92] This ended in 1926, when the minister of industry José Antonio Montalvo secretly approached Anglo-Persian to exploit the Barco concession he had previously annulled from the U.S. firm Carib Syndicate. This attempt failed when Montalvo's activities were leaked to the press, leading Anglo-Persian to withdraw in order to avoid confrontation with the Americans.[93] After this event, however, members of the Colombian elite, including Conservative leader Laureano Gómez, proposed new legislation that would nationalize the oil industry, an idea supported by members of both the Liberal and Conservative Parties who felt that the industry was too dominated by foreign firms and who did not just want to replace the Americans with the British.[94] In this environment, Montalvo proposed to Congress an increase in royalties and taxes paid by SONJ and a new "Oil Emergency" law, which would give the government unlimited powers over the oil industry until a new, more detailed legislation was written.[95] In addition, Montalvo showed Congress and the press documents proving legal irregularities in SONJ's Barco concession, which provided grounds for its annulment. SONJ challenged the legality of Montalvo's law and his arguments on the Barco concession supported again by the U.S. government, which encouraged investors not to buy Colombian bonds. Facing this challenge, in 1929 Montalvo sought an alliance with the Colombian elite, but this effort proved disappointing. Despite the sympathy they had previously shown to the idea of a nationalist policy, they responded to Montalvo that they did not want to antagonize and alienate the foreign firms or the U.S. government.[96]

Montalvo's nationalist initiatives by no means coincide with what populist governments did then and in the following decades in other Latin American countries. In 1927, when the oil labor unions went on strike against SONJ in the midst of his own nationalist campaign, he personally contacted SONJ, imploring them not to give in to the workers' demands, declared the strike illegal, and openly supported military repression.[97] In fact, the strike in the end barely affected the firm's operations.[98] Contrary to what other populist leaders did, Montalvo rejected the offers made by the left wing of the Liberal Party to support his cause.[99] Therefore, even in the times when the government developed its most aggressive nationalist initiative toward oil multinationals, Colombia was not following the populist path seen elsewhere in those years.[100]

The global economic crisis also increased SONJ's bargaining power. The price of Colombian bonds fell dramatically after the country decided to default on its foreign debt in 1930.[101] At that point, SONJ took advantage of the situation and bought a significant percentage of those bonds at very low prices, something that gave the firm strong leverage to pressure the government to write a friendly legislation.[102]

The Colombian elite reinforced the view they had about the type of policy needed toward oil multinationals with the start of the Great Depression. In 1930, when the opposition Liberal Party won the elections, the government of President Olaya Herrera immediately sought to convince U.S. oil companies that they were safe in Colombia by proposing changes in the oil legislation.[103] In addition, several New York banks had advised Olaya Herrera that without changes in the oil legislation the possibility of future loans was at risk.[104] The new law eliminated the requirements of a 25 percent domestic workforce in the oil industry, the obligation to fully comply with Colombian legislation without diplomatic arbitration, and the possibility to terminate operations before the concession deadline. It also decreased royalties from 12.5–6 percent to 11.2–2 percent, decreased taxation on private property from 8–4 percent to 8–1 percent, and decreased taxes on pipeline operations by 50 percent.[105] In addition, Olaya Herrera annulled Montalvo's previous annulment of the Barco concession, allowing the South American Gulf Company to operate it.[106] Shifting from previous flirtations with the idea of a nationalization of the oil industry, the domestic elite, in particular the increasingly important industrial bourgeoisie from Medellín, celebrated this new legislation.[107]

Conclusion

This chapter advances the concept of "export protectionism" to understand the type of policies followed by the Colombian government toward the export sector and foreign investors during the 1922–34 period. We find a continuum of this model before and after the beginning of the Great Depression, with the export protectionist model being furthered by the government with the crisis. This means that the coming of the Great Depression did not translate into the adoption of a protectionist economic model, but it provided the government with the arguments to reinforce the already-existing model of government interventionism in the economy aimed to protect the export sector. As happened in other Latin American countries, the export sector was crucial for Colombia's post–Great Depression economic recovery, and the government policies aimed to maximize the export sector performance. The approaches the government followed in dealing with the three main Colombian export industries (coffee, oil, and bananas), however, were not the same. Government policy was determined by the degree of participation of the national bourgeoisie in a particular sector, which was also determined by the technological entry barriers existing in each one of these three industries. Whereas in the low entry barrier coffee sector the domestic bourgeoisie managed to control production, the banana planters depended on the foreign investors' transportation infrastructure, and in the oil industry the domestic bourgeoisie achieved little presence beyond land speculation. The type of presence of the national bourgeoisie also affected the way in which each one of these industries defended their interests. The coffee sector managed to create a symbiotic relationship with the Colombian state and became a parallel economic policy agency. The banana sector did not have the national bourgeoisie participating in it, but rather a regional and weak one that had little success in influencing economic policy. Moreover, these politically weak banana planters who provided fruit to the foreign multinational wanted the relatively contradictory goal of having the government control the foreign firm's perceived abuses, while at the same time advocating for limited control of the industry itself. The government gave little help to the domestic planters and gave complete support to foreign investors both before and after 1929. Finally, the lack of presence of the national bourgeoisie in the oil industry led the oil firms to try to influence economic policy through diplomatic pressure. Given the lack of presence of the Colombian elite, the pre-1929 Conservative government aggressively sought to increase domestic benefits of the oil industry through higher taxes, royalties, and laws permitting expropriation—similar to what populist governments in other Latin American countries did, but without seeking an alliance with the working class.

The main effect of the Great Depression was to create a consistent policy toward the three export sectors. The government developed policies to protect the interests of the FNCC and the oil and banana multinationals. Even though the national elite were still not participating in oil exploitation, the nascent industrial bourgeoisie wanted cheap energy sources and respect for the oil multinationals' property rights. In short, even though the Colombian government changed hands in 1930 to a working-class-supported Liberal Party that had been in opposition for decades, the Great Depression showed a consolidation of the export protectionist system instituted before the crisis.

Notes

The authors thank Rory Miller, Tetsuji Okazaki, Walter Friedman, Sergio Castellanos, the participants of the European Business History Conference (Paris, 2012), and two anonymous referees for feedback on previous versions of this essay. We are also thankful for the research assistantship of Ishva Minefee.

1 Ronald Findlay and Kevin O' Rourke, "Commodity Market Integration, 1500–2000," in *Globalization in Historical Perspective*, ed. Michael Bordo, Alan Taylor, and Jeffrey Williamson (Chicago: University of Chicago Press, 2003), 43–49; Geoffrey Jones, *Multinationals and Global Capitalism* (Oxford: Oxford University Press, 2005), 16–42.

2 Dietmar Rothermund, *The Global Impact of the Great Depression, 1929–1939* (New York: Routledge, 2003).

3 Luis Bértola and Jeffrey Williamson, "Globalization in Latin America before 1940," in *The Cambridge Economic History of Latin America*, vol. 2, ed. Victor Bulmer-Thomas, John Coatsworth, and Roberto Cortés Conde (Cambridge: Cambridge University Press, 2006), 47.

4 Robert Kaufman and Barbara Stallings, "The Political Economy of Latin American Populism," in *The Macroeconomics of Populism in Latin America*, ed, Rudiger Dornbusch and Sebastián Edwards (Chicago: University of Chicago Press, 1991), 15; Jolle Demmers, Alex Fernández, and Barbara Hogenboom, *Miraculous Metamorphoses: The Neo-Liberalisation of Latin American Populism*

(New York: Palgrave, 2001), 4; Michael Monteón, *Latin America and the Origins of Its Twenty-First Century* (Santa Barbara, CA: ABC-CLIO, 2010), 90–93; Robert Levine, *Father of the Poor? Vargas and His Era* (Cambridge: Cambridge University Press, 1998), 8; Thomas O'Brien, *The Century of US Capitalism in Latin America* (Albuquerque: University of New Mexico Press, 1999), 73–99.

5 Michael Clemens and Jeffrey Williamson, "Why Were Latin America's Tariffs So Much Higher than Asia's before 1950?," *Revista de Historia Económica* 30, no. 1 (2012): 11–44; John Coatsworth and Jeffrey Williamson, "Always Protectionist? Latin American Tariffs from Independence to Great Depression," *Journal of Latin American Studies* 36, no. 2: 205–32; Eliana Cardoso and Ann Helwege, *Latin America's Economy: Diversity, Trends, and Conflicts* (Cambridge, MA: MIT Press, 1995), 47–48; Enrique Cárdenas, José Antonio Ocampo, and Rosemary Thorp, "Introduction," in *An Economic History of Twentieth-Century Latin America*, vol. 1, ed. Enrique Cárdenas, José Antonio Ocampo, and Rosemary Thorp (New York: Palgrave, 2000), 5–10; Stephen Haber, "The Political Economy of Industrialization," in Bulmer-Thomas, Coatsworth, and Cortés Conde, *Cambridge Economic History*, 537–84.

6 Victor Bulmer-Thomas, *The Economic History of Latin America since Independence* (Cambridge: Cambridge University Press, 1994), 213–16; Cárdenas, Ocampo, and Thorp, "Introduction," 25.

7 A populist movement was created within the Liberal Party under the leadership of Jorge Eliécer Gaitán in the 1930s. Gaitán, however, was never elected and was assassinated in 1948 at the peak of his political career.

8 Colombia was briefly ruled by a military dictator between 1953 and 1957. By twentieth-century Latin American standards this is an anomaly. By no means does this imply that twentieth-century Colombian politics were stable. Liberals and Conservatives fought an undeclared civil war from 1948 to 1957, when they agreed on a shared power system (the Frente Nacional) that lasted for sixteen years (1958–74). For the following decades, most political instability came from rebel left-wing groups, the illegal drug mafia, and right-wing paramilitary.

9 For a good overview of these conflicts during the nineteenth century, see Marco Palacios, *Entre la legitimidad y la violencia: Colombia, 1875–1994* (Bogotá: Norma, 2003).

10 José Antonio Ocampo, "The Colombian Economy in the 1930s," in *Latin America in the 1930s: The Role of the Periphery in World Crisis*, ed. Rosemary Thorp (London: Macmillan, 1984), 120; José Antonio Ocampo, "Crisis mundial y cambio structural (1929–1945)," in *Historia económica de Colombia*, ed. José Antonio Ocampo (Bogotá: Siglo XXI), 219.

11 At the present time, United Fruit Company is known under the name of Chiquita Brands. Their most popular good sold in the United States and Europe are the Chiquita bananas.

12 Edith Penrose, *The Large International Firm in Developing Countries: The International Petroleum Industry* (Cambridge, MA: MIT Press, 1968), 53–87.

13 After several changes in structure and ownership, at the time of writing the Standard Oil Company of New Jersey is known as ExxonMobil.

14 This was clear in the Venezuelan case. See Miguel Tinker Salas, *The Enduring Legacy: Oil, Culture, and Society in Venezuela* (Durham, NC: Duke University Press, 2009).

15 We follow the definition of populism as a set of economic policies designed to achieve particular political goals that include (a) mobilizing support within the working and lower classes, (b) obtaining support from domestic-oriented business, (c) politically isolating foreign multinationals and landed oligarchy, and (d) increasing nominal wages. See Kaufman and Stallings, "Political Economy," 15–16.

16 Miguel Urrutia, "On the Absence of Economic Populism in Colombia," in Dornbusch and Edwards, *Macroeconomics of Populism*, 369–91.

17 Palacios, *Entre la legitimidad*, 134.

18 For detailed accounts of the political debates in the oil sector, see Jorge Villegas, *Petróleo, oligarquía e imperio* (Bogotá: Ancora, 1968); René de la Pedraja Tomán, *Historia de la energía en Colombia, 1537–1930* (Bogotá: Ancora, 1985); René de la Pedraja Tomán, *Petróleo, electricidad, carbón y política en Colombia* (Bogotá: Ancora, 1993); Marcelo Bucheli, "Negotiating under the Monroe Doctrine: Weetman Pearson and the Origins of US Control of Colombian Oil," *Business History Review* 83, no. 3 (autumn 2008): 529–53. For the political debates on the banana industry, see Catherine LeGrand, "El conflicto de las bananeras," in *Nueva Historia de Colombia*, vol. 3, ed. Alvaro Tirado Mejía (Bogotá: Planeta, 1989); Marcelo Bucheli, *Bananas and Business: The United Fruit Company in Colombia, 1899–2000* (New York: New York University Press, 2005), 92–95; Judith White, "The United Fruit Company in the Santa Marta Banana Zone: Conflicts of the '20s" (MS thesis, Oxford University, 1971); Richard Sharpless, *Gaitán of Colombia: A Political Biography* (Pittsburgh: University of Pittsburgh Press, 1978), 59.

19 For an application of the theory of collective action for Latin America, see Ben Ross Schneider, *Business Politics and the State in Twentieth-Century Latin America* (Cambridge: Cambridge University Press, 2004).

20 Rosemary Thorp, "Has the Coffee Federation Become Redundant? Collective Action and the Market in Colombian Development," in *Group Behaviour and Development: Is the Market Destroying Cooperation?*, ed. Judith Heyer, Frances Stewart, and Rosemary Thorp (Oxford: Oxford University Press, 2002), 145–60; Schneider, *Business Politics*, 131–39. Mancur Olson's argument is developed in *The Logic of Collective Action* (Cambridge, MA: Harvard University Press, 1965).

21 Mancur Olson, "The Exploitation of Agriculture," in *Coffee, Institutions, and*

Economic Development, ed. Diego Pizano and José Chalarca (Bogotá: FNCC, 1997), 25–34.

22 Some historians find a continuum in terms of government interventionism in the economy from colonial times to the twentieth century. See Palacios, *Entre la legitimidad*, 133; José Antonio Ocampo, "Crisis mundial," 217.

23 Charles Bergquist, *Coffee and Conflict in Colombia, 1886–1910* (Durham, NC: Duke University Press, 1978); Jesús Antonio Bejarano, "El despegue cafetero (1900–1928)," in Ocampo, *Historia económica*, 137, 176; Palacios, *Entre la legitimidad*, 65–69.

24 Salomón Kalmanovitz, *Economía y nación* (Bogotá: Siglo XXI, 1985), 251–54; Bejarano, "Despegue cafetero," 186–90.

25 Bejarano, "Despegue cafetero," 186–90; Kalmanovitz, *Economía y nación*, 258–59; Bucheli, "Negotiating under the Monroe Doctrine."

26 Robert Bates, *Open-Economy Politics: The Political Economy of the World Coffee Trade* (Princeton, NJ: Princeton University Press, 1997), 57–58; Roberto Junguito and Hernán Rincón, "La política fiscal en el siglo XX en Colombia," in *Economía colombiana del siglo XX*, ed. James Robinson and Miguel Urrutia (Bogotá: Fondo de Cultura Económica, 2007), 246–48; Alfonso Patiño Roselli, *La prosperidad a debe y la gran crisis, 1925–1935* (Bogotá: Banco de la República, 1981); Bejarano, "Despegue cafetero," 195–200. For a detailed account of the foreign mission led by Edwin Kemmerer that led to the creation of modern economic institutions in Colombia, see Paul Drake, *The Money Doctor in the Andes: US Advisors, Investors, and Economic Reform in Latin America from World War I to the Great Depression* (Durham, NC: Duke University Press, 1989).

27 Bates, *Open-Economy Politics*, 57–58.

28 Kalmanovitz, *Economía y nación*, 275–82.

29 Ocampo, "Crisis mundial," 217.

30 José Antonio Ocampo et al., "La consolidación del capitalismo moderno (1945–1986)," in Ocampo, *Historia económica*, 243–48; Ocampo, "Crisis mundial," 218–20.

31 While from 1929 to 1931 the Colombian real GDP fell 2.4 percent, in the case of Argentina, Chile, and Mexico it fell 14, 27, and 16 percent, respectively; see Fabio Sánchez, "Aspectos monetarios de la gran depresión en Colombia: Política y evidencia empírica 1928–1936," *Cuadernos de Economía* 10, no. 14 (1990): 195–232.

32 Miguel Urrutia, "Cincuenta años de desarrollo económico," in *Ensayos sobre historia económica*, ed. Miguel Urrutia (Bogotá: Fedesarrollo, 1980), 181–94; Ocampo, "Crisis mundial," 220–22.

33 Andrés Fernández, "Essays on Business Cycles in Emerging Economies" (PhD diss., Rutgers University, 2010); Ocampo, "Colombian Economy," 117–43.

34 Fabio Sánchez, Andrés Fernández, and Armando Armenta, "Historia monetaria de Colombia en el siglo XX: Grandes tendencias y episodios relevantes," in Robinson and Urrutia, *Economía colombiana*, 335–40.

35 For the pre–coffee era booms and busts, see Jorge Orlando Melo, "Las vicisitudes del modelo liberal (1850–1899)," in Ocampo, *Historia económica*, 119–72; Kalmanovitz, *Economía y nación*, 174–77.

36 Bergquist, *Coffee and Conflict*.

37 José Antonio Ocampo and María Mercedes Botero, "Coffee and the Origins of Modern Economic Development in Colombia," Cárdenas, Ocampo, and Thorp, *Economic History*, 181.

38 Palacios, *Entre la legitimidad*, 82–83.

39 Absalón Machado, *El café: De la aparcería al capitalismo* (Bogotá: Punta de Lanza, 1977), 82–83.

40 Machado, *El café*, 222–26.

41 Marco Palacios, *El café en Colombia: Una historia económica, social y política* (Bogotá: Planeta, 2002), 408.

42 Machado, *El café*, 227.

43 Palacios, *El café en Colombia*, 413.

44 Mariano Arango, *El café en Colombia, 1930–1958: Producción, circulación y política* (Bogotá: Carlos Valencia Editores, 1982); Mariano Arango, *Política económica e intereses cafeteros* (Medellín: Universidad de Antioquia, 1979); Machado, *El café*; Bates, *Open-Economy Politics*.

45 Roberto Junguito and Diego Pizano, *Instituciones e instrumentos de la política cafetera en Colombia* (Bogotá: Fondo Cultural Cafetero, 1997), 28–32.

46 Silverio Pérez Gómez, ed., *Los propósitos de la industria cafetera colombiana, 1850–1986* (Bogotá: Federación Nacional de Cafeteros de Colombia, 1987), 124–25. As Pérez Gómez shows in the primary documents he reproduces, besides the Coffee Congress, during the 1920s the *cafeteros* repeatedly requested government support (132).

47 Pérez Gómez, *Los propósitos*, 147–50, 172–73.

48 Pérez Gómez, *Los propósitos*, 155–56, 160. The term "mild coffee" is used for most coffee beans grown outside Brazil (whose coffee bean is known as "robusta"). See Vernon D. Wickizer, *Coffee, Tea, and Cocoa: An Economic and Political Analysis* (Stanford, CA: Food Research Institute of Stanford University, 1951), 45.

49 Bates, *Open-Economy Politics*, 60; Schneider, *Business Politics*, 131–32; Thorp, "Coffee Federation," 147–48.

50 Thorp, "Coffee Federation," 148.

51 Junguito and Pizano, *Instituciones e instrumentos*, 6–8.

52 Junguito and Pizano, *Instituciones e instrumentos*, 28–30.

53 Palacios, *El café en Colombia*, 417–18.

54 Palacios, *El café en Colombia*, 402–3.

55 Bates, *Open-Economy Politics*, 64.

56 Arango, *Política económica*, 60–63; Bates, *Open-Economy Politics*, 64.

57 Fidel Cuéllar, *El crédito cafetero en Colombia* (Bogotá: Universidad Nacional and Universidad de los Andes, 2004), 46–48.

58 Cuéllar, *El crédito cafetero*, 50–57.

59 Palacios, *El café en Colombia*, 438.

60 Palacios, *El café en Colombia*, 426–45; Junguito and Pizano, *Instituciones e instrumentos*, 1–33.

61 Junguito and Pizano, *Instituciones e instrumentos*, 42–67.

62 Silverio Pérez Gómez, *Los jefes de estado ante al industria cafetera* (Bogotá: FNCC, 1994), 3–4; Arango, *Política económica*, 65.

63 Palacios, *El café en Colombia*, 440.

64 Bates, *Open-Economy Politics*, 70; Palacios, *El café en Colombia*, 426–30.

65 Junguito and Pizano, *Instituciones e instrumentos*, 69; Palacios, *El café en Colombia*, 430–45; Arango, *El café en Colombia, 1930–1958*, 237–68; Arango, *Política económica*, 60–73.

66 For analyses on UFC's continental operations, see Marcelo Bucheli, "Multinational Corporations, Totalitarian Regimes, and Economic Nationalism: United Fruit Company in Central America, 1899–1975," *Business History* 50, no. 4 (2008): 433–54; Marcelo Bucheli, "United Fruit Company in Latin America," in *Banana Wars: Power, Production, and History in the Americas*, ed. Steve Striffler and Mark Moberg (Durham, NC: Duke University Press, 2003), 80–101.

67 Marcelo Bucheli and Ian Read, "Banana Boats and Baby Food: The Banana in US History," in *From Silver to Cocaine*, ed. Steven Topik, Carlos Marichal, and Zephyr Frank (Durham, NC: Duke University Press, 2006), 204–27; John Soluri, *Banana Cultures* (Austin: University of Texas Press, 2005).

68 Bucheli, *Bananas and Business*, 150–51.

69 Eduardo Posada-Carbó, *The Colombian Caribbean: A Regional History, 1850–1970* (Oxford: Oxford University Press, 1996), 53–54.

70 Marcelo Bucheli, "Enforcing Business Contracts in South America: The United Fruit Company and the Colombian Banana Planters in the Twentieth Century," *Business History Review* 78, no. 2 (summer 2004): 181–212.

71 Bucheli, *Bananas and Business*, 93, 156–57.

72 Bucheli, *Bananas and Business*, 91–92.

73 Bucheli, *Bananas and Business*, 96–98.

74 LeGrand, "El conflicto de las bananeras"; Gabriel Fonnegra, *Bananeras: Un testimonio vivo* (Bogotá: Círculo de Lectores, 1986); White, "United Fruit Company."

75 Bucheli, *Bananas and Business*, 98–100. The Colombian government eventually supported the Colombian banana planters in the 1960s, when technology decreased the industry's entry barriers and the growers benefited from better collective action mechanisms by belonging to the Antioquia industrial sector; see Bucheli, "Enforcing Business Contracts." We find the opposite type of policies toward these multinationals during the Great Depression, when the Standard Fruit and Steamship Company (the world's second-largest banana multinational after UFC) was forced to give major concessions at the regional level

in Mexico, when it confronted the ruthless but charismatic Tomás Garrido Canabal, governor of Tabasco. See Stan Ridgeway, "Monoculture, Monopoly, and the Mexican Revolution: Tomás Garrido Canabal and the Standard Fruit Company in Tabasco (1920–1935)," *Mexican Studies/Estudios Mexicanos* 17, no. 1 (2001): 143–69. In Central America, a general concerted intergovernmental effort to constrain the banana multinationals' operations took place in the 1970s; see Marcelo Bucheli and Min-Young Kim, "Political Institutional Change, Obsolescing Legitimacy, and Multinational Corporations: The Case of the Central American Banana Industry," *Management International Review* 52, no. 6 (2012): 847–77; Bucheli, "Multinational Corporations."

76 For an analysis of SONJ's role in creating economic nationalism in Latin America, see Jonathan Brown, "Jersey Standard and the Politics of Latin American Oil Production, 1911–1930," in *Latin American Oil Companies and the Politics of Energy*, ed. John Wirth (Lincoln: University of Nebraska Press, 1985), 1–50.

77 Xavier Durán, "El petróleo en Colombia, 1900–1950: Especuladores y empresas multinacionales," in *Ecopetrol: Energía limpia para el futuro*, ed. Juan Benavides (Bogotá: Villegas, 2011), 31–36.

78 Durán, "El petróleo en Colombia," 46.

79 María Teresa Ripoll, *La actividad comercial de Diego Martínez Camargo, 1890–1937* (Cartagena: Banco de la República, 1999); Durán, "El petróleo en Colombia," 26–30.

80 This is particularly clear after the creation of ANDI, Colombia's main industrial association. See Eduardo Sáenz Rovner, *Colombia años cincuenta: Industriales, política y democracia* (Bogotá: Universidad Nacional, 2002), 55–56.

81 Kalmanovitz, *Economía y nación*, 250–51.

82 Alfonso López Michelsen, "La cuestión del canal desde la secesión de Panamá hasta el Tratado de Montería," in Tirado Mejía, *Nueva Historia de Colombia*, 154–59; Stephen Randall, *Colombia and the United States: Hegemony and Interdependence* (Athens: University of Georgia Press, 1992), 90.

83 Durán, "El petróleo en Colombia," 39.

84 Peter Calvert, "The Murray Contract: An Episode in International Finance and Diplomacy," *Pacific Historical Review* 35 (1966): 203–24; Richard Lael, *Arrogant Diplomacy: US Policy toward Colombia, 1903–1922* (Wilmington, DE: Scholarly Resources, 1987), 88; Bucheli, "Negotiating under the Monroe Doctrine."

85 George Gibb and Evelyn Knowlton, *The Resurgent Years: History of Standard Oil Company (New Jersey), 1911–1927* (New York: Harper and Brothers, 1956), 39–370.

86 López Michelsen, "La cuestión," 164.

87 Mira Wilkins, "Multinational Oil Companies in South America in the 1920s: Argentina, Bolivia, Brazil, Chile, Colombia, Ecuador, and Peru," *Business History Review* 48, no. 3 (1974): 430; Mira Wilkins, *The Maturing of Multinational*

Enterprise: American Business Abroad from 1914 to 1970 (Cambridge, MA: Harvard University Press, 1974), 27; López Michelsen, "La cuestión," 164.

88 Germán Colmenares, "Ospina y Abadía: La política en el decenio de los veinte," in Tirado Mejía, *Nueva Historia de Colombia*, 243–51.

89 After acquiring Tropical, Standard rapidly accelerated its new subsidiary activities in Colombia. See "Standard Oil Co. Has Acquired Tropical Oil," *Wall Street Journal*, January 20, 1920, 10; "Large South American Oil Merger Completed," *Wall Street Journal*, August 23, 1920, 2; "Develop South American Oil," *Wall Street Journal*, October 21, 1920, 3; "Standard Oil to Drill Twenty Wells in Colombia," *Wall Street Journal*, November 30, 1920, 9; "International Petroleum Progresses in Colombia," *Wall Street Journal*, February 2, 1921, 3.

90 Durán, "El petróleo in Colombia," 41–42.

91 Colombia, Ministerio de Minas y Petróleos, *Memoria 1944* (Bogotá: Imprenta Nacional, 1944), 44–88.

92 Marcelo Bucheli, "Canadian Multinational Corporations and Economic Nationalism: The Case of Imperial Oil Limited in Alberta (Canada) and Colombia, 1899–1938," *Entreprises et Histoire* 54 (April 2009): 80–81.

93 Fred Rippy, *The Capitalists and Colombia* (New York: Vanguard, 1931), 135; George Philip, *Oil and Politics in Latin America* (Cambridge: Cambridge University Press, 1982), 35; de la Pedraja Tomán, *Petróleo*, 23–25.

94 James Henderson, *Modernization in Colombia: The Laureano Gómez Years* (Gainsville: University Press of Florida, 2001), 147–48; Villegas, *Petróleo, oligarquía e imperio*, 129–32.

95 Villegas, *Petróleo, oligarquía e imperio*, 123–25.

96 De la Pedraja Tomán, *Petróleo*, 28–33.

97 Colombia, Ministerio de Industrias, *Memoria Presentada al Congreso de 1927* (Bogotá: Imprenta Nacional, 1927), 48–54; Efraín Estrada, *Sucesos Colombianos 1925–1950* (Medellín: Universidad de Antioquia), 173.

98 Bucheli, "Canadian Multinational Corporations," 83.

99 Estrada, *Sucesos Colombianos 1925–1950*, 229, 243.

100 For a comparison of the Colombian policies with the more business-hostile ones in Mexico and the business-friendly ones in Venezuela, see Marcelo Bucheli and Ruth Aguilera, "Political Survival, Energy Policies, and Multinational Corporations: A Historical Study for Standard Oil of New Jersey in Colombia, Mexico, and Venezuela in the Twentieth Century," *Management International Review* 50, no. 3 (2010): 347–78.

101 Drake, *Money Doctor in the Andes*, 33–34.

102 De la Pedraja Tomán, *Petróleo*, 54; "Teagle Denies Conflict of Interests of SO, Colombian Bond Group," *Wall Street Journal*, March 4, 1937, 12.

103 Olaya's election was seen as positive in Washington. See Wilkins, *Maturing of Multinational Enterprise*, 223; "Colombian Good Sense," *Wall Street Journal*, February 20, 1930, 1.

104 De la Pedraja, *Petróleo*, 40–46.

105 Jorge Villegas, *Petróleo Colombiano Ganancia Gringa* (Bogotá: Tigre de Papel, 1971), 68.

106 Estrada, *Sucesos Colombianos 1925–1950*, 348–59; "Criticizes Colombia for Its Policy on Oil: Olaya Says Firm Line Is Needed to End Impression of Hostility to Foreign Capital," *New York Times*, January 31, 1930, 9; "Bogotá Clears Way for Big Oil Trade: New Legislation and Contract for Barco Concession Are Signed in Colombia," and "Old Dispute Is Settled: American Company Wins," *New York Times*, March 5, 1931, 10; "Colombia Hails Oil Deal," *New York Times*, March 6, 1931, 11; "Colombia Takes Up Barco Contract," *Wall Street Journal*, April 7, 1931, 3; "Terms of Gulf's Barco Oil Pact," *Wall Street Journal*, June 24, 1931, 13. The British company Lobitos Oilfields Co. also acquired some concession lands in the Santander region, but it later transferred them to Tropical. See Colombia, Ministerio de Industrias, *Memoria*, vol. 1 (Bogota: Imprenta Nacional, 1933), 103.

107 Palacios, *Entre la legitimidad*, 183.

CHAPTER 6

Political Transition in

an Age of Extremes:

Venezuela in the 1930s

Doug Yarrington

The strictly economic effects of the Great Depression in Venezuela were less severe than in most of the Americas. While the world slump accelerated the decline of the nation's agricultural export sector, the relatively quick recovery of the global oil market salvaged Venezuela's economy and state finances. One result was that while governments fell in one Latin American nation after another in the early 1930s, Venezuela remained under the rule of Juan Vicente Gómez (1908–35). Denounced by critics for his repression, corruption, and alleged subservience to foreign interests, Gómez had nonetheless ended a century of civil war and laid the foundation for a modern state well before the onset of the global crisis. His effective management of the state apparatus, along with the good fortune of huge petroleum reserves, allowed him to survive the downturn of the early 1930s and rule until his death.

But while it avoided a full-blown economic crisis, Venezuela could not remain untouched by the global processes that the Depression unleashed. In particular, the ideological polarization that was intensified in much of the world reverberated powerfully there once Gómez's death opened the nation to comparatively free political debate. During the crucial period of the post-Gómez transition, from late 1935 to early 1937, Venezuela emerged from a quarter century of censorship and repression into the storm of opposing ideologies that was already raging across much of the globe. It thus fell to Gómez's successor, General Eleazar López Contreras, a man of conservative instincts in the mold of a nineteenth-century liberal, to attempt to lead Venezuela toward democracy during the years that epitomized the twentieth century as an "age of extremes."[1]

As historian Steve Ellner has explained, interpretations of this transition tend to fall into two categories. One group of scholars, following the argument of Rómulo Betancourt's widely influential *Venezuela, política y petroleo* (1956), presents López's government as a continuation of the Gómez system because of its alliance with conservative economic interests and its restrictions on opposition groups. Revisionists, by contrast, emphasize López's success in eliminating the worst abuses of the Gómez dictatorship and his adherence to constitutional norms, arguing that he initiated Venezuela's transition to democracy. Writing in the mid-1990s, Ellner noted that each interpretation contains a political subtext. Those who follow the analysis of Betancourt, himself a prominent leader of the Left in the 1930s, implicitly criticize López for delaying the "true" democratization of later decades. Conversely, those who praise López often convey disillusionment with the "pacted" democracy initiated in 1958 by the Pact of Punto Fijo, the system that was crumbling as Ellner wrote.[2]

This chapter seeks to place Venezuela's transition of the mid-1930s more squarely in the context of its own era while not ignoring the longer perspective afforded by recent developments.[3] An analysis of how Venezuelans in the 1930s understood and debated this era of change requires, first of all, an understanding of how they experienced the governing practices of the Gómez regime. I argue that for many who lived through the Gómez dictatorship it was defined primarily by corruption and political terror. By greatly curtailing these abuses and initiating gradual reforms, López satisfied basic demands for change and created a sense of rupture with the past. Meanwhile, leftists' use of increasingly confrontational tactics in pursuit of a more far-reaching transformation raised the concern, by the second half of 1936, that they were pushing the nation toward crisis, a concern accentuated by the outbreak of the Spanish Civil War. Thus, by early 1937 many Venezuelans were ready to accept a decision by López to exclude the Left from national politics in order to ensure a peaceful transition to limited democracy. As I suggest at the end of the chapter, López's desire to consolidate democracy by excluding his most determined opponents suggests that he had more in common with later democrats than either his detractors or defenders have acknowledged. The post-Gómez transition, profoundly marked by the ideological disputes of the 1930s, initiated a long-lasting pattern of exclusionary democratic regimes.

The Political Economy of the Gómez Regime

When, in 1908, Gómez seized control of Venezuela, it was an agrarian nation dependent on exports of coffee, cacao, and cattle hides and still controlled by coalitions of caudillos. The national army lacked professional training and equipment, and the treasury was in perpetual disarray. Reforms of these institutions over the next decade and a half provided two of the most important pillars of the Gomecista state and remained the basis of the dictator's power until his death. Significantly, the modernization of the national military (1910–13), as well as reforms of the treasury (1913–22), were carried out before the definite onset of the oil boom in 1925, the first year that petroleum exports exceeded those of coffee. Thus, Gómez and his allies initially established the power of the central state without the aid of large petroleum revenues.[4]

Many Venezuelans experienced Gomecista state formation primarily as a process characterized by predatory corruption and political repression. These practices, while not new to Venezuela, became increasingly systematic and difficult to resist as the Gomecistas subdued regional power holders and formed a centralized state. In particular, practices that I refer to as predatory corruption—the use of public power for personal enrichment through the extraction of resources directly from the governed—cemented alliances among Gómez and his top allies while also defining much of the day-to-day relationship between the state and society.[5]

Gomecista control of the cattle industry became one of the most emblematic examples of the regime's profiteering. Gómez, an avid rancher and cattle merchant before entering politics, used his political power to control the nation's cattle trade and urban meat markets. As president he maintained the loyalty of his key collaborators by facilitating their participation in the cattle sector and other monopolistic enterprises. State governors and military commanders often became Gómez's business associates, purchasing ranches and livestock in partnership with the dictator and using their control over municipal slaughterhouses to monopolize markets and sell their product at inflated prices. Aside from gouging consumers, Gómez and his allies forced ranchers and merchants to sell them land and cattle at prices well below their market value.

Other Gomecista rackets similarly involved monopolies, coerced transactions, and cooperation among officials at different levels of administration. For example, despite the treasury reforms, the regime continued to collect liquor taxes through a revenue-farming system that provided lucrative perquisites to leading Gomecistas, usually state governors and the district officials they appointed. Like tax farmers throughout history, Venezuelan recipients of these concessions profited not only by collecting more in revenue than they paid the treasury, but also by abusing their authority to monopolize the production and sale of liquor in their jurisdictions, force competitors out of business, and sell their product at inflated prices. Meanwhile, localities endured additional forms of predatory corruption at the hands of various rulers, such as district officials who imposed unauthorized fines, mayors who controlled local food markets, or networks of officials who appropriated public lands cultivated by peasant settlers. Such predatory forms of enrichment consolidated ties among Gomecistas while alienating citizens from the increasingly powerful state.

The oil boom that began in the 1920s gave the regime a new source of revenue and spoils, one that did not require the extraction of resources directly from the populace. Petroleum was exploited through a system of concessions granted to Venezuelan citizens, who then sold them to foreign oil companies. Concession recipients included some strongmen of the regime, as well as friends and relatives of Gómez who did not hold prominent political positions.[6] The financial returns from especially productive concessions could be fabulous but did not necessarily eclipse earnings from other sources of profiteering. A careful analysis of Gómez's personal fortune suggests that only 10–15 percent came directly from oil.[7] Similarly, a state governor who squeezed all potential profit from a liquor tax contract over a period of years might earn more from this one source than from all but the richest of the oil concessions.[8] Nevertheless, oil money benefited Gómez and his associates in various ways, not only through concessions. The Ministry of Interior Relations managed a notorious slush fund that regularly made payments to supporters and friends, the value of which rose dramatically as oil revenues increased.[9] Thus, the system of spoils that gave the Gomecista state much of its cohesion included both predatory practices—in which resources were extracted directly from the populace—and financial manipulations, such as the oil concessions and cash payments to supporters, which privatized national wealth but did not extract resources directly from citizens, a distinction to which we will return when examining the post-Gómez transition.

The final hallmark of the Gomecista state was the system of surveillance and political prisons. Aided by a network of spies and informants, the army and police hunted down the regime's real and imagined opponents. Political offenders were usually confined to La Rotunda prison in Caracas or the Castillo Libertador in Puerto Cabello, often with heavy iron shackles on their ankles; some were tortured or killed. The prisons also played their part in the system of predatory corruption. Those who refused to sell Gómez their properties at the prices he set were sometimes jailed, and the families of political prisoners had to bribe officials in order for their loved ones to receive even a minimal diet of wretched food. As stories of degradation and horror leaked out from the prisons beginning in the mid-1910s, a "psychosis of fear" gripped Venezuela.[10]

Opposition movements—caudillo revolts, student protests, and conspiracies of young army officers—broke out periodically from 1913 onward, with the most serious challenges concentrated in 1928–29. In February 1928, students affiliated with the Federation of Venezuelan Students (Federación de Estudiantes de Venezuela, FEV) in Caracas transformed a university festival into a protest for political and economic freedom.[11] When police detained the leaders, larger student protests erupted, and over two hundred were arrested. Men and women of all classes then took to the streets in support of the students, and Gómez, surprised by this open defiance, freed the young men from prison.[12] Thus was born the "generation of 1928," the extraordinary group of students—including Rómulo Betancourt, Raul Leoni, Jóvito Villalba, Rodolfo Quintero, and Miguel Otero Silva—who would influence politics and intellectual life for more than four decades. Gómez's ideologues branded the dissidents "Communists" and revised the constitution to ban Communist propaganda, but at the time few of the students adhered to any formal ideology. Some of them joined an uprising led by young army officers in April that loyal military forces only narrowly defeated; others participated in caudillo revolts, which were soundly defeated by late 1929. Fortunately for Gómez and his allies, the high tide of this political challenge had passed when the global economic crisis struck.

The Great Depression severely damaged the agricultural export economy, in which many Venezuelans made their living.[13] The 70 percent decline in the price of coffee between 1928 and 1934 proved catastrophic for many Venezuelan producers. The government provided hacendados with credit through the new Agricultural and Livestock Bank, but many recipients invested the funds in urban real estate or commerce and allowed the bank to take their mortgaged farms. Export crops continued to be widely cultivated by large and small producers, but the profitability of these enterprises never recovered. Comparable coffee economies, such as Costa Rica and Colombia, weathered the Depression more successfully than Venezuela, where growers faced particular obstacles that compounded the effects of the market slump.[14] Since the late nineteenth century, observers had noted that Venezuelan coffee trees produced average yields considerably lower than those in Central America or other regions of South America, owing in part to poor farming techniques but primarily to Venezuelans' cultivation of lands only marginally suited to coffee. Moreover, developments associated with the slump increased the value of the Venezuelan *bolívar*, which inflicted yet more damage on agricultural exporters. The devaluation of the U.S. dollar and the relatively quick recovery of Venezuelan oil exports combined to raise the exchange value of the bolívar, which Gómez's government, in 1934, decided to maintain at the rate of 3.93 bolívares to the dollar, a substantial appreciation over the 1928–29 rate of 5.24 bolívares.[15] This made sense in light of the state's increasing dependence on taxes collected from the oil companies in domestic currency, but it increased the burden on exporters while also decreasing incentives for industrialization by suppressing prices of imported goods.[16] Even without the shock of the Depression, agriculture would eventually have had to confront the consequences of low productivity and the national economy's reorientation toward petroleum, but the crisis concentrated the effects of these developments in a few short years.

The strength of the petroleum sector, as well as Gómez's fiscal management, averted a macrolevel crisis in the economy. The oil boom that began in the mid-1920s had allowed the regime to accumulate treasury reserves of 100 million bolívares by 1929, providing a cushion when the crisis hit.[17] The export price of a barrel of oil fell from $1.97 in 1929 to $0.78 in 1933, but it recovered somewhat, to $1.11, in 1936. More importantly, the volume of oil exports, which recovered to pre-Depression levels in 1934, rose to 139 million barrels in 1935, Venezuela's highest ever, and then to 150 million barrels in 1936.[18] Thus, the decline in export earnings and government revenues, while substantial in the early 1930s, proved manageable for the regime. Gómez also imposed various economies in state finances in the early 1930s, even eliminating some of his collaborators' perquisites. Gomecista officials, perhaps seeking to compensate for these new restrictions on their illicit enrichment, began to muscle their way into private enterprises they had previously left unmolested.[19] As a result, the British minister soon noted "a certain murmuring" against the regime among leading businessmen "which had even become more or less public" by the end of 1933,[20] though no new revolts broke out.

The immediate economic effects of the Depression, then, were considerable but not transformative. The more important long-term consequences of the Depression were political and, in a sense, indirect, in that they first took shape outside Venezuela. The ideological polarization intensified by the slump in much of the world could not be debated within Venezuela while Gómez lived, but exiled activists freely explored radical ideologies from the 1920s onward and would inject them into national politics following the dictator's death. In particular, two groups of Venezuelan leftists, one allied with the Comintern and another that was independent of it, were influenced by the currents of Marxism and nationalism rippling through Latin America. Gustavo Machado, the most prominent Venezuelan with ties to the Comintern, had been exiled by Gómez while still a teenager, later participated in the establishment of Cuba's Communist Party, and served under Augusto César Sandino in Nicaragua. He and other Venezuelan exiles established the Venezuelan Revolutionary Party (Partido Revolucionario Venezolano, PRV) in Mexico in the 1920s; in 1931 their allies in Venezuela established the smaller Communist Party of Venezuela (Partido Comunista de Venezuela, PCV), which became a member of the Comintern in 1935.[21] Some students who participated in the 1928 protests, such as Rodolfo Quintero and Miguel Otero Silva, became leading members of Venezuela's Communist faction.

A second group of young exiles gravitated toward a revolutionary Marxist analysis of Venezuela but maintained their independence from the Comintern and thus remained separate from Machado's PRV and the PCV. This group revolved around Rómulo Betancourt and other veterans of the 1928 protests, as well as older activists and intellectuals.[22] Dubbing themselves the Revolutionary Grouping of the Left (Agrupación Revolucionaria de Izquierda, ARDI), they gathered in Colombia in March of 1931 to issue their first proclamation, the Plan of Barranquilla. Betancourt—pugnacious, bespectacled, and the primary author of the plan—argued that Venezuela would gain little from overthrowing Gómez unless it also uprooted the configuration of interests that provided the foundation of his regime. Gomecismo was not simply a system of personalist rule, ARDI insisted, but rather a structural alliance of latifundistas, caudillos, and foreign capital that could survive without Gómez. The plan therefore called for agrarian reform, empowerment of the proletariat, and reforms to end the detrimental effects of "foreign capitalist penetration."[23] By emphasizing the structural under-pinnings of Gomecista power, the declaration marked a clear advance over opposition proclamations that never ventured beyond personal diatribes against Gómez. But ARDI's analysis also set a very high standard for an acceptable post-Gómez transition. Anything short of a transformation of existing power structures could be rejected as a perpetuation of Gomecismo.

In their subsequent years of exile, Betancourt and his circle continued to absorb diverse influences—Peruvian Aprismo, Mexico's evolving revo-lution, and various strands of European Marxism—while moving further to the left. Betancourt settled in Costa Rica, where he aided in organiz-ing the Costa Rican Communist Party, which at the time was not affiliated with the Comintern. In a 1932 pamphlet, he addressed one of the issues left unresolved in the Plan of Barranquilla, the relationship between ARDI and the bourgeoisie. Betancourt confessed that ARDI had hesitated to de-nounce Venezuelan entrepreneurs because some had supported the students in 1928. But he now concluded that true revolutionaries must issue a "frank and concrete declaration of war" against the bourgeoisie as a class in order to create "a new kind of State, anti-imperialist and Socialist, an instrument of the people for the achievement of Social Justice."[24] By late 1935, Betan-court and his associates were actively exploring the possibility of a popular front alliance with Machado and the Communists.[25] The death of Gómez on December 17, 1935, interrupted these plans as the exiles planned their return.

López Contreras and the Protests of 1935–36

Gómez's Minister of War, General Eleazar López Contreras, became interim president by a vote of the cabinet soon after the dictator's demise. Catholic educated, gentlemanly, and (like Gómez) a native of the state of Táchira, López had the virtue of being acceptable both to veteran Gomecista generals and to younger, more professionalized army officers.[26] In 1899, at the age of 16, López had joined the uprising led by Cipriano Castro and Gómez and went on to make his career in the army. But unlike many Gomecista officers, López supported the professional training and promotion of young officers. He also developed a reputation for administrative honesty amid the regime's corruption, and he enhanced his standing with the public when, in April 1928, he exercised restraint in putting down the rebellion of junior officers and students, limiting the bloodshed. Although clearly uncomfortable with the regime's most abusive practices, he never wavered in his personal loyalty to the dictator, and Gómez's appointment of López as minister of war in 1931 established him as the favored successor. As he assumed the presidency in late 1935, López was not identified with any faction or ideology; indeed, throughout his term of office he refrained from joining or establishing a full-fledged political party, claiming that his policies derived inspiration only from the ideals of Simón Bolívar.[27] Despite such platitudes, López had developed the razor-sharp political instincts required for survival in a highly politicized army, and they served him well as president.

The nation over which López presided was virtually without political or labor organizations in late 1935. Because Gómez had banned all political parties, only the clandestine, miniscule PCV operated on Venezuelan soil. Similarly, the dictatorship had suppressed virtually all labor organization, so that, despite occasional unrest among peasants, oil workers, and urban labor under Gómez, only a few small unions existed. As David and Ruth Berins Collier demonstrate, the extent of unionization in Venezuela in 1935 was lower than the levels achieved years earlier in Mexico, Brazil, Argentina, Uruguay, Chile, Cuba, Peru, and Colombia.[28]

This lack of political and labor organization highlights the spontaneous, popular nature of the protests that swept across Venezuela in late 1935 and early 1936.[29] Two days after Gómez's death, riots broke out in Caracas and soon spread to other cities. Crowds sacked the businesses and homes of leading Gomecista officials. Eager again to minimize fatalities, López was cautious in his use of the police and army to repress the protesters, who generally directed their fury at property rather than people.[30] In the countryside, peasants and workers attacked estates belonging to Gomecistas, burning crops, slaughtering livestock, destroying fences, and invading farmland.[31] Protestors often targeted the fruits of the regime's predatory practices, such as Gómez's properties in the central states of Aragua, Carabobo, and Guárico. Similar attacks against the properties of Gomecistas occurred in the western state of Lara, where the transfer of public lands to the regime's allies had dispossessed peasant cultivators.[32] The worst of the violence occurred in the oil zones of the western state of Zulia and its capital, Maracaibo, where dozens of people died, the oil companies' property was attacked, and foreigners took refuge on nearby ships.[33] As protests raged across the nation, Venezuela appeared ripe for the organization of a multiclass populist movement—or, perhaps, for civil war.

A Precarious Consensus

López quickly signaled his readiness to embrace orderly change. With a series of substantive and symbolic reforms, he dissociated himself from the old regime. He allowed the return of political exiles, freed political prisoners, and ordered the demolition of La Rotunda, the notorious prison in Caracas. With his approval, fifteen tons of chains and shackles from the equally infamous Castillo Libertador in Puerto Cabello were loaded onto a barge and dumped into the sea, while on shore a crowd listened to a speech by Andrés Eloy Blanco, a former prisoner and gifted poet.[34] López also moved to end the worst forms of predatory corruption by dismantling Gomecista monopolies affecting everything from beef and fish to the lottery.[35] By early February, according to British diplomats, there were "rumours of discontent among officers of the army who have been deprived of their illegal perquisites, and are now forced to live on rather meagre rates of pay."[36] Financial corruption certainly continued, but the coercive extraction of resources directly from citizens by abusive officials—one of the hallmarks of the Gómez system—was greatly curtailed.[37] By restricting predatory corruption and closing political prisons, López created a sense of rupture with the past. Venezuelans announcing their support for the new president simultaneously denounced the "dreadful tyranny" of the regime he had faithfully served.[38] Although some hated figures from the old regime continued to serve in his government, López himself ceased to be a "Gomecista" in the political lexicon of early 1936.

As the president distanced himself from his former allies, gradually removing many of them from official positions, the press was filled with speculation regarding the ideology or emerging political group toward which López might gravitate. López clearly sought to identify himself with the liberal tradition that had dominated Venezuelan political discourse since Bolívar, but nineteenth-century liberalism was widely considered an anachronism, discredited by the Depression and incapable of responding to the nation's evident need for economic and political modernization. Socialism, Italian Fascism, and Roosevelt's New Deal provided points of reference for political debate, and each had its advocates. Ramón Díaz Sánchez, a former judge, political moderate, and careful observer of the transition, noted that Venezuela in 1936 was suddenly subject to "the political fanaticism that had gathered intensity and velocity in the world while Venezuelans groaned beneath the iron fist of Juan Vicente Gómez."[39]

Pressures on López to define the direction of his government soon reached a climax. On the morning of February 14, police fired on a crowd that had gathered in the Plaza Bolívar of Caracas to protest censorship measures imposed by the governor of the federal district. That afternoon, Jóvito Villalba, a veteran of the 1928 student protests and president of the newly reorganized FEV, led an angry crowd of 50,000 to the presidential palace. To calm their outrage, López promised to dismiss the governor of Caracas, expand political freedoms, and pursue social and economic reforms. A week later, he issued the February Program, in which he outlined "the reforms necessary to root out gradually the vices of the past."[40] Specifically, López promised to promote labor rights, administrative honesty, education, economic development, technical assistance to agriculture, public health, and social welfare. López even called for a "study of the problems related to large landholdings and their division and distribution."[41] The February Program thus included many of the reforms called for by the FEV and other civic groups since the death of Gómez.

Political organizations of the Left, Right, and Center sprang up in the weeks that followed. Despite the constitution's prohibition against Communist propaganda, Rodolfo Quintero and other Communists were permitted to establish the Progressive Republican Party (Partido Republicano Progresista, PRP). Its program called for the confiscation of Gómez's property, land redistribution, higher taxes on oil companies, a state-owned refinery, cancellation of oil concessions secured through bribery, and voting rights for men and women over 18 years of age, as well as milder reforms that echoed López's February Program. In line with the Comintern's policy of creating popular front alliances, the PRP announced its willingness to ally with all groups dedicated to eradicating Gomecismo.[42] Meanwhile, Betancourt and other former members of ARDI established the Venezuelan Organization (Organización Venezolana, ORVE), which proclaimed its intention to "unite Venezuelans rather than divide them."[43] ORVE's manifesto retreated from the militant declarations of its leaders before Gómez's death. The main points of its platform were virtually indistinguishable from López's February Program, though many conservatives suspected that ORVE, as well as the PRP, harbored more radical ambitions. In the political center, progressive members of the bourgeoisie formed the National Republican Union (Unión Nacional Republicana, UNR). Measured in its reformist tone, supportive of the February Program, and open to cooperation with the Left, the UNR represented "the more enlightened opinion of upper-class *caraqueños*."[44] The Right, outraged by official toleration of the Left and alarmed at the prospect of its rapprochement with López, formed several small parties dedicated to denouncing Marxism. But most of the new organizations converged around the February Program's promise of reform and modernization. Indeed, in the heady days of late February and early March, it appeared that if ORVE and the PRP created mass organizations, they could pressure López to fulfill his reformist promises.

Conservative Resurgence and Exclusionary Democracy

Ultimately, however, the PRP, ORVE, and other leftist forces failed to control the direction of the post-Gómez transition, for a number of reasons. Left-wing leaders made several tactical errors that shifted debate away from the reforms needed to eradicate Gomecismo—a focus that favored their desire for far-reaching change—toward a highly polarized debate dominated by the theme of anti-Communism, which unified conservatives and many moderates who increasingly feared the destabilizing effects of unbridled political mobilization. Catholic students without ties to the Gómez regime played a prominent role in this conservative resurgence; their version of anti-Communism, based on the Church's reformist social doctrine rather than Gomecista reaction, aided López in carving out a new space distinct from both the old regime and the Left. Moreover, international events heightened many Venezuelans' suspicions of radical ideologies of the Right and Left and allowed López to position himself as the only guarantor of a peaceful transition to a post-Gómez, constitutional regime.

The first miscalculation by leaders of ORVE and the PRP was their acceptance of the reconvening of the existing Congress, composed primarily of Gomecistas, as scheduled in April 1936.[45] Leftist leaders, widely popular after their February victories, accepted López's argument that Congress had to meet in order to elect a president for the new term of office beginning in late April and thus preserve the "constitutional thread." Some leftists urged their leaders instead to demand new congressional elections and a direct presidential election, but ORVE and the PRP (as well as the more moderate UNR) decided that there was not sufficient time to organize elections before the current presidential term expired; they also believed that López's election was inevitable in any event, and that a break in the constitutional order might destabilize politics and allow hard-line Gomecistas (who were clearly dissatisfied with López) to take power. The hard-liners mentioned repeatedly in the press included José María García, León Jurado, Vincencio Pérez Soto, and Félix Galavís, all of whom had served Gómez as military commanders and state governors, had participated fully in the regime's predatory rackets, and continued to exercise influence in the army. With López the only man capable of holding the hard-liners in check, leftist leaders accepted the reconvening of Congress to elect him to a full term as president, hoping that the legislators would then bow to public opinion by disbanding and calling for new elections.[46]

But the Congress did otherwise. Once it elected López, it remained in session and enacted legislation that included reformist measures but on the whole empowered conservative interests. Perhaps most importantly, it produced the Constitution of 1936, which dramatically restricted voting rights. Whereas under the previous constitution all males over 21 could vote, the new charter introduced a literacy requirement, disenfranchising two-thirds of the male population, while retaining the system of indirect presidential elections and the ban on Communist activity.[47] Thus, the moderation demonstrated by leftist leaders in their acceptance of the Gomecista Congress facilitated the creation of the institutional basis for conservative dominance.

ORVE's attempt to regain the political initiative by proposing educational reforms proved to be another miscalculation, one that allowed the Right to regroup and broaden its appeal. In late April 1936, a recently elected acting senator, Luis Beltrán Prieto Figueroa, a teacher, ORVE activist, and organizer of the "militantly anticlerical" Venezuelan Federation of Teachers (Federación Venezolana de Maestros, FVM), proposed a national education law.[48] The legislation would establish the principle of state control over all schools, including Catholic schools, which enrolled a significant portion of Venezuela's secondary students. As Prieto explained, his proposed law would establish education as "an exclusive function of the State . . . [that] cannot be at the mercy of private institutions or persons" in a modern society.[49] The proposal provoked a tirade of criticism in Congress (where it had no chance of passing) and in the Catholic press. The Left now stood accused of attempting to establish "Socialist" education patterned after Mexico.[50] In truth, the Left's anticlericalism drew inspiration largely from nineteenth-century liberalism, but conservatives seized the opportunity to portray the initiative as a move to deprive parents and the Church of their proper role in children's moral and intellectual formation.[51] Soon after the Senate's defeat of the bill, the whole debate was reignited when a team of Chilean educators contracted by ORVE adherents in the Ministry of Education formulated recommendations that broadly paralleled Prieto's proposal. Venezuelan conservatives had previously attempted to tar Betancourt and ORVE as Communists by pointing to their activities in exile and arguing that their cooperation with López masked more radical long-term intentions; the education debate gave such accusations an immediacy they had previously lacked and led to the mobilization of lay Catholics. Thousands of middle- and upper-class Catholic women marched and signed petitions in defense of religious education over the course of 1936. Díaz Sánchez noted that the Left's anticlerical campaign provided "the most effective element of cohesion among the dispersed reactionary sectors."[52]

Catholic students untainted by Gomecista affiliations assumed an especially prominent role in the anti-Communist movement. The Venezuelan Catholic Church, though historically weak in comparison to much of Latin America, had gained in institutional strength under Gómez, despite occasional squabbles with the dictator. Growing Catholic schools in Caracas and other cities became important centers of activity for Catholic Action, the movement organized by the Vatican to strengthen the religious and social commitment of the laity in an increasingly secular world, where left-wing ideologies allegedly formed an especially potent threat to the faith. Catholic Youth, an arm of Catholic Action organized in Venezuela in 1933, proved to be an effective means for spreading Catholic social doctrine, which advocated moderate reforms to alleviate the harsher effects of unfettered capitalism, defuse class conflict, and undermine Socialism's appeal to the working class.[53] Rafael Caldera Rodríguez, a devout and intellectually astute pupil at a Jesuit-run school in Caracas, had served as the first secretary of Catholic Youth and in 1936 was a 20-year-old law student affiliated with the FEV. When the latter organization supported Prieto's legislation and also called for the expulsion of the Jesuit order, whose members had publicly denounced the proposed education law, Caldera and other Catholic students broke away from the FEV and formed the National Student Union (Unión Nacional Estudiantil, UNE).[54]

For students on both sides of the schism, the domestic issues that impelled their division were framed within an international context increasingly dominated by developments in Spain. The 1936 electoral victory of the Spanish Left, united in a popular front, triggered a wave of attacks on churches, clergy, and religious icons across Spain early in the year, repeating the pattern of violence that had erupted periodically since the declaration of the Republic in 1931. Many FEV members enthusiastically supported the Spanish Left, horrifying Venezuelan Catholic students, including Caldera, who followed events in Spain closely. Caldera came to admire José María Gil Robles, a prominent Catholic leader of Spain's moderate Right who believed that his country was no longer divided between monarchists and republicans but rather between Marxists and their opponents.[55] Caldera's belief in an international struggle between Catholicism and Communism had been strengthened when, in late 1933, he attended a Catholic Action congress in Rome of Spanish and Latin American student leaders, including future Chilean president Eduardo Frei Montalva.[56] Gomecista officials, while sympathetic to social Catholicism's anti-Communist goals, were sufficiently leery of its reformist message that they censored Caldera's mail following his return and questioned him regarding one vaguely suspicious letter from a Peruvian student.[57] Once Gómez died and ideological debate began over the direction and extent of change in Venezuela, Catholic students led by Caldera were determined to steer a reformist path that reflected Church teachings. Like Betancourt and ORVE, Caldera and the UNE supported the February Program, but the issues of education, Jesuit expulsion, and the Spanish crisis made cooperation impossible.

Caldera became a leading voice in defining a conservative reformist position, denouncing the Left as inherently revolutionary and Gomecismo as reactionary. In late May, he published a widely read article denouncing cooperation between the PRP and ORVE, charging that it would lead to a popular front alliance as advocated by the Comintern. Within such an alliance, the Communists would dominate as they did in France and Spain, he argued, and attempt an outright revolution. Caldera called on López to organize a multiclass party dedicated to moderate reform. Venezuela could then choose between "total revolution, and with it civil war and the death of the Republic; or gradual evolution, by means of an effective progress that can only be achieved through order, justice, and stability."[58] Although Lopez never formed the party that Caldera advocated or embraced social Catholicism as a governing ideology, he did cultivate Catholic support by subsidizing the UNE's publications and occasionally attending its gatherings.[59] Caldera himself was hired in the National Labor Office to help draft a new labor law.

While Caldera's warning of leftist revolution and civil war may have struck some as an exaggeration, events soon rendered his prediction more plausible. The Left called a one-day general strike on June 9 to protest Congress's passage of the Lara Law, which restricted political organizing, and to demand elections for a constituent assembly. The initial success of the strike led ORVE and PRP leaders into a fatal error—they extended the strike, as Ellner writes, "for another 24 hours and then indefinitely. . . . With no end in sight, the strike call was widely interpreted as a summons to popular insurrection."[60] Leftist leaders reversed themselves on June 13 and ended the strike, but the specter of insurrection had already alienated important allies. The moderate UNR ceased its cooperation with the Left, and the centrist Caracas press—which had occasionally sympathized with ORVE—now turned against it. Moderates like Mariano Picón Salas resigned from ORVE, which moved into more open confrontation with López, a development applauded by the PRP.[61]

The polarization of mid-1936 was deepened by conservatives' reaction against the increasingly visible activism of progressive women. Although male ORVE leaders lagged behind their PRP counterparts in addressing issues of gender, female activists linked with all major left-wing groups advocated for equal voting rights, legal protections for women, incorporation of women into labor unions, and increased female access to education, including family planning information. The most prominent women's group, the Women's Cultural Association (Agrupación Cultural Feminina, ACF), had organized shortly before Gomez's death and soon incorporated women affiliated with both ORVE and the PRP. The ACF included many teachers working for educational reform, and it supported the June strike. According to Ana Senior, an early ACF activist, some Venezuelans reacted negatively as she and her colleagues "took to the streets fighting for women's rights, helping unions, supporting the Spanish republic; and so they came to brand us as a group of crazy women, prostitutes."[62] Conservatives, especially the Catholic hierarchy, recoiled at this growing visibility of left-wing women who challenged traditionally gendered relations of power.

Amid these deepening divisions, López continued to mix reform with constraints on political activity. He approved the new constitution, which limited the vote to literate males, in mid-July, but the charter also provided for the confiscation of Gómez's property, thus satisfying a popular demand. By late 1936, the government had begun to parcel some of the confiscated farmland to peasant cultivators.[63] Also in mid-July, López signed the new labor law, which clearly strengthened workers' right to organize, bargain, and strike. In the remaining months of 1936, 109 new unions, with 56,000 members, received legal recognition. Nevertheless, as the Colliers argue, the legislation tilted in the direction of top-down control of labor by emphasizing "restraints" over "inducements."[64] The law's requirements proved especially burdensome for peasant unions, only three of which won legal recognition in 1936, despite the intense peasant mobilization of the post-Gómez protests.[65] The peasant and labor unions established in 1936 included those allied with ORVE or the PRP, on the left, and those allied with the conservative General Union of Workers (Unión General de Trabajadores, UGT), which advocated "apolitical unionism" while denouncing Communism.[66] In both its content and effect, then, the 1936 labor law reflected the conservative path of labor incorporation advocated by Caldera, who, despite his youth, helped to write the legislation.[67]

Only days after López signed the law, Nationalist generals in Spain rebelled against their popular front government, initiating a civil war driven by social and political tensions that had become ever more violent since the fall of the monarchy in 1931. Much of the Western world perceived the Spanish Civil War as a transnational struggle between Fascism and Communism as Germany and Italy provided aid to the Nationalists and the Soviet Union assisted the Republicans. But as Mark Falcoff observes, many Latin Americans viewed it in more general terms as "a contest between two roads to modernization," which broadly mirrored the political options then being debated in Spain's former colonies—that is, whether modernization could be achieved within the context of existing institutions or whether it required revolutionary transformations of the state and society.[68]

Throughout the second half of 1936, Venezuelans across the political spectrum asked whether the Spanish conflict might presage their own future. They noted that the very issues dividing the *madre patria*—anticlericalism, education, agrarian reform, unionism, the political role of the military, and women's rights—were polarizing politics in Venezuela. Writing in *Ahora*, Antonio Arráiz, a veteran of the 1928 protests and now a Socialist, argued that politics in Venezuela "have followed a curve parallel to the march of events in Spain. Many of us have predicted that the war will have immediate consequences in the Hispanic American nations, particularly ours."[69] Betancourt, in one of the most militant commentaries on the Spanish Civil War, argued that it was only the latest conflict to demonstrate that "liberties are fought for and won in pitched battle, at the cost of sacrifices whose measure cannot be negotiated. . . . Spain, bleeding and heroic, hard-fighting and immense, gives the whole world an example of how to die and how to struggle for Liberty."[70]

On the moderate right, the Catholic student periodical *UNE* also portrayed the war as vitally relevant for Venezuela. But rather than celebrate the conflict as an inspiring example, the paper's editorials suggested that the Spanish experience constituted a warning for Venezuela: "Spain, we repeat, continues to be our mother. Her problems, apart from inevitable specific differences, are in large part our very problems. With maternal exaltedness (*excelsitud*) she suffers in her own body the sorrows of a grave experience, for the purpose of enabling her children to avoid tremendous upheaval." Furthermore, the editors cautioned, "the triumph or failure of Russia on Spanish soil signifies the triumph or failure of Russia on American soil."[71] The *UNE*'s support for Francisco Franco was sometimes tempered by its distaste for his allies in Nazi Germany and the Spanish Falange, but the organization enthusiastically embraced his anti-Communist crusade nonetheless. Catholic students repeatedly denounced the dangers that a Republican victory would hold for both Spain and Venezuela.[72]

Engagement with the Spanish conflict was not confined to the press or small circles of political activists. In Caracas theaters, newsreel images of Franco and his army provoked cheers from the expensive seats and whistles of derision from the galleries. The exchanges occasionally became so boisterous that the police intervened.[73] In addition, supporters of the Republicans and Nationalists held competing rallies to raise funds to send to the peninsula. The anti-Communist fervor at conservative events led some participants to raise an arm in the Fascist salute, as Caldera recalled with disapproval years later.[74]

The historian Victor Sanz, though sympathetic to the Spanish Left, argues that "a very broad sector" of Venezuelans did not support either side in Spain.[75] They found the Spanish Right too reminiscent of their own history of *caudillismo*, and they feared the Spanish Left as too radical. Thus, their primary reaction to the war was sorrow at the "fratricide," as well as a desire to avoid a similar tragedy in Venezuela.[76] Although Sanz refrains from arguing that perceptions of Spain shaped the Venezuelan transition of the 1930s, his analysis suggests that—to the extent they became a frame for Venezuelans to interpret their own politics—such perceptions ultimately worked against the Left.[77] For Venezuelans questioning whether mass politics and free ideological debate could be reconciled with the peaceful pursuit of modernization, Spain provided a cautionary tale.[78] Few followed Betancourt in embracing the prospect of a violent political struggle, which increasingly appeared to be the only way the Venezuelan Left could achieve power.

In August, as hard-line Gomecistas called for stronger measures against the Left, López took steps to further isolate the PRP, ORVE, and other progressive groups.[79] He began by denouncing leftist leaders as "professional agitators" and then, on September 12, 1936, called on "the honorable people of Venezuela" to organize "in defense of the sacred interests of the fatherland."[80] On September 20, López warmly received leaders of the newly formed League of National Defense at the presidential palace and praised their anti-Communist orientation. The head of the League was Juan Bautista Araujo, an anti-Gómez caudillo, but Caldera, the young *letrado*, served as its chief spokesman. Addressing the president directly, Caldera dismissed the widely held opinion that López could subdue the Left only with the aid of the Gomecistas. Noting that "the Venezuelan people were all humiliated" under the dictatorship and that they rejected the Gomecistas' return to power, Caldera assured López, "You can combat the Communists with the bulk of the Venezuelan population, with the truly honorable and patriotic population of our country."[81] The PRP's *El Popular* sought to discredit the League by characterizing its members as "servants of Gomecista barbarism, old men and adolescents with their consciences mortgaged to the Company of Jesus, mercenaries of Wall Street, traitors to the working class, large landowners and caudillos."[82] Nonetheless, with López's support the League became a leading organization in the anti-Communist movement. Like the UNE, it pointed to Spain as an example of the damage done by the "social gangrene" of Communism, which threatened to create in Venezuela the same "state of mourning, desolation, and ruin" that prevailed in the mother country.[83]

López's decision to ally himself firmly with the anti-Communist cause placed the Left clearly on the defensive. Seeking safety in unity, leftist leaders in late October moved to form a single party joining the PRP, ORVE, allied labor groups, and the FEV, but the government proved unrelenting. The National Democratic Party (Partido Democrático Nacional, PDN), as the united party of the Left was to be called, was denied legal status due to provisions in the Lara Law and the constitution's ban on Communist activity. The PDN appealed the decision to the courts, arguing that its leadership did not include Communists and noting that this distinguished it from European popular front alliances. In a less conciliatory vein, the appeal referred to PDN opponents as Gomecistas and agents of the pope plotting "a theocratic regime."[84] The courts denied the PDN's appeal in mid-December.[85]

The Left had one final opportunity to mobilize popular support. Throughout 1936, activists affiliated with the PRP and ORVE had cooperated in establishing unions among Venezuelan oil workers in Zulia. They called a strike in mid-December, citing the companies' refusal to recognize the unions and engage in collective bargaining. As some 20,000 laborers joined the walkout, nationalist sympathy for the oil workers was virtually uniform across the political spectrum.[86] Even Caldera's UNE supported the workers' struggle against foreign "imperialism," though it criticized the Left for attempting to impose "an absolute dictatorship of the unions over individual workers."[87] López allowed the strike to continue for over a month before ending it on January 22, 1937, invoking a provision in the 1936 labor law. He ordered a wage increase of one bolívar a day for workers earning nine bolívares or less, but he did not require the companies to recognize the leftist unions. Oil workers, fearing military intervention if they rejected the settlement, returned to their jobs.[88]

As it became evident that public sympathy for the striking workers had not produced greater backing for the Left, López moved decisively against his opponents. In early February, the government revoked the legal status of all significant left-wing political and labor organizations, including the PRP, ORVE, the political wing of the FEV, and opposition labor confederations, citing the ban on Communist activity.[89] Members of the outlawed groups who had won congressional seats in the elections of January 1937 were stripped of their positions.[90] In March, López ordered the arrest and exile of forty-seven opposition leaders, again invoking the legal prohibition against Communism. This assault against the political and labor organizations that had played leading roles in the post-Gómez transition provoked remarkably little opposition. The press noted a widespread sense of public unease, but an attempt by the FEV and a handful of Caracas workers to organize a strike had little impact.[91] López had accurately gauged the publicly acceptable limits of repression. He went on to enact additional moderate reforms within a liberal economic framework while continuing to suppress the Left, and in 1941 he handed over power to a successor of his own choosing, Isaías Medina Angarita, another military officer and minister of war from Táchira, confirmed through the system of restricted suffrage and indirect elections created in 1936.[92]

Conclusion

Venezuelans' passive acceptance of the 1937 crackdown on popular organizations represented a dramatic contrast to the widespread mobilization that followed the death of Gómez and culminated in the demands for democracy and economic reform in February 1936.[93] In part, the decline of the popular movement derived from its leaders' missteps—including their anticlerical initiatives, mishandling of the June strike, and increasingly harsh rhetoric—which eventually lent credence to the perception that Venezuela was following Spain down the path of polarization and conflict, an analogy that worked in favor of conservatives. The Right was thus afforded an opportunity to reconstitute itself, not under the discredited banner of Gomecismo, or as defenders of oligarchic economic interests, but rather as guardians of stability, religion, and orderly reform.

Significantly, López united conservative and moderate Venezuelans behind the cause of anti-Communism only after it ceased to be the rallying cry of the old regime. Over the course of 1936, anti-Communism had become identified increasingly with non-Gomecista political actors such as the Catholic students who were mobilized by post-Gómez developments in Venezuela and abroad. Meanwhile, López had distanced himself from the Gomecistas by ending the predatory corruption and political terror of the dictatorship and by taking steps to implement the February Program's promise of modernization. Thus, when he finally swung decisively against the Left, after months of conservative prodding, many of his compatriots still viewed him as a reformer, as some on the left noted with evident bitterness. An ORVE editorial in late November 1936 ruefully observed that most Venezuelans were "almost grateful" to a ruler who merely refrained from "exploiting or harassing them" and would accept López's government simply because it "has ceased to be the organization of pillage and embezzlement on a grand scale."[94] Even López's exclusion of those leaders most identified with the post-Gómez demand for change did not alter the widely held view that he had established, on balance, a more democratic and dignified polity. For Venezuelans emerging from a brutal dictatorship and wary of the extremist ideologies of their age, exclusionary democracy emerged as an acceptable way forward.[95]

Epilogue

Concluding his second term as president on February 2, 1999, aged and increasingly frail, Rafael Caldera's final official obligation was to attend the inauguration of Hugo Chávez Frías. The veteran anti-leftist looked on with evident apprehension as his successor took the oath of office.[96] There were obvious differences between the populist Chávez and López, the president under whom Caldera began his political career, but there were also similarities. Both were military men who invoked Bolívar to justify their political orientation; both embraced economic models that the pundits of their day had consigned to the dustbin of history; and both men, having entered the presidency with wide popular support, eventually governed from a more narrow base, demonized their opposition, and practiced a form of democratic politics perceived by their adversaries as aggressively exclusionary.

For years scholars tended either to criticize López as an autocrat or to praise him as a democrat who avoided the errors of the Punto Fijo era. Today, with Chávez's rise and political longevity generally understood as a reaction against the elitist, "pacted democracy" of *puntofijismo*, we might view López instead as the originator of an exclusionary, antipluralist tradition in Venezuela's modern democracy that has been practiced, modified, and denounced by actors across the political spectrum over the intervening years. This exclusionary impulse has taken different forms in subsequent democratic regimes—sometimes marginalizing rival parties, as in 1945–48, or containing popular pressures through a "dictatorship" of centrist parties in 1958–98, or attempting to establish a hegemonic party of the Left in more recent years—but it has been a recurring feature of Venezuelan democracy since the critical juncture of 1935–37.[97]

Notes

1 Eric Hobsbawm, *The Age of Extremes: A History of the World, 1914–1991* (New York: Pantheon, 1994).
2 Steve Ellner, "Venezuelan Revisionist Political History, 1908–1958: New Motives and Criteria for Analyzing the Past," *Latin American Research Review* 30, no. 2 (1995): 100–103.
3 I nonetheless rely extensively on works critiqued by Ellner.
4 Angel Ziems, *El gomecismo y la formación del ejército nacional* (Caracas: Ateneo de Caracas, 1979); Yolanda Segnini, *La consolidación del régimen de Juan Vicente Gómez* (Caracas: Academica Nacional de la Historia, 1982); and Miriam Korn-

blith and Luken Quintana, "Gestión fiscal y centralización del poder político en los gobiernos de Cipriano Castro y de Juan Vicente Gómez," *Politeia*, no. 10 (1981): 145–55. The treasury reforms of this period included increased professional training for treasury bureaucrats, utilization of modern methods of accounting, and increased collection of domestic taxes to reduce the state's dependence on customs receipts. The resulting increases in revenue allowed the government to begin paying down the foreign debt, which was completely repaid in 1930. Gómez-era reforms did not include creation of a central bank, which occurred in 1939–40.

5 The following two paragraphs are based on Doug Yarrington, "Cattle, Corruption, and State Formation in Venezuela during the Regime of Juan Vicente Gómez, 1908–1935," *Latin American Research Review* 39, no. 2 (2003): 9–33.

6 Brian S. McBeth, *Juan Vicente Gómez and the Oil Companies in Venezuela, 1908–1935* (Cambridge: Cambridge University Press, 1983), 45–48, 67–108.

7 Tomás Polanco Alcántara, *Juan Vicente Gómez: Aproximación a una biografía* (Caracas: Grijalbo, 1990), 472–73.

8 For liquor profits, see "Memorandum para el Sr Dn Emile Sauer," enclosed with "Data for the World's Anti-Alcoholic Congress," May 7, 1919. United States National Archives (hereafter USNA), Maracaibo Consular Post Records, 1919, vol. 114, section 811.4. Also see McBeth, *Juan Vicente Gómez*, 91.

9 "Texto íntegro de la sensacional demanda del Procurador General de la Nación," *El Universal*, May 4, 1936, in *Gobierno y época del Presidente Eleazar López Contreras: La versión de la prensa, 1936–1941*, vols. 25–30 of *Pensamiento político venezolano del siglo xx: Documentos para su estudio* (Caracas: Congreso de la República, 1986), 26:63–79. Unless otherwise noted, all newspapers cited were published in Caracas.

10 José Pareja Paz Soldán, *Juan Vicente Gómez, un fenómeno telúrico* (Caracas: Avila Gráfica, 1951), 88.

11 John Martz, "Venezuela's 'Generation of '28': The Genesis of Political Democracy," *Journal of Inter-American Studies* 6, no. 1 (1964): 17–32.

12 For women's participation in the events of 1928, see Carmen Clemente Travieso, *Mujeres venezolanas y otros reportajes* (Caracas: Avila Gráfica, 1951), 17–25.

13 Unless otherwise noted, information in this paragraph comes from William Roseberry, *Coffee and Capitalism in the Venezuelan Andes* (Austin: University of Texas Press, 1983), 128–33; Marie Price, "Hands for the Coffee: Migration, Settlement, and Trade in Western Venezuela, 1870–1930" (PhD diss., Syracuse University, 1991), 332–45; and Doug Yarrington, *A Coffee Frontier: Land, Society, and Politics in Duaca, Venezuela, 1830–1936* (Pittsburgh: University of Pittsburgh Press, 1997), 161–76.

14 Mario Samper Kutschbach, "Colombian and Costa Rican Coffee Growers from Prosperity to Crisis, 1920–1936," in *Coffee, Society and Power in Latin America*, ed. William Roseberry and Lowell Gudmundson (Baltimore: Johns Hopkins University Press, 1995), 151–80.

15 Ramón Veloz, *Economía y finanzas de Venezuela, 1830–1944* (Caracas: Academica Nacional de la Historia, 1984), 364, 382. Under the new exchange system, oil companies would sell any excess dollars (i.e., those not purchased by banks) to the Venezuelan government at the rate of 3.03 bolívares.

16 Terry Lynn Karl, *The Paradox of Plenty: Oil Booms and Petro-States* (Berkeley: University of California Press, 1997), 81.

17 Jorge Salazar-Carrillo and Bernadette West, *Oil and Development in Venezuela during the Twentieth Century* (Westport, CT: Praeger, 2004), 58.

18 Salazar-Carrillo and West, *Oil and Development in Venezuela*, 75–82.

19 Emilio Pacheco, *De Castro a López Contreras* (Caracas: Editorial Domingo Fuentes, 1984), 100–101.

20 "Memorandum on the Present Conditions, Economic and Commercial, in Venezuela," enclosed in Keeling to Simon, March 2, 1934, Public Record Office (hereafter PRO), Foreign Office (hereafter FO), 371/17618.

21 Robert J. Alexander, *The Communist Party of Venezuela* (Stanford, CA: Hoover Institution, 1969), 3–5, 197.

22 Arturo Sosa and Eloi Lengrand, *Del garibaldismo estudiantil a la izquierda criolla: Los orígenes marxistas del proyetcto de A.D., 1928–1935* (Caracas: Centauro, 1981).

23 "Plan de Barranquilla," in Sosa and Lengrand, *Del garibaldismo estudiantil*, 459–67; quotation, 465.

24 Rómulo Betancourt, "Con quién estamos y contra quién estamos," in Sosa and Lengrand, *Del garibaldismo estudiantil*, 499, 501.

25 Robert J. Alexander, *Rómulo Betancourt and the Transformation of Venezuela* (New Brunswick, NJ: Transaction Books, 1982), 64–65.

26 Winfield Burggraaff, *The Venezuelan Armed Forces in Politics, 1935–1959* (Columbia: University of Missouri Press, 1972), 28–32; E. López Contreras, *Páginas para la historia militar de Venezuela* (Caracas: Tipografía Americana, 1944), xvi–xx.

27 Luis Ricardo Dávila, *El estado y las instituciones en Venezuela, 1936–1945* (Caracas: Academia Nacional de la Historia, 1988), 87–89.

28 Ruth Berins Collier and David Collier, *Shaping the Political Arena: Critical Junctures, the Labor Movement, and Regime Dynamics in Latin America* (Princeton, NJ: Princeton University Press, 1991), 97, 99; see also 80–82; and John Duncan Powell, *Political Mobilization of the Venezuelan Peasant* (Cambridge, MA: Harvard University Press, 1971), 47–49.

29 José Manuel Hermoso, *1936: Programas vs poder* (Caracas: Editorial Kinesis, 1991), 41–44.

30 Gumercindo Torres, *Memorias de Gumercindo Torres*, ed. Jose Agustín Catalá (Caracas: Presidencia de la República, 1996), 138–39, 165.

31 E. López Contreras, *Proceso político social, 1928–1936* (Caracas: Editorial Ancora, 1955), 91–115.

32 Yarrington, *Coffee Frontier*, 181–192; Rómulo Betancourt, *Problemas venezolanos* (Santiago: Editorial Futuro, 1940), 257–60.

33 Charles Bergquist, *Labor in Latin America* (Stanford, CA: Stanford University Press, 1986), 228.

34 Naudy Suárez, "U.N.E.: Gestión de una idea revolucionaria," in *Por los legítimos ideales del estudiante venezolano*, ed. Naudy Suárez (Caracas: Editorial Arte, 1973), 14.

35 Nicholson to State Department, December 30, 1935, USNA, State Department Records, Box 5785, 831.00/1557.

36 MacGregor to Eden, February 11, 1936, PRO/FO, 371/19845.

37 Blas Bruni Celli, "Rómulo Betancourt frente a la corrupción administrativa," in *Betancourt en la historia de Venezuela del siglo xx*, ed. Ramón J. Velásquez (Caracas: Centauro, 1980), 312, 316; see also Bernard Mommer, *Global Oil and the Nation State* (Oxford: Oxford University Press, 2002), 111–14.

38 "Nuestro rumbo," *El Relator* (Trujillo), February 1, 1936.

39 Ramón Díaz Sánchez, *Transición (política y realidad en Venezuela)* (Caracas: Academia Nacional de la Historia, 1983), 85; see also Luis Barrios Cruz, "Por qué el venezolano es refractario al comunismo?," *El Universal*, May 1, 1936, in *El debate político en 1936*, vols. 14–16 of *Pensamiento político venezolano del siglo xx: Documentos para su estudio* (Caracas: Congreso de la República, 1983), 14: 451. For interesting comments on liberalism in this period, see Fernando Coronil, *The Magical State: Nature, Money, and Modernity in Venezuela* (Chicago: University of Chicago Press, 1997), 84–89.

40 "Programa de Febrero del Presidente Eleazar López Contreras," in *Programas políticas venezolanos de la primera mitad del siglo xx*, ed. Naudy Suárez Figueroa (Caracas: Universidad Católica Andrés Bello, 1977), 123–34; quotation, 125.

41 "Programa de Febrero," 130.

42 "Proyecto de Programa del Partido Republicano Progresista," in Suárez Figueroa, *Programas políticas venezolanos*, 134–41. Gustavo Machado, because of his notoriety, avoided afiliation with the PRP so as not to endanger its legal status.

43 "Manifiesto-Programa del Movimiento de Organización Venezolano," in Suárez Figueroa, *Programas políticas venezolanos*, 141–45; quotation, 143.

44 Martz, "Venezuela's 'Generation of '28,'" 25.

45 Arturo Sosa and Eloi Lengrand, "Prólogo," in *El debate político*, 14:35–36.

46 Díaz Sánchez, *Transición*, 63.

47 Martz, "Venezuela's Generation of '28,'" 30.

48 Daniel H. Levine, *Conflict and Political Change in Venezuela* (Princeton, NJ: Princeton University Press, 1973), 32; see also Alexander, *Rómulo Betancourt*, 98; and Guillermo Luque, *Educación, pueblo y ciudadanía: La educación venezolana en la primera mitad del siglo xx* (Caracas: Ministerio de la Cultura, 2006), 45–47, 87–99.

49 Luis B. Prieto Figueroa, "Qué se pretende con el Ante-proyecto de Ley Orgánica de Educación Nacional?," *Ahora*, May 3, 1936, in *El debate político*, 14:453.

50 Luque, *Educacion, pueblo y ciudadanía*, 46.

51 Sosa and Lengrand, *Del garibalidismo estudiantil*, 105–6; Levine, *Conflict and Political Change*, 66–69; and Guillermo Luque, *Educación, estado y nación: Una historia política de la educación oficial en Venezuela, 1928–1958* (Caracas: Universidad Central de Venezuela, 1999), 104–53.

52 Díaz Sánchez, *Transición*, 55.

53 Guillermo Luque, *De la Acción Católica al Partido COPEI, 1933–46* (Caracas: Universidad Central de Venezuela, 1986), 34–43.

54 Kirk A. Hawkins, "Sowing Ideas: Explaining the Origins of Christian Democratic Parties in Latin America," in *Christian Democracy in Latin America: Electoral Competition and Regime Conflicts*, ed. Scott Mainwaring and Timothy R. Scully (Stanford, CA: Stanford University Press, 2003), 104–6. Caldera and other UNE activists led the formation of COPEI, Venezuela's Christian Democratic Party, in 1946.

55 Luque, *De la Acción Católica*, 65–123, 247–51; Fredrick B. Pike, *Hispanismo, 1898–1936: Spanish Conservatives and Liberals and Their Relations with Spanish America* (Notre Dame, IN: University of Notre Dame Press, 1971), 280–83.

56 Donald Herman, *Christian Democracy in Venezuela* (Chapel Hill: University of North Carolina Press, 1980), 10–11, 18–22; and Suárez, "U.N.E.: Gestión," 35–36.

57 Rafael Caldera, *De Carabobo a Punto Fijo*, 4th ed. (Caracas: Libros Marcados, 2008), 67–68n5.

58 Rafael Caldera, "Hacia la definición electoral en Venezuela," *El Universal*, May 31, 1936, in *El debate político*, 14:613.

59 Luque, *De la Acción Católica*, 78–79, 101, 153–54; Suárez, "U.N.E.: Gestión," 28; and Antonio Arráiz, "Nubes sobre el Pacífico," *Ahora*, October 6, 1936, in *El debate político*, 15:402–3. López also invited Caldera to a private two-hour meeting at his home following the publication of the article mentioned in this paragraph, a version of which Caldera broadcast as a radio speech. See Rafael Caldera, *Al ciudadano Presidente Eleazar López Contreras, en el centenario de su nacimiento, 1883–1983* (n.p.: Fondo Editorial del Estado Táchira, 1983), 109–13.

60 Steve Ellner, "Acción Democrática—Partido Comunista de Venezuela: Rivalry on the Venezuelan Left and in Organized Labor, 1936–1948" (PhD diss., University of New Mexico, 1979), 29.

61 Ellner, "Acción Democrática," 30–38; Sosa and Lengrand, "Prólogo," 54–56, 89; Alexander, *Rómulo Betancourt*, 106–9.

62 Quoted in Elisabeth J. Friedman, *Unfinished Transitions: Women and the Gendered Development of Democracy in Venezuela, 1936–1996* (University Park: Penn State University Press, 2000), 69. This paragraph draws on Friedman, *Unfinished Transitions*, 60–73; and Alexander, *Rómulo Betancourt*, 106.

63 "La distribución de la tierra," *Ahora*, October 29, 1936, in *El debate político*, 15:525–26.

64 R. Collier and D. Collier, *Shaping the Political Arena*, 253.

65 Powell, *Political Mobilization*, 59–61.

66 Ellner, "Acción Democrática," 41–42; Luque, *De la Acción Católica*, 80–81.

67 Answering conservatives who criticized the law as too favorable to workers, Caldera argued that "the Labor Law constitutes the healthiest protection of the social body against the virus of class war." Quoted in Gerhard Cartay Ramírez, *Caldera y Betancourt, constructores de la democracia* (Caracas: Centauro, 1987), 62–63.

68 Mark Falcoff, "Preface," in *The Spanish Civil War, 1936–1939: American Hemispheric Perspectives*, ed. Mark Falcoff and Fredrick B. Pike (Lincoln: University of Nebraska Press, 1982), xiv.

69 Antonio Arráiz, "Nubes sobre el Pacífico," *Ahora*, October 6, 1936, in *El debate político*, 15:402–3.

70 Rómulo Betancourt, "¡No pasarán! Madrid será la tumba del fascismo," ORVE, November 16, 1936, in *El debate político*, 15:641.

71 "El Día de la Raza," UNE, October 12, 1936, in Suárez, *Por los legítimos ideales*, 106–7.

72 Luque, *De la Acción Católica*, 104–8; and Suárez, "U.N.E.: Gestión," 68–69.

73 Díaz Sánchez, *Transición*, 114–15.

74 Luque, *De la Acción Católica*, 251; see also 104–8.

75 Victor Sanz, *Venezuela ante la república española, 1931–1939* (Caracas: Centauro, 1997), 367.

76 Sanz, *Venezuela ante la república*, 470–73.

77 For the concept of framing, see David Snow, "Framing Processes, Ideology, and Discursive Fields," in *The Blackwell Companion to Social Movements*, ed. David Snow et al. (Oxford: Blackwell, 2004), 380–412.

78 Sanz, *Venezuela ante la república*, 384.

79 Burggraaff, *Venezuelan Armed Forces*, 43–44.

80 Sosa and Lengrand, "Prológo," 56; and "Añadimos unas palabras al márgen de las expresiones del Presidente de la República," *Ahora*, September 22, 1936, in *El debate político*, 15:336.

81 Rafael Caldera, "Discurso en la audiencia del Presidente de la República a La Liga de Defensa Nacional," *El Universal*, September 22, 1936, in *El debate político*, 15:334.

82 "La Liga de Defensa Nacional," *El Popular*, November 7, 1936, in *El debate político*, 15:571–73.

83 From a League manifesto quoted in Manuel Vicente Magallanes, *Los partidos políticos en la evolución histórica venezolana* (Caracas: n.p., 1973), 319.

84 "Alegatos ante corte a favor de la legalización del PDN," *El Popular*, December 2, 1936, in *El debate político*, 16:19–31; quotation, 24.

85 John Martz, *Acción Democrática: Evolution of a Modern Political Party in Venezuela* (Princeton, NJ: Princeton University Press, 1966), 34–38; Alexander, *Rómulo Betancourt*, 112–13.

86 Ellner, "Acción Democrática," 45–46; Bergquist, *Labor in Latin America*, 233–36.

87 "Como vemos nosotros la huelga petrolero," *UNE*, January 23, 1937, in Suárez, *Por los legítimos ideales*, 156.

88 Ellner, "Acción Democrática," 47; Edwin Lieuwen, *Petroleum in Venezuela: A History* (New York: Russell and Russell, 1954), 82.

89 Alexander, *Rómulo Betancourt*, 113–14.

90 Martz, *Acción Democrática*, 39–41.

91 "La expulsión de los comunistas," *UNE*, April 3, 1937, in Suárez, *Por los legítimos ideales*, 184; Suárez, "U.N.E.: Gestión," 27.

92 Venezuela did not abandon liberal development policies until the mid-1940s, as discussed in Karl, *Paradox of Plenty*, 83–85.

93 Hermoso, *1936: Programas vs poder*.

94 "Ante el actual gobierno, a la izquierda no le queda sino un sitio: La oposición," *ORVE*, November 29, 1936, in *El debate político*, 15:735–36.

95 I borrow the term from Karen Remmer, "Exclusionary Democracy," *Studies in Comparative International Development* 20, no. 6 (1985/86): 64–85. I use it here to refer to a political system that is formally democratic but designed or managed with the goal of preventing a particular group from achieving power.

96 Cristina Marcano and Alberto Barrera Tyszka, *Hugo Chávez* (New York: Random House, 2007), 124–25.

97 Michael Coppedge, *Strong Parties and Lame Ducks: Presidential Partyarchy and Factionalism in Venezuela* (Stanford, CA: Stanford University Press, 1994), 1–46; and Javier Corrales and Michael Penfold, *Dragon in the Tropics: Hugo Chávez and the Political Economy of Revolution in Venezuela* (Washington, DC: Brookings Institution, 2011). On "critical junctures" as periods that create long-term political patterns, see R. Collier and D. Collier, *Shaping the Political Arena*, 27–39. Their emphasis on labor's "incorporation" into politics leads the Colliers to stress the importance of the 1940s in Venezuela.

CHAPTER 7

Indigenista Dictators and the

Problematic Origins of Democracy

in Central America

Jeffrey L. Gould

During the 1930s, rightist dictatorships seized power in El Salvador, Guatemala, Honduras, and Nicaragua. These regimes all reacted to the social protests and dislocations caused by the rapid and severe drop in export income, particularly in the coffee industry. The regimes attempted with a large measure of success to disrupt the nascent alliance between the Left and Indians by crushing the former and co-opting the latter. The ideologies of *mestizaje* and *indigenismo* aided that process of regime consolidation and leftist quarantine from its erstwhile (potential) allies.

During the 1920s, throughout Central America (with major caveats in the Nicaraguan case), there was a general, if mild, tendency toward the democratization of society, politics, and government.[1] It is therefore hard to imagine the triumph of the rightist military regimes in the early and mid-1930s without the social dislocations wrought by the first years of the Great Depression. Before turning to the Depression's impact on ethnic relations, let us review the economic data, policies, and consequences of the period. The Great Depression's impact on Central America had much to do with the dramatic decline of coffee and banana prices during the late 1920s and early 1930s. In El Salvador coffee accounted for 90 percent of export value, and in Costa Rica and Guatemala bananas and coffee accounted for the same proportion of exports (coffee accounted for 50 percent of export earnings in Nicaragua). World coffee prices dropped from $0.22 in 1929 to $0.08 in 1931. As a direct consequence of the price drop, the value of exports declined precipitously. In El Salvador, the value of coffee exports dropped from $22.7 million in 1928 to $10.8 million in 1931 and to a low of $6.4 million in 1932. By 1935, coffee exports had rebounded sufficiently to account for $12.1 million in income. In Guatemala, the value of exports dropped by 40 percent from 1928 to 1932. The volume of exports also declined in Central America as a whole, from 369,000 quintals (100 pounds) in 1928 to 285,000 in 1932, with Guatemala and El Salvador registering the most intense fluctuations.[2]

The impact on wage earners was devastatingly harsh. Coffee growers responded to the crisis across the region by slashing wages on the average by 50 percent. Although the decline in the cost of living probably mitigated their situation somewhat, at least during the first years of the Depression, the wage cuts brought workers' incomes below subsistence levels.[3] The sharp fall in coffee production translated directly into a decrease in the seasonal labor force, and the overall economic slowdown created more urban unemployment.[4] Similarly, the decline in government revenues from export taxes and tariffs caused a drop in government employment and public employee wages throughout the region. In Guatemala, the most extreme case, government expenditures were sliced in half from 1928 to 1932. During those same years, in El Salvador expenditures dropped nearly as much and in Nicaragua they declined by a third.

Central American governments responded proactively to the crisis. As Victor Bulmer-Thomas notes, "Coffee production could be influenced through variations on export duties, the availability of credit, exchange rate changes and special funds. All these instruments were used by one or other republic in the Depression and the impact of low world prices on profitability was also mitigated by the reduction of labour costs."[5] Such governmental support of the coffee industry brought about a fairly rapid recovery and, as Bulmer-Thomas remarks, set a precedent for future interventions (and the popular expectations for them). In Guatemala and El Salvador the value of agricultural exports during the late 1930s surpassed that of the late 1920s.

Several isthmian countries stopped making payments on their external debt and imposed a domestic debt moratorium, measures that alleviated the crises in government expenditures, allowing in the Salvadoran case, for example, the payment of government employees in 1932, and directly prevented foreclosures on coffee fincas. The Salvadoran, Costa Rican, and Nicaraguan (in 1936) governments devalued their currency to help coffee exporters, and the Guatemalan government lowered its export tax.

Government policies throughout the region aimed to promote import substitution in manufacturing and agriculture. Unlike in other countries in the hemisphere, there was only limited success with industrialization. Yet, the sharp increase in domestic-use agriculture in the second half of the 1930s served to reduce dependence on imported foodstuffs (20 percent of imports in the 1920s). Here, government-imposed tariffs and rural road construction projects (in Guatemala with forced labor) served to increase domestic production by 400 percent during the decade.[6]

Bulmer-Thomas argues for a revisionist view of the Great Depression suggesting that, in part owing to governmental intervention, its impact was "less severe than previously thought."[7] He is probably on strong ground in at least one crucial respect: the recovery in terms of macroeconomic indicators was quite rapid, and by the mid-1930s domestic agriculture production was high and export volume and values had recuperated significantly. Bulmer-Thomas correctly underscores the importance of pro-coffee governmental responses to the crisis. Yet, this view understates the devastating effects on the laboring classes, particularly during the earliest years of the Depression. This harsh impact is amply documented in British and U.S. consular reports throughout the region and a range of governmental and labor documents. For example, the British Consul in Nicaragua wrote in 1932 that its population "is mainly on the very margin of existence."[8] Whereas the rise to power of the military regimes was a prophylactic response to the social and political consequences of that rapid immiseration, the subsequent financial and economic recovery from such dramatic depths may have garnered the caudillos some measure of popular support. The authoritarian governments' efforts to support the coffee elite also involved a broadening and strengthening of the state's centralizing power and its greater intrusion into the lives of its citizens.[9]

The Great Depression was also a time of cultural change, intimately connected to the economic and political changes outlined above. Yet continuities also marked the period's nationalist discourses and practices. Since the dawn of the century, mestizaje, understood as a nation-building myth of race mixture and as a cultural process of "deindianization," contributed substantially to Central American nationalist ideologies and played a key role in shaping political culture. The discourse and associated practices of cultural mestizaje, especially the loss of ethnic markers, continued into the 1930s, provoking tensions within the communities and, at the same time, tending to cut off democratic forces from those Indians who adhered to traditional cultural and political forms.

Throughout the 1920s and 1930s, Central American elite promotion of mestizaje did not break with fundamental liberal precepts but rather muted some of its more blatant forms of anti-indigenous racism and facilitated the incorporation of some subaltern groups into the national polity. In addition to mestizaje, *obrerismo*, the radical democratic language of artisan workers, also expanded the power and reach of liberalism. In general, these relatively new ideologies challenged and threatened traditional ideologies of class and racial privilege and exclusion. Most significantly, the acceptance of an imagined mestizo nation made explicit, public forms of racism less acceptable and coincided with a societal shift from biological to cultural racism.[10] Yet, there were hidden political and cultural costs of this component of nation building in the twentieth century, in particular, the problematic origins of democratic discourse.

The world crisis, as noted above, had devastating consequences for most Central Americans, especially those Indians involved in the coffee economy as smallholders or laborers. In decisive moments during the decade, most notably in El Salvador, indigenous people protested against land taxes, forced labor, low wages, land expropriation, and perceived attacks on their religion. Despite often harsh, even barbaric repression as in El Salvador, this was an era in which Mexican currents of indigenismo made their entry into the isthmus and, in certain instances, influenced state policy. Here, we follow common usage of the term, as a discourse generated by non-Indians that focuses on Indians and on their integration into national society and in so doing aims to overcome extreme forms of exploitation, segregation, and land loss. There was significant variation within indigenismo, ranging from a strictly educational and assimilationist agenda to a recognition of the need to end special forms of exploitation of Indians.[11] Yet, even in its most radical form, in Mexico, Cárdenas emphasized the integration of Indians into the dominant culture, "Mexicanizing" Indians as opposed to "indigenizing" Mexicans.[12] At the same time, indigenismo in all of its forms was compatible with various forms of mestizaje as a key component of nationalist ideology.

A comparative study of mestizaje and ethnic relations in Central America should take into account the myriad ways in which the policies of one country influenced those of another. In this essay, we can offer but one suggestive example. In 1945 Clemente Marroquín Rojas, a Guatemalan journalist and leader of the democratic revolutionary forces, wrote,

> The Indian groups that had been strong . . . have by now almost entirely disappeared. . . . You have to realize that El Salvador is a nation of *mestizos*; there are only a few hundred pure Indians remaining. In El Salvador the Indian problem has almost disappeared, and for that reason, El Salva-

dor, a nation with a million fewer inhabitants than Guatemala, is physically and economically stronger than Guatemala . . . because the Indian problem resolves itself when the Indian disappears or becomes civilized. . . . The problem can only be resolved by racial mixture between them [ladino and Indian] and by taking away their indigenous culture in order to place them within a more advanced culture.[13]

It is remarkable that Marroquín Rojas, a democratic leader, could utter these words without the slightest reference to the massacres of 1932 that significantly accelerated the process of mestizaje. This omission is symptomatic of the profound separation between the Central American democratic forces and the indigenous peoples. Marroquín Rojas's homage to Salvadoran mestizaje also emanated from one of the more reactionary currents of indigenismo: Marroquín argued for solution of the "Indian problem" as the suppression of indigenous culture.

In all countries, the percentage of indigenous inhabitants was still significant at the turn of the century (an estimated 35 percent in Nicaragua, 25 percent in Salvador, 20–25 percent in Honduras, and close to 70 percent in Guatemala). By the 1920s cultural mestizaje had already advanced notably in the middle isthmus. In western Honduras and western Nicaragua virtually all inhabitants had ceased to speak indigenous languages by the turn of the century. Similarly, by 1930, the majority of indigenous Salvadorans no longer spoke Nahuatl as their principal language. Moreover, a significant minority were monolingual Spanish speakers. The salience of other ethnic markers such as clothing was also diminishing in certain microregions (e.g., Jinotega and Boaco in Nicaragua, Intibucá and Gracias in Honduras, and la Libertad in El Salvador). There existed a continuum of indigenous identities and communal practices across the middle isthmus. Typically, these ranged from monolingual Nahuatl speakers in Santo Domingo de Guzmán, El Salvador, to people ten miles away in Sonzacate who bore no identifiable ethnic markers yet were considered indígenas by their ladino neighbors. Not only does this enormous variation complicate analysis, but it also greatly facilitated the advance of mestizaje as discourse and practice, holding an example of "civilization" both to more traditional indigenous populations and to ideologues of mestizaje and anthropologists alike.

The rural mobilization, insurrection, and massacre of 1932 were among the most significant events in modern Central American history. As argued elsewhere, the mobilization and insurrection derived from the militant and contradictory responses by western Salvadoran campesinos to the discourse and practice of mestizaje. Unlike in the rest of the isthmus, in El Salvador ethnic militants lived among those who participated in a process of cultural mestizaje. In western Guatemala, there were also signs of ethnic militancy, but processes of ethnic homogenization had advanced far less than elsewhere on the isthmus (including the eastern highlands of Guatemala). In western Nicaragua and western Honduras, during the early twentieth century, at the moment when their land, labor, and community autonomy were under siege, the Indians had largely lost their ethnic markers of language and dress. Ethnic militancy was less of an option given that for both Indians and ladinos those effaced markers were synonymous with indigenous identity. Moreover, the Nicaraguan and Honduran indigenous communities were far more dispersed than in El Salvador or Guatemala. For the Salvadorans, as we shall see, both ethnic militants and those who long ago had shed their indigenous identity joined forces in a mobilization for land redistribution, labor rights, and political autonomy.

The Salvadoran mobilization of 1930 and 1931 was remarkable precisely because it involved rural workers and peasants of such variegated forms of identities, ranging from Nahuatl speakers to those who considered Indians, at best, to be distant ancestors. Fundamentally, the campesinos accepted leftist messages more readily owing to a 50 percent wage cut and a substantial loss of access to land during the early years of the crisis.

The mobilization and insurrection took place primarily in the three western departments of the country: Ahuachapán, La Libertad, and Sonsonate. Although in elite and diplomatic eyes most of the rural inhabitants in the region were "indios," the ethnic makeup of the western part of the country was quite complex. In La Libertad and Ahuachapán, for example, the overwhelming majority of the rural population did not consider themselves to be Indians, despite the indigenous identity of many of their grandparents.[14] Indeed, as Salomé Torres, a survivor of the massacre, recalled, "The only Indians lived in Izalco and Nahuizalco. They were the only ones who spoke Nahuatl and used Indian dress."[15]

The expansion of the coffee industry severely affected the nineteenth-century resident indigenous population of La Libertad, as many (including Torres's grandparents) lost access to land and became laborers on coffee plantations. By 1930, the large majority of coffee workers shared Torres's perspective: "Indians" lived in the towns of Nahuizalco and Izalco in the department of Sonsonate and had nothing to do with their own identities. Those whom I interviewed in the late 1990s, who had been children or adolescents in 1930, allowed that perhaps their grandparents had been "Indians" or "naturales."

As I noted in *To Die in This Way*, the Nicaraguan highland communities that the coffee industry had transformed or absorbed became centers of the radical labor movement four decades later.[16] It seems probable that in La Libertad, as in the Nicaraguan communities, the memory of primitive accumulation—the early twentieth-century ladino appropriation of former communal landholdings—and the shared cultural codes with urban artisans, especially language, facilitated the circulation and acceptance of leftist ideas. Throughout 1930 and 1931, feverish union organizing spread across the coffee plantations of La Libertad, and major strikes broke out there in December 1931 and January 1932.

The Communist labor organizer Jorge Fernandez Anaya compared the situation in Guatemala with El Salvador. In the latter country, he recalled in a 1988 interview, "not all the rural workers were Indians, and although not all of them spoke Spanish, there were always interpreters and in any event it was easier to talk with the Indians of El Salvador than with those in Guatemala."[17] For Fernandez Anaya, the Salvadoran Indian and ladino rural workers had a highly developed capacity for understanding their class interests.

Ethnic relations and identities in Ahuachapán were similar to those in La Libertad. An analogous process of coffee and mestizaje had transformed the areas in and around the departmental capital so that most residents lacked an indigenous identity at the start of the mobilization.[18] The only indigenous presence was in the municipality of Tacuba, where Indians represented 60 percent of the population. In eastern Ahuachapán, ladinos made up the large majority of the population, many of whom were phenotypically "mulatto." According to local legend, maroons who had escaped from Guatemala founded the city of Atiquizaya (population 15,000 in 1915).[19]

In Sonsonate, ethnic relations and identities were dramatically different, and it is there that the discourse of ethnic militancy circulated, in part in response to the advance of cultural mestizaje that among its effects placed Nahuatl language as a marker of inferior status. Religion and religious conflict constituted one area that conditioned the emergence of ethnic revitalization. Father Conte, a Paulist missionary and sharp observer of ethnic relations during the early twentieth century, recounted several incidents that revealed how religion accentuated a deep chasm between Indians and ladinos.[20] To cite one example, in 1912, an indigenous group in the highlands of Jayaque seized a priest who had appropriated a sacred image and turned him over to the municipal authorities for arrest.[21]

Similarly, in the 1920s, in the municipality of Nahuizalco, sharp conflicts erupted between local priests and Indians over the latter's religious practices. As in other parts of Central America, priests, for reasons of profit and purity, attempted to appropriate indigenous religious images. In addition to religious conflict, Indians and ladinos confronted each other over local political control. Throughout the first decades of the twentieth century the two groups battled for control over the municipalities of Nahuizalco (80– 90 percent indigenous) and Izalco (50 percent indigenous). Given the minority status of the ladinos in Nahuizalco, their political control depended on alliances with nontraditionalist Indians on the one hand and national political elites on the other. In addition, landlords depended to some degree on clientelistic relations. Traditionalist political struggles by the late 1920s intersected with class-based organizing among indigenous and ladino coffee laborers.

This language of indigenous militancy was part of a hidden transcript and as such is difficult to trace.[22] One example comes from the utterance of an inebriated nahuizalqueño to an Italian journalist at a wedding: "We the true Indians, the Indian kings! The pure ones . . . we know what the white people do not. We await our time. We are the owners of the mountains, the valleys, the coffee plantations, the houses . . . everything you can see."[23] The Left could in a sense appropriate these forms of ethnic militancy principally because its egalitarian and emancipatory language resounded as a rebuke to ladino arrogance and disrespect. By 1931, when the Socorro Rojo Internacional (SRI) became its primary organizing vehicle, the banners of land reform easily meshed with the vision of indigenous land rights. Finally, the Left forged electoral alliances with the local indigenous leaders who sought to overturn local ladino rule.

Thus, the leftist mobilization benefited from the contradictory responses to mestizaje sketched above. Yet, the movement had severe limitations even in the western departments, by far its strongest base of support. Particularly in the municipality of Izalco, in *cantones* where both Indians and ladino campesinos resided, cultural tensions impeded the growth of a united movement. The Indians strongly resented the ladinos as recent immigrants who had occupied ancestral land and generally excluded them from their union and SRI organizations. The ladino campesinos experienced the mobilization and the insurrection as threats; they voluntarily participated in the counterrevolutionary movement, including in the massacres.[24] Many of the ladinos were smallholders but also worked on the coffee plantations. Despite the enormous growth of the rural labor movement from 1929 to 1931, it probably did not encompass the majority of the coffee plantation seasonal labor force. Ladinos from the bi-ethnic cantons of Izalco and Juayúa constituted a substantial part of the nonorganized workforce.

Indigenous labor activists, however, had little difficulty connecting with ladino coffee workers on the plantations. In reference to his organizational work in two Izalqueño cantones in 1930, a ladino carpenter and labor organizer stated, "The Indians understood really well. Juan Hernández and other compañeros from Cuyagualo went themselves to San Julián [a plantation] in order to organize the workers."[25] In other words, on large coffee plantations (San Julián, for example), ethnic divisions were far less salient than in Nahuizalco or Izalco.

Despite the remarkable ability of indigenous and ladino leftist militants to transcend sharp ethnic divisions, those became consequential once again in the reconstruction of the events by the indigenous survivors of the 1932 massacre. Thus, to cite one critical example, informants exonerated Indians from any participation in the insurrection, blaming any looting and violence on "los mulatos" from the Atiquizaya region.[26]

Six decades of military rule conditioned these recollections. Survivors reworked the participation of nonindigenous people from Atiquizaya and Turín in the movement, enabling the suppression of the indigenous subject in the insurrection (as opposed to the mobilization). Ladino elites, ladino Communists, and the ladino military became equally guilty as perpetrators of the massacre. The suppression of indigenous participation in the fragmented collective memories of the survivors had serious consequences for the development of local political culture.[27]

The insurrection of January 22, 1932, was in large part a response to electoral fraud (as well as the abrogation of elections) and violent repression. On December 2, 1931, a military coup deposed reformist president Arturo

Araujo, whose administration during nine months had been unable to cope with the high level of rural mobilization. Two days later, General Maximiliano Hernández Martínez, vice president and minister of war, assumed power. After initially making some moves to placate the leftist labor movement, by the end of the year he aligned himself with the landed elite. He thwarted leftist electoral aspirations and then crushed their protests.

The military massacres in January and February 1932 did not target the Salvadoran indigenous population in general, but they did result in the deaths of thousands of Indians in the region where the insurrection had triumphed (notably Nahuizalco, Juayúa, Tacuba, and Izalco). The insurrections, involving five to seven thousand Indians and ladinos in roughly equal proportion, had triumphed there owing to the resentments caused by the fraudulent denial of Indian Left victories in the January 3–4 municipal elections. In other Indian areas such as Santo Domingo Guzmán (located outside the coffee belt) where the mobilization did not prosper, there was no repression. In another area south of San Salvador, where Indians had participated in an unsuccessful attack on the capital, the military engaged in selective repression and chose not to engage in mass killings.[28] In the months and years following la Matanza, the military and the Church carefully orchestrated a retelling of the history that blamed the Communists for the killings and exculpated the "innocent" Indians. The refrain "they killed the just for the sinners," rooted in military discourse, became a trope synthesizing the survivors' account of the massacre. The refrain suggested that Indians had not participated in the movement and, at the same time, refused to name the perpetrators of the massacre.

Through this reconstruction of history in the traumatized minds of the survivors, the military was able to chart a course whereby they became the protectors of Indians against those who would further disrupt society, whether through land grabs or through democratic opposition to the dictatorship. Mestizaje as national-level discourse and everyday forms of cultural reproduction continued to gather force, following la Matanza. Moreover, the Hernández Martínez regime attempted to strike an alliance with the surviving indigenous people. For example, the National Guard lieutenant, in charge of the Indian school for orphans of the massacre, unsuccessfully pushed for Nahuatl language instruction. He also attempted to institute Nahuatl language instruction in all of the area schools but failed as a result of a lack of resources.[29] Along similar lines, the Hernández Martínez regime, in 1935, enacted a law making it illegal for a municipality to change a name from its autochthonous one. This was a response to a trend exemplified by the indigenous-dominated municipality Cuisnahuat, which wished to drop its indigenous name and substitute it with "San Lucas."[30] Without making too much of this decree, it is, at the least, paradoxical: a regime whose conduct may be legitimately described as genocidal attempted to "rescue" an indigenous town from its own tendency toward ladinization. The regime also favored Indians with more concrete support, in particular, in land conflicts with ladinos. Hernández Martínez also supported small-holders faced with foreclosure and parceled out very small quantities of land in Ahuachapán and La Libertad.[31] Defeated and traumatized Indians made for good allies for a military regime ready to exonerate them for past activities and to offer them limited support in their daily battle for survival.

As stated above, sharp ethnic divisions and a discourse and cultural practices of mestizaje existed before the Great Depression. Those tendencies would have continued in some form regardless of the economic crisis, perhaps in analogous form to those described below with respect to Nicaragua. The inevitable ethnic conflicts would have remained local and probably insignificant faced with the broad currents of mestizaje that converted, as it were, the indigenous into the nonindigenous. However, the Depression created the conditions for the rapid growth of a radical labor and campesino movement that allied with Indian traditionalists. The state, in turn, responded with increasingly repressive measures, culminating in the tragedy of January 1932.

Nicaragua

In the early twentieth century, the growth of mestizaje as a Nicaraguan national discourse that emphasized ethnic homogeneity greatly facilitated ladino triumphs over indigenous communities. Typically local elites used that discourse and the commonsense evidence about the lack of salient ethnic markers to challenge the authenticity of indigenous communities. Although the regional elite of the Central Highlands were not of great political importance during the 1920s, land, labor, and political conflict took place in an economically strategic area, especially the coffee zone of Matagalpa. The battle for control over its resources had devastating consequences for the indigenous population. By 1920, in western and central Nicaragua, indigenous peoples had lost control of all municipal governments. Well before that date, Nicaraguan indigenous identities had been wrapped up in an allegiance to the institution of the Comunidad Indígena and in opposition to ladinos who were attempting to expropriate its land and thwart its political autonomy.

Although Augusto César Sandino's nationalist resistance to the United States Marine intervention had an important impact on the region's indigenous population, it did not directly support indigenous demands. Sandino's silence with respect to the Comunidades derived from his nationalist project. Sandino was crafting a popular nationalistic discourse, in effect reinventing a nation that had become the "patrimony of oligarchs and traitors."[32] Most fundamentally, Sandino was a product and producer of the discourse of mestizaje. Despite his sincere commitment to the "indo hispano" race and more concretely aiding the Miskito and Sumos, Sandino could not break free from his civilizing mission, "to do whatever necessary to civilize these Indians who are the marrow of our race."[33]

Sandino's *indohispanismo* certainly facilitated his recruitment of Indians and non-Indians. Similarly, the blurring of ethnic boundaries among Sandino's social bases of support undoubtedly prevented the kind of anti-indigenous repression following his assassination in 1934 that had scorched the Salvadoran countryside two years earlier.

Nevertheless, it is important to recognize the political and cultural cost of his project. Part of the cost surely was unintended—the political disenfranchisement of the Comunidades that accompanied the decline of the Conservative Party, delegitimized in the course of the Sandinista struggle. His failure to support the Comunidades was particularly problematic in that unique conjuncture where indigenous groups were in a position to rebound from decades of political, cultural, and economic losses.

During the 1930s, the myth of mestizaje in Nicaragua favored the consolidation of the Somoza regime in various respects. Somoza, a mestizo himself, could easily combine *obrerista* and mestizaje-inflected nationalist rhetoric and consequently bolster his own legitimacy as a popular leader. In 1936, Somoza supported the first major urban strike movement in Nicaragua's history and in so doing earned significant support for his rise to power later that year. Upward of 10,000 workers launched a solidarity strike with taxi drivers (Managua's population was 80,000). Rather than carrying out President Sacasa's orders to repress the strike, Somoza negotiated successfully with the labor leaders.[34] Similarly, striking sugar mill and plantation workers at the Ingenio San Antonio, the largest enterprise in the country, shouted "Viva Somoza" when they staged rallies.[35]

Mestizaje contributed to the fragmentation of the opposition to the emerging Somocista regime. Ironically, it was during the 1930s that indigenismo, as a more or less coherent program to promote fundamental rights for indigenous people, emerged as a serious political discourse. As in Mexico, indigenismo formed part of a fundamentally assimilationist agenda, yet compared to earlier periods, Nicaraguan Indians finally became visible with positive valences, no longer completely subsumed within the discourse of mestizaje. Responding to the power of indigenista discourse, as well as to the need for potential votes and political support, Somoza offered limited support to indigenous communities in conflict with ladinos. In 1934, the government, under Somoza's influence, promulgated a law that finally abolished the seasonal debt peonage, still practiced in Matagalpa (shortly following the approval of a similar law in Guatemala). In 1935, the government formally prohibited the sale of ejidal and communal lands and enacted a tax on hacienda lands to promote indigenous education in 1937.[36] Moreover, the Somoza regime offered some limited support to leadership groups of the surviving Comunidades Indígenas and in so doing cultivated political support that in some cases would last decades. It should be noted that these political victories for indigenous people took place following the disarticulation of the Sandinista movement and decades after most of the Comunidades had lost any significant degree of political, cultural, and economic autonomy.

Moreover, as elsewhere in Latin America, the most ardent defenders of Indians, national intellectuals who rhetorically and even politically valorized Indians, had little local knowledge of their relations with local ladinos. The progressive indigenistas had no real contact with the isolated remnants of the Comunidades who lacked the means to forge alliances with other indigenous groups or with the nascent labor movement that would acquire importance during the following decade.

The U.S. interventions in Nicaragua set its historical development apart from its neighbors. Thus, the Great Depression affected its political and cultural development less directly. Although the crisis undoubtedly aided Somoza's rise to power, previously, thanks to the United States, he was already well positioned as the head of the National Guard. And the Liberal caudillo was, in turn, uniquely capable and determined to expand his bases of popular (clientelistic) support to include the Comunidades Indigenas. Unlike in El Salvador before 1932 or Guatemala throughout much of the twentieth century, the indigenous groups of central and western Nicaragua posed no threat to the state or to local ladino power groups. The defeat of the 1881 rebellion in Matagalpa and other locales, along with the failure of the Sandino movement to mobilize the Comunidades, impeded the growth of a unified Indian movement in defense of its land and labor. It was precisely the lack of such a threat that permitted the Nicaraguan government to make concessions to individual Comunidades and indigenous groups.

Guatemala

The roots of the differences between mestizaje in Guatemala and in the other Central American countries are related to their different patterns of colonization. For Christopher Lutz and George Lovell, following Murdo MacLeod, viewed from the point of view of Spanish interests, colonial Guatemala could be divided into core and peripheral regions.[37] Most of eastern and coastal Guatemala was suitable to sugar cane and indigo cultivation and thus formed part of the core region, areas of extensive Spanish and *casta* settlement. For lack of economic motive, Spaniards tended not to settle in the western highlands.[38] Finally, for climatic reasons, the highlands area had a relatively dense population that was less affected by diseases that accompanied the conquest. Moreover, the Indians were not subjected to the slavery (and death in transit to Peru) that decimated the indigenous populations of Honduras and Nicaragua. Whatever the precise relation between the above factors, there is little doubt that with the exception of western Salvador, at the dawn of the independence era, Guatemala stood alone as a densely populated, overwhelmingly indigenous region (western Honduras was predominantly indigenous but not densely populated).[39]

One cannot overestimate the importance of the large indigenous majority in Guatemala, when attempting to understand its divergent discourses of mestizaje and indigenous policies in contrast to the rest of Central America. Beyond the sheer demographic factor, it is worth highlighting that Guatemala did not suffer the military-political defeats that Indians endured in El Salvador, Honduras, and Nicaragua. Owing to the maintenance of a strategic threat (exemplified by the 1837 Carrera rebellion), the Guatemalan state and the coffee elite perpetuated a "colonial compact" that allowed for a degree of indigenous cultural and political autonomy in return for political deference and extra economic coercion in labor relations.

In order to foment a labor supply for the coffee industry after the triumph of the Liberal Revolution of 1871, the Guatemalan elite devised a series of measures that Arturo Taracena argues amounted to a policy of "dissimu-lated segregation."[40] Upon retaking power, the Liberals were faced with an apparently insoluble contradiction. On the one hand, their ideology de-manded policies of homogenization, integration, and equal treatment of universal citizens. On the other, the necessity of a "cheap and abundant sea-sonal labor for coffee" and cultural realities dictated the need for "dissimu-lated segregation."[41] Such a policy made it virtually impossible to construct a discourse of mestizaje similar to that of Mexico or the middle isthmus. The Liberal regime decreed a series of "secondary laws," a set of more or less formal discriminatory and segregationist practices that ensured both military dominance over a strategic threat and a steady supply of indigenous labor.[42] These laws and practices related to labor, land, education, military conscription, and citizenship. Taracena forcefully argues that the Liberals undermined their own universalistic principals in order "to guarantee in-digenous labor and the distribution of communal land" for the benefit of the coffee industry. Yet, perhaps there was a more politically strategic dimen-sion to "la segregación solapada," for in Guatemala the indigenous peoples had not been subjected politically to the same degree, nor had they been de-feated militarily as decisively, as had the minority indigenous populations of the other countries following rebellions: following Indian rebellions in western El Salvador (allied with poor ladinos, 1932); in Intibucá, Honduras (1926); and in Matagalpa, Nicaragua (1881). In Guatemala, then, the state and its agrarian elite allies needed to prolong what David McCreery calls "the colonial compact" whereby the indigenous communities maintained a high level of political and cultural autonomy in exchange for their accep-tance of the political and economic rules of the game.[43] Perhaps one could add that such an acceptance included an implicit prohibition of intraethnic unity beyond municipal boundaries.

The above system combining the secondary laws and the "colonial com-pact" continued until the Depression, when the Ubico regime (1931–44) began to make concessions to indigenous groups on key labor issues and to politically represent itself within the communities through *intendentes*. In so doing, Ubico weakened the local ladino elite economically by eliminat-ing any role for the *habilitadores* (middle men) and politically by displacing local politicians. Several events took place earlier in the decade that shaped those measures.

At around noon on July 28, 1930, some two thousand Indians gathered in the plaza of the Totonicapán, a departmental capital in the western highlands, to protest an upward revision in the land tax. The local authorities reported that the Indians "engaged in an armed attack against the army barracks." Soldiers opened fire, "killing three persons and wounding a number."[44] The protesters dispersed, and reinforcements arrived from Quetzaltenango and the capital. The government decried the armed attack on the barracks by "Indian hordes," but there was no independent verification of such an event. It used the protest as a pretext to suspend constitutional guarantees to peaceful assembly and free speech. Although admitting that the armed threat in Totonicipan had been "laughable," the authorities suspended the guarantees because they "had information of the existence of seditious movements . . . (that) threaten to cause an uprising in other towns." The U.S. ambassador, Sheldon Whitehouse, relayed President Chacón's words to the State Department and concluded that the suspension of guarantees aimed to "control the press and to cope better with the feeling of unrest and dissatisfaction with the Government which exists throughout the country at the present time."[45]

There is no evidence of any serious threats to the government, much less any coordination among different indigenous communities or between them and the nascent labor movement. The miniscule Communist Party (three hundred members) did, however, try to forge organizational links in the countryside. In 1931, Jorge Fernández Anaya, the Mexican Communist organizer, spent a month in a hacienda in the department of Totonicapán. During that period, thanks to the assistance of a multilingual interpreter, he managed to organize a strike to abolish payment in scrip. According to Fernandez Anaya in an interview in the 1980s, the strike involved workers from several haciendas and from several linguistic groups. Although "there were many 'indios' taken prisoner," the strikers prevailed and the hacendados henceforth paid with money. The Mexican Communist's reflections on his organizing experience on the hacienda are revealing. First, he states that the level of internal repression on the hacienda was so intense that, in order to avoid capture, he became a virtual prisoner in a large hut. The interpreter/organizer would "look for people so that I would tell them things and they would tell others who were organized in different nuclei. And then people would talk and then tell the *peones* what one wanted."[46] In effect, Fernandez Anaya situated himself at the apex of a preexisting cellular organization that apparently had nothing to do with a formal union structure. He listened to the indigenous workers: "I realized that they wanted some kind of salvation and they saw that in money payment."[47] He also reflected some of the urban ladino bias that predominated in the ranks of organized labor. Referring to the indigenous laborers as "indios" (as did the government), he bemoaned their "cultural backwardness," which led them to apparently have no concern beyond payment in money. Fernandez Anaya, as noted earlier, suggested that the Salvadoran Indians were far more advanced, accessible, and thus available for union organization.

Although the Mexican Communist was correct that linguistic barriers were undeniably more substantial in Guatemala than in El Salvador, there is another reading of his statements: ladino leftists in El Salvador successfully overcame significant ethnic/cultural prejudices during the period of mobilization. Jorge Ubico's rise to power in 1931 squelched any possibility for their Guatemalan counterparts to accomplish a similar personal and collective transformation in the countryside.[48] His regime systematically arrested labor activists and Communist Party militants in 1931. Using the pretext of the Salvadoran insurrection, he completed the job in February 1932, when he arrested over two hundred militants.[49] Yet, as suggested above, Ubico promoted policies that gained him some support among the indigenous population. In Momostenango in Totonicapán, the Indians called him "tatanol" (big father).[50]

The regime's abolition of debt peonage in 1934 (prompted to some degree by international and indigenista criticism) allowed Ubico to claim that he had "rescued [the Indians] from slavery."[51] The impact of the abolition was tempered by the imposition of harsh vagrancy laws that obliged the landless and *minifundistas* to work 100–150 days a year on plantations or road crews. Some indigenous workers apparently viewed these measures as more than just debt peonage in part because poor ladinos were also affected and because the hated habilitadores lost out. David McCreery argues that in a broader sense Ubico's vagrancy law "hastened a process of socioeconomic differentiation within the indigenous population, already accelerated by forced participation in the coffee economy."[52] McCreery points to the availability of cheaper, local labor for wealthier indigenous peasants, since many of their poorer neighbors preferred to stay home rather than journey to the coast for the coffee, sugar, or cotton harvests. This accessibility probably contributed to the increase in foodstuff production in the latter part of the 1930s, highlighted by Bulmer-Thomas.[53] Moreover, the elimination of the habilitadores and their associates opened up new economic possibilities for Indians.

Although the abolition of debt peonage may have benefited Ubico politically, the vagrancy law did encounter some resistance. The U.S. ambassador to Guatemala reported, in 1936, that in Nebaj, Quiché, Indians reacted to police efforts to enforce the law by attacking the police station. In response, "reinforcements were sent from nearby towns and as punishment eight of the leaders of the Indians were summarily executed."[54] The ambassador went on to predict further unrest among the Indians but doubted that a "really serious opposition movement" would emerge given the Indians' lack of cohesive leadership. In the border department of San Marcos, Cindy Forster uncovered substantial evidence of passive resistance during the 1930s and of the willingness of indigenous workers to join unions in the early 1940s, while still under Ubico's rule.[55]

Despite the uneven reception of the vagrancy law, Ubico was able to consolidate a significant degree of support among the highlands Indians through a populist political style characterized by lightening visits (often on motorcycle) that allowed him to intervene in local problems.[56] Before the installation of the intendente system, local indigenous leaders had to work in subordinate fashion with local ladinos who were invariably "elected" as mayors. The intendentes, outsiders who were directly appointed by Ubico, tended to undermine local ladino authority. The Ubico regime also instituted policies of *cedulación* (identity cards) that gave a material basis to the idea of indigenous citizenship, as did their increased recruitment into the military.

If Ubico was moderately successful at forging a clientelistic political base among indigenous people, he was less successful at creating a coherent discourse about Indians and their place in Guatemalan society or in the national imaginary. Recent studies suggest that during the 1920s and 1930s mestizaje in its Mexican and Nicaraguan variants remained largely absent in Guatemala. Arturo Taracena and Ramón González suggest that the discourse of mestizaje was used to integrate nonwhite ladinos into the nation still controlled by criollos and thus to foster a strategic non-Indian alliance.[57] Yet, there do seem to have been minor ideological changes in the 1930s that accompanied Ubico's clientelistic policies. As American anthropologists and archaeologists established their presence, the notions of Mayan greatness and the value of the "pure Indian" began to circulate in middle-class and elite circles. Similarly, there were calls for increased European immigration with the vague and contradictory hope of creating mixed-race offspring (Germans in Alta Verapaz and San Marcos were well advanced in this regard).[58]

Ubico wanted to foster a strong peasant foodstuff sector, as well as provide labor for the coffee plantations. Yet he also had visions of expanding the state's power, and in pursuing that aim he ended the prerogatives of ladino (and some indigenous) intermediaries, who had benefited from the policies of "segregación solapada." Thus, the Ubico regime's policy toward Indians combined a program of state centralization with a sui generis form of indigenismo.

The Depression influenced these political and cultural developments, albeit somewhat indirectly. As suggested above, it is doubtful that Ubico would have seized power if it had not been for the threat of popular mobilization provoked in part by economic distress. Similarly, economic dislocations probably affected the ability of local ladino groups to resist their displacement by the regime. Finally, inspired by the fascist examples and by the fear of revolution, the new regime sought new ways to integrate the nation, distinguishing itself from its Liberal oligarchic predecessors. A modest indigenismo with its associated ethnic ideologies formed part of Ubico's new authoritarianism.

Conclusion: The Political Consequences of 1930s Indigenismo

Notwithstanding the absence of any national-level Indian policy, during the 1930s, the Guatemalan, Nicaraguan, and Salvadoran governments each made tactical moves and gestures that favored individual or small groups of Indians in conflicts with local ladinos. Paradoxically, these limited forms of state intervention on behalf of the indigenous communities were particularly consequential in El Salvador, where, as noted above, in the aftermath of the traumatic massacres of 1932, the military regime was able to discursively shift the blame onto the Communists and invent themselves as protectors of the Indians.[59] Indigenista rhetoric and policies bolstered the region's dictatorial regimes and had significant political ramifications.

In 1944, the Guatemalan and Salvadoran policies toward indigenous groups paid political dividends. Following the student-led overthrow of Jorge Ubico, General Federico Ponce became interim president, announcing putatively free elections to be held in December. Ponce, opposed in the presidential race by the democrat Juan José Arévalo, attempted to mobilize Ubico's base of support among the indigenous people. In some areas of the highlands, the Ponce regime announced an "abolition" of the *libreto* system, requiring workers to turn in the work cards often in exchange for registering as a member of the Progressive Liberal (Ubiquista) Party. Similarly, the regime circulated the idea that the government would distribute the recently nationalized plantations (expropriated from German nationals) to Indian workers and villagers. They warned, however, of ladino and Arevalista opposition to such a redistributive policy. On September 15, 1944, some four thousand Indians, armed with machetes, paraded on the streets of the capital in support of Ponce and against the democratic opposition.[60] For weeks, the regime kept the Indians quartered on the outskirts of the city. Growing resentment against the regime's manipulation of the electoral process, including their potential provocation of an indigenous rebellion, culminated in the revolutionary overthrow of the government on October 20. Junior officers, students, teachers, and workers participated in the successful armed movement. Ponce resigned, and the revolutionary leadership called for elections that inaugurated a ten-year period of democracy.

On October 22, in the municipality of Patzicía, Chimaltenango, pro-Ponce Indians rose up in rebellion, killing a dozen ladino men. In response, local vigilantes and troops executed perhaps three hundred Indians. Although the specific local spark is unknown, it seems likely that Ponce's defeat had symbolized the end of indigenous hopes for land reform. Evidence for this thesis is provided by the stirrings of similar movements in other locales in the western highlands.[61]

It is intriguing, if not ironic, that the promise of land reform probably ignited these abortive rebellions against a revolution that would eight years later carry out a major agrarian reform, directly benefiting the highlands Indians. Although land reform, per se, was not at the time at the forefront of the revolutionary agenda, there were a few figures within the democratic coalition who did promote that goal.[62]

The political disjuncture between the democratic forces and the indigenous population revealed by the democratic revolution of 1944 was a constant throughout modern Central American history. In El Salvador, during the same year, a similar story played out. Following the overthrow of Hernández Martínez in the spring of 1944, a democratic movement emerged, led by Arturo Romero, who gained a massive following among students and, to a lesser degree, among workers and the ladino poor peasantry. On the day following the triumph of the democratic revolution in Guatemala, conservative sectors of the military led by Osmín Aguirre overthrew the provisional government that had been guiding the electoral process. Both the landed elite and also Indians backed this Salvadoran Thermidor. Rooted in a decade of informal alliance with the military against the local ladino elite, some western Indians armed with machetes terrorized the local ladino populations with threats of vengeance for the massacres of 1932.[63] It is still unclear to what extent indigenous support for the regime proved decisive in its victory against the progressive, democratic forces. Similarly, in Nicaragua, the indigenous alliances with Conservatives were integral to their survival well into the twentieth century. Relying upon that alliance, central highlands Indians successfully thwarted numerous efforts to abolish the Comunidades Indígenas and occasionally managed to resist elite land grabs. During that same period, however, ladinos deployed the discourse of democracy and liberalism in their assault on indigenous land. In the 1930s, with the Comunidades largely defeated in their struggles for land and political autonomy, the Somoza regime was able to co-opt indigenous leadership from Matagalpa to Subtiava (León). Their support for Somocista Liberalism led to the historic defeat of Emiliano Chamorro, the Conservative caudillo, in his senatorial race in Matagalpa in 1934. As late as the 1970s, the Sandinista movement had to wage sharp political battles with the Somocista leadership and its ample base of support within the Comunidades Indígenas of Subtiava, Matagalpa, and Jinotega.[64]

The dramatic political transformations of indigenous communities throughout Central America during the first half of the twentieth century are related to the problematic origins of democracy in Central America. For twentieth-century ladino leftists, indigenous support for Somoza and their participation in the antidemocratic movements of 1944 all strike the same chord: Indians are conservatives, opportunists, or "gobiernistas." Yet, those same historical moments should be viewed from the other side, as part of the massive silencing of indigenous voices that conditioned the origins of democratic politics in the region. Those origins, shrouded in bad faith and ignorance, have acted like a dormant virus flaring up precisely at those moments when the Left and the indigenous populations have had the greatest possibilities to achieve their shared goals, as in Nicaragua and Guatemala in the late 1970s and early 1980s. The relationship is no healthier today.

Notes

1 This essay does not focus on Costa Rica, a country that suffered equally from the Depression but had a stronger democratic institutional framework to withstand its political effects. Its ethnic relations were so distinct as to warrant exclusion from this consideration. Honduras is also excluded owing primarily to

a relative lack of research on indigenous-ladino relations in its western departments during the 1930s. For preliminary research, see Darío Euraque, *Estado, poder, nacionalidad, y raza en la historia de Honduras* (Tegucigalpa: Ediciones Subirana, 1996); and Jeffrey Gould, "Proyectos del Estado-nación y la supresión de la pluralidad cultural: Perspectivas históricas," in *Memorias del Mestizaje: Cultura Política en Centroamérica de 1920 al presente*, ed. Darío Euraque, Jeffrey L. Gould, and Charles R. Hale (Antigua: CIRMA, 2004), 388–91.

2 Edelberto Torres-Rivas, *Interpretación del Desarrollo Social Centroamericano* (San José: EDUCA, 1977), 283–84. Torres-Rivas derives his data from Vernon Wickizer, *The World Coffee Economy* (Stanford: Stanford University Press, 1943). Victor Bulmer-Thomas presents a chart based on data from the League of Nations suggesting only minor production declines during this same period.

3 Jeffrey L. Gould and Aldo Lauria, *To Rise in Darkness: Revolution, Repression, and Memory in El Salvador, 1920–1932* (Durham, NC: Duke University Press, 2008), 20–31.

4 Ambassador Sheldon Whitehouse to the Secretary of State, March 12, 1930, U.S. State Department 814:00/1007, reports on the "present critical financial situation and . . . lack of work."

5 Victor Bulmer-Thomas, "Central America during the Inter-War Period," in *An Economic History of Twentieth-Century Latin America: Latin America in the 1930s*, vol. 2, ed. Rosemary Thorp (New York: Palgrave, 2000), 257. Naturally, the lowering of wages required governmental support in particular to repress any forms of resistance.

6 Bulmer-Thomas, "Central America," 260.

7 Bulmer-Thomas, "Central America," 265.

8 Cited in Jeffrey Gould, *To Lead as Equals: Rural Protest and Political Consciousness in Chinandega, Nicaragua, 1912–1979* (Chapel Hill: University of North Carolina Press, 1990), 38. In El Salvador, in August 1931, the U.S. consul noted, "It is evident that the purchasing power of the laboring classes, especially in the rural districts, has been distinctly curtailed. The ragged experience of the workers is notable." Cited in Gould and Lauria, *To Rise in Darkness*, 20.

9 See Eric Ching, "Patronage and Politics under General Maximiliano Martínez, 1931–1939: The Local Roots of Military Authoritarianism in El Salvador," in *Landscapes of Struggle: Politics, Society, and Community in El Salvador*, ed. Aldo Lauria and Leigh Binford (Pittsburgh: University of Pittsburgh Press, 2004).

10 See Etienne Balibar and Immanuel Wallerstein, *Race, Nation, Class: Ambiguous Identities* (London: Verso, 1991); and Clara Arenas, Charles Hale, and Gustavo Palma, *Racismo en Guatemala? Abriendo El Debate sobre un tema tabú* (Guatemala: AVANCSO, 1999).

11 On indigenismo, see Alan Knight, "Racism, Revolution, and Indigenismo: Mexico 1910–1940," in *The Idea of Race in Latin America, 1870–1940*, ed. Richard Graham et al. (Austin: University of Texas Press, 1990), 77.

12 See Knight, "Racism, Revolution, and Indigenismo."

13 Cited in Arturo Taracena, *Etnicidad, Estado y Nación en Guatemala, 1944–1985*, vol. 2 (Antigua: CIRMA, 2004), 39.

14 Gould and Lauria, *To Rise in Darkness*, 99–131.

15 Salomé Torres, interview by author, El Cacao, Sonsonate, 2001.

16 Jeffrey L. Gould, *To Die in This Way: Nicaraguan Indians and the Myth of Mestizaje, 1880–1965* (Durham, NC: Duke University Press, 1998), 56–57.

17 Carlos Figueroa Ibarra, "El 'Bolchevique Mexicano' de la Centroamérica de los veinte" (interview with Jorge Fernández Anaya), *Memoria* 4, no. 31 (September–October 1990): 217.

18 Gobernador de Ahuachapán al ministro de Gobernación, 1892 and 1931, Archivo General de la Nación, El Salvador, Colección Gobernación.

19 Antonio Conte, *Treinta Años en Tierras Salvadoreñas*, vol. 2 (San Miguel: El Progreso, 1934), 190.

20 Conte, *Treinta Años*, 2:97.

21 Gould and Lauria, *To Rise in Darkness*, 109–10.

22 James Scott, *Domination and the Arts of Resistance: Hidden Transcripts* (New Haven, CT: Yale University Press, 1990).

23 Mario Appelius, *Le Terre Che Tremano* (Verona: A. Mondadori, 1929), 113–14. During the insurrection, Nahuizalco residents reported that the rebels shouted "Viva los indios de Nahuizalco!"

24 Sotero Linares, interview by author, Las Higueras, Izalco, 2001.

25 Fabián Mojica, interview by author, Sonzacate, 1999.

26 Andrés Pérez, interview by author, Pushtan, Nahuizalco, 2001.

27 Jeffrey L. Gould, "Revolutionary Nationalism and Local Memories in El Salvador," in *Reclaiming the Political in Latin American History: Essays from the North*, ed. Gilbert Joseph (Durham, NC: Duke University Press, 2001), 147–57.

28 See Gould and Lauria, *To Rise in Darkness*, 209–39.

29 *El Heraldo de Sonsonate*, August 13, 1932. It is extremely doubtful that Nahuatl was taught systematically at the school.

30 San Lucas had reportedly saved a leftist leader from execution and also saved the town.

31 Everett Wilson, *La Crisis de Integración Nacional en El Salvador, 1919–1935* (San Salvador: Concultura, 1935), 228–29. The regime gave out some three hundred housing lots in La Libertad and sixty *caballerías* (45 hectares) for the rural poor.

32 *Augusto C. Sandino: el Pensamiento Vivo*, vol. 1, ed. Sergio Ramirez (Managua: Editorial Nueva Nicaragua, 1981), 151, 168. See especially the important work of Michael Schroeder, "'To Defend Our Nation's Honor': Toward a Social and Cultural History of the Sandino Rebellion in Nicaragua, 1927–1934" (PhD diss., University of Michigan, 1993). Also see Volker Wunderich's work, for example, *Sandino en la Costa* (Managua: Editorial Nueva Nicaragua, 1989).

33 José Román, *Maldito País* (Managua: Ediciones la Pez y la Serpiente, 1983), 104.

34 See Gould, *To Lead as Equals*, 39.

35 Gould, *To Lead as Equals*. They shouted the slogan in conjunction with "Abajo O'Reardon," the manager whom they sought to replace with a pro-union employee. They also fought for a 50 percent raise. Ultimately Somoza did not directly support the strikers despite their strong support for him, and they lost.

36 See Gould, *To Die in This Way*, 181–92.

37 Christopher Lutz and George Lovell, "Core and Periphery in Colonial Guatemala," in *Guatemalan Indians and the State: 1540–1988*, ed. Carol A. Smith (Austin: University of Texas Press, 1990), 38–45.

38 Moreover, this divide also reflected a crucial distinction in the realm of spiritual conquest. The religious orders in the highlands, such as the Dominicans and Franciscans, generally more sensitive to indigenous culture, tended to work in the peripheral regions.

39 See especially Richard Adams's argument in "The Conquest Tradition of Mesoamerica," *The Americas*, October 1989, about how the distinct conquest traditions in Mesoamerica (e.g., Guatemala and western El Salvador), in turn related to the forms of preconquest settlement, shaped the development and survival of the indigenous populations.

40 Taracena, *Etnicidad, Estado y Nación*, 1:267–337.

41 Taracena, *Etnicidad, Estado y Nación*, 1:37–38.

42 Taracena, *Etnicidad, Estado y Nación*, 1:37–38.

43 David McCreery, *Rural Guatemala* (Stanford, CA: Stanford University Press, 1994), 326.

44 Ambassador Sheldon Whitehouse to the Secretary of State, July 29, 1930, U.S. State: 814.00/1014; July 31, 1930, U.S. State 814:00/1015.

45 Ambassador Sheldon Whitehouse to the Secretary of State, July 31, 1930, U.S. State 814:00/1015.

46 Figueroa Ibarra, "El 'Bolchevique Mexicano,'" 221.

47 Figueroa Ibarra, "El 'Bolchevique Mexicano,'" 221.

48 On organizing efforts among coffee workers in San Marcos during the early 1930s, see Cindy Forster, *The Time of Freedom: Campesino Workers in Guatemala's October Revolution* (Pittsburgh: University of Pittsburgh Press, 2001), 22–23.

49 Carlos Figueroa Ibarra, "Marxismo, Sociedad y Movimiento Sindical en Guatemala," *Anuario de Estudios Centroamericanos* 16, no. 1 (1990): 77–78.

50 Robert Carmack, *Rebels of Highland Guatemala: The Quiche-Maya of Momostenango* (Norman: University of Oklahoma Press, 1995), 193.

51 Victor Bulmer-Thomas, "La Crisis de la Economía de Agroexportación (1930–1945)," in *Historia General de Centroamerica*, vol. 4, *Las Repúblicas Agroexportadoras*, ed. Víctor Hugo Acuña Ortega (Madrid: FLACSO, 1993), 367. Chester Jones, *Guatemala: Past and Present* (Minneapolis: University of Minnesota Press, 1940), 162, notes the objection of the International Labor Conference in Geneva in 1932 to the existing laws.

52 David McCreery, "Wage Labor, Free Labor, and Vagrancy Laws: The Tran-

sition to Capitalism in Guatemala, 1920–1945," in *Coffee, Society and Power in Latin America*, ed. William Roseberry, Lowell Gudmundson, and Mario Samper (Baltimore: Johns Hopkins University Press, 1995), 223.

53 Bulmer-Thomas, "Central America during the Inter-War Period," 259–62.

54 Letter from Ambassador Fay Allen Des Portes to the Secretary of State, August 17, 1936, U.S. State Dept. 814.504/33.

55 Forster, *Time of Freedom*, 80–81, 138–41. Also see Jones, *Guatemala: Past and Present*, 165. Jones notes one form of passive resistance, claiming a status as *comerciante* since only agricultural labor was affected by the law. He also suggests that the law led to an increase in rural wages.

56 "Populist political style" does not imply populist discourses or policies characteristic of Perón or even Somoza, but rather a nonelite style of political campaigning.

57 See Jorge Ramón González Ponciano, "La visible invisibilidad de la blancura y el ladino como no blanco en Guatemala," in Euraque, Gould, and Hale, *Memorias del Mestizaje*, 111–32; Arturo Taracena, "Guatemala: El debate historiográfico en torno al *mestizaje*, 1970–2000," in Euraque, Gould, and Hale, *Memorias del Mestizaje*, 79–110.

58 See the documentary film *Los Civilizadores: Alemanes en Guatemala*, directed by Uli Stelzner (Germany, 1998).

59 Gould and Lauria, *To Rise in Darkness*, 209–61. Also see work by Patricia Alvarenga, "Los Indígenas y el Estado: Alianzas y estrategias políticas en la construcción del poder local en El Salvador, 1920–1944," in Euraque, Gould, and Hale, *Memorias del Mestizaje*, 388–91; Erik Ching and Virginia Tilley, "The Indians, the Military, and the Rebellion of 1932 in El Salvador," in *Journal of Latin American Studies* 30, no. 1 (1998): 121–56.

60 Sergio Tischler Visquerra, *Guatemala 1944: Crisis y Revolución* (Guatemala: Universidad de San Carlos, 1998), 251.

61 See Charles R. Hale, *Mas Que un Indio: Racial Ambivalence and Neoliberal Multiculturalism in Guatemala* (Santa Fe, NM: School of American Research, 2006), 146–47. Hale notes that the memories of supposed indigenous licentiousness and barbarity enter a realm of atavistic fears at the core of what he calls the ladino "political imaginary." The political imaginary refers to "thoughts, premises, and images that are set apart from the explicit analytical and sensory realms, though potentially present in both." For Hale, this imaginary has long shaped ladino responses to indigenous movements.

62 Forster, *Time of Freedom*, 76–81.

63 Patricia Alvarenga, "Los Indígenas y el Estado: Alianzas y estrategias políticas en la construcción del poder local en El Salvador, 1920–1944," in Euraque, Gould, and Hale, *Memorias del Mestizaje*, 388–91.

64 See Gould, *To Die in This Way*, 245–66.

CHAPTER 8

The Character and Consequences
of the Great Depression in Mexico
Alan Knight

It is a roughly consensual and—more importantly—correct view that the
evolution of Mexico's political economy during the 1930s was the product
of two intersecting forces, one endogenous and one exogenous: the Revolution and the Great Depression. The comingling of these two causal streams
(apologies for the abrupt change of metaphor) created the distinct political
economy of the decade, an important part of which was the administration/
project/ideology loosely known as Cardenismo.[1] However, even this consensual formulation demands serious clarification, since the two streams,
the Revolution and the Depression, are themselves fearfully complicated
(and the subject of a good deal of lively debate).[2] Also, the endogenous/
exogenous distinction is by no means clear-cut, particularly for those who
choose to see the Revolution itself as the product of foreign penetration,
oppression, instigation, or manipulation.[3] Since I do not share that view, I
consider the endogenous/exogenous distinction as analytically useful, even
if it is not watertight (in which respect, of course, it resembles a vast number of historical and social-scientific concepts).

Furthermore, it is particularly useful in the context of this book, as we
compare different countries in Latin America. Since Mexico alone experienced a major social revolution in the early twentieth century, its historical
experience was, in that sense, unique; and, to the extent that the Revolution had an economic dimension, which it did (it was not just a narrowly
political revolution), there is a revolutionary economic story to be told, a
story that is in a number of ways distinct within the continent. In this respect, the comparison between Mexico and the rest of Latin America is an
exercise in contrast that, in particular, involves Mexican policy responses.
On the other hand, as an international phenomenon whose causes lay be-

yond Mexico and therefore affected all of Latin America, the Great Depression presented common threats and challenges, in which respect Mexico and Latin America—or, more strictly, some countries, regions, or sectors in Latin America—are suitable for comparison.[4] The similarities are more evident, I would argue, in terms of prior economic structures (exports, manufacturing, subsistence agriculture, etc.) and the way that the (exogenous) force of the Depression impacted upon them. When it comes to policy, Mexico appears more peculiar.

If I rejig my earlier hydraulic metaphor, the scenario could be sketched in these terms: in 1929 an earthquake on Wall Street (followed by further serious tremors in Europe in 1931) launched a tidal wave across Latin America. The different countries—and regions and sectors—withstood the battering to different degrees, depending on their particular topography. Low-lying islands were swamped; some high ground survived and, over time, may even have benefited from the fortuitous rearrangement of the coastline. Thus, the first task is to trace that economic topography, which was in many ways a structural given. However, the human reaction to inundation also counted, so we must secondly consider policy responses—which takes us away from structural (economic) givens and toward more voluntaristic (political) decisions. In the Mexican case, these decisions were sometimes (but not always) distinctive by virtue of being "revolutionary," being made by "revolutionaries" who were running a "revolutionary" state, and experimenting with "revolutionary" policies.

The analytical payoff of this exercise is twofold. On the one hand, an examination of the Mexican case can help us formulate general conclusions about the Depression (both impact and responses) in Latin America as a whole.[5] However, as a Mexicanist, I would stress a different, perhaps more original, benefit. Evaluations of the Mexican Revolution—which, of course, came thick and fast in 2010, the year of the centenary—are often couched in narrow, even nationalistic, terms. By that I mean not that the Revolution is deliriously celebrated (in fact, delirious celebration was notably absent in 2010, especially in official circles), but rather that it is examined in isolation, with scant reference to other Latin American countries (or others in the world for that matter).[6] Often this may not matter, but any general survey of the Revolution, especially one that purports to address both causality and consequences, requires yardsticks for comparison, and useful yardsticks can often be found in Latin America. After all, most of the usually cited causes of the Revolution (authoritarian government, political centralization, land concentration, declining real wages, economic recession, the rise of cities and the middle class) are to be found elsewhere in Latin America in this period, but they did not produce social revolutions. Furthermore, regarding outcome, Mexicanists must be careful not to assume that all post-1910 (or post-1917, or post-1920) processes were necessarily products of the thaumaturgical power of the Revolution, since some—such as increased literacy, urbanization, unionization, industrialization, and consumerism—are also to be found elsewhere in Latin America, where no such thaumaturgical power was at work. The Mexico/rest of Latin America comparison, therefore, should at least help Mexicanists sort out what is genuinely revolutionary and what is not, thus avoiding the old historiographical fallacy of *post hoc ergo propter hoc*, of attributing to the Revolution, the endogenous force, causal power that either came from outside (exogenously) or represented long-term trends, whether endo- or exogenous, predating the Revolution of 1910.

So what follows divides fairly neatly into (1) the impact of the Depression (which requires an early 1930s focus and stresses socioeconomic structures) and (2) the policy responses of the Mexican revolutionary government—a story of "agency," which I further divide into (a) short-term responses, relating to economic management, and (b) medium-term policies, which involve social and economic reform. This story takes us into the later 1930s and—as I note in conclusion—even beyond.

If the Wall Street Crash signaled the start of the Depression, there were clear premonitions—or structural weaknesses, if you prefer—in Mexico prior to 1930, as there were in other primary-producing economies in Latin America and the world.[7] Having recovered fairly briskly from the economic (and demographic) trauma of the armed revolution—by 1920 GDP had surpassed 1910 levels—Mexico weathered the severe postwar recession of 1920–21 and resumed a trajectory of respectable growth through the mid-1920s.[8] The regime was now more stable, the serious military rebellion of 1923 having been defeated; government finances were on a surer footing; and, under the ruthless but statesmanlike President Calles (1924–28), the regime embarked on a series of institutional and infrastructural reforms (the creation of a central bank, of national irrigation and road commissions, and of an extensive labor arbitration system).[9] Externally, Mexico made efforts to resume foreign debt payments, but these proved short-lived and vulnerable to the vicissitudes of external trade, which still provided the bulk of government revenue (and, of course, foreign exchange).[10] Since defaulting in 1913, Mexico, unlike most Latin American countries, had no access to foreign credit; therefore, it sat out the 1920s "dance of the millions" (which, in light of events in the 1930s, was probably a good thing). Foreign direct investment did not, however, dry up. It took a hit from the Revolution and the decline of the oil industry after 1921, but even as oil declined and mining leveled out, fresh investment in banking and manufacturing, now overwhelmingly American, flowed into Mexico.[11]

Meanwhile, the structure of foreign trade was not "revolutionized" by the Revolution; Mexico remained an exporter of primary products, especially minerals. This relative continuity in terms of Mexico's foreign trade, rightly stressed by recent economic historians, did not mean, however, that the Revolution, prior to the 1930s, lacked an economic dimension.[12] It is true that the more eye-catching change was political: the replacement of the old narrowly based, oligarchic, authoritarian and personalist Porfirian regime with a more broadly based, popular, populist and nationalist regime, staffed by parvenu politicos, many of whom had risen through the ranks of the revolutionary army, and who, whether for reasons of idealism or Realpolitik, sought to forge alliances with the new mass organizations of workers and peasants. The nature of the new regime—by definition a political matter—would over time have important economic consequences, especially after 1930, but we should note that, in more strictly economic terms too, the Revolution had already had economic consequences, even if these were less obvious. The structure of foreign trade remained broadly the same, but the flow of foreign investment changed, as direct private investment diminished and, to an extent, changed course, from mining to manufacturing, while, as already mentioned, lending to the Mexican government halted altogether. Internally, there was a substantial, if often informal, shift in class relations, a shift that some revisionist histories of the Revolution have chosen to overlook or seriously underestimate. Though official land reform was limited and piecemeal (outside, for example, the Zapatista state of Morelos, where it was rapid and sweeping), the effects of both actual and potential land distribution were significant; a good many landlords had gone bust or fallen on hard times; and peasants, many now possessed of both collective organization and available weaponry, could press their cause in ways that had been unimaginable just a decade before. In the industrial sector, too, the precocious and rapid rise of labor unions represented a sharp departure from the late Porfiriato (when workers had been mown down at Cananea and Río Blanco); and, alongside the more cautious labor reformism (evident under Madero and greatly accelerated by Obregón and Calles, again for reasons of both idealism and, more likely, Realpolitik), there existed a more radical grassroots militancy, notable, for example, in the textile industry — what Jeffrey Bortz has called the "revolution within the revolution."[13] Necessarily, I would argue, a substantial political revolution carried social and economic consequences, but the latter were much more evident domestically (for example, in industrial and agrarian class relations) than externally, with respect to foreign trade and investment. When foreign observers denounced Mexican "Bolshevism," they were usually thinking (if they were thinking at all) of uppity workers and peasants and the encouragement they received from demagogic politicos; in fact, with the important exception of the oil companies, they had relatively little to complain about concerning Mexico's external trade relations or treatment of foreign interests per se.[14] Nevertheless, "Bolshevism" was, within Latin America, a largely Mexican phenomenon, hence the concern that Mexico might export the contagion to hitherto safe and sound regions like Central America.[15]

If this was the general panorama, two conjunctural features of the later 1920s should be mentioned, one global, one peculiar to Mexico. During the later 1920s, the terms of trade disadvantaged primary producers; a major cause appears to have been the distortions created by the First World War that led to overproduction of primary products, notably wheat, sugar, and some nonprecious minerals.[16] One consequence was a revival of agricultural protectionism, evident in the disastrous Smoot-Hawley Tariff of 1930.[17] In Mexico, meanwhile, Calles blundered into the Cristero War (1926–29), which ravaged the center-west of the country, while driving up government expenditure on the military (which, because of the legacy of the Revolution, was already high).[18] By 1927 the Mexican economy had stalled; the Cristero War was raging; the government faced a deficit; and conflicts over oil, anticlericalism, and Central America soured U.S.-Mexican relations. The United States, now represented in Mexico by the suave and shrewd banker Dwight Morrow, opted for conciliation; and Calles, too, responded pragmatically, even conservatively. Though he could not end the Cristero War, his immediate successor, interim president Portes Gil, did so, in 1929; meanwhile, Calles and Morrow got along well, the oil dispute was diplomatically fudged, and a renewed effort was made to resume foreign debt payments.[19] Domestically, Calles reined in the land reform, pronouncing it a costly failure (President Ortiz Rubio, in 1930, effectively declared it dead); the state also restrained organized labor and cracked down on the (fairly minor)

Communist Party.[20] Foreign observers applauded the newfound moderation of the "Bolshevik" Calles.[21]

Thus, by 1930, when Ortiz Rubio assumed the presidency, as the first elected candidate of the new "official" revolutionary party, Mexican politics was tending to track to the right; the early promises of the Revolution, patchily implemented during the 1920s, seemed to be losing their allure; and, after a brief lull following the end of the Cristero War in 1929, the state—still informally controlled by *jefe máximo* Calles—resumed its onslaught on the Catholic Church in the early 1930s. In Mexico, as in the United States, changing mentalities remained a higher priority than changing the mode of production.

The onset of the Great Depression changed all that. We cannot explore the counterfactual scenario with any confidence, but it seems plausible that, if the Wall Street Crash and the Depression had been averted, the current course of Mexican political and economic evolution would have continued, in the direction of broadly pro-business policy, the "diplomacy of ham and eggs," and an official emphasis on cultural rather than economic policy (thus, anticlericalism rather than land and labor reform).[22] In blunt terms, Mexico would have remained in Callista rather than Cardenista mode. But in Mexico, as in the United States, the Depression brought a radical shift: from Hoover to FDR and—perhaps even more consequentially—from Calles to Cárdenas.

That shift related largely to domestic policy; and, of course, Cárdenas did not take office until the end of 1934. The first task, therefore, is to examine the impact of the Depression, as it struck an economy already suffering from several years of sluggish growth. And here I can follow, in large measure, the excellent analysis of Enrique Cárdenas (no relation, by the way).[23] Since, as I have said, "the Depression" is a complex phenomenon, some disaggregation is needed. I shall look first at the decline of foreign trade and its consequences in Mexico, including labor, welfare, and government finances. Then I shall address short-term government reactions (particularly with respect to budgetary and monetary policy). Finally, this will lead to a broader discussion of social and political consequences, involving both "bottom-up" protest and mobilization and "top-down" regime responses.[24] At the outset, Mexico appears as a victim of exogenous shocks (and here comparison with the rest of Latin America is important, by way of evaluating the scale and character of the shocks); however, as we weave our way through short-term government reactions and longer-term sociopolitical consequences, we see a more creative Mexico, displaying—to use the cliché—collective agency, and, within Latin America, a sometimes distinctive and successful collective agency.

Mexico was "hit early and hard" by the Depression, chiefly because of its close relationship with the United States, where the slump was sudden, severe, and prolonged.[25] Thus, one distinctly Mexican experience was the repatriation of over 300,000 migrant workers from the United States.[26] Of course, other Latin American countries experienced flows of labor migration (and consequent social tensions: for example, Cuba and the Dominican Republic), but in Mexico the scale was greater.[27] Between 1928 and 1932, too, the value of exports fell by 63 percent (more than, say, Brazil [44 percent] or Argentina [40 percent], but less than Chile [83 percent]).[28] On the other hand, exports provided a smaller share of GDP in Mexico than in Argentina or Chile (12 percent compared to 27 percent and 30 percent respectively), and Mexico also had good fortune in the famous "commodity lottery."[29] First, Mexico did not depend excessively on a single volatile export; second, Mexico's diverse export basket included two primary commodities that rode out the Depression rather better than others: silver and oil.[30] Silver was still Mexico's biggest single export, but whereas industrial minerals—such as copper—were hard-hit, silver benefited from its role as potential coinage, as well as from U.S. efforts to maintain silver prices to the advantage of U.S. producers in the West.[31] Mexico could thus piggyback on American price supports (rather as Colombia could benefit from Brazilian efforts to support the price of coffee). Oil prices were globally sustained by robust demand, the product of the automobile revolution; and while Mexican oil production had declined after the heady peak of 1921, there was a modest revival in the 1930s, thanks largely to the Aguila Company's Poza Rica strike.[32]

Furthermore, as Cárdenas shows, the nature of the export sector's linkages with the rest of the economy served as a shock absorber. Neither silver nor oil was a labor-intensive industry; thus, a fall in foreign earnings did not translate into a sharp drop in income (the obvious comparisons would be Brazilian coffee or Cuban sugar).[33] Similarly, the "enclave" character of these two industries meant that a fall in exports did not produce a dramatic fall in demand within Mexico.[34] Thus, two happy circumstances combined: the fall in exports, though sharp, was not as extreme or as prolonged as in some Latin American cases; and the effects of the fall were limited by the lack of linkages, again as compared to other cases. The reverse side of the enclave coin, we might say, was Mexico's large subsistence sector. In 1930 two-thirds of the population lived in communities of less than 2,500, and 69 percent of the economically active population worked in agriculture.[35] Commercial agriculture—coffee, henequen, cotton—suffered from the Depression, but subsistence agriculture remained partially insulated from the vicissitudes of the business cycle.[36] Surplus workers—their numbers increased by the 300,000 returning from the United States—could to some extent be absorbed in the subsistence sector (they could, it was said, "go back to the *quelite*"), returning to the 70,000 villages scattered across the face of the country where—in the absence of state social security systems—local and family self-help remained the principal source of welfare.[37] Of course, the subsistence sector was vulnerable to a quite different kind of shock: climatic conditions, including frosts, floods, and droughts, which were an ancient feature of Mexican rain-fed agriculture and which were still crucial in the 1920s and 1930s. It so happened that, regarding the basic staple of corn, 1929 and 1930 were bad years, which necessitated compensating imports; but the early 1930s were much better.[38]

Thus, perhaps for the last time in its long history, rural Mexico served as a sponge to soak up unemployment and compensate for the downswing in the urban, industrial, export economy.[39] Mexico possessed one final structural advantage in the face of depression: a reasonably developed industrial base, catering chiefly to domestic demand for consumer goods (in particular textiles). As export earnings (and, with them, the value of the peso) fell, the country's capacity to import declined, to the advantage of domestic industry. Initially, of course, depressed demand hit consumer industries (textiles, beer, cigarettes), while producer goods (such as steel and cement) were less affected; however, after 1932, as domestic demand recovered, Mexico underwent a significant process of import substitution, and manufacturing industry became the chief motor of growth.[40] In this respect, Mexico differed sharply from the United States: structurally, Mexico was poised to exploit the (industrializing, import-substituting) opportunities afforded by the Depression, while the United States stood at a different (more advanced) point in its economic trajectory, which made it vulnerable to prolonged recession.[41] In the United States, the business cycle and the long-term trend combined to produce unemployment and deflation; in Mexico, the trend (incipient industrialization) was accelerated by the cyclical downturn.

All the effects of the Depression mentioned thus far related to structural features of the Mexican economy; they were, we could say, "regime-blind," politically neutral. As a result, comparisons with other Latin American economies can be made with some confidence: Mexico was vulnerable because of its dependence on the United States, although, with respect to silver purchases, this dependence proved advantageous, as did Mexico's fortunes in the "commodity lottery" (compared, say, to Chile's). The enclave-like character of the export sector (mining and oil), coupled with the size of the subsistence sector, cushioned the economy against exogenous shocks (even when they involved a large repatriation of Mexican migrant workers). In this respect, Mexico resembled peasant/agrarian economies like Peru; however, unlike them, and more like Argentina and Brazil, Mexico had a substantial industrial base that could rapidly crank up import substitution production.[42]

So far, so structural. Not a single human, not a single purposive policy, has been mentioned. Now let me turn to government reactions to the Depression. These fall under two chief headings. The first, short-term, perhaps "tactical" responses relate to monetary and fiscal policy. Here, again, Mexico grappled with problems that, mutatis mutandis, were evident elsewhere in Latin America; however, there is now some indication of a heterodox approach, perhaps the product of "revolutionary" thinking. Even more clearly, the second set of medium-term responses, socioeconomic and, perhaps, "strategic," are strongly influenced by Mexico's distinctive revolutionary stance (hence, within Latin America, they stand out as unusual). These relate to three areas of policy: land reform, labor reform, and economic nationalism.

As the Latin American country with the closest economic relations with the United States (perhaps bar Cuba), Mexico rapidly felt the impact of the U.S. recession, which, as I have said, came on the heels of several years of relative economic stagnation in Mexico. Export earnings fell by over 60 percent, but—for the reasons already suggested—GDP fell by only (!) 18 percent.[43] Government income, still heavily dependent on foreign trade, dropped by 34 percent.[44] In response, the Ortiz Rubio administration—a weak administration, headed by a puppet president, reluctantly beholden to the *jefe máximo*, Calles—adopted orthodox, pro-cyclical policies. Between 1929 and 1932 government spending was cut by 23 percent; in consequence, Mexico did not run a deficit, but contrived substantial surpluses in 1930 and 1931 and a balanced budget in 1932 (deficits occurred in 1933 and 1936–40, as will be seen).[45] Mexico effectively quit the gold standard in July 1931 but, for several months, strove to retain a link to gold, which had a strongly deflationary—an "asphixiating"—effect; between 1929 and 1931 the money supply declined by 60 percent.[46] In this respect, the Ortiz Rubio/Calles administration emulated the "orthodox" policies evident in most countries: in the face of recession, governments clung doggedly to gold, slashed public expenditure, and strove to balance budgets.[47] In so doing, it is clear, they aggravated the problem.

However, Mexico made a rapid switch to heterodox policies in early 1932. The change came with the return of Alberto J. Pani—then Mexican ambassador to Spain—to the Ministry of Finance (Hacienda) early in 1932.[48] Pani, from a well-to-do family that had fallen on (somewhat) hard times as a result of the Revolution (which he had supported), was highly educated, cultured, and endowed with a "million-dollar smile" and "a particular fondness for oil paintings."[49] He was also a leading "revolutionary" politico-técnico; he had served as minister of industry and commerce under Carranza, in the desperate years 1917–18, as foreign minister in 1921–23, and as minister of finance in 1923–27, until a bizarre—and possibly contrived—sexual scandal cost him his job.[50] As finance minister in the mid-1920s—under President Calles—he had embarked on a series of financial and economic reforms that, he alleged, his more conservative successor, Montes de Oca, then foolishly abandoned.[51] Pani traveled from Madrid to Mexico, clear about the new direction he would follow: in part a revival of his old project, in part a response—and, he stressed, a rapid response—to the current problems provoked by the Depression.[52] In the course of 1932 Pani, with Calles's support, definitively took Mexico off the gold standard, boosted the supply of silver pesos, and used Mexico's accumulating silver reserve as a basis for a new issue of paper currency. The Montes de Oca-Lamont agreement on foreign debt repayments, which Pani considered a further disastrous deflationary measure, was allowed to lapse.[53] Pani also fortified the Banco de Mexico, turning it into a functioning central bank at the heart of the banking system. The money supply grew rapidly, yet there were no immediately inflationary effects. Credit became more abundant, and the peso stabilized. In the course of 1932, therefore, the Mexican economy bottomed out and began a rapid recovery.[54] Pani's reflationary policies were not the sole reason, of course; the structural factors previously mentioned also played a part. But, together, they produced a rapid and sustained recovery, which contrasted with the more sluggish performance of the U.S. economy and of several major Latin American economies.[55]

Two aspects of Pani's policies are of particular interest—although, since they have not, to my knowledge, been systematically researched, there are no clear-cut answers. First, how and why did Pani hit upon these presciently Keynesian policies (expanding the money supply and enabling the government to increase public spending)?[56] He was clearly a smart, if arrogant, and highly experienced politico-financier. But then so were many of the architects of the Great Depression, such as Montague Norman and Josiah Strong, who clung doggedly to orthodox pro-cyclical policies.[57] As ambassador to France and Spain in 1927–31, Pani had firsthand knowledge of events in Europe, which no doubt widened his already-broad horizons. During this time, he had clearly been thinking carefully about Mexico's deteriorating economy (hence his long missives to Calles in 1931), and so, on returning to office, he was poised to act. Mexico's financial circumstances were also highly relevant. As a result of the Revolution (and Pani, though he stood on the right of the "revolutionary family," was a genuine revolutionary veteran), Mexico had been cut off from foreign credit since 1914, and efforts to repay both the foreign debt and the foreign claims for revolutionary damages had largely failed—owing to lack of commitment, the disgruntled foreign creditors claimed. Pani himself consigned the latest short-lived agreement to the rubbish bin. As a result, Mexico had no foreign credit and—unlike, say, Argentina, long schooled in the virtues of sound finance—felt less obligation to service its foreign debt (or to meet other obligations, such as inflated foreign claims for revolutionary damages).[58] Not only did this save money, but it also made Mexico less vulnerable to peso devaluations, since the dollar-denominated foreign debt had been effectively shelved.[59] More broadly, we could hypothesize that the financial upheaval of the Revolution made policy makers like Pani more creative and less risk averse. Postrevolutionary Mexico was condemned to be unorthodox, so why not make a virtue of unorthodoxy?

The second interesting feature of Mexican Keynesianism was the rapid and, it seems, smooth switch to paper currency. During the Revolution, Mexico had drowned in a polychromatic tide of paper money, churned out by rival governments and factions.[60] By 1916 paper money had lost all value and transactions—if they were not on a barter basis—required dollars or scarce silver pesos. As the economy revived in the early 1920s, silver pesos returned to circulation, but they provided an insufficient money supply, while paper banknotes were almost nonexistent. Pani therefore sought to reflate the economy by issuing notes, on the basis of silver reserves; as a result, the money supply at the end of 1932 was 31 percent greater than it had been a year before, and the ratio of coins to notes stood at 47:11. By 1936 the money supply had grown by a further 76 percent, and the ratio now stood at 28:38.[61] The new paper pesos were, it seems, widely accepted (unlike some previous monetary issues in Mexican history, which had generated serious protests).[62] Why, given the hyperinflation of the 1910s and the suspicion of paper money that ensued, did Mexicans readily return to banknotes?[63] Why does this significant conversion to paper money scarcely show up in the standard histories and—perhaps even more surprisingly—in local anthropological accounts?[64] The logical answer must be that it was not hugely contentious. Since such acceptance depends on confidence, it seems likely that there was sufficient confidence in (1) the Banco de México's reserves, which underwrote the paper issue; (2) the stability and coherence of the government (paper pesos were used to pay public employees and were obligatory for the payment of government bills); and (3) the newfound vigor of the Mexican economy, which generated not only consumer and investment confidence but also a strong demand for pesos.[65] It also seems likely that, while small-denomination coins were still used for petty transactions—for example, in the bustling markets of Oaxaca or Michoacan—the new notes fueled the burgeoning urban and commercial economy.[66] Peasants and day laborers did not go around with piles of silver pesos jingling in the pockets of their baggy cotton trousers; hence, we might assume, a switch from silver to paper did not immediately affect many of the population in terms of their daily transactions.[67] Whatever the cause(s), the apparently smooth acceptance of paper money was a tacit vote of confidence in the regime, a conspicuously ignored tribute to its growing stability and even legitimacy.

Irrespective of causes, the switch to paper succeeded. Beginning in 1932, Mexico experienced four years of rapid growth (and low inflation), which in turn boosted government income and facilitated the ambitious reforms of the mid-1930s; despite a minor recession in 1937, and further troubles occasioned by the oil expropriation of 1938 and the onset of the Second World War, the economy bounced back in 1939–40.[68] Inflation now became a more serious—though by no means a massive—problem. However, the Mexican state possessed the proven will and capacity to engage in countercyclical policy, without lurching—as some have alleged—into irresponsible "economic populism."[69] Thus, Mexico's economic performance throughout the "depression decade" was, by international standards, positive and sustained. Compared to its Latin American peers, it did better than Argentina and Uruguay, and about as well as Brazil, where, we might note, countercyclical "proto-Keynesian" policy also flourished, although perhaps for rather different reasons.[70] Clearly, the fact of a "revolutionary" regime could not, of itself, work economic miracles; growth required investment, which, in turn, depended on a measure of business confidence; the revolutionary state therefore had to strike a balance between, on the one hand, social reforms and popular legitimation and, on the other, maintaining that confidence within what was still a largely market/capitalist economy, located on the doorstep of the world's biggest market/capitalist country.[71] The trade-off between, as it is sometimes called, "legitimation" and "accumulation" is, of course, a feature of all capitalist societies and regimes, but it is particularly acute in those that claim a revolutionary origin and have to respond to vocal popular demands. Note, for example, the decline and fall of the Bolivian revolutionary regime of the 1950s—a regime that, in the eyes of historical actors and analysts alike, bears comparison with revolutionary Mexico.[72] It is these domestic demands and outcomes that, in conclusion, I now address.

Mexico's socioeconomic reforms in the 1930s were unusual within the Latin American context. In order of "unusualness," we could list three main items: land reform, labor reform, and economic nationalism. The first was, for a Latin American country, both unusual and unprecedented; no other country emulated the Cardenista reparto until the 1950s, when Bolivia made a more tepid attempt and Cuba embarked on a more radical socialist and collectivist experiment. For the 1930s, therefore, the Mexican agrarian reform was highly unusual, and while the Depression gave it definite impetus, its origins were clearly revolutionary and thus peculiar to Mexico. The story, though crucial, is well known and can be quickly summarized. Land hunger had fueled the popular revolution of 1910, and after the 1917 Constitution (Article 27) had created a formal commitment to agrarian reform, a long, complicated, and at times violent struggle ensued, as *agraristas* battled for their rights and landlords and their conservative political allies resisted. During the 1920s, a piecemeal reparto took place—much more sweeping and radical in some states than others—and, in consequence, agriculture suffered from sustained tension and uncertainty.[73] By 1930, when Calles and his puppet president Ortiz Rubio began to halt the reparto, some 673,000 *ejidatarios* had received land; these constituted perhaps 20 percent of the economically active population in agriculture and generated 11 percent of agricultural output.[74] This initial reparto was sufficient to weaken and worry the landlord class, but not to satisfy pent-up peasant demands. Some observers therefore advocated an immediate end to land reform; others called for a rapid and radical acceleration. The result, as Eyler Simpson expertly showed, was an impasse, which satisfied neither side (and this, we might add, was a zero-sum game in which it was impossible for both sides to emerge as winners).[75]

The onset of the Depression prompted a renewed reparto for several reasons. Unemployment, declining real wages, and the mass repatriation of Mexican workers from the United States contributed to mounting misery and social tension.[76] De facto land seizures occurred in defiance of government policy: in Tamaulipas, for example, the official view was that "further agrarian dotations will not be made," but, not for the first or last time in Mexican history, formal policy diverged from informal practice; hence, in late 1931 an observer commented on "the continued presence of agraristas (in some cases armed) whose petitions for ejidos have been refused, but whom the proper authorities either cannot or will not forcibly eject from the lands where they have taken up squatters' rights."[77] Whether for reasons of disinterested idealism (and, though it is historiographically unfashionable, we should grant some of the revolutionary leadership their idealistic inclinations) or because of baser political motives (the desire to defuse social tensions, while building a political base among the ejidatarios), politicos now saw greater advantages in espousing the agrarista cause. In some cases, such as Cárdenas, we can detect a measure of idealism; in others, Realpolitik—an opportunistic decision to board the agrarista bandwagon—probably predominated.[78] This was particularly clear as Cárdenas, the new president, squared up to his old mentor, Calles, in 1935/36: agrarismo was a proud badge of Cardenismo, a means to elicit presidential favor and popular support.

Furthermore, the landlord class, weakened through the 1920s, was now in straitened circumstances, as foreign markets dried up and agricultural prices fell. Some went bust, and few were prepared to put up the kind of vigorous (in her case, suicidal) resistance to agrarianism that Rosalie Evans had mounted in the 1920s.[79] Hence, some of the Laguna cotton planters succumbed to the great reparto of 1936 in a spirit of resigned stoicism. Others, like William Jenkins, the sugar baron of Atencingo, rolled with the punch; effected a controlled, top-down reparto; and salvaged their fortunes, at the expense of surrendering their sprawling landholdings.[80] Thus, one important consequence of the 1930s land reform was a marked shift of capital and entrepreneurship from agriculture to industry and services. Far from destroying capitalism, land reform (of the Mexican kind) potentially benefited it. Indeed, this was appreciated by percipient politicos at the time. It is important to note that the renewed commitment to land reform preceded Cárdenas's inauguration. Cárdenas, a true believer, greatly accelerated and radicalized the reparto, personally pushing it forward, espousing the new collective ejido, and, in doing so, stimulating further agrarian demands and mobilization.[81] But his predecessor, the much more conservative and pro-business president Abelardo Rodríguez, had already signaled a shift in policy, particularly with the new Agrarian Code of 1934, which enabled hacienda peons to petition for land for the first time.[82] Rodríguez no doubt wished to dampen social tensions, but, as a canny businessman, he was also acutely conscious of the weakness of Mexico's domestic market, both structurally and contingently: a controlled land reform, especially at a time when agriculture was depressed, would boost domestic purchasing power to the advantage of Mexican industry.[83] And industry was the most dynamic sector of the economy, the motor that would power Mexico out of recession and into the sunlit uplands of prosperity.

Land reform was the most important item of government policy in the 1930s, affecting the majority of the population and thus the entire economy. Its results have been hotly debated. Where ejidos produced profitable crops and received adequate government support (credit, training, education), they were successful: the classic case would be the Laguna. Where they had to deal with flagging markets, an indifferent (or hard-up) government, and a hostile local environment, as in Yucatán, they were much less successful. Overall, the land reform was a political success but a mixed economic story. Above all, once Cárdenas left office, its fortunes fast declined. By the 1940s agrarianism was unfashionable and underfunded; increasingly, it became a populist official stratagem rather than a radical project for the socioeconomic transformation of society.

A somewhat similar story unfolded with respect to labor reform: that is, the recognition of trade union rights, wage hikes, and other benefits. These were not peculiar to Mexico, since, during the 1930s, we encounter ostensibly pro-labor policies elsewhere: with Vargas in Brazil, Batista in Cuba, and even Somoza in Nicaragua.[84] But the Mexican variant was more radical, since Mexican unions had emerged from the Revolution with precocious vigor; thus, within the (minority) unionized sector, demands not just for higher wages (monetary and "social") but also for substantial powers to hire and fire, which crimped managerial autonomy and thus alarmed business, became commonplace. Again, the Depression greatly accelerated a prior ("revolutionary") process, and that process meant that the Mexican version of 1930s labor reform would be unusually militant by Latin American standards.

Again, therefore, the Depression catalyzed previous socioeconomic demands. The Confederacíon Regional Obrera Mexicana (CROM), the dominant labor confederation of the 1920s, whose fortunes had slumped after the assassination of Obregón in 1928, was supplanted by the more radical Confederacíon de Trabajadores de México (CTM), whose official slogan advocated "a classless society" (competition between the two continued to provoke serious violence during the 1930s, chiefly in the textile towns of Veracruz).[85] Domestic political factors thus conspired with the Depression to bring about this shift in labor organization and ideology.[86] Greater labor militancy became evident soon after 1930; official strike figures, which reflect government policy as much as grassroots activism, are, in this sense, misleading, since they fail to grasp the upswell of militancy, for example, in the crucial mining sector.[87] However, official figures do suggest how, from late 1934, the incoming Cárdenas administration gave the green light for strike action and, to the alarm of both business and the urban middle class, strikes came thick and fast in 1935.[88] The battle for power between Calles and Cárdenas accelerated this process. To a greater extent than in other Latin American countries, therefore, labor organized, mobilized, and made substantial gains, with respect to not only wages (monetary and "social") but also union power, which, in some key industries, like oil, trespassed on managerial prerogatives, while also achieving substantial political leverage.[89] At the same time, labor unions forged close ties with peasant organizations, playing an important role in rural mobilization, for example, in the Laguna.[90]

Again, therefore, the prior experience of the Revolution, which had engendered an unusually militant labor movement, gave the Mexican response to the Depression an unusually radical edge. We should also note that, even before Cárdenas assumed the presidency, official policy had shifted in a (moderate) pro-labor direction. The old alliance between the state and the labor unions had been well established, under the auspices of Calles and Morones, in the 1920s; hence, in terms of labor as well as agrarianism, the 1930s saw a radical reformulation of the *political* status quo ante, prompted in large measure by the stresses of the Depression. But there was also an *economic* rationale, and, as in the case of land reform, there were clear intimations of economic laborism (as well as economic agrarianism) prior to December 1934. The new Federal Labour Law, designed to achieve greater central regulation of labor relations, was promulgated in 1931, at the depth of the Depression. It set up a nationwide system of tripartite labor arbitration, which would avert conflicts and boost wages; soon after, President Rodríguez took steps to raise and enforce the minimum wage, in a deliberate attempt to bolster domestic purchasing power. Though a successful businessman himself, he judged that firms could pay higher wages, and that higher wages would boost demand and, in turn, benefit business.[91] Again, Cárdenas radicalized and extended an existing policy, introducing a paid seventh day (in effect, a 17 percent pay raise), while supporting, conditionally at least, trade union demands for better pay and conditions. As I have said, the regime, even in its radical Cardenista incarnation, could not dramatically increase real wages overnight. However, there is good evidence that real wages grew, especially in the unionized sectors of the economy, during the early and mid-1930s (as they had done in the mid-1920s); after 1937, as inflation picked up, the picture is more mixed.[92] Taken as a whole, however, the 1930s were a relatively good period for real wages and popular consumption, which becomes even clearer if comparisons are drawn with the inflationary 1940s, when the more conservative administrations of Avila Camacho and (a fortiori) Alemán constrained wage demands and cracked down on labor militancy.[93] The wage levels attained in 1939 were not recovered until the early 1950s, when *desarrollo estabilizador* and the "economic miracle" got under way.[94]

Lastly, the 1930s were a decade of economic nationalism around the world, as tariffs were raised, flows of foreign investment were dammed, and *desarrollo hacia adentro* became the norm (whether by chance or by conscious design and decision). We have already noted a brisk process of import substitution industrialization (ISI) in Mexico; in part a product of circumstances (the declining peso, the loss of foreign exchange, the collapse of once-profitable foreign enterprise), this process also responded to political decisions. Economic nationalism could, of course, cohabit with contrasting political models and ideologies: Fascism, Communism, managed corporate capitalism, and British liberal imperialism. Mexico shared in the global inward turn, but, again, its version was colored by its immediate revolutionary past. The Revolution of 1910 was not, as often alleged, a movement motivated by powerful sentiments of xenophobia and, specifically, anti-Americanism. Apart from some specific pockets of xenophobia (where the victims tended to be immigrant entrepreneurial communities—Spaniards, Chinese, and later Jews—rather than the big Anglo-American enterprises), the chief thrust of the Revolution, exemplified by the Sonoran dynasty of the 1920s, was to achieve a better and more balanced relationship with foreign (especially American) capital, with respect to taxation, sovereignty, and regulation.[95] As Calles declared, more than once, he did not seek to expel productive foreign capital; rather, he wanted to rejig the terms on which that capital came to Mexico and extracted profits: productive investment (e.g., in manufacturing) was preferred to parasitic.[96]

Even in the more radical climate of the 1930s, this was also the position taken by President Cárdenas, and one with which organized labor usually agreed.[97] In part, therefore, the "nationalization" of the Mexican economy in the 1930s was less a product of virulent sentiment than of inescapable circumstances. Where productive foreign investment was forthcoming, the regime welcomed it; thus, even as the old enclaves of mining and oil declined, fresh investment—Colgate-Palmolive, Ford, GM, IT&T—flowed into Mexico in the 1930s, anticipating the flood of the 1950s and 1960s.[98] Of course, there was one outstanding case of economic nationalism: the oil expropriation of March 1938. But, as I have argued elsewhere (and it is not, I think, a hugely contentious argument), oil was a special case (mining, which was much more important, continued relatively unaffected), and it was a special case by virtue of the militancy of the oil workers and, we could say, the countermilitancy of the oil companies, who, true to form, decided to hold the line in Mexico, to defy both union and government, and, ultimately, to flout the sovereignty of the host country and to question the personal honor of the president (something it was unwise to do when the president was Lázaro Cárdenas).[99] We should note, too, that the state takeover of the bankrupt National Railways aroused much less protest and passion; oil was special by virtue of being both profitable and politically salient. The expropriation of March 1938 was as much an assertion of political will—a bold answer to the question, who rules in Mexico?—as of rational economic calculation. It was also a decision taken in the confident belief that neither Britain nor the United States was in a position to take severe reprisals; the international context of the 1930s provided a window of opportunity that had not existed in the 1920s and that, with the onset of the Cold War, would close with a resounding clump.[100]

The expropriation resulted in the formation of PEMEX, the first major state oil company in the "Third World." But since the expropriation was unusual, a product of particular circumstances, political as well as economic, it cannot be taken as typical of the times. In fact, even at the height of radical

Cardenismo, the state's role in the economy was carefully circumscribed. The state certainly sought to regulate the economy — witness the Federal Labour Code, the Six Year Plan, the Agrarian Code, the state commissions responsible for roads and irrigation, and the burgeoning central bank — and the state also embarked on extensive public works (again, roads and irrigation were key), hence the loose allegations of Cardenista "Communism," which recycled older allegations of Callista "Bolshevism." But, in fact, state planning was haphazard and ineffectual, while the state's role in the economy remained quite modest: central government taxes represented only 5.0 percent of GDP in 1930, rising to just 5.7 percent in 1940 (note the comparable figures for Argentina, 7.2 percent and 9.0 percent; for Brazil, 8.9 percent and 9.8 percent; and for an average of France, Italy, and the United Kingdom, 17.2 percent and 17.5 percent).[101] As a result, the Cárdenas administration, bent on ambitious land, labor, and educational reforms, soon encountered financial constraints. By 1936–37 the government deficit was growing (which, given the recession of 1937, was no bad thing), and after the shock of the oil expropriation, Cárdenas reined in public spending. Indeed, the final lame-duck period of his presidency witnessed efforts — partly successful — to curb inflation and the deficit, even at the expense of offending erstwhile supporters. Cardenismo was not Communism; it was not even "economic populism."

Thus, as Nora Hamilton has convincingly argued, by the late 1930s the regime had hit the "limits of state autonomy" — structural buffers that inhibited continued social reform and the state spending that went with it.[102] Of course, the train driver could have steamed ahead, breaking the buffers, and careering through the Grand Central Station of capitalism. But neither Cárdenas, nor his pragmatic minister of finance, Eduardo Suárez, nor the great majority of the "revolutionary" political elite were prepared to risk such a train wreck. Ultimately, the regime remained within the limits of national and global capitalism, taxing, regulating, and reforming, but always within the broad — and often demanding — disciplines of the market. Cárdenas was no Stalin, and the Mexican state was no totalitarian Leviathan; indeed, it would only start to assume Leviathanesque characteristics some forty years later, with the "neopopulist" excesses of President Echeverría and the hypertrophied oil- and debt-fueled state of the 1970s.[103] The Mexican regime of the 1930s went further down the road of state-sponsored social reform than any Latin American state of the period, particularly with respect to land reform, and it did so, of course, because of the prior experience of the Revolution and the continued popular demands—and political opportunities—that the Revolution left in its wake.[104] As a result, while the macroeconomic performance of Mexico in that decade bears close comparison with other Latin American countries—and hence can be fruitfully analyzed in terms of the usual conceptual suspects (external shocks, the commodity lottery, ISI, enhanced state intervention)—domestic policies diverged and were more distinctive, particularly regarding labor and, above all, land reform. These policies, while greatly stimulated by the Depression, owed their origins to the Revolution; hence, they were weaker or entirely absent in comparable Latin American countries. And the ensuing mix also gave Mexico a distinct politico-economic trajectory during the postwar years, when, even if the broad patterns of economic growth (ISI, urbanization, renewed foreign investment) were shared, for example, with Argentina and Brazil, the Mexican model was unusual by virtue of its stable, civilian, "institutionally populist" regime, a product (as it kept reminding us) of the epic Revolution. Which is another way of saying, in the face of some half-baked revisionism, that the Revolution mattered, not only by wreaking destruction in the 1910s but also by achieving constructive—and, for many, positive—results after 1917, particularly, I would conclude, in the 1930s.[105]

Notes

1 However, as I shall argue below, the Depression and the radical policy responses it elicited preceded Cárdenas's taking office in 1934, and the retreat from Cardenista radicalism similarly preceded Cárdenas's leaving office at the end of 1940.

2 The complexity of the Revolution is the one thing that all students of the process agree upon; to assert complexity (and to deny that the Revolution was monolithic) is, therefore, a necessary, rather ritual, starting point, not a bold new departure. The same is no doubt true of the Great Depression, which, Garraty observes, was "a worldwide phenomenon composed of an infinite number of separate but related events"; John A. Garraty, *The Great Depression* (New York: Anchor Books, 1987), 2.

3 John Mason Hart is probably the most weighty and insistent exponent of this traditional view; see his *Revolutionary Mexico* (Berkeley: University of California Press, 1987) and *Empire and Revolution* (Berkeley: University of California Press, 2002), part 3.

4 In the words of Daniel Díaz Fuentes, the Great Depression in Latin America "was an imported product"; Daniel Díaz Fuentes, *Las políticas fiscales latinoamericanas frente a la Gran Depresión* (Madrid: Ministerio de Economía y Ha-

cienda, 1993), 25. The alert reader will note that here I have switched from "the Americas" to "Latin America" (the focus of most of this book), since the Depression in the United States was—"and on this many authors agree"—endogenous ("almost entirely homemade"), not the result of external shocks; Michael A. Bernstein, *The Great Depression: Delayed Recovery and Economic Change in America, 1929–39* (Cambridge: Cambridge University Press, 1987), 3, the second quote being from Gottfried Haberler. In what follows I chiefly use countries as units of analysis, but we should be aware that, when the Depression struck, many Latin American countries, Mexico included, were still only partially integrated and contained major regional diversities and divergences that—for want of space—cannot be easily accommodated in a single essay. The point is stressed by Alan Knight, "Export-Led Growth in Mexico, c. 1900–30," and Paulo Drinot, "Peru, 1994–1930: A Beggar Sitting on a Bench of Gold," in *An Economic History of Twentieth-Century Latin America*, vol. 1, *The Export Age: The Latin American Economies in the Late Nineteenth and Early Twentieth Centuries*, ed. Enrique Cárdenas, José Antonio Campo and Rosemary Thorp (Basingstoke, UK: Palgrave, 2000), 119–21, 152–53. On Mexico, see also Susan M. Gauss, *Made in Mexico: Regions, Nation, and the State in the Rise of Mexican Industrialism, 1920s-1940s* (University Park: Penn State University Press, 2010), chaps. 2, 4, and 6.

5 Some—perhaps economists rather than historians—may also wish to argue that a study of the Depression of the 1930s will better prepare today's policy makers as they grapple with more recent recessions. While I have my doubts about the practical utility of history, even economic history, I would not deny that a sound—not superficial—knowledge of prior "conjunctures" may at least forewarn policy makers and broaden their horizons; indeed, the recent management of the U.S. Federal Reserve under Ben Bernanke may afford an interesting test of such historically informed policy making.

6 The obvious comparison would be between Mexico and other revolutionary states, especially contemporaneous ones that lived through the 1930s Depression. Of course, there were none in Latin America, and the Soviet example is radically different (I touch on both points later). A better comparison, far beyond the scope of this essay, might be China under the GMD.

7 I stress "signaled" rather than "caused" since there is widespread debate, hinging on major questions of economic theory and history, concerning the causes of the Great Depression and the role of the Wall Street Crash among those causes; useful surveys can be found in Garraty, *Great Depression*, chap. 1, and Charles P. Kindleberger, *Manias, Panics and Crashes*, 4th ed. (New York: John Wiley, 2000), 62–68. However, that debate chiefly—and I assume correctly—concerns the developed economies and their interrelations and, above all, stresses the central role of the United States ("many authors agree that the United States led the rest of the world into recession"; Bernstein, *Great Depression*, 3).

8 Sandra Kuntz Ficker, "De las reformas liberales a la gran depresión," in *Historia*

ecónomica general de México, coord. Sandra Kuntz Ficker (Mexico: El Colegio de México, 2010), 301–11. During the upswing in 1921–26, GDP grew at 2.68 percent a year; Graciela Márquez, "Evolución y estructura del PIB, 1921–2010," in Kuntz Ficker, Historia económica general de México, 553.

9 Enrique Krauze, Jean Meyer, and Cayetano Reyes, Historia de la Revolución Mexicana, 1924–28: La reconstrucción económica (México: El Colegio de México, 1977), remains a good overview.

10 See Luis Aboites, Excepciones y privilegios: Modernización tributaria y centralización en México, 1922–1972 (México: El Colegio de México, 2003), 37, 40, which shows that in 1925 94 percent of federal taxation was indirect. Of this, foreign trade (chiefly export taxes) accounted for 39 percent (rising to 48 percent in 1930); however, taxes on "natural resources" (oil and minerals, largely for export) also accounted for 16 percent. Income tax, introduced in the teeth of strenuous opposition in 1924, generated only 5 percent; see Aboites, Excepciones y privilegios, chap. 4. On Mexico's stuttering efforts to resume debt payments, see Robert Freeman Smith, The United States and Revolutionary Nationalism in Mexico, 1916–32 (Chicago: University of Chicago Press, 1972), chaps. 8 and 9; and Carlos Marichal, A Century of Debt Crises in Latin America (Princeton, NJ: Princeton University Press, 1989), 224–26.

11 Krauze, Meyer, and Reyes, Historia de la Revolución Mexicana, 289–90; Paolo Riguzzi, "México y la economía internacional, 1870–1930," in Kuntz Ficker, Historia económica general de México, 404. Díaz Fuentes, Las políticas fiscales, 22, following H. E. Peters, gives illustrative figures of U.S. investment flows to Latin America in the 1920s; Argentina received $808 million, Mexico $694 million, and Brazil $557 million. However, while investment in Argentina and Brazil involved both direct and indirect investment (in the ratio of 44:56 and 38:62, respectively), investment in Mexico was wholly direct; hence, Mexico was the biggest recipient of direct U.S. investment during the decade.

12 Sandra Kuntz Ficker, "The Export Boom of the Mexican Revolution: Characteristics and Contributing Factors," Journal of Latin American Studies 36, no. 2 (2004): 267–96.

13 Jeffrey Bortz, Revolution within the Revolution (Stanford, CA: Stanford University Press, 2008).

14 The boss of the Mexican Light and Power Company, a major British enterprise based in Mexico City, when asked if he was worried by "apparent threats of nationalization," replied "that he was not unduly alarmed and that view was shared by the majority of the remaining foreign companies who are operating in this country"; Monson to FO, August 24, 1933, FO371/16580, A6750.

15 Jürgen Buchenau, In the Shadow of the Giant: The Making of Mexico's Central American Policy, 1876–1930 (Tuscaloosa: University of Alabama Press, 1996), chap. 7.

16 Derek W. Aldcroft, From Versailles to Wall Street, 1919–29 (London: Penguin Books, 1977), chap. 9.

17 Charles P. Kindleberger, *Comparative Political Economy: A Retrospective* (Cambridge, MA: MIT Press, 2000), 409. On the impact of the Smoot-Hawley Tariff on Mexico, see Paolo Riguzzi, *Reciprocidad imposible? La política del comercio entre México y Estados Unidos, 1857–1938* (México: El Colegio Mexiquense, 2004), 243–44.

18 In 1910 the Díaz government devoted 20 percent of government spending to the military; by 1921 this had risen to a peak of 53 percent, which was followed by an irregular decline: 31 percent in 1925, 37 percent in 1929, and 25 percent in 1933. The Porfirian "low" was finally surpassed (downward) in 1936. See James W. Wilkie, *The Mexican Revolution: Federal Expenditure and Social Change since 1910* (Berkeley: University of California Press, 1973), 109.

19 Smith, *United States and Revolutionary Nationalism*, 244–59.

20 Lorenzo Meyer, *Historia de la Revolución Mexicana, 1928–34: El conflicto social y los gobiernos del maximato* (México: El Colegio de México, 1978), 210, 216–17, 222–23; see also Daniela Spenser, *The Impossible Triangle: Mexico, Russia and the United States in the 1920s* (Durham, NC: Duke University Press, 1999), 187–90, which notes that Mexico's "Red Scare" of 1930 was "out of all proportion to reality" (in other words, it resembled most "red scares").

21 Arnaldo Córdova, *La ideología de la Revolución Mexicana* (México: Ediciones Era, 1973), 394–401.

22 Counterfactuals often raise historians' hackles; however, they can prove useful, not by virtue of floating fanciful "alternative worlds," but rather by helping us sift the "structural" from the "contingent"—what was, in some sense, set in stone, "over-determined," refractory to agency, and what, in contrast, was amenable to intelligent political management. Aldcroft, *From Versailles to Wall Street*, 284, sums it up well: "some degree of recession was inevitable in 1929–30; that it developed into a global crisis of such intensity can be attributed not only to the convergence of a combination of unfavorable circumstances, but also to the fact that governments resorted to policies which made things worse." See also Córdova, *La ideología de la Revolución Mexicana*, 379.

23 Enrique Cárdenas, *La industrialización mexicana durante la gran depresión* (México: El Colegio de México, 1987). I would also like to thank Enrique Cárdenas for some helpful comments on this chapter (personal communication, February 2012).

24 "Top-down" and "bottom-up" have now become standard concepts in modern Mexican history, not least as analyses of the state and state building have tended to supplant older class-based approaches.

25 Stephen H. Haber, *Industry and Underdevelopment: The Industrialization of Mexico, 1890–1940* (Stanford, CA: Stanford University Press, 1989), 169. In 1928 the United States took 70 percent of Mexico's exports, a figure exceeded only by Cuba (75 percent) and Colombia (78 percent) among the larger Latin American economies; Sandra Kuntz Ficker, *El comercio exterior de México en la era del capitalismo liberal, 1870–1929* (México: El Colegio de México, 2007), 153.

26 Víctor Urquidi, *Otro siglo perdido* (Mexico: FCE, 2005), 71, gives the standard figure of 312,000. For a more detailed breakdown, see Abraham Hoffman, *Unwanted Mexican Americans in the Great Depression* (Tucson: University of Arizona Press, 1974), 174–75. As the Americans forced Mexicans south across the border, so the Mexicans expelled Chinese migrants back to the north (though in much fewer numbers, since there were fewer of them).

27 During the 1930s, Haitians in Cuba were "attacked . . . persecuted and expelled," but at least most survived. In the Dominican Republic, however, Trujillo "ordered a massacre," in which some 12,000 Haitians died; César J. Ayala, *American Sugar Kingdom* (Chapel Hill: University of North Carolina Press, 1999), 240. Of course, the correct comparison with Mexico would be Haiti itself, which had to reabsorb a substantial number of returned migrants.

28 Victor Bulmer-Thomas, *The Economic History of Latin America since Independence* (Cambridge: Cambridge University Press, 1994), 207.

29 Urquidi, *Otro siglo perdido*, 70, following Angus Maddison, *Two Crises: Latin America and Asia 1929–38 and 1973–83* (Paris: Development Center Studies, OECD, 1985), table 6. These figures put Mexico on a par with Brazil. Bulmer-Thomas, *Economic History of Latin America*, 195, gives a much higher (1928) figure for Mexico of 31 percent. B. R. Mitchell, *International Historical Statistics: The Americas and Australasia* (Detroit: Gale Research Co., 1983), 545, 889, gives figures of 18 percent for 1928 and 21 percent for 1929, which roughly square with Kuntz Ficker, *El comercio exterior*, 75, with an average for 1920–29 of 19 percent. The chief discrepancy arises because Bulmer-Thomas uses 1970 prices, while Maddison and Mitchell use current prices. This still does not explain the (smaller) discrepancy between Maddison and Mitchell.

30 Cárdenas, *La industrialización mexicana*, 37.

31 Riguzzi, *Reciprocidad imposible?*, 260–63.

32 Mexican oil production peaked in 1921 at 193 million barrels; by 1929 production had fallen to 45 million, and in 1932—coincidentally the trough of the Depression—it bottomed out at 33 million. There followed steady annual growth, which, by 1937, the year before the expropriation, had reached 47 million; Lorenzo Meyer, *Mexico and the United States in the Oil Controversy* (Austin: University of Texas Press, 1977), 9.

33 The total labor force in mining (not just silver) was 90,000 in 1927, falling to 45,000 in 1932; and in petroleum, 14,000. Meyer, *Historia de la Revolución Mexicana*, 44, 55.

34 Cárdenas, *La industrialización mexicana*, 24–28, assesses the enclave nature of mining and petroleum, showing that mining (at 81 percent of returned value in 1926) had tighter linkages with the domestic economy (via wages, inputs, and taxes) than petroleum (at 39 percent).

35 Cárdenas, *La industrialización mexicana*, 16.

36 Urquidi, *Otro siglo perdido*, 71, refers to the "vuelta al quelite," *quelite* being an edible wild plant. The figure for rural communities (with a population of less

than two thousand) is taken from Eyler N. Simpson, *The Ejido: Mexico's Way Out* (Chapel Hill: University of North Carolina Press, 1937), 587. Haber, *Industry and Underdevelopment*, 173, notes that the potential "buffering" effect of the subsistence sector had been reinforced by the (piecemeal but significant) agrarian reform of the 1920s.

37 As the Russian agrarian economist Alexander Chayanov pointed out (*On the Theory of the Peasant Economy*, edited by Daniel Thorner, Basile Kerblay, and R. E. F. Smith [Madison: University of Wisconsin Press, 1986]), peasant production can—by means of exploiting unpaid family labor—weather economic downturns that would ruin commercial farms. Thus, in early 1933 Tamaulipas experienced a "noticeable increase in agriculture . . . more particularly by smallholders than by large farmers. The low value of farm products and cattle has hurt the large farmer, whereas it has encouraged the smallholder to raise products for personal use"; Tampico report in Monson to FO, March 9, 1933, FO371/16580, A2367.

38 Mexican corn production in millions of metric tons: 2.1 in 1927, 2.2 in 1928, 1.5 in 1929, 1.4 in 1930, 2.1 in 1931, 2.0 in 1932, and 1.9 in 1933 (figures from Simpson, *Ejido*, 673). The Banco Nacional de México *Examen de la situación ecónomica de México*, no. 63, December 31, 1930, corroborates the year's bad harvest but, rather on the lines of Marie Antoinette, optimistically argues that the decline in corn production partly reflected urban consumption patterns: "thanks to their higher wages, workers now find themselves able to eat bread instead of tortillas."

39 Thus, during the serious stagflation of the 1980s, "returning to the *quelite*" was no longer a systemic option for Mexicans facing hard times; rather, they relied on urban self-help, migration and migrants' remittances, and a measure of state social security.

40 Between 1932, the low point in the cycle, and 1940, Mexican GDP grew by 55 percent (5 percent a year), while industry grew by 118 percent (10.2 percent a year) and agriculture only by 24 percent (2.8 percent a year); Cárdenas, *La industrialización mexicana*, 40, and chaps. 5 and 6; and Haber, *Industry and Underdevelopment*, 156–70, 176–89.

41 This is the central argument of Bernstein, *Great Depression*, 2, 31, 39, and chap. 2.

42 Thus, if we look at the trajectory of the Mexican economy in the 1930s, it quite closely resembles Brazil's; see Marichal, *Century of Debt Crises*, 209, regarding exports; and Díaz Fuentes, *Las políticas fiscales*, 28, for GDP figures.

43 Cárdenas, *La industrialización mexicana*, 34.

44 Cárdenas, *La industrialización mexicana*, 225.

45 Cárdenas, *La industrialización mexicana*, 225; cf. Wilkie, *Mexican Revolution*, 22.

46 Alberto J. Pani, *Apuntes autobiográficos*, vol. 2 (1950; repr., Mexico: INEHRM, 2003), 146. Pani, who played a major part in resolving the crisis, was hardly

objective, but he was certainly well informed and, as events showed, broadly correct. See also Cárdenas, *La industrialización mexicana*, 34.

47 Garraty, *Great Depression*, 18, 23, 36–37, 42–43, 47.

48 Significantly, the call came not from President Ortiz Rubio but from *jefe máximo* Calles; an official telegram from the puppet president followed a few days later. In office, Pani recalls that, whenever he proposed a major decision, the president asked, "Have you consulted General Calles yet?" Pani, *Apuntes autobiograficos*, 2:148–49.

49 J. W. F. Dulles, *Yesterday in Mexico* (Austin: University of Texas University Press, 1961), 60–61. Rosalie Evans, battling to save her hacienda from agraristas and "Bolsheviks," concurred, in her usual dyspeptic way: she found Pani to be a "little, unctuous, very prosperous (since the Revolution), black [*sic*] Mexican, with an agreeable manner"; Rosalie Evans, *Cartas desde México* (Mexico: Colección Testimonio, 1986), 249.

50 Roderic A. Camp, *Mexican Political Biographies, 1884–1935* (Austin: University of Texas Press, 1991), 164; see also Gauss, *Made in Mexico*, 28–32. While negotiating Mexico's foreign debt settlement in the United States in 1927, Pani was arrested for supposed contravention of the Mann Act, since he had traveled across state lines in the company of two nubile young Catalan ladies. The young ladies do not seem to have been unwilling; it is possible that the arrest was contrived by Pani's political enemies, who included Adolfo de la Huerta. President Calles, while accepting Pani's resignation, famously addressed Congress, asking if they would prefer to have "a cabinet of eunuchs"; Dulles, *Yesterday in Mexico*, 286.

51 And, while serving in Europe, he kept up a brisk correspondence with Calles, expressing his forthright views; Dulles, *Yesterday in Mexico*, 507–8; Pani, *Apuntes autobiograficos*, 2:142–47.

52 The story of Pani's policies in 1932–33 draws on Cárdenas, *La industrialización mexicana*, 55–59; Pani, *Apuntes autobiograficos*, 2:149–61; and Dulles, *Yesterday in Mexico*, 515–17.

53 In his September 1933 message to Congress, Pani boasted that, regarding the foreign debt, his "policy. . . . had been, he was glad to say, diametrically opposed to that pursued by previous administrations"; Farquhar to FO, September 14, 1933, FO371/16580, A7187.

54 Cárdenas, *La industrialización mexicana*, 190; Díaz Fuentes, *Las políticas fiscales*, 38, gives figures that show that Mexican GDP reached a low of 81 in 1932 (1929 = 100); by 1935, the 1929 level had been recovered, and by 1936 clearly surpassed (1936 = 111).

55 Bulmer-Thomas, *Economic History of Latin America*, 212, includes Mexico among the "fast-recovery group" (of eight Latin American countries); p. 219 gives average annual rates of GDP growth for 1932–39: 6.5 percent in Chile, 6.2 percent in Mexico, 4.8 percent in Brazil and Colombia, 4.4 percent in Argentina, and 0.1 percent in Uruguay.

56 Since "prescient Keynesianism" may be questioned (Haber, *Industry and Underdevelopment*, 170, warns that "we should . . . be careful not to speak of Keynesianism before Keynes; . . . the Mexican government pursued the policies that it did because it had little choice"), it is worth citing Pani's lengthy message to Congress of September 1933, in which, summing up policy since 1925, he severely criticized the resumption of foreign debt payments, the sharp cuts in government and military salaries, and "the failure of the Bank of Mexico to put in circulation sufficient quantity of paper money," all of which produced "acute monetary deflation," and all of which Pani—in a deliberate U-turn (see n. 53)—reversed in 1932; Farquhar to FO, September 14, 1933, FO371/16580, A7187. This seems to me strong evidence of what Díaz Fuentes, *Las políticas fiscales*, 43, calls "Keynesianism avant la lettre." Of course, it depends on what "Keynesianism avant la lettre" or "Keynesianism before Keynes" is meant to mean: while it is true that Keynes's *General Theory* (1936) was not published in Mexico until 1942 (see Sarah Babb, *Managing Mexico* [Princeton, NJ: Princeton University Press, 2001], 57–58), that does not mean that some smart worldly wise people—like Alberto J. Pani—might not have picked up a prior smattering of Keynesianism; and, to do that, it was never necessary to wade through *General Theory*, given that Keynes had previously penned strong and readable critiques of the gold standard and related orthodoxies. See John Maynard Keynes, *Essays in Persuasion* (1931; repr., New York: W. W. Norton, 1963).

57 Liaquat Ahamed, *Lords of Finance: The Bankers Who Broke the World* (London: Penguin Books, 2009).

58 For a sympathetic analysis of Argentine priorities in the 1930s, see H. S. Ferns, *The Argentine Republic, 1516–1971* (Newton Abbot: Davis and Charles, 1973), 120, 138; Marichal, *Century of Debt Crises*, 211, refers, more critically, to "the folly of a loyal debtor"; see also Díaz Fuentes, *Las políticas fiscales*, 48.

59 Furthermore, when the debt and damages were finally settled, in the 1940s, in a cozy atmosphere of wartime cooperation, Mexico got a very good deal, whereby liabilities were scaled down by as much as 90 percent; such, in Marichal's words, were "the benefits of procrastination"; Marichal, *Century of Debt Crises*, 224, 227.

60 Edwin W. Kemmerer, *Inflation and Revolution: Mexico's Experience of 1912–17* (Princeton, NJ: Princeton University Press, 1940).

61 Cárdenas, *La industrialización mexicana*, 77, 212.

62 The vicissitudes of the copper currency had provoked serious protests and violence in the mid-1830s; and again, during Manuel González's presidency (1880–84), the issue of paper currency provoked a panic and flight to silver.

63 Robert Redfield, *The Folk Culture of Yucatán* (Chicago: Chicago University Press, 1941), 164–65.

64 A historical *argumentum ex silentio* is always risky: it assumes that the primary sources are a fair reflection of reality and that relevant primary sources have

been thoroughly scrutinized (for "sounds" that may break the "silence"). But, in this case, even when local studies focus closely on markets and petty transactions (see n. 66), I have encountered no perturbations caused by the post-1932 currency shifts.

65 Cárdenas, *La industrialización mexicana*, 77. Confidence in Pani himself was apparent in his rapturous reception by Congress in September 1933 and the tremor that went through the banking system when he suddenly left office a month later; however, his heavyweight successor—none other than *jefe máximo* Calles himself—soon steadied the markets; Monson to FO, September 6 and October 5, 1933, FO371/16580, A7052, A7711.

66 Detailed studies of 1930s markets in these states are given by Ralph L. Beals, *Cherán: A Sierra Tarascan Village* (1946; repr., New York: Cooper Square, 1973), 58–91; and Bronislaw Malinowski and Julio de la Fuente, *Malinowski in Mexico: The Economics of a Mexican Market System* (London: Routledge and Kegan Paul, 1982), chap. 7.

67 As a rural schoolteacher recalled, back in the 1930s things were cheap, but no one had much money anyway: "only the rich had those 0.720 silver pesos"; *Los Maestros y la Cultura Nacional, 1920–1952*, vol. 4, *Centro* (México: SEP, 1987), 134.

68 Cárdenas, *La industrialización mexicana*, 59–65.

69 Cf. Rudiger Dornbusch and Sebastian Edwards, *The Macroeconomics of Populism in Latin America* (Chicago: University of Chicago Press, 1991), which rather too casually includes Cárdenas (and other "classic" populists of the 1930s and 1940s, including Vargas and Perón) in its indictment of profligate "economic populism." For a convincing refutation, see Enrique Cárdenas, "El mito del gesto público deficitario en México (1934–56)," *El Trimestre Económico* 75, no. 4 (October–December 2008): 809–40.

70 Like Mexico, Brazil pursued anticyclical policies, running sizable deficits through the 1930s. However, at least two factors were different: Brazil channeled funds to the crucial coffee sector, to the benefit of coffee planters; and, as a genuine fiscal federation, the Brazilian regime involved multiple official actors. The Mexican fiscal system, in contrast, was highly centralized (and under Pani became more centralized; Gauss, *Made in Mexico*, 47, 50), and while the Vargas government subsidized coffee plantations, the Cárdenas government expropriated them.

71 Alan Knight, "La revolución mexicana: Su dimensión económica," in Kuntz Ficker, *Historia económica general de México*, 490.

72 Alan Knight, "The Domestic Dynamics of the Mexican and Bolivian Revolutions," in *Proclaiming Revolution: Bolivia in Comparative Perspective*, ed. Merilee S. Grindle and Pilar Domingo (Cambridge, MA: Harvard University Press, 2003), 54–90.

73 Thus, in Morelos, 59 percent of agricultural property (by area) and 62 percent (by value) was in the ejidal sector by 1930. While these were unusually high

figures, other states in central Mexico now possessed sizable ejidos (for example: Tlaxcala, 19 percent and 21 percent; Puebla, 18 percent and 16 percent; Guerrero, 10 percent and 18 percent). Other states—notably in the north—had been barely touched by official land reform. See Meyer, *Historia de la Revolución Mexicana*, 190–91. The monthly reports of the Banco Nacional de México contain repeated references to the uncertainty generated by agrarian claims and conflicts through the later 1920s and 1930s; *Examen de la situación económica de México, 1925–76* (Mexico: Banamex, 1978), 32, 35, 45, 46, 82, 100, 109.

74 Though Calles and (for what it mattered) Ortiz Rubio were both committed to winding up the land reform, some state governors/bosses—such as Cárdenas (Michoacan) and, even more clearly, Tejeda (Veracruz)—continued to promote agrarianism, and since Mexico was a federation in political (if not fiscal) terms, such state actors had a good deal of leeway; *Examen de la situación económica*, 93, 100. See also Simpson, *Ejido*, 613, 700. I have roughly calculated that the agricultural economically active population was about 3.5 million.

75 Simpson, *Ejido*, chap. 24.

76 Thus, regions, perhaps particularly in the north, where economic activity was already flaccid had to deal with an influx of unemployed migrants: for example, in the major cotton zone of the Laguna, which, in 1930, was coincidentally suffering from drought and where "a large number" of returned migrants "were wandering through the city (of Torreón) and the railway marshalling yards, begging for help"; Maria Vargas Lobsinger, *La Comarca Lagunera* (Mexico: UNAM, 1999), 128–29. It is not coincidental that the Laguna became the site of major popular—including Communist—mobilization, leading to the radical land reform of October 1936.

77 Report of Consul Macy, Tampico, January 6, 1932, State Department Records, Internal Affairs of Mexico, 1930–39, 812.5200/960; or, again, report of Consul Hinke, Mazatlán, September 15, 1932, 812.5200/908, noting that ejidal petitions had doubled during 1931–32. British Foreign Office records contain several similar examples.

78 For example, in Tlaxcala; Raymond Buve, "State Governors and Peasant Mobilization in Tlaxcala," in *Caudillo and Peasant in the Mexican Revolution*, ed. D. A. Brading (Cambridge: Cambridge University Press, 1980), 233–44.

79 Timothy Henderson, *The Worm in the Wheat: Rosalie Evans and Agrarian Struggle in the Puebla-Tlaxcala Valley of Mexico, 1906–1927* (Durham, NC: Duke University Press, 1998).

80 David Ronfeldt, *Atencingo* (Stanford, CA: Stanford University Press, 1973).

81 There was, in other words, a clear "demonstration effect," as agrarian activists—even in unpropitious environments like los Altos de Jalisco—saw what was going on elsewhere and realized that "the Centre" (the federal government) was sympathetic to their cause; see Ann L. Craig, *The First Agraristas* (Berkeley: University of California Press, 1983), chap. 4.

82 Simpson, *Ejido*, 455–62; Francisco Javier Gaxiola, *El Presidente Rodríguez (1932–*

34) (Mexico: Editorial "Cultura," 1938), 450–64; Farquhar to FO, July 28, 1933, FCO371/16580, A6244.

83 Abelardo Rodríguez, *Autobiografía* (Mexico: Novaro Editores, 1962), 153. Concerns about the "congenital weakness" of the domestic market were well established; *Examen de la situación ecónomica*, 122. As the adjective "congenital" suggests, this was not just a conjunctural question of the Depression, important though that was; problems of weak demand and, as a result, industrial overproduction (e.g., of textiles) predated the Revolution.

84 Hobart Spalding, *Organized Labor in Latin America* (New York: New York University Press, 1977), 94.

85 Report of Consul Willson, Veracruz, April 16, 1937, State Department Records, 812.504/1652. As an anonymous reader of this manuscript rightly pointed out, the assumption that the CTM (and Lombardo) were more radical than the CROM (and Morones), though commonly made, should perhaps be questioned, since rhetoric and practice often diverged; furthermore, the CROM of the 1920s often carried a genuinely radical and popular thrust (see Bortz, *Revolution within the Revolution*). However, I would stick to the conventional view that the transition from CROMista to CTMista hegemony in the labor movement (a transition that coincided with the Depression, 1928–36) did represent a radicalization, and not just in terms of rhetoric.

86 U.S. Ambassador Josephus Daniels, who was sympathetic to the Cárdenas administration, saw the CTM as favoring "an extreme socialistic form of government"; Report of May 16, 1936, State Department Records, 812.504/1584. Of course, the public discourse of the CTM (as voiced by Lombardo Toledano) and its actual practice (as effected by the likes of Fidel Velázquez) tended to differ.

87 Marcos Tonatiuh Aguila M., *Economía y trabajo en la minería mexicana* (Mexico: UAM, 2004), 85–106.

88 *Examen de la situación económica*, 146–47 (March 1935: railways, trams, oil, miners, and a "general strike" in Puebla), 149–51 (May 1935: trams, light and power, miners, railways), 151–52 (June 1935: telephonists, paper workers, in short, an "epidemic of strikes"). Official strike figures are misleading, since they record only "legal," i.e., officially recognized, strikes (and sometimes fail to cover the whole country); however, those figures also shot up in 1934–35, as a result of both increased industrial conflict and the administration's more pro-labor stance; see Guadalupe Rivera Marín, *El mercado de trabajo* (Mexico: Fondo de Cultura Económica, 1955), 226. The same source, on p. 230, also shows a tendency for strikes to be settled in favor of the unions rather than the companies.

89 Joe C. Ashby, *Organized Labor and the Mexican Revolution under Lázaro Cárdenas* (Chapel Hill: University of North Carolina Press, 1963), remains one of the best studies.

90 Report of Consul Park, Torreón, May 13, 1936, State Department Records, 812.504/583.

91 *Examen de la situación económica*, 128–29; Rodríguez, *Autobiografía*, 152–54,

which recounts how the textile bosses—their sales flaccid and their warehouses full—had opposed raising the minimum wage, but within "six to eight weeks of raising wages, the warehouses were empty and their factories were starting to work at full capacity," so "the same industrialists, the most recalcitrant, who had most resisted raising wages, gave me a banquet to . . . thank me for what had been done, with such good results for everyone."

92 The most careful study of industrial production, productivity, and wages in the revolutionary period is that of Aurora Gómez-Galvarriato on the textile industry, which shows that the balance of power tipped decisively in favor of organized labor, resulting in a 131 percent increase in real wages during the 1920s; Aurora Gómez-Galvarriato, "Measuring the Impact of Institutional Change in Capital-Labor Relations in the Mexican Textile Industry, 1900–1930," in *The Mexican Economy, 1870–1930*, ed. Jeffrey L. Bortz and Stephen Haber (Stanford, CA: Stanford University Press, 2002), 315. Unfortunately, this study stops in 1930. However, the underlying dynamics (strong unions and tariff protection) were, if anything, reinforced during the 1930s; it was not until the 1940s that those dynamics were decisively reversed, at least with respect to union power. Aguila, *Economía y trabajo*, 132, shows rising real wages in mining at least until 1937, followed by a brief plateau, and then a sharp decline after 1940. U.S. consular reports frequently attest to the power of unions and consequent wage hikes; see, e.g., Macy, Tampico, August 22, 1936, and Blohm, Chihuahua, November 3, 1937, State Department Records, 812.504/1617, 1687. We should note, however, that these cases relate to sectors—textiles, mining, oil—where unions were strong; "disorganized" labor—of which there was a lot—probably fared less well.

93 As the American consul in Chihuahua observed, as the Spanish Civil War broke out, raising fears that a similar conflict might arise in Mexico, "the Mexican laborer . . . will not . . . take up arms so long as a labor government is in power, as he congratulates himself upon doing quite well under the present national regime"; Report of Consul Blohm, Chihuahua, October 19, 1936, State Department Records, 812.504/1627. We should add that workers could benefit because industry, especially manufacturing industry, was growing and paying a good rate of return to investors; Haber, *Industry and Underdevelopment*, 183. Real wages aside, there is also some (far from clear-cut) evidence that improved living standards in the 1930s began to produce biometric effects; Moramay López-Alonso, "Living Standards of the Mexican Laboring Classes, 1850–1950: An Anthropometric Approach," in *Living Standards in Latin American History*, ed. Ricardo D. Salvatore, John H. Coatsworth, and Amílcar E. Challú (Cambridge, MA: Harvard University Press, 2010), 91.

94 Jeffrey M. Bortz, *El salario en México* (Mexico: El Caballito, 1986), charts the sustained decline of real wages (in Mexico City) through the 1940s. See also Rivera Marín, *El mercado de trabajo*, 141, which gives a fall of one-third in real wages between 1940, the last year of the Cárdenas administration, and 1944.

95 Report of Consul Smale, Ensenada, August 31, 1937, State Department Records, 812.504/1671. This could be rephrased, in the terminology of studies of imperialism, by saying that Mexico's "collaborating elite" wanted to redefine the terms of the collaborative bargain between them, the local "hosts," and foreign—increasingly, American—capital.

96 Córdova, *La ideología de la Revolución Mexicana*, 385; Gauss, *Made in Mexico*, 41.

97 Though "radical," the trade unions were not strictly xenophobic: they wanted to cream off benefits from themselves, without necessarily driving the gringos out of Mexico; Report of Consul Blohm, Chihuahua, November 3, 1937, State Department Reports, 812.504/1687. Even when the gringos were driven out—at the time of the March 1938 oil expropriation—it was done with remarkably little confrontation or violence.

98 Gauss, *Made in Mexico*, 35–36. By the later 1930s, as the government failed to meet rising demands for agricultural (ejidal) credit, the Anderson Clayton company became a major supplier, especially in the north, and did so with tacit official encouragement; Nicole Mottier, "What Agricultural Credit and Debt Can Tell Us about the State in Mid-century Mexico," American Historical Association Meeting, Chicago, January 2012.

99 Alan Knight, "The Politics of the Expropriation," in *The Mexican Petroleum Industry in the Twentieth-Century*, ed. Jonathan C. Brown and Alan Knight (Austin: University of Texas Press, 1992), 90–128.

100 Hence the fate of Mossadegh and Arbenz in 1953 and 1954.

101 Gauss, *Made in Mexico*, 15–16, 48–51; Aboites, *Excepciones y privilegios*, 397 (I have summed the three European countries since the individual figures are very close). What the Mexican figures make clear is that the growth of the state's role in the economy in the 1930s was essentially to do with regulation rather than ownership. Even when the state paid for roads or dams, they were built by private companies (some, it is true, closely linked to prominent *políticos*).

102 Nora Hamilton, *The Limits of State Autonomy: Post-Revolutionary Mexico* (Princeton, NJ: Princeton University Press, 1982).

103 Alan Knight, "Cárdenas and Echeverría: Two 'Populist' Presidents Compared," in *Populism in Twentieth-Century Mexico*, ed. Amelia M. Kiddle and María L. O. Muñoz (Tucson: University of Arizona Press, 2010), 15–37.

104 Carleton Beals, *America South* (Philadelphia: J. B. Lippincott, 1937), 265. A sort of land reform was essayed in Colombia in the 1930s, but it fell far short of the Mexican counterpart; Albert O. Hirschman, *Journeys towards Progress* (New York: Doubleday, 1965), chap. 2. In the Dominican Republic, too, Trujillo initiated a "land distribution campaign" in 1934, which formed part of his broader pro-peasant, populist, and nationalist (including xenophobic) project. The results—in terms of peasant land acquisition—were real, but less radical and more piecemeal than the contemporary Cardenista reparto; furthermore,

after World War II, Trujillo changed his tune and became, in the eyes of the Dominican peasantry, "an agent of their dispossession, dislocation and disillusionment"; see the excellent analysis of Richard Lee Turits, *The Foundations of Despotism: Peasants, the Trujillo Regime and Modernity in Dominican History* (Stanford, CA: Stanford University Press, 2003), 90–143, 245.

105 The centennial of 2010 produced quite a crop of such revisionism, often in the form of glossy magazines, which chose to commemorate the 1910 Revolution by exploding "myths" and thus deflating the whole business; a representative example, probably no worse than many, is Alejandro Rosas, coord., *Las dos caras de la historia: Revolución mexicana: El tiempo del caos* (Mexico: Grijalbo, 2010), which, on p. 11, rather gives the game away when it states that the book is "an exercise in historical investigation *and literary imagination*" (emphasis added).

CHAPTER 9

Cuba: Depression, Imperialism,

and Revolution, 1920–1940

Gillian McGillivray

When the U.S. commodities market plummeted in October 1929, investors may have perceived it as simply a deeper dip in the roller coaster that sugar prices had been riding for over a decade. Cuba's economy and society hinged largely around the mercurial price of sugar because it represented 80–90 percent of national agricultural production and exports.[1] World War I and Prohibition in the United States had focused more investments (alongside sugar and tobacco) into tourism, gambling, and prostitution rings, but profits from these also slumped after the U.S. economic crash. This chapter will highlight some of the significant cultural and political changes that began in the 1920s and deepened under the impact of the Great Depression in the 1930s, including the nationalist embrace of Afro-Cuban culture; women achieving suffrage; the forging of nationwide associations for landowners, cane farmers, and workers; and, more generally, an increase of state intervention in economy and society as exemplified by the creation of a national sugar institute and a labor ministry.[2]

Many of these changes related to those taking place elsewhere: culturally, the *vogue nègre* began to thrive in Europe; flappers, jazz, and the Harlem Renaissance flourished in the United States; samba and *mestiçagem* rose to prominence in Brazil; and Mexico and other countries of the Americas embraced *indigenismo-mestizaje* as racial "mixing" alternatives to the social Darwinism and positivism that had condemned all but French, German, and Anglo-Saxons to the bottom of the civilization ladder.[3] Politically, the increasing intervention of the Cuban state in economy and society was similar to Franklin Roosevelt's New Deal and Lázaro Cárdenas's nationalization of oil and creation of corporatist bodies for trade unions and farmers in Mexico. Two specifically Cuban features of the 1920s and 1930s were

(1) the Cuban state's high level of intervention in the economy that tilted the balance of power from U.S.-owned sugar companies toward Cuban mill owners, cane farmers, and workers; and (2) the extent to which U.S. influence continued to constrain formal political policy on the island.

The initially popular nationalist Machado regime (1925–33) introduced protection for Cuban farmers and industrialists, as well as massive public works projects. The regime aimed to cooperate with other nations to better control world sugar prices and to create alternate means of growth besides sugar. In particular, the regime introduced import substitution of light consumer goods and sought to create an island oasis for tourists, using tourism to pay for civic improvements in port facilities, sewage, and water supplies that would benefit wealthy neighborhoods and country clubs, as well as casinos and hotels.[4] Even before the 1929 stock market crash severely undermined these efforts, the fraudulent renewal of Gerardo Machado's presidential term in 1928, combined with extensive graft—funded by ever-larger loans from U.S. banks—prompted massive opposition to what had become a dictatorship.

After the 1929 crash, sugar prices dropped to an average of 1.47 cents per pound—half of the already low 1927 average of 2.96 cents. In 1930, the United States, which consumed some 75 percent of Cuba's sugar, passed the Smoot-Hawley Tariff, which shifted much of the U.S. market away from Cuba toward domestic beet sugar producers and the insular territories of Puerto Rico, Hawaii, and the Philippines. Cuban intellectual Herminio Portell Vilá reflected on this protectionism in a language that eloquently captures Cuban nationalist sentiment: "A difference of half a cent in the tariff . . . represents the difference between a national tragedy in which everything is cut, from the nation's budget to the . . . alms handed to a beggar, and a so-called state of prosperity, whose benefits never reach the people as a whole or profit Cuba as a nation."[5] Strict cane quotas limited the total production of sugar, but other countries increased production, offsetting Cuba's painful efforts to curb the world supply. Prices resumed a downward spiral, and by 1930 the crop restriction was hurting the mill owners almost as much as workers and farmers. Since less sugar was being sold at lower prices, workers lost jobs, farmers lost income, and mill owners lost profits. Cutbacks on public works and a downturn in the number of tourists simultaneously reduced employment alternatives.

To put down the opposition groups born of economic and political frustration, Machado relied upon U.S. funds, the secret police, and Rural

Guard soldiers. Veterans of the 1895–98 Second War for Independence tried to overthrow the government in 1931, but Machado's army repressed the movement. Students and middle-class professionals organized a University Student Directorate (DEU) and "ABC" secret cells that responded to Machado's repression with manifestos and terrorism; Communist leaders (who followed directives from Joseph Stalin's Russia) or Trotskyist leaders (who believed in the exiled Russian's Bolshevik and Leninist principles) organized workers clandestinely. Machado's well-funded secret police force and army targeted them all. The *ley de fuga* became a common tactic whereby secret service or policemen would round up suspects for interrogation, set them free, and then claim that they had to shoot the suspects for trying to run away. Soldiers in the countryside were equally brutal with any workers or professionals suspected of organizing unions or opposition groups: the Rural Guard would expel them from their homes, put them into prison, and sometimes torture and lynch them.

A critical April 19, 1933, editorial in the *Nation* correctly asserted that "Machado has been maintained in office against the obvious will of the Cuban people by the financial support of our great corporations. More heavily loaded with per capita debt charges than any other Latin American country, Cuba . . . has been unable to revolt or default. Machado would doubtless have fallen in 1930 but for the $50,000,000 lent him by the Chase bank." The interpretation is powerfully expressed in an adjacent cartoon image where "Wall Street" strings hold up a machine-gun-toting Machado puppet that stands over a chained "*Cuba Libre*." Cuban presidents since 1902 had practiced graft and repression to varying degrees, but none before Machado had engaged in corruption under such dire economic conditions or employed such extensive state terrorism that included the murder of middle-class journalists, students, and political activists.

Nationalist politics could not survive the Great Depression, nor could the capitalist welfare that had reigned in the countryside.[6] Large U.S. corporations like the Cuban-American Sugar Company and the Cuba Company, which had managed to weather the 1920s without deficits, began to lose money in 1930. Sugar baron Manuel Rionda wrote to his Tuinucú sugar mill manager Oliver Doty in 1929: "Fortunately, the sales last summer show a profit of $194,000.00 . . . but even this does not permit us to continue paying dividends, so then: (1) out with the idea of paying the cane farmers but just what they are entitled to; (2) we must cut down expenses; (3) we must cut down our staff. . . . Tuinucú must change its methods, or stop paying dividends, which alternative shall it be?"[7] This was a rhetorical question: to Rionda it was obvious that capitalist welfare was a luxury. Among other things, his mills stopped paying pensions in 1932 and reduced the monthly salaries of the most fortunate employees (those with jobs during the "dead season" between harvests) by 82 percent.

Field workers suffered the worst cutbacks during the Depression. A September 1932 report from Oriente Province's Punta Alegre Sugar Company observed that "the average daily pay for 1932 was 40 percent less than the averages back in 1910, and some 30 percent less than the seven-year period from 1910–1917."[8] The British Embassy in Havana asserted one year later that wages had been steadily declining since 1929, adding that it was "probably no exaggeration to say that field workers are worse off in some respects today than in the days of slavery. They are expected to work 10 or 11 hours a day for 25 cents, with seldom more than 100 days' work in the year."[9]

Companies also espoused a strategy of shortening the milling season: from an average of almost five months a year in 1925, the harvest declined to just over two months in 1933. Mills maintained this intense, two-month harvesting system through the 1950s, with the resulting national underemployment an underlying cause of Cuba's revolutions. Many mills had to close altogether: there were 163 active in 1929, but only 125 in 1933.[10]

Mills across the island cut jobs, salaries, the milling season, and the budgets for schools, medical services, and power. The educational expenses at the Cuban-American Sugar Company's massive Chaparra and Delicias plantations fell from the 1929–30 level of $41,690 to $9,050 by 1933–34. The company gave fewer discounts for medical services and stopped paying for doctors and teachers in more rural areas. Workers and farmers flooded the general manager's office with letters and petitions pleading for the return of schools, teachers, and doctors to their communities in the cane farm towns and mill towns. One asked for access to land "on the former 'Campo Sport' [to] cultivate corn, sweet potatoes, beans etc. I am an old employee of the Analysis Department Central Office, and have six small children to give food."[11] Company archives reveal the striking contrast between the lives of these workers and their administrators. While one new manager requested a list of luxury furniture to be shipped from the United States and his dog "couriered" from his former place of employment, another was called to a meeting in Havana to discuss preparations for the Yacht Club's National Sailing Regatta.

The rest of this chapter will show that such injustices, greatly amplified by the Great Depression, lay at the core of the 1933 Revolution against Machado. Communities across the countryside organized a clear rejection of the local system of rule that was based on repression, control, and capricious welfare. Simultaneously, urban residents including bus drivers, students, teachers, soldiers, and feminists protested against a system of rule based on U.S. meddling; cronyism (in politics, business, and the military); and gender, racial, and economic inequalities. Rural and urban protestors precipitated a fundamental change in Cuba: "new elements, represented by the students, younger professional men and heroic women, for the first time fearlessly threw themselves into a political struggle," and they, together with rural workers and farmers, prompted the beginning of nationalist, class-based politics that overshadowed the caudillo networks that had reigned since Cuba's 1895–98 Second War for Independence.[12] By 1940, the pressure for social rights and democratic reforms arising out of influences including Spanish Republicanism, Mexican populism, and the Comintern's Popular Front strategy led soldier-turned-army-chief-turned-presidential-candidate Fulgencio Batista to institutionalize the 1933 reforms in one of the hemisphere's most progressive constitutions.[13]

Sugar, Tourism, and Afrocubanismo

Back in 1902–3, the nascent Cuban republic had signed reciprocity treaties with the United States that rendered the island's economy practically dependent on exporting a single product, unrefined sugar, to a single market, the United States, while entrenching low tariffs for nearly all imports from that same market. The competition from mass-produced U.S. goods inhibited the development of domestic industries such as soap or shoes in the newly independent nation, and U.S. investments focused almost exclusively on sugar production and related infrastructure. When World War I essentially removed European beet sugar from the world market, investors pushed even more cane sugar plantings into virgin forests. By 1925, Cuba produced nearly one-quarter of the world's sugar—five million tons, up from one million in 1904.[14]

As mentioned above, sugar mill companies (including those owned by U.S. corporations) provided housing, schooling, medical clinics, and parks for workers, cane farmers, and their families on an ad hoc basis, favoring upper-level employees and adjusting benefits year to year according to profit levels. When sugar sold at high prices, as it did during World War I, Cubans in the cities and in the countryside benefited from a booming economy. Thus, they tolerated a high level of U.S. investment and interference in the economic and political spheres. But speculation and the consequent crash in sugar prices in 1920–21 led to major wage and social spending cutbacks and sparked increasing nationalism and popular mobilization for change across the island. Those who suffered most were the Cuban workers, cane farmers, and small Cuban mill owners, not the U.S. corporations, which had access to credit from North American banks and economies of scale that allowed them to better weather the economic storm.

Cane farmers mounted a successful campaign for government protection by drawing on gendered and racialized nationalist arguments. After the death of poet José Martí and mulatto general Antonio Maceo in the 1895–98 Second War for Independence, the vision that they propagated of Cubans as "more than white, black, or mulatto" had been superseded by an elite desire to "whiten" the island.[15] Cuban nationalists tended to idealize Cuba as a white, Hispanic woman who needed to be protected; cartoonists depicted the "typical Cuban" as a white, bearded country bumpkin named Liborio.[16] Despite insisting upon a universal male suffrage that included Afro-Cuban voters, Cubans agreed to the U.S.-inspired 1902 ban against nonwhite immigration, allowed Spaniards to remain and keep their resources after the war, and let some 900,000 more Spaniards settle on the island between 1900 and 1929.[17]

Cane farmers—many of them former sugar mill owners unable to consolidate and modernize their mills after the destruction of 1895–98; others, these newer Spanish immigrants—cast themselves as white Cuban fathers unable to feed and clothe their wives and children because of greedy U.S.-owned sugar mills underpaying for cane, or rapacious North American banks repossessing their lands. The cane farmer category stretched from very rich absentee landowners who hired sharecroppers and managers to run their estates to very humble sharecropping families: the rich were able to use their literacy and access to the press and the legislature in Havana to emphasize the collective image of the poor, suffering cane farming father in need of state protection. This *guajiro* (rural Hispanic peasant) nationalism could tap into Western European middle-class romanticization of "the folk" in the form of Biedermeier art and the peasant heroes of ballets and operas.[18]

In March 1922, the government passed a law to regulate contracts between cane farmers and sugar mill owners regarding land rental and the sale and milling of cane. According to the civil code, products cultivated on rented or sharecropped lands officially belonged to the landowner, but the new laws made cane and its derivatives independent of the land, fortifying the position of cane farmers to solicit credit and loans by using the cane as guarantee for loans. This would help cane farmers (a vast majority of them Cuban or Spanish immigrants) to get loans and credit directly from banks instead of leaving them perennially dependent on sugar mill owners (many of whom were foreign—U.S. corporations owned thirteen of the nineteen largest sugar mills, producing 48 percent of sugar in 1921).[19] The most important aspect of the new 1922 law was that it fixed the maximum number of years for contracts so that cane farmers would no longer be chained to sugar mills for indefinite periods.

Another more assertive government move into the previously laissez-faire sugar economy came in 1923 with the passage of the Tarafa (or "Railroad Consolidation") Law that prohibited the construction of new private ports or railroads for moving sugar: this would put the brakes on the reckless expansion of sugar companies that saw some forty-five new sugar mills destroy Cuba's forests between 1914 and 1920.[20]

Besides fostering a boom and bust in the sugar economy that ushered in a first wave of anti-imperialism and protection for Cuban farmers, World War I and postwar prosperity in the United States prompted a boom in the number of tourists going to Cuba. U.S. hotel operators, retail merchants, and shipping and railroad interests organized a Cuban Commercial Association in 1914, and the Cuban government created the National Tourist Commission in 1919. Travel became easier with improvements in rail, steamship, and (after 1921) airline transportation. Havana boasted one of the world's first international airports, which received hundreds of flights per week from cities including Miami, New York, Houston, and Chicago. A larger postwar U.S. middle class with more disposable income and leisure time traveled to Cuba to pursue popular pastimes banned by conservative U.S. legislators, including horse track betting in the 1910s and the consumption of alcohol in the 1920s. For North Americans, Cuba became a place where they could do things that were considered morally suspect, at best, in their hometowns.[21]

An increasing number of U.S. tourists flocking to the island—up from some 33,000 in 1914 to 90,000 in 1928 and altogether more than two million between 1920 and 1940—helped to forge an image of "Cuba" that was dramatically different from the Cuban elite's white Hispanic woman or the cartoonist and cane farmers' white Hispanic peasant. U.S. cartoonists consistently caricatured the Cuban nation as a black child in need of advice from the tall white Uncle Sam, and tourism and music promoters marketed sexy Hispanic and mulatta women and Afro-Cuban men dancing to the exotic and primitive jungle beat of tom-tom drums.[22]

Until the 1920s, many Cuban elites inspired by social Darwinism encouraged white immigration and appropriated and imitated French and Anglo-Saxon "high culture," downplaying African, indigenous, or Iberian influences. When American bartenders, cooks, hotel owners, and tourists swamped the island with U.S. cultural products, a Cuban scientific and artistic movement known as Afrocubanismo sought to erect an authentically Cuban culture.[23] As other scholars have pointed out, the "exaltation of autochthonous cultural symbols cannot be separated from the antagonistic relationship between the United States and Cuba in the first republic."[24] Just as Cuban elites had accepted *danzón* despite its African elements in response to the U.S. occupation of 1898–1902, mainstream national culture embraced *son* music, *poesía mulata*, and *vanguardia* paintings and sculptures that incorporated "black motifs" into Cuban culture in a complex response to the pressures of U.S. tourism and the commercialization of radio and phonographs. Robin Moore emphasizes how middle-class whites appropriated black music and dance through a "stylization" process that "purified" them to make them "respectable," distancing them from the authentic Afro-Cuban performances.[25]

Vera Kutzinski interprets the poetic and literary creation of *mestizaje* as "the site where men of European and African ancestry rhetorically reconcile their differences and . . . give birth to the paternalistic political fiction of a national multiculture" while simultaneously reinforcing racial hierarchies.[26] Alejandro de la Fuente correctly asserts that despite these ambiguities, Afrocubanismo was "nothing short of a cultural and ideological revolution": the dominant discourse embraced the mulatta and mestiza as essential to the Cuban identity, and many Afro-Cubans and politically progressive artists and intellectuals used the discourse to point out racial, social, and gender inequalities.[27]

Although Machado did not remove the Zayas regime's 1922 legislation that banned all performances of African-influenced dances and music, the president did openly invite son musicians to his birthday party and legalized son music, now conceived as Cuba's "weapon against [American] jazz."[28] The regime also invested more resources into education, effectively narrowing the gap between black and white literacy while increasing overall literacy. Whereas only 30 percent of blacks were literate in 1899 (and 39.7 percent of whites), by 1931, 71.5 percent of blacks were literate, approximating the 74.3 percent of whites.[29]

Besides this "cultural" nationalism, the Machado regime flirted with economic nationalism. Machado's 1927 tariff reform encouraged import substitution and diversification, but because of the 1902 treaty with the United States, it affected mainly light consumer goods of European origins. Production of eggs, poultry, meat, butter, cheese, and condensed milk increased, and more large factories owned by the likes of Ford, Coca-Cola, and Armour established branch plants in Havana, but dependence on sugar persisted.[30] The regime tried to raise the price of sugar by limiting supply: the 1926 Verdeja Act limited the 1927 crop to 4,500,000 tons and assigned quotas to individual mills and cane farmers—ostensibly to protect the Cuban owners of small and medium-sized sugar mills and farms. Sugar's price did increase for several months, but it declined again in 1928 upon the return to pre–World War I levels of European beet sugar and the dramatic expansion of supply from Java and the Soviet Union.[31]

At least in its early years, the Machado regime thus sought to contain worker and farmer mobilization through cultural nationalism, economic diversification, and sugar quotas. The president alternated between repression and co-option: sending in the Rural Guard to end a strike on one occasion, while on another asking a mediator to convince workers to return to work in exchange for a few, minimal reforms. Machado certainly hoarded money for himself and his cronies, but he also funneled export taxes, payoffs from capitalists seeking contracts, and extremely large loans from Wall Street banks into education and public works programs such as a national highway system and a new capitol building in Havana. Both efforts signaled Machado's intention to give the Cuban state a more prominent role in economics and politics. The symbolic architectural importance of a new capitol building is self-explanatory. Since the railroads were almost all foreign owned, the highway would give Cubans a way to move sugar without losing so much profit to foreign companies.

Machado prolonged his presidential term in 1928 in the name of political and economic stability. He attempted to maintain his legitimacy by supporting "blacks" as a political category through music, education, and the *Sociedades de Color*, and women's groups by promising the vote if they supported his reelection.[32] The problem was that there was no real election, and his incumbency deprived Cubans of a political avenue for protest. Urban and rural clandestine opposition movements grew, and Machado's regime responded with violence.

Depression and Dictatorship in the Countryside and the City

The hardships of the Great Depression prompted small farmers and field and factory worker representatives from thirty-two sugar mills across the island to meet in Santa Clara in December 1932 to constitute the National Union of Sugar Industry Workers (SNOIA), despite the military repression under Machado. The number of mills represented had grown to 102 by the second meeting of SNOIA, held the following May at Camagüey. Worker manifestos emphasized the need for solidarity across sectors: railroad workers could refuse to run the trains bringing soldiers to repress a strike; dockworkers could refuse to load sugar produced by strikebreakers; soldiers could decline to repress workers; cane farmers could complete a production blockade against a company; and merchants, farmers, and other residents near the mills could provide sustenance for striking workers. They also encouraged industrial mill workers and agricultural laborers to form strike committees together, coordinating mill and field strikes, and they included a special request to women, urging them to form "Aid Committees" to provide for basic needs and "Anti-Eviction Committees" to protect strikers and their families.[33]

Only a select few wanted to join a union in those years because, as one former worker put it, "[that] meant losing one's job, and the majority of workers had families with no alternative means of support."[34] With the help of the Rural Guard or private security forces, companies would expel anyone accused of organizing a union from their homes, together with their families. This was an effective way to use the apparent worker benefit of housing as a means of control. Crime reports from Cuban-American sugar mills reveal that workers preferred the safer alternative of anonymous sabotage during 1932 and 1933. Workers stole or destroyed telephone wires, wood, bridges, and other materials. They placed obstacles in the way of company trains; left the doors open on cane trains so that cane would fall out; and burned, among other things, private security force barracks, cane train bridges, and a slaughterhouse. In March 1933 someone even made an attempt on the life of the general manager. The most common and dramatic action was to set the cane fields on fire. American press sources reported in March 1933 that 200,000,000 pounds of cane had been torched in the eastern province of Oriente alone.[35] Cubans came up with ingenious ways to light the fires clandestinely, for example, by slipping into the cane fields at night and scattering balls of phosphorus covered with wax. The next day, the sun would melt the wax and set light to the phosphorus, with the arsonist long gone. Two other methods were to wire a brand to the tail of a snake and let it dash in agony through the cane fields, or to soak a large tree rat in oil and release it with its fur on fire.[36]

Sabotage could not fill empty stomachs: the Spanish ambassador in Havana described the consequent "caravans of hunger" that came streaming into the capital city in search of jobs, food, and a place to settle their families.[37] But urban employers were also cutting back on jobs and salaries. Given that sugar was the base of the Cuban economy, the sale of most goods and services depended on Cubans gaining wages and profits from sugar. Furthermore, from almost $26 million in 1928–29, tourist dollars plunged to under $5 million in 1933–34.[38] The Great Depression thus devastated the entire Cuban economy. Estimated national income fell from 708 million pesos in 1925 to only 294 million in 1933.[39] In the city and countryside, Cubans responded with strikes and unemployment marches.

Workers across the country staged a general strike on August 5, 1933, in support of the Havana bus drivers who refused to pay Machado's transportation taxes. The masses paralyzed the Cuban economy, and they should be credited for the fall of Machado. But before the strike could achieve its ultimate goal of ousting Machado *and* his congress and army, on August 12 several officers from that very army escorted him to the airport and named another caudillo, Carlos Manuel de Céspedes, as his successor. The officers acted upon the advice of a U.S. mediator, Assistant Secretary of State Sumner Welles, and their appointment of a new president left Machado's congress intact along with much of his army. Despite the mass participation in the strike, the events of early August resembled more a palace coup than a revolutionary change for Cuba. This was mainly due to U.S. diplomatic meddling.

Workers and middle-class Cubans nevertheless seized the opportunity to flood the streets and celebrate Machado's departure. Contemporary descriptions in the U.S. press allow for a historian's analysis of the moral economy of Depression-era Havana. The throngs were quick to target and attack the most notorious elite supporters of the dictatorship, as well as its foot soldiers, the secret police. Impoverished and hungry Cubans also used the celebrations to take food and goods from the elite associated with the dictatorship. Finally, workers and students renewed strikes and protests when they realized that there had not been a significant change in the government.

Middle-class Cuban mobs began by attacking symbols of the dictator-ship. Students tore down street signs reading *Avenida del Presidente Machado* and replaced them with new ones that bore the name of a student who had fallen victim to the *machadato*. Others stole typewriters and destroyed the headquarters of the regime's newspaper for slander and propaganda, the *Heraldo de Cuba*. The barbershop where Machado had his hair cut was targeted because its owner ran a string of pornographic theatres for him. Thousands of lower- and middle-class Cubans descended upon the Presidential Palace and the houses of twenty-eight notorious Machado supporters. The crowd "was not chiefly interested in looting. Time and time again, when someone started to carry away a piece of furniture which was intact, he would be met with the cry, 'no, no, it is dirty, dirty,' and the axe would fall upon it." Cubans forced their way into the lower floor of the palace, smashed furniture, and tore up trees and plants in the garden. Someone hung a "For Rent" sign on the main entrance. At the Machado supporters' homes, the crowds de-stroyed furniture and china. They threw oranges and mangoes at paintings, tossed books out of the windows, broke down doors, and threw debris into the street. These actions reveal that at least middle-class residents of Havana mainly desired to expose and destroy the lies, luxurious excesses, and cor-ruption of the rich few.[40]

Besides this rejection of corruption and excess, some clearly sought re-venge and others desperately needed sustenance. There were many "mob re-prisals" against leaders of Machado's *porra* killing squad. As one U.S. journal-ist wrote, "The relief felt by a long-suffering people expressed itself in blood . . . the *porristas* had it coming to them. They had murdered wantonly."[41] An August 28, 1933, *Time* article described someone placing a cigar between the teeth of former police chief Antonio Ainciart's corpse as jubilant indi-viduals hung it by the neck from an arc light. The crowds made a bonfire beneath the corpse and danced around it as the rope burned through. When an ambulance arrived to take away the corpse, the crowds shouted "Dump Ainciart into the sea! He is not fit to be buried in the cemetery with human beings." This is reminiscent of the statements that the crowds made about the items in *Machadista* homes: evidently Cubans rejected the excessive vio-lence, power, and luxury of the few as "dirty" in the context of depression and political dictatorship.

Hudson Strode, of the progressive U.S. journal the *New Republic*, noticed that while middle-class Cubans waved palm fronds stolen from the presi-dential garden at the American Embassy, thanking Sumner Welles for helping to rid the island of Machado, another "more grimly ecstatic" group looted the palace and *Machadista* houses for food. They lugged off a prize hog, butchered it into small pieces, and distributed it among hungry bystanders "who rushed off with bloody joints and hunks of meat into the side streets to seek . . . charcoal fires for the cooking." Poor Cubans may, in fact, have been genuinely interested in taking some of the furniture and goods that middle-class Cubans had the luxury of destroying with the statement "No, it is dirty." At least in one case, a poor Afro-Cuban woman had the wherewithal to justify taking something in terms that middle-class protesters could accept. She took Machado's linen from the Presidential Palace and waved them to the crowd, declaring that "she deserved them because she was a taxpayer."[42]

A New Deal for Cuba?

President de Céspedes did not bring any immediate relief to the extreme poverty, nor did he significantly reform either the political or military underpinnings of the Machado dictatorship. As the incident of palm frond wavers mentioned above suggests, many Cubans believed that de Céspedes had come into office largely as the result of Welles's mediation. According to a popular saying, de Céspedes bore a "Made in the U.S.A." label. Therefore, the popular classes continued to use strikes and protests through August to demand speedy justice, revenge, and a more equitable distribution of goods. Riding on this popular wave of protest, Sergeant Fulgencio Batista, other soldiers, and a group of radical students, professors, and journalists led a bloodless coup against ex-*machadista* officers and President de Céspedes on September 5, 1933. This motley group represented the first nationalist-populist coalition in Cuba and it was not recognized by U.S. power. Professor Ramón Grau San Martín became provisional president, and Sergeant Batista began his meteoric rise to power in the background.

Grau and his co-conspirators—the University Student Directorate and the sergeants—broadcast an English-language message to Americans in the *New York Times* on October 8, 1933, explaining that they wanted to give Cuba a "New Deal" like the one Roosevelt was implementing in the United States. "We can no longer tolerate puppet governments born of monopolies and concessions," Grau declared, because they make Cuba merely "a sweatshop for the privileged few. . . . Our success will mean a new Cuba, born of new ideals. . . . We are called radicals because we are closely following the tracks of your own National Recovery Act; we are called Communist because we endeavor to return the buying power of the Cuban people." The Student Directorate's speech was far more threatening, proclaiming the revolutionary goal to "conquer economic and political freedom."[43]

Although this development alarmed U.S. policy makers, they did not want to jeopardize their new Good Neighbor Policy. After helping to free Cuba from Spain in 1898, U.S. policy makers had insisted upon the inclusion of the Platt Amendment to the Cuban constitution that allowed for U.S. intervention whenever large-scale political struggle threatened order on the island. Based on this justification, marines had occupied the island during or after the contested elections of 1906, 1912, 1917, and 1921; but in 1933, the Roosevelt administration assembled the Latin American ambassadors in Washington to tell them that there would be no "intervention." Ironically, he proceeded to announce that the United States would not recognize the Grau regime until it proved its popularity and ability to maintain order, and he sent twenty-nine ships to surround Cuba's shores. The United States thus created an overbearing challenge for Cubans who wanted significant nationalist change: nonrecognition undermined Grau's legitimacy, and the naval presence encouraged opposition groups to court U.S. intervention.

The Grau regime forged ahead regardless, introducing a series of reforms that responded directly to the popular demands of the mobilized masses. Grau repealed the Platt Amendment—at least from the Cuban side (the United States did not acknowledge the repeal). He formalized women's suffrage, even though the first real elections would not be held until 1940. He lowered utility and interest rates, a popular nationalist move because U.S. capitalists owned most utilities and banks. He gave autonomy to the universities that the dictatorship had closed.[44] The government also sponsored the inauguration of a National Cane Farmer Association and a program of land reform that guaranteed cane farmers the permanent right to stay on the land they cultivated.[45] Again, this was significant because most farmers were Cuban, and many of the sugar mill owners from whom they rented land were American. The Cubans did not gain full ownership of the land, but at least they had more security because landowners could not evict them.

For workers, the regime established a Labor Ministry to arbitrate strikes, workers' compensation, a minimum wage, an eight-hour workday, and a forty-eight-hour workweek. The reforms symbolized a great deal to laborers. For the first time the state had pledged to intervene in more than a repressive or ad hoc way between capitalists and labor. The eight-hour day meant an end to the brutal twelve-hour work regime whereby men and women had to work one six-hour shift, lose up to an hour walking home to eat and sleep for four hours, and then trek back to work before the bell rang to signal the start of another six-hour shift.

The Grau regime also approved a Nationalization of Labor decree that required Cuban nationality for 50 percent of all employees and allocated to Cubans 50 percent of all salaries in industry, commerce, and agriculture. This extremely popular decree promised to end the practice whereby foreigners' family members or foreign professionals got positions that Cubans could fill, leaving only the worst-paid and most difficult jobs for nationals. Great numbers of Afro-Cubans—who suffered the worst discrimination—staged demonstrations to support the law and to demand that the ratio be increased from 50 to 80 percent.

Companion legislation ruled that only Cubans could lead unions on the island, not foreign citizens. Working-class Cubans participated enthusiastically in the effort to rid the island of foreigners, whom they perceived as competition for scarce jobs. This confounded Communist and Trotskyist union organizers. Many were Spanish citizens themselves, and all hoped to forge class solidarity across national and ethnic barriers. When these unions published manifestos and newspaper articles condemning the laws as a fascist effort to divide the working classes, mobs stormed the newspapers and targeted their union headquarters.[46]

Despite the regime's efforts to satisfy popular aspirations, forces on both ends of the political spectrum threatened its existence. From the left, the above-mentioned unions, the Communist "National Congress of Cuban Workers" (CNOC), and the Trotskyist "Federation of Havana Workers" (FOH) perceived the regime as middle-class, nationalist, and Fascist, along the lines of Adolf Hitler's Germany, and there were certainly elements of truth to this interpretation. Grau's radical young minister of the interior, Antonio Guiteras, introduced several concrete social reforms, but many members of Grau's coalition did not support them. As the administration neared its hundredth day in power, army chief Fulgencio Batista, his U.S. allies, and traditional Cuban politicians challenged the regime from the right. Batista had consolidated his control over the armed forces, and soldiers consequently fraternized less with workers and students.[47] The U.S. State Department, by continuing to deny official recognition, deprived the regime of political economic stability, and the U.S. embassy secretly encouraged Batista to find a more traditional political alternative to Grau.

Despite its internal divisions, the 1933 Revolution provided a significant opening for labor mobilization. At least for a brief period, the armed forces and state leaders pledged their allegiance to the popular classes and the Cuban nation. Workers certainly rose to the occasion. Sugar workers across the island had already participated in the June, July, and August strikes that forced Machado to leave; some of them were members of the Communist sugar workers' union mentioned above (SNOIA). Machado's departure on August 12 elicited outbursts in smaller cities and mill towns across the island similar to those in Havana, combining jubilation, looting, and destruction of newspapers and notorious *machadista* homes. But most sugar mills did not erupt into full-scale revolutionary mobilization until Batista led the sergeants' revolt in September. Only then could workers take advantage of the collapse in the power of the forces of repression—the Rural Guard.

A revolutionary avalanche took place on sugar mills across the country after Machado's exile. Workers forced management to leave many mills, and different political groups competed to organize and lead the mobilized sugar workers, including the "Guiterista" students and new labor ministry officials who supported the left wing of the Grau San Martín regime, the "Bolchevique-Leninista" (Trotskyist) FOH, and the (Communist) CNOC. Despite the manifesto wars generated by these parties, workers on the ground at most mills appeared to maintain the unity necessary to win their demands.

In general, like their poor and working-class counterparts in the cities, sugar workers reacted to the fall of Machado with irony, humor, and dignity against the local power holders. Workers at the Tacajó sugar mill devised a most creative act of vengeance: they installed a loudspeaker that rang a bell on the street corner near an administrator's house so that he could feel what it was like to be sleep-deprived.[48] Inspired by examples from the 1917 Russian Revolution, field and factory workers and some small cane farmers organized *soviets* to take over, protect, and run several mills from September 1933 through January 1934. These *soviets* constituted elaborate experiments in political, juridical, and economic life. Strike committees took over crude and refined sugar stocks and sold them to pay workers' salaries, to purchase food for families living at the mills, and to stock up on rifles for armed self-defense groups. In the case of Mabay, committees distributed tools, machinery, and over 250 acres of land to farmers and workers. Workers operated the mill without upper-management oversight, opened schools, and established a Justice Tribunal.[49] A remarkable feature of this revolutionary occupation of sugar mills is that one of the primary goals of strike committees and worker "red guards" was to protect the mills from any form of destruction or sabotage. It seemed that they wanted to prove that they were not savages, but rather Cuban citizens, worthy of a larger share of sugar profits. They used the fall months of September to December to prepare the fields and mills for the January harvest.

Those not needed for work at the mills marched in flying brigades from mill to mill to support their comrades to gain demands from other mills. For example, over three thousand workers and farmers armed with sticks and machetes marched from the Tacajó and Baguanos mills to Santa Lucía to free the workers from the company and Rural Guard tyranny in that eastern Cuban enclave. Upon meeting a group of marchers, a Rural Guard sergeant advised them to elect a fifteen-person committee to go to speak to the mill administrators. The leader said that "he would have to wait for the rest" to see if they would agree. When the sergeant climbed a tree and saw men as far as the eye could see, he stepped aside and allowed them to destroy the sentry post and to break the entry gate chains that symbolized the company's extreme control over its residents. Workers from all three mills marched through the town, raising the Cuban flag and the Soviet red flag. They also sang the national anthem and the Communist "Internationale."[50]

Like the workers of Santa Lucía, Tacajó, and Baguanos, workers at the mills owned by Manuel Rionda broke the system of company control. In response to the "wave of communism," Rionda's nephew Higinio Fanjul suggested sprinkling some cash around because the fundamental cause of the problems was hunger, and "no one deserve[d] the blame more than [U.S. president Herbert] Hoover and Smoot [of the Smoot-Hawley Tariff]."[51] In a remarkable gesture, given the extreme poverty and hunger, workers rejected the $1,000 per week Rionda offered to distribute to "those faithful, old employees who have found themselves without work for no fault of their own."[52] The strike committee ordered Tuinucú's 87-year-old philanthropic matron Isidora Rionda, and the system of dependence and charity that she represented, to leave the mill. When she did not leave, they took away her servants.[53] "In all the mills," Higinio Fanjul wrote, "all of the pigs, chickens, and provisions are running out."[54] Most mills had strike committees that set up soup kitchens to distribute such food equitably to all residents who remained on the occupied mills. The removal of servants and redistribution of food and goods, though short-lived, constituted a very revolutionary effort to create a more equitable society.[55]

Rionda adopted the attitude that the companies might as well concede whichever demands his nephews considered reasonable in order to avoid any damage. As far as he was concerned, none of the contracts were worth the paper they were written on "until Cuba has a strong government."[56] Two days later, his nephew José reported back on a meeting at the new Labor Ministry office in Havana with Tuinucú strike representatives. The powerful letter captures the radical change that the 1933 Revolution brought to the island:

> They were much harsher than I thought they would be, and one can say that the "feeling [sentimiento]" of the old Tuinucú has disappeared. This is a changed Cuba. The workers are perfectly organized and united, everywhere, and marked by communist tendencies. The Government is weak, and can give only minimal guarantees to capital and property. It has placed itself on labor's side to get their support, and that is why the workers feel so strong, ruling the roost, and imposing conditions . . . and these are the children of those who worked with us in harmony, and who received so many favors from Tuinucú.[57]

Favors no longer sufficed. Workers wanted contracts and government legislation that established fixed social and economic rights, and the 1933 Revolution provided them with the opportunity to win these. Interior Minister Guiteras told Tuinucú worker Agustín Valdivia at a meeting in Holguin to "squeeze these people [apriete a esta gente]," esta gente meaning the Rionda family interests on the island, which were very large at the time.[58] Precisely to avoid this kind of grouping—workers from all the Rionda mills versus the companies—Manuel advised his nephews to schedule the meetings in Havana with workers from the various mills for different days. Even though they were kept apart, the workers from all of the mills nevertheless succeeded in winning most of their demands, including higher salaries than the minimum wage later established by President Carlos Mendieta in January 1934. He set it at $1.00 per day in the cities and sugar mills, yet Tuinucú had to continue to pay $1.20.[59]

Despite the owners' repeated references to Communism, the worker manifestos that remain in the Santiago provincial archives in Eastern Cuba reveal many political factions competing for leadership. The CNOC-affiliated

Communist SNOIA led the union at Delicias and the Juan Claro port, while the FOH-affiliated Trotskyist Partido Bolchevique-Leninista led workers at Chaparra and Puerto Padre. The Communists (Partido Comunista de Cuba) maintained an extremely sectarian stance, attacking the Grau-Guiteras-Batista regime as "bourgeois" and the Trotskyists as divisive opportunists. On the other hand, the Trotskyist FOH manifestos spoke more of events in Havana and Europe than Puerto Padre; they criticized the Cuban Communist Party (PCC) and CNOC for attacking the 50 percent law only through manifestos, not through strikes. Despite their differences, the manifesto battles between the CNOC and FOH clearly indicate that the two organizations completely rejected the Grau regime's populist reforms.

Workers had to decide whether to negotiate with the company and the state during the Grau interregnum. The Guiteristas, whom navy officers seemed to think led the workers at Puerto Padre, were the only organization that supported the populist regime and advocated using its new legislation. The radical Minister of the Interior Guiteras worked hard to try to establish more links with Cuban workers to counter Batista's growing power, but the CNOC rejected his requests for support. The FOH toned down its attack on the regime only after its Spanish leaders were exiled and replaced with Cubans, in accordance with Grau's new labor law.

It is understandable that neither Communists nor Trotskyists recognized Guiteras's sincerity: every pro-worker act he carried through risked being reversed by one of Batista's counteracts. For example, Guiteras would set workers free from jail, but Batista would put them back. In late 1933, while Guiteras's newly created, pro-worker Ministry of Labor engaged in strike mediation and helped workers form militias to defend themselves and their government, Batista and his soldiers toured the country breaking strikes on U.S.-owned plantations to win the support of U.S. ambassador Sumner Welles.[60]

The massive Cuban-American Sugar Company determined that it would grant no reforms and would pay the same wages in 1933–34 as it had in 1932–33 despite national minimum wage decrees to the contrary. On December 19, the company stated that it would be unable to harvest the 1933–34 season. It closed the hospital, bakery, butcher shop, and other food shops. Department heads were told to leave their posts, and telegraph, telephone, hospital, and other public services were closed. Workers responded by issuing a manifesto calling for solidarity for the locked-out workers of Chaparra and Delicias and a boycott of the Chaparra Light and Power Company, which continued to operate through the strike. The same manifesto explicitly called on the Grau regime to fulfill its rhetoric: "You will be our real defender when you do not allow us workers to be trampled, as we are now."[61]

Interior Minister Guiteras stepped up to the challenge. On December 22, 1933, he ordered the mayor and local authorities at Puerto Padre to take possession of the power plant, hospital, and commercial departments at Chaparra and Delicias. This included the general stores, slaughterhouse, ice plant, butcher shops, and bakeries. A U.S. diplomat communicated the Cuban Department of Agriculture's message that they were taken over "on the ground of public need, *since they were the only plants existing on the lands of this Company, from which from 40,000 to 60,000 people could secure service and products suitable to their needs*" (emphasis added).[62] He had sent a letter two days earlier reporting that "Doctor Carlos Hevia, Secretary of Agriculture of de facto Government, . . . said in effect: 'If they do not grind and we do not do anything about it, you can easily understand that the one hundred thousand inhabitants of the district will take matters into their own hands.'" A January 11, 1934, confidential follow-up report stated point-blank, "The recent difficulties at Chaparra and Delicias . . . arise from the fact that the Company [pays] average field wages of only about fifteen cents a day."[63]

British reports provide a broader picture of company-state relations under the Grau regime that help clarify Guiteras's December intervention. A November 1, 1933, report stated that many companies had stopped paying taxes, assuming that the regime would soon fall without U.S. recognition. These companies refused to accept Grau's pro-worker decrees and waited in expectation for a counterrevolution. The report's astute conclusion was that "the sugar crop is the supreme test of the administration."[64] A December memorandum indicated that the administration might triumph. Guiteras's action at Chaparra, it explained, "has caused other sugar mill owners to modify their attitude towards the Government[;] some of them [had been] about to issue an ultimatum to the effect that they would be compelled to close down unless the Workmen's Insurance Law was satisfactorily amended."[65] Guiteras's intervention at Chaparra sent a strong message to these mill owners: reform or lose your company.

Containing and Institutionalizing Revolution: 1934–40

An early January report from the American consul at Antilla reveals that he had not figured out what the British author of the October memo had, namely, that social and political struggle in Cuba tended to fit around the sugar harvest. "Nominally," the report reads, "the various strikes which have occurred throughout the sugar mills all over the country have resulted in a higher scale of wages, which have not been put into effect as the crop of 1934 has not yet begun. It is believed, at this writing, that the majority of sugar mills will not operate this year not only on account of the wage demands being made by unionized labor but, also, on account of the political and economic chaos at present existing in Cuba."[66] Cuba depended too heavily on sugar to let this prophecy come true. Batista and his soldiers were willing to stand by and watch, and even join sugar workers in September and October, but they opted for repression as the harvest approached in November and December.

Batista shifted his support from Grau San Martín to Carlos Mendieta on January 15 as a way to encourage mills to begin the sugar harvest, prevent U.S. invasion, and respond to Cuban and U.S. capitalists' entreaties for order and peace on the island. Almost immediately, the United States granted recognition to the new conservative president (and Batista) and officially recognized the annulment of the Platt Amendment. Middle-class nationalists thus got their way, but workers had a harder time. Immediately upon taking power, the Mendieta-Batista regime began to repress workers both physically and legally under the motto *Habrá zafra o habrá sangre* ("There will be harvest, or there will be blood"). One of the new regime's first decrees returned Chaparra and Delicias to the Cuban-American Sugar Company. The army and Rural Guard stormed union headquarters at Puerto Padre and throughout the island, took papers and furniture, jailed or evicted labor leaders from sugar mills, and declared unions illegal.

Nevertheless, because of the massive popular mobilization that had taken place during the 1933 Revolution, even these repressive measures had to be carried out through legislation disguised as "compromises" between capital and labor. For example, Decree #3, passed on February 7, 1934, allowed workers to strike, but required them to give eight days' notice before they did so. The law took away the element of spontaneity that made strikes effective. It also gave the companies time to rally together strikebreakers and to evict or exile the leaders of the strike before it began. Communists, Trotskyists, and Guiteristas all advocated the rejection of this controlling social legislation, but they had no choice but to modify their stance after the failure of a general strike in March 1935. The government repressed the walkout with extreme force, and shortly thereafter the SNOIA began to advocate working from within the system to avoid more violence. The SNOIA issued circulars explaining how to make unions legal and trained unions to combat the legalese that companies were using to get around legislation.

The Mendieta-Batista government passed a series of decrees to save cane farmers, including an August 17, 1934, moratorium to help them pay off their debts. The directives were complemented by a series of minimum-wage laws introduced for workers in agriculture and industry. Finally, the 1937 Law of Sugar Coordination permanently established a new system: protection for tenant cane farmers on the land they worked and profit sharing between workers, cane farmers, and mill owners according to a sliding scale that moved with the price of sugar. New regulations set the starting dates for grinding, minimum cane production quotas for each cane farmer and mill (effectively protecting small and medium farmers and small Cuban mill owners), the size of bags, the ports of shipment, wage rates in all categories of employment, and a high fixed percentage of sugar due to cane farmers in exchange for their cane (47 percent of sugar produced if the cane yielded over 12 percent of sucrose, and 48 percent if it yielded over 13 percent). Between 1939 and 1949, mill owners complained that costs for labor and cane farmers increased by 300 percent, but thanks to a new U.S. sugar quota in 1934, official average prices also increased by 290 percent; the International Bank for Reconstruction and Development reported that "when pressed," most mill owners admitted that it was still worth producing sugar even though profits were lower than the pre-1939 levels.[67]

Conclusion

In the end, the Great Depression and the nationalist, social reformist movements that it ushered in helped Afro-Cubans, women, workers, and cane farmers to create a new Cuba. The break with tradition is demonstrated at both the national political level and the local mill community level. At least at a symbolic level, Afro-Cuban culture was no longer completely shunned, and Afro-Cuban and women's rights were enshrined in the 1940 constitution.[68] The state, which included the president and his cabinet, judges, prosecutors, the military, and the new Ministry of Labor, became mediators who tried to ensure that workers, cane farmers, and sugar mill owners got their fair share of sugar industry profits. At the national level, each group created an association to lobby for spoils, and locally the representatives of these associations, or unions in the workers' case, went to the state mediators (lawyers, judges, Ministry of Labor representatives, and governors).

The state thus entered the sugar mills to an unprecedented degree, and Batista's soldiers, at least until his 1952 coup, were not merely oppressive forces. They became key players on the local scene, soliciting bribes, marrying into local families, and teaching at schools, among other activities.

The 1933 revolutionaries did not necessarily want to abolish sugar production on the island, but they did not agree with a status quo that prioritized it above any other political, social, or economic aspect of life. Participants in the sugar economy—cane farmers and workers—wanted a larger share of the profits, and students, industrialists, professionals, Afro-Cubans, and feminists sought a more diverse economy and egalitarian society. Overall, those who participated in the 1933 Revolution wanted greater access to political and economic power.

When Batista's power base shifted in the late 1930s, partly owing to the Spanish Civil War's reverberations and partly inspired by Cardenista Mexico, more profound popular nationalist reform did come. Cubans and Spaniards on the island staged massive Popular Front demonstrations for the release of political prisoners and against dictator Francisco Franco. Cuban labor leaders and army chief Batista also visited and received visits from populist Mexico in 1938 and 1939. The Spanish Civil War and Mexico's Cardenista model encouraged a populist alliance between President Batista, cane farmers, and Cuban Communist workers in the late 1930s that significantly altered political, social, and economic structures. Organized labor, women, and cane farmers finally won a place in the Cuban political arena alongside military men and Cuban and U.S. capitalists and politicians.

The positive worker legislation passed in the late 1930s and early 1940s demonstrates this triumph, as do Cuba's democratic elections of 1940 and 1944. The change is also reflected in the fact that the most influential labor confederation switched from advocating rejection of Cuban state institutions to promoting engagement and negotiation from within. This very change reveals the transformation mass popular mobilization provoked in the Cuban state: from openly repressive dictatorship in 1932 to "populist democratic" regimes from 1933 to 1952. The quotation marks around "populist democratic" are there because the inclusion of popular groups varied immensely during the period. The early years included top-down labor legislation combined with extreme repression. The far more significant inclusion of popular groups came when Batista shifted to the left during the 1937–44 period. His shift can be explained by the popular rejection of military dictatorship on the island, reflected in popular demonstrations against Franco, his visits to Mexico (alongside union leaders) that offered a functional example of leftist populism in Latin America, and the Comintern and Allies' pressure for "middle-class, worker, and farmer" Popular Fronts against Fascism advocated during World War II. Batista's adversary Ramon Grau San Martín's *Auténtico* party, which ruled from 1944 to 1952, introduced a highly insidious form of populism that divided labor unions from within and undermined some of the power that workers had accumulated.[69] Finally, Batista's 1952 coup against the *Auténticos* ushered in a dictatorship reminiscent of the Machado years in its dependence on U.S. tourism, loans, and military repression.

At the local level in the countryside, paternalism and minimal capitalist welfare lasted only as long as the profits were good. Mill owners and managers overestimated the number of cutbacks mill residents would accept. When the Great Depression exposed the fragility of capitalist welfare, workers and cane farmers in Cuba, like their lower- and middle-class counterparts elsewhere in the Western Hemisphere, demanded more formal, lasting reform and protection from the state. The transition from the capitalist welfare programs to legislated welfare under the populist governments of the 1930s and 1940s was rocky, but Cuba was not alone. The island fits into the larger American hemispheric pattern more than most studies recognize. What was different was the level of state intervention in the sugar industry that rendered it "one of the most thoroughly controlled industries in the world," as well as the level of U.S. meddling that seems to be due in large part to the intransigent U.S. imperialists who advised the State Department from Cuba during these years (first Ambassador Sumner Welles and then Franklin Roosevelt's personal representative Jefferson Caffery).[70]

This chapter has emphasized the important changes that Cubans initiated during and after the Great Depression, but the U.S. role in precluding more extensive national reform should not be ignored. One can read with historical irony the 1934 *Literary Digest* summary of the mainstream U.S. press's take on Batista: "There is nothing in the little brown man's character to justify appellations of 'Little Napoleon' or 'Emperor Batista.' He is smart but has none of the makings of a dictator so far as political ambition is concerned. . . . Long experience in close contact with army leaders taught him . . . the danger of rising too high in a Latin-American republic. He is of the people and his inclination is to support the Government which will do the most for the masses."[71] In contrast, *Foreign Policy Review* associate Charles A. Thomson foresaw with prophetic accuracy the rise of the

"Batista Dictatorship." (In an impressive analytical coup, he came up with this label almost twenty years before it became common shorthand in the political discourse of Cuba.) Thomson's January 1936 retrospective observed that nonrecognition had been a powerful instrument in the hands of the Roosevelt administration. Refusal to recognize the Grau regime, he argued, "helped to doom, as it now appears, the most promising opportunity for a constructive solution of the Cuban problem. . . . The forces of protest have been driven underground . . . but whether to disappear or to reappear in more aggressive form, the future alone will decide."[72] They did reappear, with a vengeance, in 1959. Upon the triumph of that revolution, which also largely began as a middle-class movement, workers carried out extensive land reform and nationalization.[73] As in 1933, their actions preceded and made essential the reformist legislation that followed.

Notes

1 Tobacco exports exceeded sugar just after the wars for independence in 1899, but by 1919 tobacco accounted for only 8.3 percent of the value of total exports. Cuba, Dirección General del Censo, *Censo de la República de Cuba, 1919* (Havana: Maza Arroyo y Caso, 1920), 231. For more on tobacco, see Jean Stubbs, *Tobacco on the Periphery: A Case Study of Cuban Labour History* (Cambridge: Cambridge University Press, 1985).

2 The National Sugar Export Corporation was the "single seller" in 1929 and began to regulate quotas within the island and for export between 1931 and 1935 before these tasks were taken over by the Cuban Sugar Stabilization Institute (ICAE) in 1935. See Alan Dye, *Cuban Sugar in the Age of Mass Production, 1899–1929* (Stanford, CA: Stanford University Press, 1998); and Oscar Zanetti Lecuona, *Las manos en el dulce* (Havana: Editorial de Ciencias Sociales, 2004).

3 See Robin D. Moore, *Nationalizing Blackness: Afrocubanismo and Artistic Revolution in Havana, 1920–1940* (Pittsburgh: University of Pittsburgh Press, 1997); Gregory T. Cushman, "De qué color es el oro? Race, Environment, and the History of Cuban National Music, 1898–1958," *Latin American Music Review* 26, no. 2 (2005), 164–94; Hermano Vianna, *The Mystery of Samba: Popular Music and National Identity in Brazil*, trans. John Charles Chasteen (Chapel Hill: University of North Carolina Press, 1999).

4 See Rosalie Schwartz, *Pleasure Island: Tourism and Temptation in Cuba* (Lincoln: University of Nebraska Press, 1997).

5 Herminio Portell Vilá, quoted in "By Way of Prologue" to Fernando Ortiz, *Cuban Counterpoint: Tobacco and Sugar* (New York: A. A. Knopf, 1947), xix. Spanish edition: *Contrapunteo cubano del tabaco y el azúcar* (Havana: Jesús Montero, 1940).

6 "Capitalist welfare" can be considered the predecessor to the social welfare that many states began to provide for citizens in the 1930s: it combined elements of traditional paternalism with new Fordist initiatives whereby companies provided health care, education, and housing for workers.

7 Manuel Rionda to Oliver Doty, January 31, 1929. Braga Brothers Collection, Special Collections, Smathers Library, University of Florida, Gainesville (hereafter BBC), Record Group (RG) 2, Series (S) 10, file: Tuinucú, Colonos—A&L.

8 Punta Alegre Sugar Company to R. B. Wood, September 15, 1932, Provincial Archives of Las Tunas, Cuban American Sugar Company Collection (hereafter APLT, CASC), leg. 7, exp. 77.

9 Public Record Office, Foreign Office, London (hereafter PRO, FO) 371/16575, Document 304, memo re: labour agitation, 27 Sept. 1933.

10 Barry Carr, "Mill Occupations and Soviets: The Mobilisation of Sugar Workers in Cuba 1917–1933," *Journal of Latin American Studies* 28 (1996): 132.

11 Original letter is in broken English. Chaparra, Cándido Fernández to Mr. H. M. Hicks, Auxiliary General Manager, July 20, 1932, Chaparra, APLT, CASC, leg. 50, exp. 558.

12 The quotation is from a remarkably progressive report of the [U.S.] Commission on Cuban Affairs called *Problems of the New Cuba* (Foreign Policy Association, 1935), 11.

13 Samuel Farber, *Revolution and Reaction in Cuba, 1933–1960: A Political Sociology from Machado to Castro* (Middletown, CT: Wesleyan University Press, 1976), 94; Robert Whitney, "The Architect of the Cuban State: Fulgencio Batista and Populism in Cuba, 1937–1940," *Journal of Latin American Studies* 32 (2000): 435–59.

14 It remained at roughly this level of production claiming between 20 and 25 percent of the market until 1931, at which point it dove down to below 12 percent of the world market, where it remained until after World War II. Brian Pollitt, "The Cuban Sugar Economy in the 1930s," in *The World Sugar Economy in War and Depression, 1914–40*, ed. Bill Albert and Adrian Graves (London: Routledge, 1988), 97; Manuel Moreno Fraginals, *El Ingenio* (Havana: Editorial de Ciencias Sociales, 1978), 3:39–40.

15 See Ada Ferrer, *Insurgent Cuba: Race, Nation, and Revolution, 1868–1898* (Chapel Hill: University of North Carolina Press, 1999); Alejandro de la Fuente, *A Nation for All: Race, Inequality, and Politics in Twentieth-Century Cuba* (Pittsburgh: University of Pittsburgh Press, 2001); Aline Helg, *Our Rightful Share* (Chapel Hill: University of North Carolina Press, 1995); Frank Guridy, *Forging Diaspora: Afro-Cubans and African Americans in a World of Empire and Jim Crow* (Chapel Hill: University of North Carolina, 2010).

16 Cushman, "De qué color es el oro?," 169.

17 Aline Helg, "Race in Argentina and Cuba, 1880–1930: Theory, Policies, and Popular Reaction," in *The Idea of Race in Latin America*, ed. Richard Graham (Austin: University of Texas Press, 1990). The total population of Cuba in-

creased from 1,572,797 in 1899 to 3,962,344 in 1931. Report of the Commission on Cuban Affairs, *Problems of the New Cuba*, 25.

18 Moore, *Nationalizing Blackness*, 131.

19 Muriel McAvoy, *Sugar Baron: Manuel Rionda and the Fortunes of Pre-Castro Cuba* (Gainesville: University of Florida Press, 2003), 162.

20 Zanetti Lecuona, *Las manos en el dulce*, 53–54; Reinaldo Funes, "El *boom* azucarero durante la Primera Guerra Mundial y su impacto sobre zonas boscosas de Cuba," in *Cuba: De colonia a república*, ed. Martín Rodrigo (Madrid: Biblioteca Nueva, 2006), 230.

21 Louis A. Pérez Jr., *On Becoming Cuban: Identity, Nationality, and Culture* (Chapel Hill: University of North Carolina Press, 1999), 167.

22 Pérez, *On Becoming Cuban*, 166–67; and Schwartz, *Pleasure Island*. Robin Moore suggests that pro-independence playwrights had used the *mulata* as symbol for the Cuban nation earlier, in the late nineteenth century, but theirs was a far more subtle and critical symbol than that of the U.S. music and tourism promoters; Moore, *Nationalizing Blackness*, 44.

23 De la Fuente, *Nation for All*, 180.

24 Vera Kutzinski, *Sugar's Secrets: Race and the Erotics of Cuban Nationalism*, in de la Fuente, *Nation for All*, 180. See also Jules R. Benjamin, "The Machadato and Cuban Nationalism, 1928–1932," *Hispanic American Historical Review* 55, no. 1 (February 1975): 66–91.

25 Moore, *Nationalizing Blackness*, 135.

26 Vera M. Kutzinski, *Sugar's Secrets: Race and the Erotics of Cuban Nationalism* (Charlottesville: University Press of Virginia, 1993), 12–13.

27 De la Fuente, *Nation for All*, 182–85.

28 Moore, *Nationalizing Blackness*, 31, 104–5.

29 De la Fuente, *Nation for All*, 141–42.

30 Julio Le Riverend, *Historia económica de Cuba* (Havana: Instituto Cubano del Libro, n.d.), 597; McAvoy, *Sugar Baron*, 183.

31 Report of the Commission on Cuban Affairs, *Problems of the New Cuba*, 241.

32 Lynn Stoner, *From the House to the Streets: The Cuban Woman's Movement for Legal Reform, 1898–1940* (Durham, NC: Duke University Press, 1991), 65–74; Alejandra Bronfman, *Measures of Equality: Social Science, Citizenship, and Race in Cuba, 1902–1940* (Chapel Hill: University of North Carolina Press), 139. Frank Guridy points out that Afro-Cubans paid dearly for their apparent support for Machado. He describes the racist backlash in the town of Trinidad in "'War on the Negro': Race and the Revolution of 1933," *Cuban Studies* 40 (2009): 49–73.

33 "SNOIA: Proyecto de Resolución para la II Conferencia Nacional," June 16, 1933, Instituto de Historia, Fondo: 1er Partido Marxista-Leninista y otros, leg.: Organización de los Trabajadores Sindicales Nacionales, exp.: SNOIA (hereafter IH, SNOIA), document 1/8:87/3.1/1–6.

34 Luis Merconchini, interview by Víctor Marrero, Delicias, August 21, 1990. Audio-taped interview is at the Office of the Historian of Las Tunas.
35 Workers adopted the very same strategies of sabotage during the Second War for Independence (1895–98) and the struggle against Fulgencio Batista's dictatorship (1952–59). Charles W. Hackett, side note on Cuba in his article on "Mexican Constitutional Changes," *Current History*, May 1933, 214. See also Gillian McGillivray, *Blazing Cane: Sugar Communities, Class, and State Formation in Cuba* (Durham, NC: Duke University Press, 2009).
36 The three methods are described, respectively, in Secret Police Agent Francisco Micó Urrutia's "Informe" about the cane burnings at Chaparra and Delicias forwarded by Rafael Balart Perera, Chief of Secret Police, Santiago to Governor of Santiago, forwarding, March 22, 1936, Santiago de Cuba, Provincial Archives, leg. 312, exp. 16; The Mapos Sugar Co. Case 121 in Department of Justice, Special Report of William E. Fuller, 47; George Atkinson Braga, "A Bundle of Relations," Typed Manuscript, BBC, RG 4, S. 24 (Additional), p. 47.
37 Carr, "Mill Occupations and Soviets," 133.
38 Schwartz, *Pleasure Island*, 88–89.
39 *Les Années Trente à Cuba: Actes du colloque international organizé à Paris en novembre 1980 par le Centre Interuniversitaire d'études Cubaines et L'Université de la Sorbonne-Nouvelle, Paris III* (Paris: Editions L'Harmattan, 1982), 34.
40 Hubert Herring, "The Downfall of Machado," *Current History*, October 1933, 17–18.
41 Edwin Lefevre, "Soldier and Student Control in Cuba," *(Philadelphia) Saturday Evening Post*, January 6, 1934, 36.
42 Hudson Strode, "Behind the Cuban Revolt," *New Republic*, October 4, 1933, 204–7.
43 Cited in McAvoy, *Sugar Baron*, 256.
44 For more on the impressively strong student and women's movements, see Stoner, *From the House to the Streets*; and Jaime Suchliki, *University Students and Revolution in Cuba, 1920–1968* (Coral Gables, FL: University of Miami Press, 1969).
45 Louis A. Pérez Jr., *Cuba: Between Reform and Revolution*, 2nd ed. (New York: Oxford University Press, 1995), 268.
46 The same law produced injustices and violence in the countryside as well. The targets there were the large number of English, French, and Dutch Caribbean workers who had come to Cuba during boom times to cut cane and remained settled there with their families in the 1930s. The Rural Guard practiced raids along with bounty hunters, who tracked down foreigners and deported them, often without their belongings and wages. Barry Carr, "Identity, Class, and Nation: Black Immigrant Workers, Cuban Communism, and the Sugar Insurgency 1925–1934," *Hispanic American Historical Review* 78, no. 1 (1998): 103–9.
47 Robert Whitney, *State and Revolution in Cuba: Mass Mobilization and Political*

Change, 1920–1940 (Chapel Hill: University of North Carolina Press, 2001), 105–7.

48 Octaviano Portuondo Moret, *El soviet de Tacajó: Experiencias de un estudiante de los 30* (Santiago de Cuba, 1979), 69, cited in Carr, "Mill Occupations and Soviets," 153.

49 Carr, "Mill Occupations and Soviets," 155.

50 Carr, "Mill Occupations and Soviets," 139–58; Jacobo Urbino Ochoa, Gabriel Milord Ricardo, and Dionisio Estévez Arenas, *Datos para la historia: Movimiento Obrero y Comunista, Holguín 1918–1935* (Holguin: Ediciones Holguín, 1983), 120–37.

51 Fanjul to Aurelio Portuondo, September 14, 1933, BBC, RG 2, S. 11, file: Correspondencia con Higinio Fanjul, Manuel Rasco y Cuban Trading Co., Havana.

52 Rionda, President, Tuinucú Sugar Company to Tuinucú [Comité Central], September 11, 1933, BBC, RG 2, S. 4, vol. 3.

53 Rionda to Bernardo Braga, London, September 15, 1933, BBC, RG 2, S. 4, vol. 3.

54 Higinio Fanjul to Aurelio Portuondo, September 25, 1933, BBC, RG 2, S. 11.

55 Former Tacajó worker Ursinio Rojas remembered strikers making administrators and upper-level employees eat humble food. One can almost feel his smirk as he wrote, "Sr. Hernández lost quite a bit of weight because he didn't like the 'rancho' that the union made in the soup kitchen." Ursinio Rojas, *Las Luchas Obreras en el Central Tacajó* (Havana: Editora Política, 1979), 83. Also, Carr, "Mill Occupations and Soviets," 153.

56 Manuel Rionda, New York to José Rionda, Havana, September 18, 1933, BBC, S. 2, vol. 78.

57 José Rionda to Manuel Rionda, September 30, 1933, BBC, S. 10, RG 2, S. 10, file: Tuinucú, Labor Troubles.

58 Arquímedes Valdivia Hernández, interview by author, February 1, 2000, Tuinucú.

59 Oliver Doty to Sindicato de Obreros y Empleados de la Industria Azucarera, Sección del Central Tuinucú, Tuinucú, January 11, 1935, BBC, RG 2, S. 10, file: Tuinucú, Labor Troubles.

60 José Tabares del Real, *Guiteras* (Havana: Editorial de Ciencias Sociales, 1973), 197, 282–83.

61 "Chaparra" chapter of SNOIA manifesto, n.d., Santiago de Cuba, Provincial Archives, "Tribunal de Defensa Nacional: Juicios establecidos por propaganda subversives."

62 U.S. Chargé D'Affaires Samuel S. Dickson to Secretary of State, December 30, 1933, United States National Archives (hereafter USNA), RG 59, Stack 250, Row 26, Decimal file 1900–1939, Box 1339, 337.115 SM/665 to 37.1153 CU [Re: 1933 nationalization of Cuban-American sugar mills].

63 The diplomat received this information from an American newspaper correspondent who had obtained it confidentially from one of the Company's ac-

countants. Jefferson Caffery to Secretary of State, January 11, 1934, USNA, RG 59, Stack 250, Row 26, Decimal file 1900–1939, Box 1339, 337.115 SM/665 to 37.1153 CU.

64 Mr. Grant Watson to Sir John Simon, PRO, FO 371/16575 and surrounding documents.

65 "Memorandum for the Minister re: the Situation at Chaparra," Grant Watson to Sir John Simon, December 30, 1933, PRO, FO, 277/226.

66 "Current Wages in the Antilla Consular District," January 8, 1934, in USNA, RG 59, 837.5041/63.

67 Irving P. Pflaum, "Aspects of the Cuban Economy Part II," *American Universities Field Staff Reports Service Mexico and Caribbean Area Series* 5, no. 8 (August 1960): 2.

68 See Stoner, *From the House to the Streets*; Bronfman, *Measures of Equality*; and de la Fuente, *Nation for All*.

69 See Whitney, "Architect of the Cuban State."

70 Pflaum, "Aspects of the Cuban Economy Part II," 2; and Philip Dur and Christopher Gilcrease, "U.S. Diplomacy and the Downfall of a Cuban Dictator: Machado in 1933," *Journal of Latin American Studies* 34, no. 2 (May 2002): 255–82.

71 "Cuba's Procession of Presidents," *Literary Digest*, January 27, 1934, 14.

72 Charles A. Thomson, "The Cuban Revolution: Reform and Reaction," *Foreign Policy Reports*, January 1, 1936, 276.

73 See Juan Martínez Alier, "The Peasantry and the Cuban Revolution from the Spring of 1959 to the End of 1960," chap. 5 of *Haciendas, Plantations, and Collective Farms* (London: Frank Cass, 1977), 127–47.

CHAPTER 10

The Great Depression in

Latin America: An Overview

Alan Knight

This chapter attempts a very difficult task: to advance some general thoughts about the Great Depression in Latin America, drawing not only on the chapters in this book but also on other (secondary) sources.[1] The task is difficult, given, first, the sheer complexity of the historical processes (which span over a decade and, more importantly, some twenty countries, about half of which are directly dealt with in this book) and, second, the very diverse approaches to the topic that are apparent in these pages, some being more strictly economic, or politico-economic, some sociopolitical (and not so economic), some even sociocultural.[2] This diversity prompts two initial questions, familiar—at least in theory—to historians and social scientists, but sometimes overlooked in practice. Both relate to the flight of our causal arrows: put simply, what causes what? First, to what extent did the Great Depression, by definition an *economic* phenomenon, bring political, social, and even cultural consequences (beyond the more obvious economic outcomes)?[3] In other words, to what extent were the political phenomena of the 1930s—including political instability, enhanced state building, economic dirigisme, authoritarianism, corporatism, popular frontism, nationalism, etc.—products of the Depression? Absent the Depression, would they have occurred, or occurred in such clear-cut form? Similar questions can be asked of (loosely) social and cultural phenomena: migration, urbanization, xenophobia, and, again, nationalism.

The second familiar problem that at once emerges is the old one of *post hoc ergo propter hoc* ("after this therefore because of this")—in other words, the risk of attributing to the Depression outcomes that in fact obeyed a quite different causality.[4] For example, Venezuela's halting liberalization in the later 1930s was primarily the result of Juan Vicente Gómez's death and the dissolution of his regime, not of economic pressures arising from the Depression (which, thanks to oil, had a muted impact).[5] Augusto César Sandino launched his offensive against U.S. Marines in the Segovias region of Nicaragua in 1927; at most, the Depression brought him fresh recruits among the "impoverished peasantry" of the region.[6] The radical reforms of Lázaro Cárdenas in the mid-1930s were certainly stimulated in part by the impact of the Depression on Mexico, but they would have been unthinkable without the prior Mexican Revolution and the forces and expectations that it unleashed.[7] Long-term trends, such as urbanization, industrialization, and demographic growth, were clearly affected by the Depression, too, but they were never initiated de novo, and whether the "effect" was one of acceleration or retardation is an empirical question, the answer to which may vary from case to case, country to country.

Thus, in some cases the Depression may not have been crucial, since a different causality prevailed. In others, the Depression accelerated previous trends (and, of course, measuring acceleration—and the added fuel that produces acceleration—is no easy matter; the same goes for "retardation": whose foot is on the brake pedal and with what force?). Causal connections are particularly difficult to establish as we move, let us say, from the world of political economy to that of "culture."[8] The politico-economic sequence (falling exports→falling revenue→budget deficit→government cuts and layoffs→protest and electoral losses) is both empirically demonstrable in particular cases and consonant with general patterns of causality (what we could call watered-down "covering laws").[9] It is much harder to establish such links between politico-economic trends and cultural phenomena; to suppose that such links exist and are clear-cut is to commit the "Harry Lime" fallacy.[10] Jorge Luis Borges, who first made his name as a writer in the 1930s, was hardly a product of the nationalist reaction of that decade, while Gilberto Freyre, who has better claims to embody Brazilian (or "Luso-tropical") nationalism, was no great admirer—or beneficiary—of the Vargas regime.[11] Of course, political economy and "culture" are not separate sealed compartments; but beyond banally noting—while switching to a better metaphor—that these streams of history commingle, it is hard to identify the causal connections with great confidence. So this résumé is cautiously and apologetically light on "culture."

With these caveats in mind, I offer a brief overview of the 1930s, starting with the economic impact of the Depression, then noting political responses, both short- and medium-term. By "medium-term" I mean roughly the decade of the 1930s, whereas "short-term" refers to the years of crisis, approximately 1930–33. This is not just a capitulation to "hectohistory," history mindlessly measured by decades (or centuries); it also reflects the fact that, by the second half of the decade, most Latin American economies were well out of recession, while the onset of war—at the end of the decade—created fresh shocks and reactions.[12] Of course, important "legacies" of the years of Depression survived through the 1940s and beyond, as I note, but it is difficult to attribute new phenomena of the late 1940s and 1950s—such as "populism"—to the Depression, as I comment in conclusion. At the very least there must have been many and influential intervening factors, rendering the Depression, at best, a distant and very indirect stimulus.

Great Depression Economics

Since Latin America was "one of the underdeveloped regions which had been most closely integrated into the international division of labour," the impact of the Depression was, in Celso Furtado's view, "catastrophic."[13] Indeed, the Chilean economy may have been "worse hit than any other in the world."[14] Furtado's premise seems more convincing than his conclusion. Latin America did have high trade coefficients, which made it highly vulnerable to the dramatic fall in world trade after 1929, a vulnerability compounded by the fact that, from 1927, the Wall Street bull market had been sucking U.S. investment out of the region (see table 10.1).[15]

Chile was hard hit because it depended heavily on a couple of mineral exports (copper and nitrates), both highly sensitive to world demand, hence the "staggering" collapse of export revenue in four years, which had major sociopolitical repercussions, as mentioned below.[16] Cuba, too, was highly vulnerable to the decline of sugar prices, its predicament aggravated by U.S. protectionism. After nearly touching 5 cents per pound during the First World War, the price slumped to 1.94 cents in 1929 and 1.23 cents in 1930; three years later, the Cuban sugar industry was working at 35 percent capacity, and the value of the *zafra* had fallen by three-quarters (1929–33).[17] As the case of sugar exemplifies, some primary commodity prices had been weak since the end of the postwar boom in 1921; thus, the 1929–30 shock, far from coming out of the blue (as it did for, say, U.S. stock prices), severely aggravated existing trends: cacao, like sugar, had declined through the 1920s, to the detriment of Ecuadorian exports; Bolivia suffered falling tin prices after 1927; and the same year saw wheat prices turn down, af-

Table 10.1. Trade Coefficients and Export Decline

COUNTRY	TRADE COEFFICIENT (EXPORTS + IMPORTS/ GDP, 1970 PRICES) 1928	FALL IN PURCHASING POWER OF EXPORTS, 1928–32 (%)	TRADE COEFFICIENT (1970 PRICES) 1938
Venezuela	120	0	56
Costa Rica	110	35	81
El Salvador	81	62	62
Colombia	63	35	43
Argentina	60	40	36
Chile	57*	83	45
Peru	53*	57	43
Mexico	48	63	26
Brazil	39	44	33

Source: Victor Bulmer-Thomas, *The Economic History of Latin America since Independence* (Cambridge: Cambridge University Press, 1994), 195, 197.
* 1929 data.

fecting Argentina.[18] The coffee- and banana-producing countries of Central America—being small, open economies, often heavily dependent on a single export—were also hard hit (bananas fared worse, to the detriment of Honduras and Nicaragua), while Mexico, like Bolivia and Chile, suffered from sharply falling mineral prices.[19]

However, if the impact was severe, in many cases recovery was rapid and sustained. As usual in economic history, judgments depend a great deal on the comparators being used. Compared to the United States, for example, Latin America did very well.[20] But the United States, while a commonly used comparator, is not necessarily the most suitable. Usually, it serves to denigrate Latin America's (sluggish) long-term performance; in this case, by contrast, a conjunctural comparison tends to flatter.[21] However, Latin America also did better than India and—not surprisingly—war-torn China.[22] A better point of reference might be southern or eastern Europe; however, this comparison has been rarely explored, with the signal exception of Love's perceptive analysis of economic thinking.[23]

Comparison is, therefore, a somewhat slippery business, and, as we address Latin America, it is worth distinguishing between two elements: the *severity* of the initial depression and the *rapidity* of the recovery. The United

States, for example, was hard-hit and was also slow to recover (obviously, the worst combination; it is difficult to detect a Latin American equivalent). Germany was hard-hit but recovered fast.[24] Britain, which had suffered structural recession in the 1920s, experienced a less severe shock and a less robust recovery. The Latin American pattern varied, but there are distinct "Germanic" overtones—that is, a sharp fall and a brisk recovery.

If we take Victor Bulmer-Thomas's typology of fast, medium, and slow recoverers in Latin America, we find eight countries in the "fast" category (where GDP grew by over 50 percent between the trough—usually 1931 or 1932—and 1939), three in the "medium" category (recovery of over 20 percent), and a further three in the "slow" category (where recovery was less than 20 percent; since the fast category includes Mexico and Brazil, it would represent the greater part of Latin America, whether by population or GDP).[25] However, the question of the (chronological) comparator is again relevant. In Bulmer-Thomas's scheme there is a clear correlation between the depth of the trough and the "speed" of the recovery: the eight "fast" recoverers include those economies that were hit hardest by the Depression in the first place (e.g., Mexico, Chile, and Cuba, which, between 1932 and 1939, experienced annual GDP growth rates of 6.2, 6.5, and 7.2 percent, respectively), while the "medium recovery countries" tend to be those that were less hard-hit (e.g., Argentina and Colombia, whose growth rates in the same period were 4.4 and 4.8 percent, respectively).[26] This is because Bulmer-Thomas defines recovery in terms of a comparison between GDP at the time of the trough (i.e., 1931- 32) and GDP in 1939, as mentioned above. Not surprisingly, countries that hit noticeably low troughs tend to show 50 percent or more growth some seven or eight years later, since they are starting from a lower baseline, with greater spare capacity. If comparisons are made not with the 1931–32 trough but with the pre-1930 peak (thus taking into account the scale of the Depression prior to 1932), the picture is somewhat different: now, Chile and Cuba—whose troughs were particularly severe—take longer to recover (pre-Depression GDP was not recovered until the 1940s; we could talk, therefore, of a "lost decade"), while in Brazil and Colombia recovery was achieved by 1933, and in Mexico and Argentina by 1935.[27]

Both the depth of the trough and the rapidity of the recovery depended on a variety of economic factors. There were common features. Everywhere, foreign trade declined, as did the terms of trade; domestic economies contracted (though a good deal less); government income fell and political instability grew, as I note below. Most countries quit the gold standard (to which they had only recently and often partially adhered), and all, save Argentina, Honduras, Nicaragua, and Haiti, ceased servicing their foreign debts.[28] However, Mexico's debt service since the Revolution had been, at best, sporadic, while Venezuela, having paid off its national debt (by way of commemorating the centennial of Bolívar's death), had no debt on which to default.[29] According to the arbitrary logic of the "commodity lottery," some exports performed better than others, in terms of volume and/or price.[30] Certainly Latin American mineral exporters were much harder hit by the vagaries of the "lottery." Bolivian tin exports, which accounted for three-quarters of the country's exports, fell from 47,000 to 14,400 tons between 1929 and 1933; although the Tin Producers Association agreement of 1933 stabilized prices, it did so at the cost of restricting production.[31] In Chile, copper output halved between 1929 and 1933, while prices fell by 60 percent; at the same time, "the Depression administered the *coup de grace* to the already enfeebled salitreras," whose exports fell by over 90 percent and whose labor force shrank from 60,000 to 8,000. In consequence, "people fled from the north as if it were a pesthouse," and these migrants included Bolivians who were obliged to head for home, where jobs were no easier to find.[32] In contrast, silver producers — Mexico in particular — benefited from the U.S. policy of silver purchases (and, by 1938, from U.S. geopolitical preoccupations), while the price of gold held up, to the benefit of Colombia and Peru.[33] Peruvian mineral exports thus contributed to the country's "vigorous export-led recovery."[34] But the luckiest ticket in the commodity lottery was petroleum, where demand continued to rise, above all to the advantage of Venezuela (see table 10.1) and, in smaller measure, Peru.[35]

The story for agricultural exports was also mixed. Wheat prices had declined in the 1920s, as a result of World War I overproduction, and remained "abysmally low" between 1930 and 1933, as surpluses were released on to a depressed market.[36] However, Argentina boosted corn production (which grew 48 percent by volume between 1933 and 1937, while exports increased by 67 percent), and the much-maligned Roca-Runciman pact of 1933 shored up beef exports and prices, chiefly to the benefit of the big landowners.[37] After the 1932 trough, therefore, Argentine recovery was vigorous and sustained.[38] David Rock reasonably concludes that "Argentina suffered relatively little from the Great Depression."[39]

Coffee had also experienced pre-Depression overproduction, and supply was relatively inelastic (trees continued to produce irrespective of global depression, whereas wheat fields could be left fallow or turned over to corn or pasture); however, this very inelasticity of supply could induce among coffee producers "a tendency to join together as a powerful interest group which will exert pressures on the state to undertake price support schemes in times of distress."[40] The classic case was Brazil, where the state had been creatively grappling with this problem since the coffee valorization scheme of the 1900s.[41] As prices slumped—by nearly two-thirds between 1929 and 1931—stockpiling increased and surpluses were destroyed; prices were thus stabilized between 1933 and 1937, while devaluation cushioned the impact on Brazil's coffee producers.[42] Coffee exporters elsewhere in Latin America could to some extent piggyback on Brazilian price stabilization: Colombia (which also possessed an effective coffee lobby) recovered quickly, but Central America—and Venezuela—were harder hit.[43] Again, the coffee interests lobbied for support, but Central American states lacked the will or the capacity to bolster those interests, save in the traditional strong-arm fashion: repressing labor and peasant protest.[44] Thus, in El Salvador and Guatemala, perhaps the extreme cases of "labour-repressive" agriculture, coffee planters shifted the burden of falling income onto the shoulders of their workers, cutting jobs, wages, and rations.[45]

Meanwhile, just as Colombia could, to some extent, piggyback on Brazil, so cotton producers on the Peruvian coast similarly benefited from the price support scheme instituted by the United States.[46] Sugar, in contrast, languished, in Peru and elsewhere; no dominant producer could bolster prices, and, for Cuba in particular, the battle for access to the U.S. market involved competition with domestic sugar producers and their powerful lobbies (there was, of course, no equivalent coffee producer lobby in the United States).[47] In particular, the perverse Smoot-Hawley Tariff of 1930 penalized Cuba, and the Cuban state—by 1933 racked by political upheaval—had to negotiate with a powerful and unyielding monopsonist; Argentine exporters arguably got a better deal from their British customers in 1933 than Cuban sugar producers did a year later, in their Reciprocity Treaty with the United States.[48] At the same time, the Cuban state restricted sugar production and closely regulated the domestic industry; as a result of the Depression, therefore, Cuba acquired an expanded "regulative state," as I note later.[49]

Thus, the worst scenario was to depend heavily on a single commodity for which demand and prices had fallen sharply (such as tin, copper, or sugar); by contrast, a diverse basket of exports, some buoyed by price supports and favored by inelastic demand, helped inhibit recession. Large producers—

such as Brazil's coffee sector—had some bargaining power; Brazil was also favored by the fact that it bought from those to whom it sold (namely, the United States, and increasingly Germany). Argentina, in comparison, continued to sell to Britain at a time when imports from the United States were rapidly rising, since the United States could outcompete Britain in the products of the Second Industrial Revolution (cars, chemicals, machine tools).[50] The consequent imbalance contributed to Argentina's long-term loss of economic dynamism.[51] There were also political consequences: British investors could extract concessions (e.g., regarding railway and tram revenues) in return for Argentina's qualified status as an "honorary member of the British Empire," but at the cost of stoking consumer resentment and nationalist criticism, which now became a staple of Argentine political debate.[52] Arguably, the 1930s witnessed the swan song of the old Anglo-Argentine economic liaison, before both countries spiraled into (relative) economic decline, accompanied by mutual recriminations. However, the economic record of the 1930s suggests that the swan song still had its appeal, at least for certain sectors, and from the mid-1930s, the aggregate performance of the Argentine economy, stimulated by an effective monetary policy, was very respectable, as it would remain until the late 1940s.[53]

Thus, contrasting relations with economic "metropolises" (global "significant others," we might say), combined with the crucial commodity lottery, produced very different outcomes, which can be summed up under two headings: depth and duration. In some countries (such as Brazil and Colombia) the effects of the Depression were relatively shallow and short-lived (the happiest scenario).[54] In some (e.g., Mexico) they were severe (an 18 percent fall in GDP) but, again, fairly short-lived (recovery by 1935).[55] In the worst-case scenario, they proved deep and quite durable: Chile's GDP fell by as much as 46 percent between 1929 and 1932 and did not recover its pre-Depression peak until 1940; in Cuba—whose GDP figures are notoriously elusive—GDP may have fallen by 40 percent, and recovery had to await the later 1940s.[56] It is perhaps not surprising, therefore, that these countries witnessed the most radical political responses to hard economic times, in the shape of the 1933 Revolution in Cuba and, in Chile, the short-lived Socialist Republic of 1932 and the more consequential Popular Front of 1938–41.[57] For quite different reasons the United States, a relatively closed industrial economy, suffered a serious and prolonged double-dip recession, with a 25 percent fall in GDP and a halting recovery—which depended on war-induced demand and spending in the early 1940s.[58]

Despite Latin America's relative openness, the nature and scale of the impact cannot be confined to the external sector. Two major structural features of the Latin American economies were also crucial by way of mediating the external shock. First, some countries still contained large peasant/subsistence sectors that were to a degree resistant to fluctuations in the business cycle. They were not, of course, invulnerable: by 1930, most Latin American peasant sectors were in some measure linked to the market economy as consumers, suppliers of labor, and producers (of agricultural goods and artisanal products). As (modest) consumers, they may have slightly benefited from lower prices; as laborers—migrants, jornaleros, sharecroppers—their income fell along with real wages more generally (an extreme example being the rural workers of El Salvador's coffee sector).[59] However, even if income fell (and the terms of trade tended to favor manufactured goods over agricultural products, to their disadvantage), peasants who retained access to land and who produced basic foodstuffs—corn, chile, beans, potatoes, manioc, even coffee—either for their own consumption or for sale in relatively inelastic domestic markets, suffered less than commercial farmers engaged in commercial crops, especially volatile export crops (such as the poorer Cuban colonos).[60] In much of rural Central America, foodstuffs seem to have been "quite abundant" during the Depression years. In Nicaragua—in contrast to El Salvador—the coffee sector was small and land was more abundant; thus, laid-off sugar workers "retreated into the peasant sector, as they had always done" when times were hard.[61] Campaigning in the Segovias, Sandino noted that the peasants did not lack for food (as townspeople in government-controlled communities did).[62] In Mexico, too, it seems likely that the alleged fall in agricultural (staple) production and consequent price inflation, which urban consumers blamed on feckless peasants (now *ejidatarios*, possessed of their own farm land), reflected in part increased consumption by the peasants themselves.[63]

Thus, domestic-use agriculture could, in some cases, take advantage of the conjuncture of the 1930s, as Bulmer-Thomas has stressed.[64] Subsistence peasants, by definition, produced for their own consumption and, when jobs were scarce or real wages declined, they could take partial refuge in subsistence production.[65] Indeed, as Chayanov argued, peasants could, by exploiting family labor, survive (if not prosper) in circumstances that would bankrupt commercial farms.[66] Such a phenomenon was evident, as I note, in Mexico; in Honduras, where laid-off banana workers could make a living in the country's "still extensive ejido lands"; or in Colombia, where "the peasant base of the coffee industry absorbed the cost of declining land prices and wages and responded to declining coffee prices by increasing production."[67] Thus, particularly in Mesoamerica and Andean America, large peasant sectors acted as a buffer during times of depression—a buffer largely lacking in, for example, El Salvador or Chile, where private estates dominated and the mass of unemployed workers (over 50,000 Chilean nitrate workers, for example) could not be readily absorbed into dense peasant communities.[68] Peasant families—including migrants turning their backs on depressed urban labor markets—could, in the Mexican phrase, "return to the quelite."[69] In (some of) Central America, too, the peasant sector became "a refuge for the rural unemployed masses"; thus, a "partial decadence in the monetary sector of the internal market" could be withstood "without catastrophic consequences."[70]

We have here an example of how delinking from the export and money economy could—as the simpler forms of dependency theory propose—bolster welfare, at least in hard times. Of course, agriculture faced its own crises, generated by adverse climatic conditions—frosts, droughts, floods, and pests—but these echoes of the ancient colonial (and pre-Columbian) rural economy followed a quite different and random rhythm, compared to the (relatively new) undulations of the business cycle.[71] Ecuadorian cacao production, hit by "witch's broom" disease, fell in the pre-Depression 1920s; in the following decade, banana blight caused more layoffs and hardship in Central America than the Depression itself.[72] In some cases, however, natural disasters—like the prolonged drought in the Brazilian Northeast in 1930–32 or the earthquake that devastated Chillán (Chile) and its hinterland in 1939—prompted significant government intervention and investment.[73] Though "exogenous" in terms of causality, such disasters could, in the right circumstances, contribute to enhanced state intervention.

The second structural feature is, in some senses, the mirror image of the first. By 1930 several Latin American economies had acquired significant industrial sectors, catering to the domestic market and benefiting from substantial tariff protection. The most obvious example was the textile industry, which in the larger and richer countries (Mexico, Brazil, Argentina, Chile) had grown rapidly, especially since the 1890s, and which had been additionally boosted by the First World War.[74] Where such industrial plants existed, it was possible to boost production, substituting for imports, when foreign

Table 10.2. GDP Growth and Manufacturing Output

COUNTRY	GDP GROWTH P.A. 1932-39	MANUFACTURING OUTPUT GROWTH P.A. 1932-39
Argentina	4.4	7.3
Brazil	4.8	7.6
Chile	6.5	7.7
Colombia	4.8	11.8
Mexico	6.2	11.9

Source: Victor Bulmer-Thomas, *The Economic History of Latin America since Independence* (Cambridge: Cambridge University Press, 1994), 219, 226.
p.a. = per annum.

exchange dried up. In many cases, spare capacity could be used more intensely (e.g., shifts could be increased); fresh investment was not essential.[75] Thus, the 1930s witnessed rapid increases in industrial production, which included not only textiles and other consumer goods but also, in some cases, producer goods, such as cement.[76] Between 1932 and 1939 manufacturing output grew appreciably in the larger Latin American economies, outstripping—and thus fueling—GDP growth, while also shifting the balance of domestic production toward the dynamic industrial regions, such as São Paulo (Brazil) and Monterrey (Mexico) (see table 10.2).[77]

We may contrast these cases—where the combination of an existing industrial base and a larger domestic market made a measure of import substitution industrialization (ISI) feasible—with those where ISI played little part in recovery, and recovery, to the extent that it occurred, depended on renewed exports and/or import-substituting agriculture. These would include Peru, Cuba, Venezuela, Ecuador, El Salvador, Honduras, and Nicaragua.[78] In the latter, for example, the British consul in Managua commented on the shallowness of the domestic market: coffee exports had plummeted in value, wage cuts and layoffs were widespread, and "the population is mainly on the very margin of existence."[79] It is worth noting that, when it came to ISI, "size" was a function of the domestic market (and thus of disposable incomes), not just of aggregate output or population: both Costa Rica and Uruguay—though "small"—achieved a measure of ISI, which the rest of

Central America (as well as Bolivia and Paraguay) failed to do; Venezuela, too, buoyed by oil exports, failed to take the ISI path, as did Peru, where "the reorientation of the . . . economy in the years following the Depression was slight by comparison with other Latin American countries."[80]

If we relate this industrializing story to the global comparisons mentioned above, it is clear that, given the structure of their economies circa 1930, the larger Latin American countries were well placed to take advantage of the external shock of 1930, since the fall in export income spurred a process of ISI, at least where capacity and demand made it possible. This positive response in turn reflected the fact of significant incipient industrialization—notably in the 1890s—which had been further encouraged by the First World War.[81] The Depression thus accelerated an ongoing process (it did not create something out of nothing). Furthermore, Latin America could now engage in the "easy" phase of ISI, for which the necessary inputs of capital and technology were quite limited, hence within the range of national entrepreneurs.[82] The U.S. economy, in contrast, was operating at a more advanced stage of industrial development; hence, it has been plausibly argued, it proved much harder to pull that economy out of the slough of depression.[83] ISI, accelerated, if not induced de novo, by the Depression, was thus another example of de-linking from the global economy, producing—in some measure—economic benefits, at least for some (large) sectors of society in some (large) countries. Again, dependency theorists, now widely ignored or dismissed, were not wholly barking up the wrong tree.[84]

Great Depression Politics (Conjunctural)

This broad *economic* pattern is fairly well known, and the chapters in this book do not substantially amend received (economic history) wisdom. But how do *political* and *social* responses to the Depression—which these chapters do address—stack up? First, such responses are subject to a wider range of variation and divergence. There are only so many ways of growing wheat or making widgets, while wheat and widget markets display a degree of uniformity across the globe.[85] Politics, both elite and popular, top-down and bottom-up, tends to be more skittish and idiosyncratic, susceptible to individual or small-group decision making. *Natura non facit saltem* ("Nature doesn't proceed by leaps and bounds") may have relevance for economic processes, especially the grand structural processes of demographic change, technological innovation, and direct investment; but politics certainly makes jumps—sometimes leaps in the dark—and politicians, like March hares, often enjoy cavorting about in *macho* courtship rituals.[86]

The political narrative of the 1930s is therefore punctuated by sudden and seemingly stochastic political twists and turns, some of which, for all their apparent contingency, had decisive consequences. The Argentine military coup of 1930, the first successful *golpe* of the twentieth century in that country, which ended fourteen years of representative democracy, involved "remarkably little planning" and "only small forces," most of them junior cadets.[87] The death of Juan Vicente Gómez five years later brought rapid and substantial change in Venezuelan politics. Bolivian president Daniel Salamanca's decision to go to war with Paraguay in 1932 was essentially a personal and political decision, taken "despite the clear opposition of his own high command," while the beleaguered president was in an "almost hysterical state of mind."[88] The ensuing Chaco War (1932–35), which would profoundly affect Bolivian state and society—dominating "all other considerations . . . for the whole decade from 1928 to 1938"—was essentially an individual throw of the political dice, not some ineluctable collective economic fate.[89] In the same year, President Sánchez Cerro—"perhaps [in order] to divert public opinion" from the country's economic woes—mobilized the Peruvian army in order to wrest Leticia from Colombia; in this case, however, no major war ensued.[90] Even President Lázaro Cárdenas's celebrated expropriation of the Anglo-American oil companies in 1938, a prime example of economic nationalism, which would have significant long-term consequences for Mexico's political economy and leftist/nationalist mythology, responded chiefly to considerations of national decorum and political sovereignty; it was not a direct response to the Depression, nor was it a calculated cost-benefit economic decision.[91]

These individual political decisions, for all their undoubted consequences, could have gone differently: that is, we could imagine the Argentine coup failing (plenty failed in 1930s Chile), Gómez either dying earlier or living longer, Salamanca listening to his high command and avoiding war with Paraguay, Peru and Colombia opting for war, or Cárdenas adopting a "safety-first" policy toward the intransigent oil companies, as some cabinet members counseled.[92] These are plausible *political* counterfactuals that warn against assuming an ineluctable—or "overdetermined"—causality. In contrast, many *economic* outcomes were, we could say, "overdetermined," that is, counterfactuals are fundamentally implausible (for example, that Paraguay and Honduras would rely on ISI to haul their economies out of recession or that Brazil and Mexico would eschew ISI in favor of export-led recovery). However, by its very nature, this political *histoire événementielle* is resistant to rigorous model building and sweeping cross-national generalization.[93] After all, wheat or widgets are more amenable to measurement and cross-national comparisons than military coups or presidential decisions to go to war.[94] Thus, like Díaz Alejandro, I am skeptical how far we can discern, across Latin America, common political patterns riding on the back of the common economic experience of the Depression; rather, we see a "bewildering variety of political paths" even among countries "similar in per capita income and their degree of opening to trade."[95] This is simply another way of asserting the "relative autonomy" of the political, the refusal of politics — especially short-term, conjunctural politics — to act as a simple reflex of economics (even "in the last analysis").

However, a few tentative thoughts can be advanced. The safest generalization, which has the merit of firmly tying political consequences to economic causality (and of being very roughly quantifiable), is that the Depression provoked serious political instability, evident in rapid and often unconstitutional governmental — and regime — change, not just in Latin America but also elsewhere in the world, including Spain, Germany, Greece, and Austria. The bald statistics are often cited: thirteen successful Latin American coups in the years 1930–34, followed by seven more in the rest of the decade.[96] Ecuador alone suffered fourteen coups in ten years, it is said.[97] More schematically, we can note, in ascending order of consequence, (1) constitutional/ incremental changes of government, (2) unconstitutional changes of government (usually by means of military coup), and (3) unconstitutional changes of *regime*.[98] Category (1) would include Colombia, where the Liberals returned to power in 1930 and governed (in some respects innovatively) for sixteen years (hence, the Depression ushered in the "Liberal Republic"); and Mexico, where the regime born of the Revolution endured (and, indeed, grew stronger) but veered to the left under Cárdenas, adopting radical policies of land and labor reform.[99] In Colombia, change came through the ballot box; in Mexico, though ballot boxes were used (and, indeed, were both stolen and stuffed), change derived from a broader concatenation of elite and popular political struggles, chiefly within the ranks of the regime (army, party, and allied mass organizations). The result, in both cases, was significant political innovation (and a lurch to the left), but within the terms of the political status quo ante. The pre-1930 rules of the game may have been amended, but they were not subverted.

Category (2) involves what might be called classic *golpismo*: changes of administration (but not regime, therefore not the basic "rules of the game") by unconstitutional (nonelectoral) means involving force—usually military force, but occasionally also popular violence.[100] Sánchez Cerro's ouster of Leguía in Peru in August 1930 may have indicated that "Peru was about to enter a new political era," but the immediate result was the replacement of one authoritarian leader and government by another.[101] Furthermore, Sánchez Cerro was then forced out of office in 1931, only to return later in the same year, thanks to elections that "historians have generally considered . . . fraudulent."[102] Following his assassination two years later, power passed to the moderate conservative Oscar Benavides.[103]

Getúlio Vargas's revolt of 1930 also represented an unconstitutional seizure of power, the product of elite and regional interstate rivalries, coupled with "the pressure of the world-wide economic crisis."[104] But it did not produce an immediate change of regime; at the time, it looked like "merely another chapter in the history of quarrels among the slowly changing elite," followed by another "seven years of agitated improvisation" before the Estado Novo brought genuine regime change in 1937.[105] In Bolivia, too, 1930 witnessed a violent change of government, as the army overthrew President Siles; but the change of regime—the advent of "military socialism"—came six years later, after the decisive trauma of the Chaco War.[106] The first of Ecuador's (alleged) fourteen coups occurred in 1931, with the violent—though not *very* violent—overthrow of the Ayora administration in 1931, which was swiftly followed by the fall of his military successor, Larrea Alba.[107] There followed a succession of elections, coups, and civil wars (that of August 1932 being notably severe); yet, while the first (short-lived) administration of Velasco Ibarra (1934–35) marked the advent of "the outstanding phenomenon of twentieth-century Ecuadorian politics," Velasquista populism, there was no decisive change of regime, no Ecuadorian Estado Novo.[108]

The Estado Novo—and Bolivian "military socialism"—involved violent changes of *regime*, not just of *administration*. They also came later, at a time when the immediate effects of the Depression had receded (particularly in Brazil). However, the stresses of the Depression did provoke category (3) regime change in several countries.[109] We can first identify a distinctive Southern Cone (Argentine and Uruguayan) syndrome: the overthrow of established constitutional, civilian, and democratic (and in the case of Uruguay *social*-democratic) regimes by force, and their replacement by more conservative and "oligarchic" regimes, linked to the army and roughly representative of the old landlord and exporting elites—what Paul Drake therefore calls "oligarchic retrenchment."[110] Particularly in Argentina, this political closure—or regression—proved very significant, since the use of military force to change regimes (and, at the same time, to purge and proscribe opponents—Radicals in the 1930s, Peronists in the 1960s and after) became a recurrent feature of the country's perverse political "culture." Indirectly, the Depression and its political consequences thus contributed to Argentina's "reversal of development."[111] In Chile, however, the pattern was quite different. The immediate effect of the Depression, in political terms, was the fall of authoritarian president Carlos Ibáñez and—after a confused hiatus in 1931–32—the restoration of electoral democracy. Having weathered the "remorseless plotting" of his political opponents, notably Arturo Alessandri, "General Ibáñez was defeated . . . by the Wall Street crash and the onset of the Depression."[112] Furthermore, electoral democracy remained intact (albeit initially under threat) until 1973. The Depression thus had decisive but antithetical political consequences.

At the other end of Latin America we can discern another—Central American—syndrome, also involving regime change, whereby oligarchic civilian regimes gave way to authoritarian caudillos, products of the army or, in Nicaragua, the newly created National Guard (a lineage that displays the importance of U.S. policy in the determination of political outcomes in the isthmus).[113] The pattern is not uniform (if the term may be allowed), but in four of six republics this outcome prevailed, albeit with variations. Ubico (Guatemala) and Carías (Honduras) first came to power under oligarchic/constitutional auspices, but they soon set about creating harsh but durable authoritarian regimes (Ubico, 1931–44; Carías, 1931–46); Somoza engineered his election in 1936 and, likewise, created a long-lasting regime and dynasty.[114] Ubico, Somoza, and Trujillo also cultivated a populist style of politics—vaguely demotic, without being remotely democratic. They were activist itinerant presidents who appealed to the people and flirted with social reform—at least to begin with.[115] El Salvador represents an interesting sui generis case: 1927–31 represented "the first, and some would argue the last, era of genuine democracy in the country's history" (at least prior to the 1990s), and President Arturo Araujo, democratically elected in 1931, was a progressive reformer.[116] But he was ousted by the army at the end of that year, and short-lived democracy gave way to a ferociously repressive military regime under General Maximiliano Hernández Martínez.[117] Thus, even if the point of departure—the overthrow of a progressive and democratic government—was different, the outcome was similar: enduring authoritarian regimes, personalist, in some cases populist, and eventually "sultanistic." The decade of the 1930s witnessed, as Bulmer-Thomas puts it, the "rise of authoritarian caudillismo," a phenomenon whose "main cause . . . was the depression itself."[118]

In much of Central America, therefore, the old oligarchy lost ground to personalist authoritarian strongmen, while in the Southern Cone (outside Chile) the oligarchy made a political comeback, conniving in the overthrow of democratic regimes and their replacement by conservative-military coalitions. So, in purely political terms, the Depression tended to produce a conservative and authoritarian direction of travel; Drake therefore refers to the 1930s as a "dictatorial decade," a key chapter in Huntington's "first reverse wave" (1922–42), that is, the first systematic rolling back of democracy after the early democratic gains of the pre-1914 period.[119] But this was in part a random outcome. There was no strict rule regarding Depression-induced political change; that is to say, it could involve both political opening and political closure, swerves to the left as well as to the right. In Colombia, as we have seen, the Depression helped bring the Liberals to power (constitutionally), and, under López Pumarejo, the Liberals not only adopted progressive socioeconomic policies but also mobilized wider sectors of the population (in other words, we see political opening—some might wish to call it "empowerment"—rather than closure).[120] Had the Liberals been in power in 1930, a Conservative comeback might have been on the cards (as in Argentina and Uruguay).

In Cuba, too, the violent overthrow of Machado, which clearly stemmed from the regime's failure to address the severe problems of the Depression, stimulated widespread popular mobilization, involving students, peasants, and workers, which, for a time in 1933, threatened a form of social revolution.[121] And even when Batista and the army rolled back this threat, the ensuing regime, for all its corruption, embodied a measure of populist reform, which Batista himself continued when he was elected president in 1940.[122] In Chile, too, the Depression unseated president-dictator Carlos Ibáñez and prompted a process of re-democratization, but in a context of great political turbulence and polarization—hence the short-lived Socialist

Republic of 1932 and the more consequential Popular Front of 1938–41.[123] As mentioned above, it is surely not coincidental that the two countries that fared worst in the commodity lottery—Chile and Cuba—should have faced the greatest leftist and popular protests. These were also the two countries where economic stress had a democratizing effect, an outcome that, of course, stemmed from the fact that the Depression struck Chile and Cuba when authoritarian regimes held power. In the one Latin American country that had actually experienced a social revolution—Mexico—the Depression pushed the regime decisively (but largely peacefully) to the left, ensuring the ouster of Calles and the radical Cardenista reforms of the mid-1930s.

The simplest and most parsimonious explanation of these divergent outcomes is that the Depression, by provoking fiscal crises, job losses, and hardship, undermined incumbent governments and regimes. Whether the outcome was (again, in political terms) conservative (and disempowering?) or progressive (and empowering?) depended a great deal on the character of the political status quo ante. The Southern Cone (Argentina and Uruguay) had competitive civilian representative regimes pre-1930; their discrediting and overthrow marked a shift back to more closed oligarchic rule. In Central America, at the other extreme of Latin America, not just geographically but also in terms of economic development and social welfare, the status quo ante typically involved civilian oligarchs, who now gave way—with respect to political power at least—to authoritarian caudillos, some of remarkable political longevity. In Cuba, where the Depression was particularly severe, the fall of the oligarchic—and neocolonial—regime of Machado opened several possibilities, including social revolution and renewed U.S. intervention; the eventual outcome was a more populist, reformist regime and, as Domínguez argues, a shift from U.S. imperialism to U.S. hegemony.[124] In Colombia and Mexico there was no sharp regime change, but rather a left turn within the ranks of the regime.

The one safe generalization—which is neither novel nor revelatory—is that the Depression stressed and struck down existing governments/regimes; the direction of political travel thus depended a good deal on the nature of the political status quo ante.[125] Again, there is a pertinent recent parallel: the debt crisis of the 1980s has been (correctly) credited with encouraging the spread of democracy in Latin America; sometimes, the causal link is the supposed "elective affinity" between neoliberal state shrinking (necessitated by the debt crisis) and liberal (or "bourgeois") democracy. However, a more solid—even if somewhat stochastic—link is probably to be found in the delegitimization of incumbent regimes, which, in many Latin American countries, happened at the time to be authoritarian (for example, Argentina, Brazil, Chile, Uruguay, and Mexico).[126] It seems less likely that the Depression of the 1930s and the debt crisis of the 1980s were ideologically discriminating than that they were anti-incumbent.

Even if the political instability provoked by the Depression was in many cases conjunctural and exogenous (rather than structural and endogenous), that did not mean it was inconsequential. Conjunctural events can have lasting—even structural—consequences.[127] Some Depression-induced changes—such as the ouster of the Radicals in Argentina—had lasting consequences, tossing the army into politics and fostering a more divisive and exclusionary politics that would endure well into the postwar period.[128] Conversely, the overthrow of Ibáñez in 1931 and the election of Alessandri in 1932 inaugurated over forty years of democratic civilian government in Chile.[129] Apart from such lasting institutional outcomes, the years of depression also created some enduring myths and symbols. Revolutionary upheaval in Cuba—though it did not translate into a full-fledged social revolution—left a legacy that later Cuban radicals, including Castro and the 26th of July Movement, would profitably draw upon.[130] In Central America, the violent repression of the 1932 leftist/Indian revolt in El Salvador and the construction of the Somoza regime/dynasty after 1936 marked decisive watersheds in political history; and when the resulting authoritarian systems came under sustained attack in the 1970s and 1980s, it is significant that the armed opposition fought under the names of Sandino and Farabundo Martí, heroes and martyrs of the 1930s.[131] Even where greater continuity prevailed—as in Mexico—the shift from Callismo to Cardenismo was also consequential, since Cardenismo brought with it a sweeping land reform, a reformulation of the alliance between the state and organized labor, oil nationalization, and a measure of détente between church and state; Cardenismo also became a fundamental point of reference for the Mexican nationalist Left, both elite and popular.[132] Especially for the Left, it seems, the 1930s were a fertile seedbed of heroic myths and memories.

But remember *post hoc, ergo propter hoc*. Some major political changes clearly cannot be attributed to the Depression. Juan Vicente Gómez did not die of economic causes, and Venezuela, blessed with oil, did not suffer serious macroeconomic troubles; the political mobilization of the 1930s therefore defies economistic explanation. But, elsewhere, much of the political instability of the early 1930s derived at least in part from economic

Table 10.3. Percentage of Government Revenue Derived from Import and Export Duties, 1929

Argentina	47	Costa Rica	65	Nicaragua	60
Bolivia	46	Cuba	55	Paraguay	59
Brazil	44*	El Salvador	63	Peru	35
Chile	54	Guatemala	61	Uruguay	41
Colombia	55	Mexico	41	Venezuela	51

Source: Victor Bulmer-Thomas, *The Economic History of Latin America since Independence* (Cambridge: Cambridge University Press, 1994), 182, 110.
* Federal revenue.

tensions and grievances. The causal sequence—somewhat "stylized," as economists like to say—is clear. Workers in the export sector—Bolivian and Mexican miners, day laborers on the coffee and banana plantations of Central America, workers in the Chilean nitrate fields—faced layoffs and wage cuts.[133] Throughout Latin America, the drop in exports and export earnings diminished government revenue, which still depended heavily on foreign trade taxes, albeit somewhat less than it had a generation earlier (see table 10.3).[134]

Strapped for cash, governments had difficulty servicing the public debt and felt obliged to cut public spending; this in turn meant fewer public works and fewer jobs. In some cases public penury reached such a point that state employees went unpaid or—in the case of Honduras—were (allegedly) paid in postage stamps. If the unpaid state employees included the army—as in Peru—the spur to rebellion was all the greater: the coup that ousted Peruvian president Leguía in August 1930 involved junior army officers aggrieved over "the precipitous decline in their salaries as a result of the depression."[135] As already noted, Argentina, well schooled in the principles of orthodoxy and concerned to maintain its creditworthiness, serviced both its foreign and domestic debt with what Marichal calls "Swiss punctuality."[136] Argentina's debt servicing rose from 6 to 16 percent of government expenditure, but this deflationary trend was offset by a heterodox monetary policy that boosted domestic confidence and stimulated revival.[137] Elsewhere, defaults were the norm, starting with Peru and Bolivia; in Mexico, default mattered less, since it had been the norm since 1913.[138] When it came to monetary policy, most governments strove to cling to the gold standard, even "with misguided stubbornness," as in the case of Chile; but orthodoxy proved untenable, especially after Britain quit the gold standard in September 1931, and the key question now became how governments, freed from their "golden fetters," would respond to their newfound freedom.[139]

In the small republics of Central America, governments cut budgets so severely that, by the mid-1930s, Guatemala and El Salvador actually ran small budget surpluses. However, since those budgets were primarily dedicated to maintaining an oppressive state and its forces of repression (as well as doling out patrimonial rewards to favored clients), it is arguable that cuts were less consequential than they would have been if education, welfare, and/or useful public works were priorities.[140] Such "passive" reactions to the Depression—government cuts and, for better or worse, a continued reliance on export recovery—thus characterized the poorer economies of "Indo-America."[141]

In contrast, Mexico adopted heterodox policies, suspending debt payments (which had been intermittent anyway) and engaging in (proto?)-Keynesian reflationary policies, at least after 1932.[142] The money supply expanded, social reforms (land and labor) boosted demand, and public works (chiefly road building) created jobs. Brazil, too, resorted to deficit financing—not because Vargas was an unorthodox proto-Keynesian, which he wasn't, but rather because politico-economic circumstances favored such policies.[143] One measure that stood ready to hand was the state purchase of coffee surpluses, which had a powerful reflationary impact; furthermore, Brazil's political system permitted pump priming at the state as well as the federal level.[144] It is not coincidental that Brazil and Mexico—favored, as they also were, by sizable domestic markets—made more rapid and sustained recoveries.[145] In Colombia, too, the money supply was boosted, and by the later 1930s the Colombian finance minister, Carlos Lleras Restrepo, was openly espousing the "Keynesian heresy": "a government deficit was not necessarily a bad thing . . . it could help to reactivate the economy."[146] One element of "[re]active" strategy—crucial if hard to evaluate with any precision—was a government commitment to experiment and intervention, which countered fatalism and engendered a measure of confidence, not least among business.[147] Cárdenas was not much liked by Mexican big business, but it could not be denied that his policies—which involved a judicious balance between social reform and respect for the market—redounded to their benefit.[148] The same, of course, was true of FDR: his economic grasp was tenuous, his policy often inconsistent, but, by stressing the creative role of government, he countered the notion that nothing could be done, and, in place of fear, fatalism, and quiescence, he offered "action, action."[149]

Great Depression Politics (Structural)

These were conjunctural responses; it remains to consider the structural changes that were associated with the Depression.[150] Of course, the conjunctural/structural distinction is not clear-cut. Incremental conjunctural shifts can eventually add up to structural transformations. The most obvious example is the role of the state. It is often argued that the Depression marked a sea change in the role of the state, both in Latin America and elsewhere in the world.[151] In the simplest terms, laissez-faire gave way to dirigisme. Certainly there is good evidence of a shift in official thinking. The Mexican Six Year Plan of 1934 stressed "the central . . . role of the state in directing and restructuring society," while in Brazil, too, an incremental growth of state intervention in the economy—including the heterodox policies just mentioned—prefaced the more thorough and purposive extension of state power under the Estado Novo, which, in emulation of European totalitarianism, extended beyond the economy to include the nation's culture and identity.[152] In Bolivia, the military took power in 1936, pledging—in the words of General and President David Toro—"to implant state socialism."[153] Even in Argentina, where the commitment to laissez-faire and elite suspicion of a strong state were stronger, the economic plans hatched in the 1930s and early 1940s involved greater tariff protection and state regulation of the economy, particularly in the area of monetary policy, while the 1940 Plan Pinedo, drawn up by the then finance minister, committed the state to an "ambitious scheme for promoting national industry" by means of an industrial development bank, state marketing of agricultural surpluses, and the purchase of the British-owned railways. Though voted down in the Chamber of Deputies, the plan clearly prefigured later Peronist policy.[154] In Cuba, state regulation of the sugar economy grew apace in the 1930s, while the 1940 constitution granted the state extensive powers, particularly regarding labor relations and wage bargaining.[155] Perhaps the most radical, if ephemeral, project of statist development was hatched by Chile's socialist government of 1932, which set out "to reorganize the Chilean economy along strongly dirigiste lines," with a national economic council coordinating a series of public corporations responsible for "agriculture, mining, industry, transportation (and) foreign trade."[156]

This quick résumé of statist initiatives (which could easily be extended) suggests two immediate conclusions: first, the commitment to dirigisme spanned the whole political spectrum and embraced democratic, authoritarian, military, and "revolutionary" regimes; and second, rhetoric often outran reality—irrespective of discursive claims and ambitious paper projects, the Latin American states could not become Leviathans overnight (on the contrary, their fiscal and administrative capacities were usually quite limited, as we shall see), while powerful groups in civil society (including businessmen and the church) were leery of official commitments to statism and "socialism" and were disposed to resist them.[157]

Nevertheless, there was a marked tendency for the role of the state to grow, under regimes of both the Left and Right. The tendency was clearest (almost by definition) where, in Díaz Alejandro's terms, "reactive" policies prevailed and where the size of the economy and depth of the market made state promotion of industry more feasible (e.g., Mexico, Brazil, Chile, and Argentina). By contrast, Central American states were largely "passive," although Somoza did court organized labor and introduce modest social reforms.[158] Peru, too, was something of an exception (in part, perhaps, because of the collapse and disgrace of Leguía's developmentalist regime in 1930): exports revived, ISI was very limited, and tariff hikes were avoided. Economic liberalism retained its appeal in (largely conservative) policy-making circles; state intervention, by way of industrial promotion and development banks, had to await the 1940s and, even then, was half-hearted, short-lived, and "dismal" in its delivery.[159] Even where the statist rhetoric was shrill, the practical commitment to intervention was often piecemeal and pragmatic, driven by political pressures as much as any grand economic vision (Vargas being the quintessential example; Cárdenas, too, was much more prudent and pragmatic than his radical image often suggests).[160] Nevertheless, we can discern, amid the groping, experimentation, and often-exaggerated rhetoric, a shift (to call it "paradigmatic" is tempting but probably wrong) toward greater state intervention in the economy, toward ISI, and—given growing export pessimism—away from the old reliance on export-led growth (*desarrollo hacia afuera*). Prebisch and Pinedo in Argentina were perhaps the most sophisticated exponents of this policy shift, which, before long, would crystallize in the postwar orthodoxy of CEPALismo.[161] Again, the Depression did not induce this new policy mix ex nihilo: there was a very old tradition of tariff protection and state intervention in Latin America, and, more proximately, the First World War had

Table 10.4 Central Government Spending as a Percentage of GDP

COUNTRY	1900	1910	1920	1930	1940	1950	1960
USA	2.8	2.0	6.9	3.7	9.1	14.0	18.2
Cuba	—	7.3*	5.0**	10.3	12.7	11.6	14.8§
Mexico	4.7	3.6	4.1	6.0	7.4	8.8	13.0
Guatemala	—	—	6.2†	11.5	10.7	7.3	8.9
Peru	3.6	4.4	4.5	11.5‡	6.6	11.3	13.3
Venezuela	—	—	10.3	10.7	12.1	18.2	26.1
Argentina	10.6	8.9	5.2	11.4	11.0	14.0	12.5
Brazil	14.0	13.0	12.5	11.4	9.6	8.7	9.5

Source: Figures calculated according to the Montevideo-Oxford Latin American Economic History Data Base (http://moxlad.fcs.edu.uy/en.html).
* 1911.   ** 1919.   § 1958.   † 1925.   ‡ 1928.

underlined the fragility of *desarrollo hacia afuera*.[162] But it would probably be fair to say that the Depression—preceded by one world war and succeeded by another—was instrumental in fostering this new statist and "structural-ist" approach.

The immediate effect of this new approach should not be exaggerated.[163] The growth of state powers during the 1930s is clear, in very general terms, but the rate of growth and its impact are hard to measure. It should, in theory, be possible to plot the state's upward trajectory: for example, by tracking state spending as a share of GDP. In fact, the figures are often hard to obtain and may be largely unreliable.[164] What they do show, in a few salient cases, is indeed a growth in relative state expenditure (see table 10.4).[165]

Accuracy aside, these figures are potentially misleading in several re-spects: they indicate state spending, not state revenue, and they reflect cen-tral government spending, which, especially in genuinely federal systems like those of the United States or Brazil, is only part of the story.[166] But they offer a rough guideline, from which we can extract a few solid conclusions (again, conclusions that are probably neither novel nor revelatory). First, as the U.S. figures show, war, especially "total war," significantly boosted state spending (hence the rise from 2.8 to 6.9 percent in 1900–1920 and from 9.1 to 14.0 percent in 1940–50). The Latin America countries show no such war-induced increase; even those that participated in the Second World War did so on a very limited scale in military terms, while intra–Latin American wars were few and relatively minor (the Chaco War being the major exception). By the same token, the kind of enhanced "prewar" arms spending—sometimes referred to as "military Keynesianism"—which, for example, boosted output in Germany and Japan, played little role in Latin America.[167] Total wars may also elicit new "social pacts," binding government and citizens in a joint war effort and thus affording the basis for enduring welfare states, as in Western Europe (and, to a lesser extent, the United States). No such phenomenon occurred in Latin America, which helps explain the relatively low levels of state spending (and taxation) and the corresponding weakness of Latin American welfare regimes.[168]

Secondly, wars would be less significant if, postwar, there was a "return to normalcy," as Calvin Coolidge eloquently put it, but state spending in fact tends to be "downwardly sticky"; thus, once it has risen, it is hard to repress (the same was true of wages after the First World War). Of course, the major belligerents did convert from war to peace economies after 1945, but state spending never returned to prewar levels: the welfare state and the Cold War—those odd kissing cousins—saw to that. So, too, in Latin America, where the growth of state spending was more gradual (and not war induced), increases were rarely reversed. The increments of the 1930s therefore tended to become permanent.

However, two additional facts are important. First, the increments of the 1930s were quite modest and built on earlier increases in state spending. As table 10.4 shows, state spending did not suddenly spike; thus, to take a couple of good examples, to see Cárdenas and Vargas as profligate economic populists, bent on building huge hypertrophied states, is fundamentally wrong; it is to use—and to traduce—history in the cause of contemporary economic advocacy.[169] The statism of the 1930s was also clearly incremental. Contrary to some hoary myths, Latin America states were never consistently committed to laissez-faire principles or policies; their "liberalism" was often highly illiberal (for example, involving state subsidies of infrastructure and heavy-handed control of the labor force); and, since they depended on foreign trade taxes for the bulk of their revenue, a commitment to thoroughgoing free trade would have meant fiscal suicide. Therefore, even during the region's so-called liberal heyday (roughly 1860–1914), states maintained high (revenue) tariffs and, in other respects, intervened in the economy.[170] They intervened, in part, to create the supposed preconditions of economic liberalism (breaking up corporate property and inducing—even forcing—workers to enter the labor market). These illiberal means, since they favored powerful interests (not least the government itself), tended to endure.

Means became ends. Thus, while the 1930s certainly witnessed a retreat from principles of laissez-faire, this was no sudden and dramatic fall from grace, but rather a further compromising of an already-flawed economic liberalism. Tariffs went up, but they did not have to be introduced de novo; indeed, since tariffs were rising around the world, it seems likely that, in relative terms, Latin American protectionism may actually have decreased.

There is no need to postulate some murky Latin American corporate/ Catholic/paternalist/patrimonial id, concealed beneath the superficial super-ego of liberalism, to explain this shift.[171] Circumstances changed, *desarrollo hacia afuera* looked a less attractive bet, domestic lobbies clamored for protection, and, of course, ruling elites usually prefer state-enhancing policies to those that involve an abdication of their power and patronage. So, the recourse to greater state intervention was easily comprehensible (it had worldwide parallels, far away from the Catholic and corporate culture of Latin America), and it was incremental, building on established policies of protection and government intervention. It was also quite modest. Revolutionary Mexico, which might be expected to be in the van of economic statism, nudged up the state's role in the economy from 4.1 percent of GDP in 1920 to 6.0 percent in 1930 and 7.4 percent in 1940.[172] Incremental growth continued for decades, even after the revolution lost its radical momentum: the real spurt in statism, which led to the gross Leviathan of the late Partido Revolucionario Institucional, did not come until the 1970s and early 1980s.[173] We also see modest incremental growth in such dissimilar cases as Venezuela and Guatemala; in Argentina central government spending remained roughly static, while in Brazil it fell somewhat, and in Peru it declined significantly—as the spending splurge of the Leguía regime came to a sorry end in 1930. In terms of the growth of the state, therefore, the decade of the 1930s was an important episode, but it was no more than an episode in a long story; the dirigiste jalopy—it was still far from a juggernaut—gathered speed, but it did not have to execute a sudden U-turn.[174]

Of course, the figures of state spending relative to GDP do not tell the whole story, though at least they tell a story that is potentially measurable, and thus amenable to evaluations that go beyond loose semantic comparisons—"bigger," "growing," "stronger," and so on. Many elements of enhanced state power did not show up in the balance sheet; they involved increased control and regulation of fiscal and monetary policy, of foreign assets, and of the labor movement (hence, in the case of Cuba, Domínguez's "regulative state," mentioned above).[175] Indeed, Bolivia's military socialists set out to construct a radical, nationalist, reformist regime while paradoxically promising "a balanced budget and a frugal administration."[176] States now played a much greater role in the regulation of exchange rates, foreign trade, and, in some measure, foreign investments. Central banks—again, several of them creations of the 1920s—acquired and wielded additional powers.[177] In Latin America, as in the rest of the world, tariffs edged up, as already mentioned; however, as governments and growing manufacturing lobbies espoused the cause of industrialization, so revenue tariffs tended to give way to (ISI) protective tariffs, coupled with protective quotas and subsidies. The 1945 conference at Chapultepec, Mexico, confirmed that tariffs and ISI were here to stay.[178] The United States, while allergic to state intervention in Latin America, could tolerate higher tariff barriers, so long as U.S. corporations could vault over them and establish profitable subsidiaries within protected national markets. ISI thus acquired a measure of self-sustaining momentum, reflecting shifts in economic power (roughly from rural to urban, landlord to industrialist), as well as congruent shifts in geographical locus (the rise of Monterrey and São Paulo, the hypertrophy of Buenos Aires and Santiago, the shift of population from the Argentine interior to the littoral).[179]

The second element of state intervention involved the regulation—and occasionally expropriation—of foreign assets. As the figures of state economic intervention suggest, regulation was much more common than expropriation: no state acquired large-scale ownership of foreign firms. The biggest single transfer of property was the Mexican land reform of the 1930s: although foreign landowners suffered, the majority of the victims were Mexican, and since the agrarian bonds that they received proved virtually worthless, the transformation of their properties into *ejidos* represented a substantial loss.[180] However, that loss was more a product of the Mexican Revolution than it was of the Great Depression. Mexico also witnessed the most dramatic expropriation of foreign assets: the 1938 nationalization of the Anglo-American oil companies (for which modest compensation was later paid). Politically and economically salient, this was a rare event, without parallel in the rest of Latin America in terms of both its scale and its causes. True, Bolivia nationalized Standard Oil in 1937, but that was a minor enterprise and event in comparison.[181] In Mexico, the driving force behind the nationalization was a militant labor union (again, unparalleled in Latin America at the time), coupled with a "revolutionary" administration that— not surprisingly, in light of Mexican history—was highly sensitive to U.S.

slights of its sovereignty.[182] Oil was a special case (Mexican mining, a much larger item, was unaffected); elsewhere in Latin America, oil became the target of economic nationalist policy, involving increased regulation and taxation and the creation of infant state oil companies. However, "oil nationalism" affected oil-*importing* countries (such as Argentina, Chile, and Uruguay) more than oil *exporters* (such as Mexico, Peru, and Venezuela).[183] Outside Mexico, the labor movement counted for less: in the buoyant Venezuelan oil industry, strikes were successfully contained.[184] Mexico, in short, was a special case because of the preceding Revolution, heightened nationalism, and the consequent muscle of the labor movement.[185] In Peru, foreign oil companies remained largely untouched; in Colombia, the government, keen to promote exports, actually lowered taxes; in Ecuador, "oil nationalism" petered out and the companies "were again left in peace"; while in Venezuela, major tax hikes and labor reform had to await the postwar victory of Acción Democrática.[186]

A less dramatic but more extensive form of mild *agrarian* economic nationalism did, however, characterize the 1930s. States sought to shift the balance of power and income between domestic agriculturalists (usually, small farmers) and big foreign companies. This shift responded both to the pressure of farmers' lobbies and to perceptions that foreign companies were behaving like independent enclaves — politically and fiscally — and needed to be reined in.[187] Thus, even if radical land reform was off the agenda (outside Mexico), policies to protect farmers were widespread: in Cuba, the colonos — "la clase más cubana" — received security of tenure, rent control, and priority in the allocation of the sugar quota, as a result of which "administration cane," the sugar produced directly by the major companies, most of them American, fell from 30 percent in 1930 to 10 percent in 1948.[188] In the Dominican Republic, Trujillo also favored domestic producers — including peasants and squatters — over big foreign companies, citing Cuba as a negative example of a perverse antinational latifundismo.[189] Meanwhile, as mentioned earlier, domestic coffee lobbies in both Colombia and Central America strengthened during the 1930s, enlisting the support of the state in their dealings with foreign exporters.[190]

More systematically, states increasingly monitored and mediated labor disputes. Again, this was not necessarily an innovation: the so-called social question had preoccupied *pensadores* and policy makers since the turn of the century; the 1920s, in particular, had witnessed a slew of initiatives — in Leguía's Peru, Alessandri's Chile, and Calles's Mexico.[191] But the 1930s saw a further development of labor codes and arbitration procedures, made all the more necessary by hard times and the industrial unrest that followed. The year 1931 thus saw the adoption of national labor codes in both Mexico and Chile (countries with sizable and robust labor movements), but they also appeared (in attenuated form) in Costa Rica, Nicaragua, and Ecuador, while in Colombia, labor legislation made the president—by 1934–38 the progressive Liberal López Pumarejo—"the supreme arbiter of worker-management conflicts."[192] Colombian labor arbitration even extended into the countryside, as the National Labour Bureau extended its remit to cover squatters' disputes with landowners.[193] In general, however, labor legislation had an urban focus; it was often accompanied by state repression (the stick being bigger than the carrot), and in some countries it was largely absent. The American ambassador to Honduras rejoiced that, where he was posted, "there are . . . no Communists, no labor unions, no wage or social security laws, no income tax," but rather a reliance on "old-fashioned and orthodox virtues of hard work and frugality."[194]

At the other extreme, it was no surprise that revolutionary Mexico boasted the most militant and effective labor sector, allied, at least conditionally, to the radical Cárdenas administration and, as already noted, capable of triggering the 1938 oil crisis and expropriation.[195] In Cuba, too, Batista's alliance with organized labor—and with the Cuban Communist Party—gave labor substantial leverage: during the 1930s, an American observer later lamented, "much legislation was passed by succeeding administrations, which actively sought the support of labour"; thus, by the early 1940s "the whole machinery of government was geared to favour labour."[196] In Argentina and Brazil—especially the Brazil of the Estado Novo—the power of organized labor was less, state repression greater. But even Brazilian *peleguismo* illustrated that labor coud not be ignored and had to be appeased as well as controlled.[197] In the process, the old Latin American Anarchist tradition wilted: it proved impossible—or at least highly impolitic—to maintain a staunch independence of the state at a time when the state was flexing its muscles, not least in the domain of labor relations and economic management.[198]

Great Depression Politics (Social)

The state's increased role in labor relations, which contrasted—notably in Central America—with its relative indifference to the plight of the peasantry,[199] exemplified an important aspect of 1930s political economy, which is my final topic. States now engaged more systematically with society, and that society was undergoing important stresses and changes, some conjunctural, some structural. State engagement was, therefore, a reaction in part to bottom-up pressure, to—if you like—popular agency.

The conjunctural stresses involved widespread unemployment and falling incomes. In Chile, perhaps the worst case, employment in the nitrate sector collapsed, throwing over 50,000 workers out of jobs, while mining also declined sharply.[200] In Mexico, similar if less severe, consequences were compounded by the return of over 300,000 migrant workers from the United States.[201] Elsewhere in the region, the depression prompted the expulsion of foreign migrant workers, notably in Cuba, where, by 1937, economic nationalism spilled over into outright xenophobia, directed against Haitian and British West Indian migrant workers, who were laid off and repatriated en masse.[202] In the same year, in the Dominican Republic, Trujillo went a step further, launching a brutal pogrom of the country's Haitian migrants. Some 15,000 were expelled and a further 15,000 were killed, most of them clubbed, stabbed, or slashed with machetes, some even as they tried to flee westward across the border.[203]

But the most decisive, if less dramatic, demographic consequence of the Depression was the cutoff of European migration to the Southern Cone (Argentina, Uruguay, and southern Brazil), which ended a long cycle of massive population movements from Europe to the "neo-Europes" of South America (a cycle that was crucial not just for the recipient countries but also for Europe, especially southern Europe).[204] Thus, 1930 marked a demographic watershed, which "closed an era during which immigration contributed most to Latin American population growth and ushered in a period of rising natural increase."[205] For Argentina, in particular, this removed one of the key pillars of pre-1930 growth (the others being British investment and *desarrollo hacia afuera*). Internal migration, from the interior to Buenos Aires, gathered strength from the late 1930s; hence, the subsequent strengthening of the Argentine labor movement and its decisive alliance with Perón were, if not directly caused, certainly facilitated by this demographic turnaround.[206]

Confronting widespread unemployment, governments, at least in the short term, lacked the will or the resources to provide either jobs or effective social assistance; public works were, in fact, being curtailed, as budgets were cut. Road building, a strategic as well as economic priority, eventually picked up as economies revived and government revenue recovered;

the 1930s thus accelerated the transition from railway (and horse and *burro*) transport to cars, trucks, and buses.[207] The chief recourse of the unemployed was therefore family self-help, which, depending on circumstances, might involve a retreat into peasant farming (as already mentioned) or, contrariwise, migration from a depressed countryside into burgeoning cities. Thus, we see contrasting currents of migration, both to and from the cities: in the Southern Cone, where subsistence peasant communities were few, the flow favored the big cities (Santiago, Buenos Aires, São Paulo); in "Indo-America" (Mexico, Guatemala, Peru, Bolivia), subsistence agriculture—fortified by land reform in Mexico—could still staunch the flow and thus restrain rampant urbanization.

Hardship generated protest, of course. The 1933 Revolution in Cuba, combining economic grievances, opposition to the corrupt Machado dictatorship, and nationalism, was perhaps the perfect political storm.[208] But less focused protest occurred throughout the continent: riots and strikes in São Paulo in 1930–31; land seizures in Sumapaz, Quindío, and the Valle del Cauca (Colombia); mass demonstrations by unemployed coffee workers in San Salvador on May Day 1930.[209] In the Chilean countryside, Loveman notes, "resistance" was extensive but inchoate: it took the form of "pilferage, sabotage, strikes, work slowdowns or individual acts of violence"—in other words, all the familiar "weapons of the weak."[210] However, in the depth of the Depression concerted collective action was difficult and the authorities were often ready to resort to repression. The severity of repression varied according to the nature of the regime. The most extreme form occurred in El Salvador, where an authoritarian regime and a panicky elite set out to crush a popular, Indian and leftist ("Communist") uprising.[211] In Brazil, the Vargas regime was also ready to use the mailed fist, albeit cushioned by a sheepskin blanket.[212] In contrast, as already noted, leftist/populist regimes were more accommodating: in Mexico, the corrupt Callista CROM was supplanted by the more radical Cardenista CTM (and Luis Morones gave way to the Marxist firebrand Vicente Lombardo Toledano); in Chile, union membership doubled between 1935 and 1940; and similar growth occurred under President López in Colombia (1934–38), where Cardenismo perhaps "served as a model" for La Revolución en Marcha.[213] In each case, a buoyant Communist Party played a role—a dependent, collaborationist role—in leftist mobilization and reform, benefiting from another (global) "demonstration effect": the supposed success of the Soviet Union in outstripping the stagnant capitalist economies of Europe and the United States.

In most countries, rural political mobilization lagged behind or, as in El Salvador, was severely repressed. The chief exceptions were Mexico, where the radical Cardenista land reform reflected, in part, bottom-up pressure, and, to a lesser degree, Cuba, Chile, and Colombia.[214] We have seen how, in Cuba, small farmers (*colonos*) could press for security of tenure and better market access, appealing to nationalist sentiment. In Argentina, too, modest legislation was introduced to protect tenant farmers, while cotton farmers in northern Peru, backed by the Socialists, also secured better terms, indicative of the "increasing strength of the tenants and their consequent independence of large landowners."[215] These were undramatic incremental changes; hence, perhaps, they have been somewhat neglected. When it came to the more eye-catching radicalism of the 1930s, peasants and rural laborers often lacked effective collective organization, at least outside Mexico and, with qualifications, Cuba and Colombia. In some countries, where ethnic identities overlapped—and perhaps trumped—class divisions, urban radicalism did not easily spill over into the countryside.

In Chachapoyas, in the northern Peruvian Andes, the 1930s saw "a disintegration of the casta-based political order," as new popular forces—roughly the "middle sectors"—wrested local control from established (but declining) creole elites.[216] These political parvenus called for progressive, honest, democratic government, appealing to (urban) workers, artisans, students, and petty bourgeois *empleados*; and they echoed French Jacobinism by rejigging the calendar—1930 became "year one of the Redemption."[217] However, such radical urban movements, however democratically inclusive toward their own, were often leery about mobilizing peasants and Indians, and they remained resolutely patriarchal: urban male mestizos ran the show (as they did the flourishing local football teams), and peasants, day laborers, and Indians were largely excluded, while women, at best, enjoyed an "inactive" secondary role.[218] Even in Chile, where radical efforts were made to extend the provisions of the 1931 Labour Code into the countryside, the landed elite—and their influential lobby, the Sociedad Nacional de Agricultura—fought a tenacious rearguard action, blunting the thrust of state and leftist interventions. Indeed, in 1939, the Left tacitly agreed to halt rural mobilization and "sacrificed the rural labor force in the name of supporting the Popular Front."[219] The landed elite thus bought themselves twenty more years of rural preeminence and profit before popular mobilization resumed, with dramatic consequences, in the late 1950s.[220] Indeed, this chronology also roughly fits Bolivia and Brazil: in the former, peasant activism quickened in the 1940s and achieved decisive results—in the shape of land reform and the formation of powerful peasant unions—with the Revolution of 1952; in the latter, as in Chile, extensive (and therefore threatening) rural mobilization remained off the political agenda until the 1960s, when it served as a catalyst to military intervention.[221]

Thus, the popular radicalism of the 1930s—evident, for example, in the short-lived Chilean Socialist Republic of 1932, the contemporaneous wave of strikes in São Paulo, or university protest in Bolivia—tended to be an urban phenomenon, in which, apart from workers and artisans, the relatively new sociopolitical constituency of university students sometimes played a supportive role.[222] Student activism traced its origins back at least to the Argentine university reform movement of 1918, thus had much older roots, and of course continued to grow through the 1940s and beyond, in part reflecting the sheer growth—the "massification," if you like—of Latin American higher education.[223] It was an incremental process at best, tenuously linked to the economics of depression (or recovery); in Venezuela, student activism against the Gómez regime preceded the Depression, while in the birthplace of the student movement, Argentina, activism declined during the years of economic downturn.[224]

Women also played an important role in the popular mobilizations of the early 1930s: they participated in the "great tobacco workers' strikes" in Cuba, and they were prominent in both the São Paulo textile factory movement and the (now largely forgotten) protests that bucked paternalist control of Medellín's textile industry in the 1930s.[225] When troops moved against striking workers in ASARCO's Monterrey smelter, "fifty hot-headed women waving union flags" led the resistance.[226] It is not clear that these movements had decisive consequences, however. Though women's wages were substantially lower than men's—hence, a feminization of the labor force would have cut costs—the trend seems to have been in the other direction.[227] That is, trade union leadership, overwhelmingly male, usually favored the preservation of men's jobs and often advocated a traditional (house-bound) role for women, especially when jobs were scarce; and state policy, whether for reasons of ideology or political pragmatism, sided with macho male trade unionists, most clearly in the case of the Estado Novo.[228] Vargas, it is true, gave women the vote in 1932. But votes, under Vargas, were hardly decisive assets. And if we survey the electoral map of Latin America in the 1930s, it was not notable for the advance of female suffrage, which is essentially a story of the 1940s and 1950s.[229]

In long-term, structural terms, therefore, the Depression of the 1930s was remarkable much more for its impact on the political economy of cities and of industry, where states—some committed to ISI and most of them well aware of the advantages of state "incorporation" of organized labor—set about establishing (or reinforcing) links to urban, usually masculine, labor.[230] Such links might offer genuine "bottom-up" empowerment, or they might threaten "top-down" control and Brazilian-style peleguismo. Either way, they indicated the state's desire to engage with the labor movement, while preempting (or crushing) more radical working-class mobilization. One outcome of this engagement was the eclipse of Anarchism, whose rejectionist stance toward the state seemed anachronistic at a time when the state came bearing gifts, however modest.[231] At the same time, on the global stage, the Soviet Union seemed to prove the superiority of state socialism, while—after 1935—espousing Popular Frontism in opposition to Fascism. Both nationalist populism and international Communism thus trumped the old Anarchist tradition.[232] No equivalent process of popular mobilization combined with state engagement occurred in the countryside (outside Mexico and, to a limited extent, Cuba and Colombia). The scattered rural population, still the great majority of the Latin American population, lacked both organization (especially supralocal organization) and political leverage; furthermore, in many countries, they were darker and ethnically distinct, and urban radicals, for all their class and nationalist rhetoric, did not readily forge links of solidarity with their campesino comrades. And, of course, elites were usually keen to avoid the forging of any such links.[233]

Depression-era politics carried a strong nationalist charge, as we have seen. Again, this was nothing new; 1930s nationalism built on old foundations, its chief contribution being a greater stress on *economic* nationalism. The latter was often entirely rational and respectable and could be justified by sophisticated ("structuralist") arguments relating to the terms of trade and the protection of infant industries.[234] But the nationalism of these years easily spilled over into outright xenophobia, directed against "foreign" interests and communities, some of whom—such as the Indians of El Salvador or the Jews of the Southern Cone—were not "foreign" at all.[235] Mexico's Chinese communities—already the victims of persecution in the 1920s—were now expelled from the country en masse, while, as we have seen, Haitian migrants were driven out of Cuba and the Dominican Republic (if they were not, in the latter case, slaughtered before they could escape).[236] Unemployment and economic hard times contributed to this xenophobic reaction, which governments like Trujillo's shamelessly exploited. Migrants who competed for jobs were victimized, but so too were foreign (or allegedly foreign) businessmen who, as in the case of the Jews or some of Mexico's Chinese, were accused of abusing (national) workers. The extremism and violence associated with these episodes contrast strikingly with the peaceful manner in which, for example, Mexico expropriated the Anglo-American oil companies.[237] In part this reflected the politico-diplomatic weakness of the Jews and Chinese (and Haitians), but the contrast also suggests that social proximity (the Jews and Chinese were typically small businessmen, engaged in retailing or small-scale manufacturing) provoked greater popular hostility, which opportunistic politicos could exploit, especially in hard times. In the case of the Jews, too, the ancient strains of Catholic anti-Semitism now combined with the siren song of European Fascism to create a seductive refrain.

It is not surprising that, in many cases, 1930s nationalism assumed a fascistoid character, combining antiforeign (including anti-Semitic) attitudes and anti-imperialist discourse. Much of this was discursive froth, fashionable emulation of what looked like virile authoritarian regimes in Italy and Germany. (Again, therefore, we see a global "demonstration effect," often based on scant evidence, emanating from Italy and Germany, as well as the USSR, the common denominator being a rather desperate disillusionment with a bankrupt liberal capitalist order.) When imported into the very different ambience of Latin America, the impact of "Fascism" was varied and distinct. Mexican anti-Semites railed against Jews who were in fact few and socially marginal; more significantly, clerical conservatives—such as the Sinarquistas—found inspiration in Franco's Nationalists.[238] The Chilean Nazis were brutally repressed, their chief achievement being to help bring the Popular Front to power, while Brazil's Integralists—the biggest Fascist movement in South America in the 1930s—were exploited and finally emasculated by the cunning Getúlio Vargas (who, we might say, played the Franco to the Brazilian Falange).[239] In Bolivia, the early Movimiento Nacionalista Revolucionario (MNR) betrayed fascistic leanings, but in the context of a backward—feudal?—country, ruled by a narrow oligarchy, its nationalist program was, certainly compared to its main European Fascist counterparts, popular, progressive, and even empowering.[240]

With respect to broad social change—urbanization, industrialization, internal migration—the Depression was, therefore, one episode in a long story, an episode that is distinctive, but not necessarily crucial and formative. Similarly, 1930s state building was affected by the Depression in the ways described, but many features of the process—a larger government budget and payroll, better communications (especially roads), stronger central banks, greater intervention in the economy, and, at least in the urban sector, greater state "penetration" of society—were incremental and involved the acceleration of prior trends rather than radical innovations or dramatic U-turns. This is hardly surprising, since trends of this kind are rarely the result of sudden initiatives. However, in the more volatile world of politics, where vicissitudes are more common and can sometimes be consequential, the 1930s did witness changes, of both administrations and regimes, which were (in large part) the product of economic shocks and which also had enduring results (such as the collapse of competitive democracy in Argentina, or its reinstatement in Chile). These changes occurred in a climate that seemed propitious for state activism (which, again, was nothing new: it was a question of deploying state activism toward different ends). But the ensuing changes were remarkably diverse, perhaps because Latin America itself was—to state the blindingly obvious—remarkably diverse.[241] Diversity and experimentation were also helped by the international conjuncture: the United States was distracted by both domestic challenges and international threats, and the threats—in the 1930s, unlike the 1950s—induced a measure of restraint and tolerance, epitomized by the Good Neighbor Policy. Latin American states, even in the United States' immediate sphere of influence in the circum-Caribbean, were afforded a greater measure of autonomy, which permitted innovatively nationalist, progressive, and even radical policies—most clearly in Mexico, but also in Cuba and Colombia.[242]

Given this diversity, I am not persuaded that it makes sense to fasten onto the 1930s as the decade when, say, "populism" became the "prevalent" form of Latin American politics, under both democratic and authoritarian auspices.[243] Such a thesis exaggerates the explanatory power of the concept of "populism," while homogenizing the diverse political histories of the period.[244] It also anticipates, by a decade or two, the floruit of major populisms like Peronismo and (later) Getulismo. Furthermore, movements and administrations grouped under the "populist" heading—Cardenismo and Getulismo, perhaps Batistismo, Somocismo, and even Ubiquismo—were substantially different; they arose in different contexts and had different consequences. In Chile, where political responses to the Depression were most overtly radical, populism was weak, and it was also kept at bay by conservative elites during the *década infame* in Argentina. No historian would try to assimilate all of 1930s Europe—Hitler and Stalin, the France of the Popular Front, and the Britain of Stanley Baldwin—under a common political rubric; on the contrary, the decade was one of sharp polarization and divergence, not least because of the consequences of the Depression. What was true of the "west" was also true, mutatis mutandis, of "the extreme west" ("l'extrême occident"), Latin America.[245] A safe—not to say cowardly—conclusion to this overview of the effects of the Great Depression in the Americas might, therefore, be the following: that the effects were highly diverse; that accelerations (and retardations) of existing trends were much more common than sudden new departures; that common tendencies (falling exports, constrained budgets, political instability, state interventionism) were refracted through diverse national prisms; but that, even if skeptically deflated, the Depression was a crucial episode in the longer-term evolution of political and economic systems.

It was also—compared to Europe and the United States in the 1930s—a more positive and creative episode. In that respect, if in no other, it bears comparison with the recent global recession of post-2008. As a working-class woman from the squalid and swampy immigrant town of Berisso (Argentina) put it, "At that time things in Berisso were very bad"; but, she also recalls, "Berisso was nice in the 1930s"—a busy, bustling, young community, "with a lot of social life," which would, before long, become a bastion of Peronism.[246] At the other end of Latin America, in Mexico, comparable "communities-in-formation" formed the backbone of popular Cardenismo in the 1930s.[247] Thus, while the early "1930s were certainly years of crisis and hardship, the responses, both elite and popular, could be creative (in Díaz Alejandro's term, "reactive"), as well as constructive. In Europe, during these same years, the Depression prompted war, political regression, and social exclusion; it was, as Auden famously put it, "a low, dishonest decade"; in Britain, Richard Overy has recently argued, this was a "morbid age," infused with "a mood of despair or helplessness or sober pessimism."[248] Whatever was true of Britain or Europe, such a characterization would hardy fit Latin America in the 1930s, where, notwithstanding both the diversity of the regions and disasters that befell many of its inhabitants, it could be argued that the balance sheet of the Great Depression was mixed, that the undoubted challenges of those years often produced creative and successful responses, and that Tom Payne perhaps only exaggerated a little when he observed that crises "have their uses: they produce as much good as hurt."[249]

Notes

1 So I should stress that the chief aim of this chapter is not to sum up the preceding chapters, which are referred to only in passing, as they relate to the general overview being presented.

2 We could compare this fairly eclectic selection with the more focused — essentially economic — approach taken in Rosemary Thorp, ed., *Latin America in the 1930s: The Role of the Periphery in World Crisis* (London: Macmillan, 1984; Spanish translation, 1988), in some respects the point of departure of this volume. In part, this shift of emphasis reflects broader shifts in historiographical approaches over the past thirty years. Of course, categories like "economic," "political," "social," and "cultural" are loose — not to say "contested" — concepts; however, it is hard to get away from them (the participants in recent debates about "cultural" history are, by definition, assuming that such categories exist; see n. 8), and "looseness" and "contestedness" are standard features of a great many concepts that we, as historians or social scientists, readily and necessarily use.

3 Of course, political decisions — in the sense of decisions taken by governments and political elites — also had important economic consequences: consider the prevalent financial orthodoxy of the day or that "turning point in world history," the Smoot-Hawley Tariff of 1930; Charles Kindleberger, *The World in Depression: 1929–39* (London: Penguin, 1973), 134.

4 For a succinct summary, see David Hackett Fischer, *Historians' Fallacies* (New York: Harper and Row, 1970), 166–67.

5 Charles W. Anderson, *Politics and Economic Change in Latin America* (Princeton, NJ: D. Van Nostrand, 1967), 211; see also chap. 6 of this volume.

6 Edelbert Torres-Rivas, "Crisis and Conflict, 1930 to the Present," in *Central America since Independence*, ed. Leslie Bethell (Cambridge: Cambridge University Press, 1991), 77; Robert G. Williams, *States and Social Evolution, Coffee and the Rise of National Governments in Central America* (Chapel Hill: University of North Carolina Press, 1994), 258, proposes a rather closer connection between the Depression, peasant land seizures, National Guard repression, and the Sandino offensive.

7 Alan Knight, "The Rise and Fall of Cardenismo, c.1930–1946," in *Mexico since Independence*, ed. Leslie Bethell (Cambridge: Cambridge University Press, 1991), 245–46.

8 We return to the question of analytical categories, that of "culture" being one of the most slippery, as well as most fashionable (a dangerous combination). According to robust scientific — including anthropological — thinking, "culture" includes all information and practices that are not genetically transmitted, which would therefore include the vast bulk of "history," including "economic" history. Like most historians, however, I am here using "culture" in the narrower commonsensical sense of, roughly, art, literature, music, recreation,

religion, etc. "Cultural history," like its forerunner "social" history, is something of a ragbag, but it remains roughly distinguishable from "political" history (which has to do with the state in its many ramifications) and "economic" history (which deals with the production and exchange of material goods). Again, of course, there are major overlaps (the state is imbricated in the economy; the demand for material goods is in part culturally determined), but conceptual overlaps are common in historical analysis and do not per se disqualify the concepts being used—which are, in this case, common workaday concepts that are hard to avoid.

9 Following Carl Hempel; for a useful, if critical, résumé, see Fischer, *Historians' Fallacies*, 128–29. The "watered-down" version is closer to Hempel's probabilistic revision (whereby unalterable "laws" become strong tendencies); thus, as a general tendency, but not inevitably and invariably, governments that rely on foreign trade taxes lose income in time of recession, and governments that then slash budgets and jobs also lose political support. I omit any discussion of radical Humean scepticism regarding causality, which, if applied to history, would undermine the whole enterprise.

10 By which I mean the fallacy—famously enunciated by Harry Lime in the film *The Third Man*—that politics, war, society, and culture march forward together in lockstep, obeying a common rhythm. Needless to say, we can assert the "relative autonomy" of, say, cultural history, without going to the other extreme of denying connections between, say, culture, politics, and economics. Dickens has a lot to say about industrialization, but his work is not a product of industrialization like the railway engine.

11 Arthur Whitaker, "An Overview of the Period," in *Prologue to Perón: Argentina in Depression and War, 1930–1943*, ed. Mark Falcoff and Ronald H. Dolkart (Berkeley: University of California Press), 25–26; Peter Burke and Maria Lúcia Burke, *Gilberto Freyre: Social Theory in the Tropics* (Oxford: Peter Lang, 2008), 114–15. Regarding popular culture, we are told that the mordant tango lyrics of Enrique Santos Discépolo "distill the bitter essence of the disillusionment, the frustration of Depression-decade Argentina," but the same author notes that Discépolo had been penning similar lyrics in the (more prosperous) 1920s; Gustavo Sosa-Pujato, "Popular Culture," in Falcoff and Dolkart, *Prologue to Perón*, 143–44.

12 As Whitaker observes, "periodization by decades is highly artificial, but in the history of Argentina the decade of the 1930s"—being bookended by the onset of the Depression and the outbreak of the Second World War—"is less so than most"; Whitaker, "Overview of the Period," 29. At the other end of the Americas, in a very different political context, the end of the 1930s arguably brought the end of the radical phase of the Mexican Revolution (a phase that had been ushered in by the Depression); Alan Knight, "The End of the Mexican Revolution? From Cárdenas to Avila Camacho (1937–41)," in *Dictablanda: Politics,*

Work and Culture in Mexico, 1938–68, ed. Paul Gillingham and Ben Smith (Durham, NC: Duke University Press, 2014), 47–69.

13 Celso Furtado, *Economic Development of Latin America* (Cambridge: Cambridge University Press, 1970), 39; James Dunkerley, *Power in the Isthmus: A Political History of Modern Central America* (London: Verso, 1988), 90, uses the same adjective for Central America, as does Whitaker, discussing Argentina; Whitaker, "Overview of the Period," 29.

14 Gabriel Palma, "External Disequilibrium and Internal Industrialization: Chile, 1914–1935," in *Latin America, Economic Imperialism and the State: The Political Economy of the External Connection from Independence to the Present*, ed. Christopher Abel and Colin M. Lewis (London: Athlone Press, 1985), 328; see also Albert O. Hirschman, *Journeys toward Progress: Studies of Policy-Making in Latin America* (New York: Anchor Books, 1965), 240.

15 Heywood Fleisig, "The United States and the World Periphery during the Early Years of the Great Depression," in *The Great Depression Revisited: Essays on the Economics of the Thirties*, ed. Herman van der Wee (The Hague: Nijhoff, 1973), 149–51. The following trade data are taken from Victor Bulmer-Thomas, *The Economic History of Latin America since Independence* (Cambridge: Cambridge University Press, 1994), 195, 197. If current (1929), rather than deflated (1970), prices are used, the trade coefficients would be lower, particularly for Mexico; compare Víctor L. Urquidi, *Otro siglo perdido: Las políticas de desarrollo en América Latina (1930–2005)* (Mexico: El Colegio de México, 2005), 70, following Angus Maddison, *Two Crises: Latin America and Asia 1929–38 and 1973–83* (Paris: Development Center Studies, OECD, 1985). It is interesting to note that the degree of *closure* indicated by the falling export-to-GDP ratio for the 1930s is roughly the mirror image of the process of *opening* experienced in the 1970s and early 1980s; Eliana Cardoso and Ann Helwege, *Latin America's Economy: Diversity, Trends and Conflicts* (Cambridge, MA: MIT Press, 1995), 76, 93.

16 Simon Collier and William F. Sater, *A History of Chile, 1808–1994* (Cambridge: Cambridge University Press, 1996), 221–22; Michael Monteón, *Chile and the Great Depression: The Politics of Underdevelopment, 1927–48* (Tempe: Arizona State University Press, 1998), 36–37, 65–66.

17 Alan Dye, "Why Did Cuban Cane Growers Lose Autonomy? 1889–1920," in *Latin America and the World Economy since 1800*, ed. John H. Coatsworth and Alan M. Taylor (Cambridge, MA: Harvard University Press, 1998), 326; Oscar Zanetti Lecuona and Alejandro García Alvarez, *Sugar and Railroads: A Cuban History, 1837–1959* (Chapel Hill: University of North Carolina Press, 1998), 322–26.

18 Herbert S. Klein, *Parties and Political Change in Bolivia, 1880–1952* (Cambridge: Cambridge University Press, 1969), 108; Enrique Ayala Mora, "Ecuador since 1930," in *The Cambridge History of Latin America*, vol. 7, *Latin America since*

1930: Spanish South America, ed. Leslie Bethell (Cambridge: Cambridge University Press, 1991), 689; Bulmer-Thomas, *Economic History of Latin America*, 196. A. J. H. Latham, *The Depression and the Developing World, 1914–1939* (London: Croom Helm, 1981), 176, notes a "disastrous" downward trend in world wheat prices from about 1925, which Derek H. Aldcroft, *From Versailles to Wall Street, 1919–29* (London: Allen Lane, 1977), 226–27, attributes to enhanced production during the war, arguing that sugar suffered a similar postwar glut.

19 Victor Bulmer-Thomas, "Economic Development over the Long Run—Central America since 1929," *Journal of Latin American Studies* 15 (1983): 273; Marcos Tonatiuh Aguila M., *Economía y trabajo en la minería mexicana* (Mexico: UAM, 2004), 53–58.

20 The contrast is clearest with respect to recovery; thus, the key question regarding the United States is "what . . . accounts for the exceptional length of the depression of the 1930s"; Michael A. Bernstein, *The Great Depression: Delayed Recovery and Economic Change in America, 1929–39* (Cambridge: Cambridge University Press, 1987), 3. See also Robert Higgs, *Depression, War, and Cold War* (Oxford: Oxford University Press, 2006), whose first chapter is entitled "Regime Uncertainty: Why the Great Depression Lasted So Long . . ." Thus, in the United States, GDP fell by 29 percent between 1929 and 1932/33; by 1937 the economy had recovered to 96 percent of its previous (1929) peak, but then relapsed a further 4 percent in 1938 due to the "Roosevelt recession." It thus took a full decade (1929–39) for the economy to recover, and even then unemployment remained stubbornly high; Higgs, *Depression, War, and Cold War*, 6. As I note below, most Latin American economies returned to pre-Depression output much earlier: Brazil by 1933, Mexico by 1934, Argentina by 1935.

21 The *locus classicus* is Stephen Haber, ed., *How Latin America Fell Behind: Essays on the Economic Histories of Brazil and Mexico, 1880–1914* (Stanford, CA: Stanford University Press, 1993).

22 Latham, *Depression and the Developing World*, 156, 168.

23 Joseph L. Love, "Economic Ideas and Ideologies in Latin America since 1930," in *The Cambridge History of Latin America*, vol. 6, *Latin America since 1930: Economy, Society and Politics*, part 1, *Economy and Society*, ed. Leslie Bethell (Cambridge: Cambridge University Press, 1994), 419–20. H. Rauspach, "The Impact of the Great Depression on Eastern Europe," in van der Wee, *Great Depression Revisited*, is of little help.

24 Industrial production fell by 17 percent in the United Kingdom between 1929 and 1932, but by 42 percent in Germany and 46 percent in the United States. However, by 1937/38 UK production was 31 percent higher than in 1928/29, and German production was 22 percent higher; the comparable U.S. figure was 4 percent. David Landes, *The Unbound Prometheus: Technological Change and Industrial Development in Western Europe from 1750 to the Present* (Cambridge: Cambridge University Press, 1972), 391–94; W. Arthur Lewis, *Economic Survey, 1919–39* (London: Allen and Unwin, 1953), 61, offers similar data.

25 Bulmer-Thomas, *Economic History of Latin America*, 212. The analysis involves fourteen countries for which GDP data are available.

26 Bulmer-Thomas, *Economic History of Latin America*, 219.

27 Bulmer-Thomas, *Economic History of Latin America*, 231. Regarding Chile, see also the comments of Monteón, *Chile and the Great Depression*, 124, 129, 131.

28 During the 1920s, central banks were established in several Latin American countries, which adopted the gold exchange standard; Furtado, *Economic Development of Latin America*, 71–72; Bulmer-Thomas, *Economic History of Latin America*, 116; Carlos Marichal, *A Century of Debt Crises in Latin America: From Independence to the Great Depression, 1820–1930* (Princeton, NJ: Princeton University Press, 1989), 204. Clearly, no common causal pattern unites this odd foursome: Honduras, Nicaragua, and Haiti were under U.S. financial tutelage and hence were not independent economic actors. Argentina, in contrast, *was* an independent actor and was therefore the only major (and sovereign) Latin American state not to default on its debt.

29 Edgar Turlington, *Mexico and Her Foreign Creditors* (New York: Columbia University Press, 1930); see also chap. 6 of this volume.

30 Carlos Díaz Alejandro, "América Latina en los años treinta," in *América Latina en los años treinta: El papel de la periferia en la crisis mundial*, ed. Rosemary Thorp (México: FCE, 1988), 34.

31 Laurence Whitehead, "Bolivia since 1930," in Bethell, *Cambridge History of Latin America*, 7:515–16.

32 Collier and Sater, *History of Chile*, 218, 221; Whitehead, "Bolivia since 1930," 514, which notes that "those most closely engaged with the international economy were naturally to feel the strongest impact of the depression."

33 John Morton Blum, *From the Morgenthau Diaries: Years of Crisis, 1928–38* (Boston: Houghton Mifflin, 1959), 199–204, 493–95; Frank Safford and Marco Palacios, *Colombia: Fragmented Land, Divided Society* (Oxford: Oxford University Press, 2002), 275; Rosemary Thorp and Geoffrey Bertram, *Peru, 1890–1977: Growth and Policy in an Open Economy* (London: MacMillan, 1978), 157–59.

34 Peter Flindell Klarén, *Peru: Society and Nationhood in the Andes* (Oxford: Oxford University Press, 2000), 278.

35 Thorp and Bertram, *Peru, 1890–1977*, 163–65; Ecuador also benefited from modest oil exports; Osvaldo Hurtado, *El poder político en el Ecuador* (Quito: Editorial Planeta, 2003), 100.

36 Latham, *Depression and the Developing World*, 176–78; Kindleberger, *World in Depression*, 83, 90; Dieter Rothermund, *The Global Impact of the Great Depression, 1929–39* (London: Routledge, 1996), 38–40.

37 David Rock, *Argentina, 1516–1987: From Spanish Colonization to Alfonsín* (Berkeley: University of California Press, 1987), 232; Peter H. Smith, *Politics and Beef in Argentina: Patterns of Conflict and Change* (New York: Columbia University Press, 1969), 142–47; Roy Hora, *The Landowners of the Argentine Pampas: A Social and Political History, 1860–1945* (Oxford: Oxford University Press, 2001),

192–93, which notes that the Justo administration, coming to power in 1932, "made the salvation of cattle raising its first order of business."

38 Roberto Cortes Conde thus sees the post-Depression recovery as the beginning of a long upswing, involving 3 percent annual growth in GDP per capita, between 1933 and 1947, much higher than in the pre-Depression period (1912–27), when growth was slightly negative, and higher than the ensuing Peronist and post-Peronist years (1947–74), when growth slipped to 1.6 percent; Roberto Cortes Conde, *La economía argentina en el largo plazo* (Buenos Aires: Editorial Sudamericano), 18–19.

39 Rock, *Argentina, 1516–1987*, 231. Roy Hora, in chapter 1 of this volume, argues that the chief beneficiaries were the burgeoning urban middle class, who enjoyed social mobility and rising consumption; the urban working class of the littoral, whose numbers were swelled by migrants from the interior, did less well—until, of course, Perón took power in the late 1940s.

40 Albert O. Hirschman, *A Bias for Hope: Essays on Development in Latin America* (New Haven, CT: Yale University Press, 1971), 11. Demand for coffee in developed countries also tended to be relatively inelastic in times of depression (coffee drinkers needed their fix of caffeine); thus, coffee prices in the United States fell by only a third, prices in Brazil by nearly two-thirds; Celso Furtado, *The Economic Growth of Brazil: A Survey from Colonial to Modern Times* (Berkeley: University of California Press, 1968), 204.

41 Steven Topik, *The Political Economy of the Brazilian State, 1889–1930* (Austin: University of Texas Press, 1987), 74, 86.

42 Furtado, *Economic Growth of Brazil*, 203–13.

43 Safford and Palacios, *Colombia*, 275; Charles Bergquist, *Labor in Latin America: Comparative Essays on Chile, Argentina, Venezuela and Colombia* (Stanford, CA: Stanford University Press, 1986), 308–9. Doug Yarrington, in chapter 6 of this volume, cites the sorry plight of Venezuelan coffee; however, in aggregate terms, growing oil exports more than compensated. In Colombia, too, rising gold exports helped offset falling coffee prices.

44 Victor Bulmer-Thomas, *The Political Economy of Central America since 1920* (Cambridge: Cambridge University Press, 1987), 59–60.

45 Jeffery M. Paige, *Coffee and Power: Revolution and the Rise of Democracy in Central America* (Cambridge, MA: Harvard University Press, 1997), 107; David McCreery, *Rural Guatemala, 1760–1940* (Stanford, CA: Stanford University Press, 1994), 312–16, which also alludes to some provision of state credit for failing coffee fincas. The "labour-repressive" label derives from Barrington Moore Jr., *Social Origins of Dictatorship and Democracy: Lord and Peasant in the Making of the Modern World* (Harmondsworth: Penguin, 1967), 433–34.

46 Thorp and Bertram, *Peru, 1890–1977*, 175–76.

47 Bill Albert, "The Peruvian Sugar Industry 1918–1939: Response to World Crisis," in *The World Sugar Economy in War and Depression, 1914–1940*, ed. Bill Albert and Albert Graves (London: Routledge, 1988), 71–84; Brian Pollitt,

"The Cuban Sugar Economy in the 1930s," in Albert and Graves, *World Sugar Economy*, 97–108, offers a good overview of the Cuba case.

48 Zanetti Lecuona and García Alvarez, *Sugar and Railroads*, 322; Juan Martínez Alier, *Haciendas, Plantations and Collective Farms* (London: Frank Cass, 1977), 107–8; César J. Ayala, *American Sugar Kingdom: The Plantation Economy of the Spanish Caribbean, 1898–1934* (Chapel Hill: University of North Carolina Press, 1999), 239–41. For a revisionist—hence, quite positive—evaluation of the Roca-Runciman pact, see Peter Alhadeff, "Dependency, historiography and objections to the Roca Pact," in Abel and Lewis, *Latin America, Economic Imperialism and the State*, 367–78.

49 Jorge I. Domínguez, *Cuba: Order and Revolution* (Cambridge, MA: Harvard University Press, 1978), 84–87; Martínez Alier, *Haciendas, Plantations and Collective Farms*, 93, sees "the beginning of very heavy government interference in the economy" in the later 1920s, as sugar prices sagged; the post-1930 depression greatly accelerated this incipient process.

50 On the rapid growth of German-Brazilian trade in the 1930s (a good deal of it taking the form of bilateral deals), see Marcelo de Paiva Abreu, "The External Context," in *The Cambridge Economic History of Latin America*, vol. 2, *The Long Twentieth Century*, ed. Victor Bulmer-Thomas, John H. Coatsworth, and Roberto Cortes Conde (Cambridge: Cambridge University Press, 2006), 113–14. German trade with Central America (again, including coffee) also boomed in the 1930s, chiefly at the expense of the United States; Bulmer-Thomas, *Political Economy of Central America*, 78–79.

51 This is a major chapter in the grand story of British global commercial/financial hegemony giving way to American, a transition that, in the present context (Latin America in the 1930s), was significant—and negative—in that British overseas lending/investment tended to be countercyclical (it rose in times of domestic recession), whereas American lending was pro-cyclical, thus having the effect of exporting recession; Kindleberger, *World in Depression*, 292–93.

52 Rock, *Argentina, 1516–1987*, 225–6; Raúl García Heras, "Foreign Business–Host Government Relations: The Anglo-Argentine Tramways Co. Ltd of Buenos Aires, 1930–66," *Itinerario* 19, no. 1(1995): 85–96.

53 Cortes Conde, *La economía argentina*, 18–19. On monetary policy, see Gerardo Della Paolera and Alan M. Taylor, "Economic Recovery from the Argentine Great Depression: Institutions, Expectations and the Change of Macroeconomic Regimes," *Journal of Economic History* 59, no. 3 (1999): 567–99.

54 Brazil lost 4 percent of GDP, Colombia 2.5 percent, and both countries recovered pre-Depression levels of output by 1933. I take these figures from the Oxford Latin America Economic History Database (http://oxlad.qeh.ox.ac .uk). Other sources are in broad agreement. In the odd case of Ecuador, the same database tells us that the country experienced no depression at all, whereas Ayala Mora, "Ecuador since 1930," 690, states that "the world depression of 1929–32 had devastating consequences for the Ecuadorian economy."

When quantitative and qualitative estimates differ to this degree, what is the "lay" (non-Ecuadorianist) scholar to conclude? Despite hometown loyalty, I am inclined to accept Ayala Mora's version, which is roughly corroborated by Hurtado, *El poder político en el Ecuador*, 98–99, 317. Bulmer-Thomas, *Economic History of Latin America*, chap. 7, is brief and tentative when it comes to Ecuador (e.g., 213).

55 Enrique Cárdenas, *La industrialización de México durante la gran depresión* (México: El Colegio de México, 1987), 34, 190.

56 The Chilean figures are taken from the OXLAD database (http://oxlad.qeh.ox.ac.uk); for Cuba, I have relied on Marianne Ward and John Devereux, "The Road Not Taken: Prewar Cuban Livings Standards in Comparative Perspective" (2010), at http://econweb.umd/~davis/eventpapers/CUBA.pdf.

57 Chile being the only country outside Europe to elect a Popular Front government; Collier and Sater, *History of Chile*, 224–25, 234, 240–43; Louis A. Pérez Jr., *Cuba under the Platt Amendment* (Pittsburgh: University of Pittsburgh Press, 1986), chaps. 10 and 11; see also chap. 9 of this volume.

58 Higgs, *Depression, War, and Cold War*.

59 Paige, *Coffee and Power*, 107.

60 Pollitt, "Cuban Sugar Economy," 102.

61 Torres-Rivas, "Crisis and Conflict," 74; Jeffrey L. Gould, *To Lead as Equals: Rural Protest and Political Consciousness in Chinandega, Nicaragua, 1912–79* (Chapel Hill: University of North Carolina Press, 1990), 37–38.

62 Gregorio Selser, *Sandino: General of the Free* (New York: Monthly Review Press, 1981), 142 (of course, Sandino was also making a political point).

63 E. Alanis Patiño and E. Vargas Torres, "Observaciones sobre algunas estadísticas agrícolas," *Trimestre Económico* 12 (1945–46): 57–86.

64 Bulmer-Thomas, *Economic History of Latin America*, 224, 229. Domestic-use agriculture (DUA) could include both subsistence and commercial crops (such as coffee); at times, of course, the distinction becomes blurred and the balance between peasant family consumption, on the one hand, and sale in the market, on the other, can only be drawn in particular contexts, and even then with some difficulty.

65 An even more clear-cut case was Asia, where Latham, *Depression and the Developing World*, 185, argues that "the depression had much less effect . . . than a monsoon failure would have done."

66 A good grassroots example is provided by Vincent C. Pelosi, *Peasants on Plantations: Subaltern Strategies of Labor and Resistance in the Pisco Valley, Peru* (Durham, NC: Duke University Press, 1999), 138–49, which describes how, when cotton production fell (for a time), peasants in the Pisco Valley turned to subsistence, especially vegetable production. But this was no easy option: at best, "they found solace in a few gains," and did so by relying on "the unpaid labor of children and spouses." Elsewhere in Peru, Florencia Mallon argues, the depression, "by forcing communities to turn inward on their own resources," while

also compelling migrants to return home (to the same communities), inten-sified processes of "commodification" and internal differentiation; Florencia Mallon, *The Defense of Community in Peru's Central Highlands* (Princeton, NJ: Princeton University Press, 1983), 295, 305.

67 Dunkerley, *Power in the Isthmus*, 101; Safford and Palacios, *Colombia*, 275. Hirschman, *Journeys toward Progress*, 141, also notes how, as the Depression struck and public works were curtailed, "the unemployed drifted back to their families in the countryside." On the Atlantic coast, too, laid-off banana workers in the Santa Marta zone "moved onto idle United Fruit Company properties, cleared small fields and planted foodcrops"; Catherine Legrand, *Frontier Expansion and Peasant Protest in Colombia, 1830–1936* (Albuquerque: University of New Mexico Press, 1986), 115.

68 Paige, *Coffee and Power*, 107; Collier and Sater, *History of Chile*, 221; however, as Monteón, *Chile and the Great Depression*, 75, 88, 178, notes, the government promoted gold panning as a remedy for unemployment—a measure that pro-voked "cynical laughter" in Congress when first proposed, but which provided some 34,000 jobs and significantly boosted Chile's gold exports. With regard to the rural sector, Chile and El Salvador therefore bear comparison with other labor-surplus economies: for example, Turkey and Egypt, where the subsis-tence cushion was threadbare and the cash-strapped state responded by fiscally squeezing the rural poor; Rothermund, *Global Impact of the Great Depression*, 80–81. In contrast, Latin American states, by and large, lacked either the will or the capacity to tighten their fiscal grip on their populations, whether rich or poor.

69 Víctor L. Urquidi, *Otro siglo perdido: Las políticas de desarrollo en América Latina (1930–2005)* (Mexico: FCE, 2005), 71—"quelite" being chenopodium (goose-foot), a spinach-like wild plant of some nutritional value.

70 Torres-Rivas, "Crisis and Conflict," 74. Note that even in the—advanced, industrial—United States, President Roosevelt "dreamed of putting a million families into subsistence farming"—a quixotic notion that even found its way into his famous inaugural address; John A. Garraty, *The Great Depression* (New York: Anchor Books, 1987), 131; David M. Kennedy, *The American People in the Great Depression: Freedom from Fear*, part 1 (Oxford: Oxford University Press, 1999), 134. Today, of course, as we survey the recent world recession, this sub-sistence cushion may still exist in parts of Africa and Asia (and it might become crucial if recession belatedly hit China, reversing the massive rural-to-urban migration of recent decades), but in most of the Americas, as in Europe, it has lost all its stuffing. In other words, there is no *quelite* to return to.

71 Cities were not immune to natural disasters, of course, and some—such as the "devastating" Managua (Nicaragua) earthquake of 1931 or the 1939 quake that destroyed Chillán (Chile)—played their part in the politico-economic story of the 1930s, even if they obeyed a quite exogenous and random causality; Gould, *To Lead as Equals*, 38; Collier and Sater, *History of Chile*, 241.

72 Hurtado, *El poder político en el Ecuador*, 97; Steve Striffler, *In the Shadows of State and Capital: The United Fruit Company, Popular Struggle and Agrarian Restructuring in Ecuador, 1900–1995* (Durham, NC: Duke University Press, 2002), 23. On the other hand, Striffler points out, it was the ravages of the so-called Panama disease in Central America that induced the United Fruit Company to expand its holdings on the south coast of Ecuador in the 1930s; Striffler, *In the Shadows of State and Capital*, 55. See also Bulmer-Thomas, *Political Economy of Central America*, 59.

73 Hirschman, *Journeys toward Progress*, 63–64; Collier and Sater, *History of Chile*, 241; Jody Pavilack, *Mining for the Nation: The Politics of Chile's Coal Communities from the Popular Front to the Cold War* (University Park: Pennsylvania State University Press, 2011), 109–12.

74 Bulmer-Thomas, *Economic History of Latin America*, 134–35; Stephen A. Haber, "The Political Economy of Industrialization," in Bulmer-Thomas, Coatsworth, and Cortes Conde, *Cambridge Economic History of Latin America*, 2:539–62; Stephen A. Haber, *Industry and Underdevelopment: The Industrialization of Mexico, 1890–1940* (Stanford, CA: Stanford University Press, 1989), chap. 3; Gabriel Palma, "De una economía de exportaciones a una economía sustitutiva de importaciones: Chile, 1914–1939," in Thorp, *América Latina en los años treinta*, 71, 73–74.

75 On the other hand, where demand was buoyant, capacity could be boosted by buying secondhand manufacturing equipment from industrial countries hard hit by the Depression; Furtado, *Economic History of Brazil*, 217–18; see also Haber, *Industry and Underdevelopment*, 166–67, 177.

76 Werner Baer, *The Brazilian Economy: Its Growth and Development* (Columbus, OH: Grid, 1979), 93–96; Palma, "De una economía de exportaciones," 43, 47; Haber, *Industry and Underdevelopment*, 176; and Haber, "Political Economy of Industrialization," 562 ff.

77 Bulmer-Thomas, *Economic History of Latin America*, 219, 226, from which the data in table 10.2 are taken.

78 Bulmer-Thomas, *Economic History of Latin America*, 212, 214.

79 Gould, *To Lead as Equals*, 38 (the consular report is from November 1932).

80 Thorp and Bertram, *Peru, 1890–1977*, 147; Alfonso W. Quiroz, *Domestic and Foreign Finance in Modern Peru, 1850–1950* (Basingstoke, UK: MacMillan, 1993), 178–81, shows how, in Peru, monetary policy and government credit tended to favor agro-exporting interests, especially in the cotton sector. See also Hurtado, *El poder político en Ecuador*, 99–100; and, on the Venezuelan oil boom of the 1930s (which the death of Gómez in 1935 only briefly interrupted), B. S. McBeth, *Juan Vicente Gómez and the Oil Companies in Venezuela, 1908–35* (Cambridge: Cambridge University Press, 1983), 209–10.

81 Thus, "the growth of manufacturing industry after 1930 was a broadening and elaboration of a process that had been going on for some time," at least since the 1890s; Haber, "Political Economy of Industrialization," 562. Palma, "De

una economía de exportaciones," 70, 96–97, also stresses prior industrialization, particularly that spurred by the First World War, in the case of Chile.

82 In contrast, by the 1960s, several Latin American economies had entered the "hard" stage of ISI, which, as Guillermo O'Donnell famously argued, was associated with the onset of "bureaucratic-authoritarian regimes" (I am deliberately blurring the causal processes involved); see David Collier, "Overview of the Bureaucratic-Authoritarian Model," in *The New Authoritarianism in Latin America*, ed. David Collier (Princeton, NJ: Princeton University Press, 1979), 25–26. It is, of course, entirely reasonable to accept the easy/hard ISI distinction without buying the whole O'Donnell thesis. For a sophisticated analysis, see Hirschman, *Bias for Hope*, 85–123.

83 This is the central—and, it seems to me, persuasive—argument of Bernstein, *Great Depression*: the U.S. economy was unusually vulnerable to vicissitudes in the business cycle because "dramatic changes were taking place in the composition of consumer demand, investment demand, technology and employment requirements"; Bernstein, *Great Depression*, 36. The structural changes apparent in, say, the contemporary Brazilian or Mexican economies (whether "dramatic" or not) were much more conducive to a rapid and sustained recovery in domestic demand and employment, which in the United States had to await the war- and government-induced boom of the 1940s. The teleological implications of "advanced" are, in the circumstances, justified.

84 I make no apology for reaching again for Hirschman, *Bias for Hope*, 25–26, which, when discussing the rival merits of open versus closed economies (that is, *desarrollo hacia afuera* versus *desarrollo hacia adentro*), suggests that an optimal strategy might be "an appropriate alternation of contact and insulation, of openness to the trade and capital of the developed countries, to be followed by a period of nationalism and withdrawnness." A similarly subtle analysis of "linking" and "de-linking" is provided by Carlos F. Díaz Alejandro, "Open Economy, Closed Polity?," in *Latin America in the World Economy*, ed. Diana Tussie (Aldershot: Gower, 1983), 21–53.

85 Especially since nineteenth-century globalization had the decisive effect of integrating markets and bringing about a convergence of factor prices (all subject, of course, to political interventions in respect of tariffs, taxation, and monetary policy); see Kevin H. O'Rourke and Jeffrey G. Williamson, *Globalization and History* (Cambridge, MA: MIT Press), especially chap. 3.

86 *Pace* Schumpeter, who would place greater stress on sudden spurts, associated with creative entrepreneurialism (in other words, a sort of "punctuated" economic evolution). And these political leaps—motivated, for example, by electoral considerations—can have major economic consequences (often of a negative kind): for example, the Smoot-Hawley Tariff (see n. 3).

87 Rock, *Argentina, 1516–1987*, 215. Of course, the fact that the *golpistas* faced "only token resistance" was significant, suggesting a more pervasive disenchantment with the political status quo; however, the fact remains that the overthrow of

that status quo was the work of a small and unrepresentative minority. Paul W. Drake, *Between Tyranny and Anarchy: A History of Democracy in Latin America, 1800–2006* (Stanford, CA: Stanford University Press, 2009), 168, generalizes this phenomenon—of violent political change effected by elites, rather than by "ordinary people"—to the entire Southern Cone, including Brazil, between the 1930s and 1970s. Edgar J. Dosman, *The Life and Times of Raúl Prebisch, 1901–86* (Montreal: McGill-Queen's University Press, 2008), 68, describes "a spontaneous orgy of public acclaim" that greeted the Argentine military coup, but his principal source is a "young and rapidly rising Army officer," Colonel Juan Perón.

88 Klein, *Parties and Political Change*, 179.

89 Whitehead, "Bolivia since 1930," 517–18, who adds that "the war . . . was not deliberately planned to distract attention from the depression"; thus, it should not be facilely assumed that the Depression "caused" the war.

90 Klarén, *Peru*, 276.

91 Alan Knight, "The Politics of the Expropriation," in *The Mexican Petroleum Industry in the Twentieth Century*, ed. Jonathan C. Brown and Alan Knight (Austin: University of Texas Press, 1992), chap. 4. By 1938 the trough of the Depression was six years in the past, and while it is true that Mexico had been affected by the "Roosevelt" recession of 1937 (the second half of the "double dip"), this, if anything, militated *against* risky ventures like the oil expropriation.

92 Collier and Sater, *History of Chile*, 223, 224, 225–26, 233; these included the abortive *nacista* putsch of 1938 and the attempted military coup of 1939 ("el ariostazo"), which is well described by Joaquín Fernández, "El Ariostazo: la política por otros medios," in *XX. Historia del siglo veinte chileno* (Santiago: Vergara, 2008), 185–230.

93 Despite, we might add, the best efforts of ingenious political scientists, desperate to make the study of politics as rigorous, quantitative, and positivistic as economics—or, we should perhaps say, as economics claims to be.

94 Elections and congressional votes are another matter, and today's political scientists enjoy the advantage of studying a largely democratic Latin America, which provides ample grist to the statistical mill; eighty years ago, elections were both fewer and less fair, while ancillary quantitative data—such as opinion polls—were very rare.

95 Díaz Alejandro, "Open Economy, Closed Polity?," 31. (The observation refers particularly to Chile, Cuba, and Uruguay.)

96 Drake, *Between Tyranny and Anarchy*, 165.

97 Charles W. Anderson, *Politics and Economic Change in Latin America* (Princeton, NJ: Van Nostrand, 1967), 219–20.

98 There is, of course, a notional category (4): constitutional changes of *regime* (not just of government). The best example might be Brazil, which acquired a new—short-lived—constitution in 1934; however, while the procedure was constitutional, the new charter did not represent a decisive break with the past;

see Thomas E. Skidmore, *Politics in Brazil, 1930–64: An Experiment in Democracy* (New York: Oxford University Press, 1967), 19–20. The Cuban Constitution of 1940—the point at which Cuba "became a formal democracy"—was more consequential, but this happened, of course, a decade after the Depression began, a decade in which Cuba experienced major political changes; it is therefore hard to attribute the 1940 constitution to the Depression in any direct or proximate way; see Robert Whitney, *State and Revolution in Cuba: Mass Mobilization and Political Change, 1920–40* (Chapel Hill: University of North Carolina Press, 2001), 180.

99 Safford and Palacios, *Colombia*, 288; Knight, "Rise and Fall of Cardenismo."

100 As mentioned in n. 98, it may be a moot point when regime (as opposed to government) change takes place. These are "judgment calls" that may require detailed knowledge of the polities in question, so I am happy to defer to experts who know, better than me, when the rules of the game really changed (or did not).

101 Steve Stein, *Populism in Peru: The Emergence of the Masses and the Politics of Social Control* (Madison: University of Wisconsin Press, 1980), 18. See also Paulo Drinot, *The Allure of Labor: Workers, Race and the Making of the Peruvian State* (Durham, NC: Duke University Press, 2011), 125.

102 Stein, *Populism in Peru*, 189. Stein, it should be said, questions whether the election of 1931 was as thoroughly fraudulent as often supposed.

103 Klarén, *Peru*, 274–78.

104 Skidmore, *Politics in Brazil*, 7.

105 Skidmore, *Politics in Brazil*, 7–8.

106 Whitehead, "Bolivia since 1930," 511, 513, 521. As Klein, *Parties and Political Change*, 227–28, points out, the military thus ended fifty years of civilian oligarchic rule; furthermore, unlike many Latin American coups (see n. 87), this one was not only bloodless but also "willingly accepted by the majority of Bolivians," who saw the army as "the only viable instrument for creating the new political atmosphere and 'social justice' that all were demanding." No specific evidence is given; it is presumably an inference drawn from the events of that year.

107 Ayala Mora, "Ecuador since 1930," 693.

108 Ayala Mora, "Ecuador since 1930," 695.

109 "Immediate" is hard to define precisely: it involves both temporal and causal propinquity. Roughly, it denotes events occurring during the economic "trough" (which, as already noted, varied from country to country) and that can reasonably be attributed to economic factors.

110 Drake, *Between Tyranny and Anarchy*, 158.

111 Carlos Waisman, "Counterrevolution and Structural Change: The Case of Argentina," *International Political Science Review* 10, no. 2 (1989): 159–74, summarizes the thesis; as Waisman notes on pp. 161–62, in the fifty years after 1930 Argentina experienced nineteen years of military rule, thirteen years of Pero-

nism, and nineteen years of "restricted democracy," the latter involving pro-scription of either the Radicals or the Peronists.

112 Collier and Sater, *History of Chile*, 221; and, for a good detailed analysis, Mon-teón, *Chile and the Great Depression*, chap. 2. Francisco E. González, *Creative Destruction? Economic Crises and Democracy in Latin America* (Baltimore: Johns Hopkins University Press, 2012), 53, therefore concludes that "Chile was the only country in Latin America during the Great Depression that was able to shed an authoritarian regime"—presumably in favor of democracy (and not another authoritarian regime). Cuba (1933) would arguably fit this category too.

113 Though, as Bulmer-Thomas points out, it is really only in Nicaragua that U.S. influence proved so decisive; indeed, in El Salvador and Guatemala the United States opposed the turn of political events; Bulmer-Thomas, *Political Economy of Central America*, 67. In the Dominican Republic, however, the United States played a similarly key role, establishing the National Guard, while disarming the peasantry, both to the advantage of Rafael Trujillo; Richard Lee Turits, *Foundations of Despotism: Peasants, the Trujillo Regime, and Modernity in Domi-nican History* (Stanford, CA: Stanford University Press, 2003), 80, 82.

114 Knut Walter, *The Regime of Anasatsio Somoza, 1936–56* (Chapel Hill: University of North Carolina Press, 1993), 59–63.

115 On Trujillo, see the excellent analysis of Turits, *Foundations of Despotism*. Gould, *To Lead as Equals*, 15 and part 2, stresses "somocista populism," while Jim Handy, *Gift of the Devil: A History of Guatemala* (Boston: South End Press, 1984), 94–99, depicts Ubico as honest, popular, and paternalistic (also repres-sive and "pathologically secretive"); if he practiced "populism" (a term Handy avoids), this was an old-style caudillesque "populism," a throwback to the nine-teenth century. Dunkerley, *Power in the Isthmus*, 88, is skeptical about the use of the term in 1930s Central America, "local politics during the Depression being singularly devoid of the populist motifs often adopted elsewhere" in Latin America. On the other hand, he considers Somoza to be a "Bonapartist"; Dunkerley, *Power in the Isthmus*, 89, 103.

116 Paige, *Coffee and Power*, 110–11.

117 See chap. 7 of this volume.

118 Bulmer-Thomas, *Political Economy of Central America*, 67. Despite the "ravages of the depression," both Costa Rica and Panama (which remained under close U.S. political and financial tutelage) avoided the extremes of authoritarian caudillismo, Costa Rica adopting a "Tico version of caudillismo"; Bulmer-Thomas, *Political Economy of Central America*, 64; see also Almon R. Wright, *Panama: Tension's Child, 1502–1989* (New York: Vantage Press, 1990), 215–24.

119 I stress "purely political" because, as I shall note shortly, the *economic* policies of these new authoritarian regimes were at times innovative and scarcely "conser-vative." Drake, *Between Tyranny and Anarchy*, 165, where the author also quan-tifies the dictatorial trend: between 1928/30 and 1932/34 Latin America went

from fourteen democracies (or, in several cases, "oligarchic republics") and six dictatorships to ten "democracies" and ten dictatorships. On the "first reverse wave," see Samuel P. Huntington, *The Third Wave: Democratization in the Late Twentieth Century* (Norman: University of Oklahoma Press, 1991), 16.

120 Legrand, *Frontier Expansion*, especially chaps. 6 and 7, describes popular— peasant—mobilization and regime responses.

121 Pérez, *Cuba under the Platt Amendment*, chaps. 10 and 11; see also chap. 9 of this volume.

122 Whitney, *State and Revolution in Cuba*.

123 Collier and Sater, *History of Chile*, 224, 232, 240–42.

124 That is, a shift from forms of direct ("imperialist") control to more indirect ("hegemonic") forms; Domínguez, *Cuba*, 54.

125 A point made by Díaz Alejandro, "Open Economy, Closed Polity?," 34.

126 González, *Creative Destruction?*, 126–239.

127 It has become historiographically fashionable to attribute the Latin American Wars of Independence to Napoleon's—conjunctural and exogenous—invasion of Spain. For an interesting essay on this (recurrent?) historical phenomenon, see Emmanuel Le Roy Ladurie, "The 'Event' and the 'Long Term' in Social History: The Case of the Chouan Uprising," chap. 7 in *The Territory of the Historian* (Hassocks, UK: Harvester Press, 1979).

128 Waisman, "Counterrevolution and Structural Change."

129 Drake, *Between Tyranny and Anarchy*, 165–66.

130 Samuel Farber, *Revolution and Reaction in Cuba, 1933–1960* (Middletown, CT: Wesleyan University Press, 1976), 176–78. Bolivia's MNR also harked back to the 1930s, though the Chaco War and the military socialist regime were more consequential points of reference than the Depression per se.

131 In contrast, Costa Rica experienced no such divisive caesura in the 1930s; thus, the divergent political paths followed within Central America, while they responded to multiple causes over time, were at least partly determined by decisions taken in the 1930s. See Deborah Yashar, *Demanding Democracy: Reform and Reaction in Costa Rica and Guatemala, 1870s–1950s* (Stanford, CA: Stanford University Press, 1997), chap. 2. Dunkerley, *Power in the Isthmus*, 340–41, notes both the "superficial similarities" and the substantial differences.

132 Barry Carr, *Marxism and Communism in Twentieth-Century Mexico* (Lincoln: University of Nebraska Press, 1992), 310–12. A lesser current in the Mexican Left, which also had its roots in the 1930s, was Lombardismo, which harked back to the nationalist labor leader Vicente Lombardo Toledano; Carr, *Marxism and Communism*, 198–99.

133 Bergquist, *Labor in Latin America*, offers a useful comparative analysis: see 76–77, 95–96, 336. I touch on the social impact of the Depression later.

134 Bulmer-Thomas, *Economic History of Latin America*, 182; and, for earlier figures, 110.

135 Klarén, *Peru*, 249. In Brazil, Vargas's successful coup of 1930 also involved

widespread recruitment of disaffected junior officers and NCOs, who rose up against their commanders. In subsequent years "rebellions by enlisted men plagued the army," the rebels' motivations being both ideological and economic; Shawn C. Smallman, *Fear and Memory in the Brazilian Army and Society, 1889–1954* (Chapel Hill: University of North Carolina Press, 2002), 41–42.

136 Marichal, *Century of Debt Crises*, 211; and see n. 28. As already mentioned, Haiti, Nicaragua, and the Dominican Republic also maintained debt service payments. We should recall President Carlos Pellegrini's dogged commitment to honoring Argentina's foreign debt during the Baring crisis of the early 1890s; H. S. Ferns, *Britain and Argentina in the Nineteenth Century* (Oxford: Clarendon, 1960), 455–84.

137 Díaz Alejandro, "América Latina en los años treinta," 42; Della Paolera and Taylor, "Economic Recovery"; Rock, *Argentina, 1516–1987*, 222–23.

138 Klarén, *Peru*, 276; Marichal, *Century of Debt Crises*, 213–14.

139 Hirschman, *Journeys toward Progress*, 239–40; Barry Eichengreen, *Golden Fetters: The Gold Standard and the Great Depression, 1931–39* (New York: Oxford University Press, 1992), which refers only in passing to Latin America, 260–61, 290, but makes clear that prompt abandonment of the gold (exchange) standard was generally advantageous by way of permitting—but not guaranteeing—an expansionary monetary policy.

140 Torres-Rivas, "Crisis and Conflict," 75.

141 On the "passive"/"reactive" distinction, see Díaz Alejandro, "América Latina en los años treinta," 38, 40. Arguably, the term "reactivo"/"reactive" is somewhat misleading, since it could connote an unthinking mechanistic "reaction" to external shocks (which in fact would be closer to the "passive" category), whereas, of course, "reactive," in Díaz Alejandro's lexicon, involves a measure of creative experiment and heterodoxy. A simple and semantically neat solution would be to drop the prefix "re."

142 Daniel Díaz Fuentes, *Las políticas fiscales latinoamericanas frente a la gran depresión* (Madrid: Ministerio de Econonía y Hacienda, 1993), 67–75; see also chap. 8 of this volume.

143 Bulmer-Thomas, *Economic History of Latin America*, 206–7. On Vargas's fiscal/financial orthodoxy, see J. W. F. Dulles, *Vargas of Brazil* (Austin: University of Texas Press, 1967), 88–89.

144 Urquidi, *Otro siglo perdido*, 74–75, 80. There is some debate—notably, Furtado versus Peláez—concerning the reflationary impact of state coffee purchases; see Baer, *Brazilian Economy*, 43–45; and Díaz-Fuentes, *Las políticas fiscales*, 59–61.

145 Bulmer-Thomas, *Economic History of Latin America*, 211; Díaz-Fuentes, *Las políticas fiscales*, 75–79.

146 José Antonio Ocampo, "La economía colombiana en la década de los treinta," in Thorp, *América Latina en los años treinta*, 155–57; Safford and Palacios, *Colombia*, 289–90.

147 On fatalism (elsewhere), see Garraty, *Great Depression*, 172–77. The counterpart to fatalism, described here, is closely akin to Hirschman's "possibilism"; Hirschman, *Bias for Hope*, 28.

148 Alex M. Saragoza, *The Monterrey Elite and the Mexican State, 1880–1940* (Austin: University of Texas Press, 1988), chap. 8.

149 Kennedy, *American People in the Great Depression*, 135.

150 "Associated" is a deliberate fence-sitting verb, ambiguous with regard to causality, for reasons that should become clear.

151 For example, Rothermund, *Global Impact of the Great Depression*, chap. 10, where the chapter devoted to Latin America is entitled "The New Role of the State."

152 Nora Hamilton, *The Limits of State Autonomy: Post-Revolutionary Mexico* (Princeton, NJ: Princeton University Press, 1982), 120–21. However, as Hamilton argues—and as recent research on Cardenismo has confirmed—actual outcomes fell short of rhetorical objectives. In Brazil, the official *Revista do Serviço Público* declared, in July 1938, that "no aspect of national life can be left at the margin of state action, as the State is the sole entity capable of imprinting on each citizen a truly nationalist mark"; Daryle Williams, *Culture Wars in Brazil: The First Vargas Regime, 1930–45* (Durham, NC: Duke University Press, 2001), 69. Again, in practice, achievements rarely matched rhetoric; as Joel Wolfe, in chapter 3 of this volume, stresses, Varguista state building was never as radical in practice as it sometimes sounded, or as some historians seem to have believed. An even greater discrepancy was evident in Cuba, where Batista's Three Year Plan "promised to redistribute what was not yet produced"; Whitney, *State and Revolution in Cuba*, 158.

153 Klein, *Parties and Political Change*, 230.

154 Paul H. Lewis, *The Crisis of Argentine Capitalism* (Chapel Hill: University of North Carolina Press, 1990), 92.

155 Domínguez, *Cuba*, 88–89; Whitney, *State and Revolution in Cuba*, 180.

156 Collier and Sater, *History of Chile*, 225.

157 For further examples of enhanced state intervention, ranging from banking to labor relations, see Safford and Palacios, *Colombia*, 275–76; Hurtado, *El poder político en el Ecuador*, 101–2; Klarén, *Peru*, 270; and chaps. 4 and 6 of this volume. Note that these examples include countries (e.g., Peru, Ecuador) where dirigisme is usually discounted.

158 Gould, *To Lead as Equals*.

159 Thorp and Bertram, *Peru, 1890–1977*, 147–49, 190–91.

160 See chap. 3 of this volume; Robert M. Levene, *Father of the Poor? Vargas and His Era* (Cambridge: Cambridge University Press, 1998), 43–49, offers a corroborative "balance sheet" of the Vargas regime prior to 1937. On Cardenismo, see Alan Knight, "Cardenismo: Juggernaut or Jalopy?," *Journal of Latin America Studies* 26 (1994): 73–107.

161 See Joseph L. Love, "The Rise and Fall of Structuralism," in *Economic Doctrines*

in Latin America: Origins, Embedding and Evolution, ed. Valpy FitzGerald and Rosemary Thorp (Basingstoke, UK: Palgrave MacMillan, 2005), chap. 8; and Enrique V. Iglesias, ed., *The Legacy of Raúl Prebisch* (Washington, DC: Inter-American Development Bank, 1994).

162 John H. Coatsworth and Jeffrey G. Williamson, "Always Protectionist? Latin American Tariffs from Independence to the Great Depression," *Journal of Latin American Studies* 36, no. 2 (2004): 205–32.

163 I resort to this historiographical cliché with gritted teeth: it seems self-evident that, when it comes to writing history, nothing should be exaggerated—blown up out of proportion. "X should not be exaggerated" is therefore historian's shorthand for "I don't think X is as important as some other historians; but I am either unable or too lazy to try to measure its relative importance." It should be said, too, that historians—from flighty biographers to dour economic historians—probably tend to inflate their chosen subjects; after all, showing the relative *un*importance of a person or process is not usually the way to scholarly fame and fortune, even if it serves as a useful corrective to historiographical hype.

164 In a previous excursion into economic history I sounded off about dodgy statistical data; Alan Knight, "Export-led Growth in Mexico, c. 1900–30," in *An Economic History of Twentieth-Century Latin America*, vol. 1, *The Export Age: Latin American Economies in the Late Nineteenth and Twentieth Centuries*, ed. Enrique Cárdenas, José Antonio Ocampo, and Rosemary Thorp (Basingstoke, UK: Palgrave MacMillan, 2000), 137–41. This current excursion has not stilled earlier concerns (for a small example, see n. 54), nor has a recent informal conversation with Victor Bulmer-Thomas regarding the unreliability of some Latin American data series (October 2012).

165 Figures calculated according to the Oxford Latin American Economic History Database (http://oxlad.qeh.ox.ac.uk).

166 Spending is presumably more indicative of state power and reach, since it involves disbursements that are not necessarily covered by revenue, but by loans or expansion of the money supply (and which, depending on circumstances and criteria, may be seen as either creative deficit financing or irresponsible economic populism). Of course, the capacity to raise revenue is also a useful index of state power, in which respect most Latin American states in the 1930s were fairly deficient. The difference between central and state governments spending was less crucial in the case of Mexico, where federal income greatly exceeded—and, indeed, *increasingly* exceeded—the income of the states (and municipalities); see Luis Aboites Aguilar, *Excepciones y privilegios: Modernización tributaria y centralización en México, 1922–1972* (Mexico: El Colegio de Mexico, 2003), 39.

167 Kindleberger, *World in Depression*, 283–86; Kozo Yamamura, "Then Came the Great Depression: Japan's Interwar Years," in van der Wee, *Great Depression Revisited*, 203. Of course, Latin America imported much of its weaponry, so

arms spending would have a weaker multiplier effect than in Europe or Japan. Safford and Palacios, *Colombia*, 276, suggest that tension with Peru over Leticia "contributed to the success of [economic] recovery," by boosting spending and jobs, while calming "social and party agitation." The political argument strikes me as more convincing than the economic one.

168 At least until very recently, when welfare provision has slightly improved in several countries. Still, Latin America lags far behind the (currently imperilled) welfare states of Western Europe. Regarding the historic link between total war and social reform, two Latin American examples might be the Mexican Revolution (a civil war, of course) and, again, the Chaco War, which stimulated both popular demands and, in some measure, official efforts at social reform: as President David Toro put it in 1936, "Our social doctrine has been born in the sands of the Chaco"; Klein, *Parties and Political Change*, 233. In Paraguay, too, veterans played a role in the 1936 "Liberating Revolution," which briefly combined authoritarian politics with a commitment to social—even agrarian—reform; George Pendle, *Paraguay: A Riverside Nation* (London: Oxford University Press, 1967), 32–33.

169 Cf. Eliana Cardoso and Ann Helwege, "Populism, Profligacy, and Redistribution," in *The Macroeconomics of Populism in Latin America*, ed. Rudiger Dornbusch and Sebastian Edwards (Chicago: University of Chicago Press, 1991), 46–47 (and elsewhere in the same volume).

170 Coatsworth and Williamson, "Always Protectionist?"

171 Howard J. Wiarda, *The Soul of Latin America* (New Haven, CT: Yale University Press, 2003); David S. Landes, *The Wealth and Poverty of Nations* (New York: W. W. Norton, 1998), chap. 20.

172 Rothermund, *Global Impact of the Great Depression*, 108.

173 Alan Knight, "The Weight of the State in Modern Mexico," in *Studies in the Formation of the Nation State in Latin America*, ed. James Dunkerley (London: ILAS, 2002), 218.

174 I am recycling an old metaphor; Knight, "Cardenismo: Juggernaut or Jalopy?"

175 The point is well made by Douglas A. Chalmers, who notes that "the state is central not because it commands an exceptionally large share of GNP . . . but because it has a share in so many decisions"; Douglas A. Chalmers, "The Politicized State in Latin America," in *Authoritarianism and Corporatism in Latin America*, ed. James M. Malloy (Pittsburgh: Pittsburgh University Press, 1977), 31.

176 Klein, *Parties and Political Change*, 231.

177 Safford and Palacios, *Colombia*, 275–76; Cárdenas, *La industrialización de México*, 72–84; Della Paolera and Taylor, "Economic Recovery."

178 Daniel Cosío Villegas, *Ensayos y notas*, vol. 1 (Mexico: Editorial Hermes, 1966), 73–111.

179 Michael Snodgrass, *Deference and Defiance in Monterrey: Workers, Paternalism and Revolution in Mexico, 1890-1950* (Cambridge: Cambridge University Press,

2003), 168–69; Eli Diniz, "The Post-1910 Industrial Elite," in *Modern Brazil: Elites and Masses in Historical Perspective*, ed. Michael J. Conniff and Frank D. McCann (Lincoln: University of Nebraska Press, 1989), 105–8; see also chap. 1 of this volume. A similar shift in the politico-economic center of gravity was also taking place in Peru (from sierra to coast), but it was less a product of ISI than of changing fortunes in the "commodity lottery."

180 John J. Dwyer, *The Agrarian Dispute: The Expropriation of American-Owned Rural Land in Postrevolutionary Mexico* (Durham, NC: Duke University Press, 2008).

181 "Of symbolic importance only"; George Philip, *Oil and Politics in Latin America* (Cambridge: Cambridge University Press, 1982), 57.

182 Knight, "Politics of the Expropriation."

183 The phrase derives from Philip, *Oil and Politics*, 51. Argentina's state oil company (YPF) was well established by the 1930s; Uruguay (ANCAP, 1931) and Chile (COPEC, 1935) were products of that decade, though of much less consequence than PEMEX (Mexico, 1938).

184 Bergquist, *Labor in Latin America*, 238–41.

185 As U.S. undersecretary of state Sumner Welles (who knew Latin America well) recognized, "conditions in Mexico to which present developments were mainly due were not present in other countries to the same degree"; Philip, *Oil and Politics*, 56.

186 Thorp and Bertram, *Peru, 1890–1977*, 164–69, note that, as oil exports boomed in the later 1930s, taxes were raised, yet they remained "derisory" (whether 12 percent of exports is "derisory" is another matter); government regulation increased in the early 1940s, but by then the boom was over. On Colombia, where "oil nationalism" retreated in the 1930s, see chap. 5 of this volume; on Ecuador and Venezuela, see Philip, *Oil and Politics*, 48, 51; and Bergquist, *Labor in Latin America*, 260, 263.

187 A similar charge was leveled at the oil companies, at least in Mexico. The most egregious agrarian "enclaves" were the plantation/export complexes of the Caribbean littoral controlled, in particular, by United Fruit and Standard Fruit. However, in Central America their chief problem was not economic nationalism (which the authoritarian turn of the 1930s largely avoided), but banana diseases, which severely curtailed production and, by the late 1930s, prompted a major shift to the Pacific lowlands. In Colombia, too, where the "enclave" of Santa Marta had witnessed the bloody repression of workers in 1928, banana production also slumped, leading to a re-peasantization of the labor force; Bulmer-Thomas, *Political Economy of Central America*, 70, 75–77; Legrand, *Frontier Expansion*, 114–15.

188 Martínez-Alier, *Haciendas, Plantations and Collective Farms*, 93–103.

189 Richard Lee Turits, *Foundations of Despotism: Peasants, the Trujillo Regime and Modernity in Dominican History* (Stanford, CA: Stanford University Press, 2003), 78–79, 82–83, 135–37.

190 Bulmer-Thomas, *Economic History of Central America*, 59–60; Safford and Palacios, *Colombia*, 269–71.

191 Drinot, *The Allure of Labor*; Peter de Shazo, *Urban Workers and Labor Unions in Chile, 1902–27* (Madison: University of Wisconsin Press, 1977), chap. 8; Bergquist, *Labor in Latin America*, 65–70; Rocío Guadarrama, *Los sindicatos y la política en México: La CROM (1918–1928)* (Mexico: Ediciones Era, 1981); Barry Carr, *El movimiento obrero y la política en México, 1910–29* (2 vols.; Mexico: Sep-Setentas, 1976), vol. 2.

192 Saragoza, *Monterrey Elite*, 155–67; Brian Loveman, *Struggle in the Countryside: Politics and Rural Labor in Chile, 1919–73* (Bloomington: Indiana University Press, 1976), 72 ff.; Bulmer-Thomas, *Political Economy of Central America*, 65; Gould, *To Lead as Equals*, 39–40; Ayala Mora, "Ecuador since 1930," 696; Safford and Palacios, *Colombia*, 289. In Brazil, Vargas took advantage of serious labor unrest in São Paulo to encroach on Paulista autonomy and present the federal government as the necessary guarantor of social peace and order; Joel Wolfe, *Working Women, Working Men: São Paulo and the Rise of Brazil's Industrial Working Classes, 1900–1955* (Durham, NC: Duke University Press), 51–69.

193 Legrand, *Frontier Expansion*, 132–33.

194 Quoted in Dunkerley, *Power in the Isthmus*, 85. The ambassador, John D. Erwin, was in post from 1937 to 1947; the date of this observation is not given. Even Honduras saw a tentative effort at labour reform under President Mejía Colindres in 1931, but Congress killed it off; Bulmer-Thomas, *Political Economy of Central America*, 63–64.

195 Joe C. Ashby, *Organized Labor and the Mexican Revolution under Lázaro Cárdenas* (Chapel Hill: University of North Carolina Press, 1963), remains the best overall study. As Ashby shows, in Mexico—even more than in Colombia—labor reforms extended to the countryside, and in some celebrated cases, such as La Laguna, labor disputes were resolved by means of a sweeping land reform, with workers becoming ejidatarios.

196 Whitney, *State and Revolution in Cuba*, 180. Some allowance must be made for American hyperbole.

197 On *peleguismo* (from *pelego* — a sheepskin saddle blanket), thus the phenomenon of labor leadership that, interposed between state and sindicato, represented the Ministry of Labor more than the rank-and-file, see Wolfe, *Working Women, Working Men*, 74–81.

198 On the erosion of the textile workers' traditional anarchism, see Wolfe, *Working Women, Working Men*, 56. A similar retreat from Anarchism—exemplified in the career of CROM boss Luis Morones—was evident in Mexico too; Guadarrama, *Los sindicatos*, 122–24. There was an additional parallel: while the textile workers gravitated toward official unions, some powerful industrial unions—such as the Brazilian metalworkers or the Mexican miners and railwaymen—were more leery of the embrace of the state and, through the 1920s and 1930s, maintained a more militant independence; see Wolfe, *Working Women, Work-*

ing Men, 57; Hamilton, *Limits of State Autonomy*, 111–12, 152–61; and Ashby, *Organized Labor*, chaps. 6 and 7. *Peleguismo* also had its Mexican counterpart (though the term was coined later): *charrismo* (from *charro*, a cowboy).

199 Dunkerley, *Power in the Isthmus*, 87, notes a strengthening of large landowner-ship in Central America in the 1930s, even if the landed class lost some of their direct political leverage.

200 Collier and Sater, *History of Chile*, 221. See also chap. 2 of this volume; and, for Peru, where mining layoffs and wage cuts were also severe, see chap. 4 of this volume and Mallon, *Defense of Community*, 292–93, which notes how the min-ing companies used layoffs to purge the labor force of political activists. On the other hand, Chile's migrant nitrate workers—known for their rowdy behavior and radical politics—injected a fresh militancy into working-class communities elsewhere, for example, at the massive El Teniente copper mine; Thomas M. Klubock, *Contested Communities: Class, Gender and Politics in Chile's El Teniente Copper Mine, 1904–51* (Durham, NC: Duke University Press, 1998), 84–85.

201 Abraham Hoffman, *Unwanted Mexican Americans in the Great Depression* (Tucson: University of Arizona Press, 1974), chap. 8.

202 Whitney, *State and Revolution in Cuba*, 154–55.

203 A similar number managed to escape to Haiti. The story, which has a distinctly Balkan-ethnic-cleansing quality, is expertly told by Turits, *Foundations of Des-potism*, 161–80.

204 The term comes from Alfred Crosbie, *Ecological Imperialism: The Biological Ex-pansion of Europe, 900–1900* (Cambridge: Cambridge University Press, 2004), 4–5.

205 Joseph Merrick, "The Population of Latin America, 1930–1990," in Bethell, *Cambridge History of Latin America*, 6:6, 9. However, the Depression did not sharply affect the processes of natural increase: between the 1930s and 1940s birthrates were substantially similar, but—despite hard times—death rates continued to fall, notably in Chile, Cuba, Mexico, and all of Central America. It is hard therefore to discern any Depression-induced demographic relapse, such as occurred in the United States and some European countries (owing to a falling birthrate); Garraty, *Great Depression*, 108; Kennedy, *American People in the Great Depression*, 165.

206 Rock, *Argentina, 1516–1987*, 234–35. Thus, for the first time, the Argentine rural population declined, in absolute numbers; see chap. 1 of this volume.

207 In Argentina, the road network doubled, to the further detriment of the declin-ing British railways; Rock, *Argentina, 1516–1987*, 227. Road building spanned the continent and defied political ideology: it advanced under conservative auspices in Argentina, the Estado Novo in Brazil, the radical Cárdenas admin-istration in Mexico, and Ubico's personalist dictatorship in Guatemala. In the last three cases—Vargas, Cárdenas, and Ubico—road building, apart from pro-viding jobs, also suited peripatetic presidents, who liked to scour the country in person (Ubico on his motorbike); see chap. 3 of this volume; Levene, *Father*

of the Poor?, 58, 66; Luis González, *Historia de la Revolución Mexicana, Periodo 1934–40: Los días del Presidente Cárdenas* (Mexico: El Colegio de Mexico, 1981), 80, 268; Dunkerley, *Power in the Isthmus*, 99, 101.

208 Whitney, *State and Revolution in Cuba*, chap. 5.

209 Wolfe, *Working Women, Working Men*, 50–51; Legrand, *Frontier Expansion*, chap. 6; Paige, *Coffee and Power*, 107–10.

210 Loveman, *Struggle in the Countryside*, 145; James C. Scott, *Weapons of the Weak: Everyday Forms of Peasant Protest* (New Haven, CT: Yale University Press, 1985). Such forms of resistance are, Loveman points out, "nowhere systematically recorded"; hence, their scale and impact are hard to assess. But he gives several illustrative examples, 146–51.

211 Thus, state repression preceded—and helped provoke—the popular uprising of early 1932, which, in turn, was drowned in blood; Paige, *Coffee and Power*, 109; Dunkerley, *Power in the Isthmus*, 95–96; chap. 7 of this volume.

212 See n. 197. On Vargas's labor policy, see Wolfe, *Working Women, Working Men*; and John D. French, *The Brazilian Workers' ABC: Class Conflict and Alliances in Modern São Paulo* (Chapel Hill: University of North Carolina Press, 1992), 55, 68, 77–92.

213 Ashby, *Organized Labor*, chap. 5; Bergquist, *Labor in Latin America*, 73; David Bushnell, *The Making of Modern Colombia: A Nation in Spite of Itself* (Berkeley: University of California Press, 1993), 186–89.

214 Not least in the cotton country of the Laguna, where the Communist Party played an important part; Carr, *Marxism and Communism*, chap. 3.

215 Rock, *Argentina, 1516–1987*, 237; Thorp and Bertram, *Peru, 1890–1977*, 175, which notes that one outcome was a sharper division of labor between decentralized farm production of cotton and centralized ginning by major commercial enterprises, a trend that would continue well into the postwar period and that would be replicated in other agricultural production processing and export sectors, such as Central America's tropical fruit sector, as the big companies increasingly concentrated on processing and/or marketing, leaving production in local (farmers') hands.

216 David Nugent, *Modernity at the Edge of Empire: State, Individual and Nation in the Northern Peruviam Andes, 1885–1935* (Stanford, CA: Stanford University Press), chap. 8 ("middle sectors" on 265, 281). Since "middle sectors" is pretty vague, it is worth quoting Nugent's occupational résumé of these urban activists, p. 262: "carpenters, tailors, blacksmiths, saddlemakers, muleteers, breadmakers [*sic*], petty merchants, small shopkeepers, cantina-owners and lower-level public employees."

217 Nugent, *Modernity at the Edge of Empire*, 268, which is useful by way of dating this process of political renewal and clearly linking it to the onset of the Depression and the fall of Leguía; however, as Nugent shows, Leguía's dictatorship had already undermined elite power and status during the 1930s. It is worth noting that, unlike the original Jacobins, these activists were not anti-

clerical: they had their own patron saint, and they fought to democratize access to the local cathedral.

218 Nugent, *Modernity at the Edge of Empire*, 295–96. In the Pisco Valley, too, the "resistance" of rural cotton workers "reached its nadir" in the late 1930s, while "the political voice they looked for in the APRA and the Communist Party" grew fainter, since "both movements were diverted to industrial issues"; Pelosi, *Peasants on Plantations*, 153.

219 Loveman, *Struggle in the Countryside*, 118.

220 Loveman, *Struggle in the Countryside*, 209–10, graphically illustrates the take-off of contentious rural politics around 1960. See also Maurice Zeitlin and Richard Earl Ratcliff, *Landlords and Capitalists: The Dominant Class of Chile* (Princeton, NJ: Princeton University Press, 1988), 190–92.

221 Whitehead, "Bolivia since 1930," 538–39, 544, 549–50; Philippe Schmitter, *Interest Conflict and Political Change in Brazil* (Stanford, CA: Stanford University Press, 1971), 209–12; Shepard Forman, *The Brazilian Peasantry* (New York: Columbia University Press, 1975), 181–96.

222 Bolivia's first student congress met in 1928, advocating a radical, nationalist, and indigenista program that anticipated the Revolution of 1952, and armed students seconded the popular military coup of 1930 (for which they were duly rewarded with university autonomy and the right to elect their rectors); Klein, *Parties and Political Change*, 99–101, 111, 116.

223 Rock, *Argentina, 1516–1987*, 200.

224 See chap. 6 of this volume; Whitaker, "Overview of the Period," 15, refers to the Argentine student movement being "in a state of suspended animation" during the 1930s.

225 Jean Stubbs, *Tobacco on the Periphery: A Case Study in Cuban Labour History, 1860–1958* (Cambridge: Cambridge University Press, 1985), 129–36; Wolfe, *Working Women, Working Men*, 54–55; Ann Farnsworth-Alvear, *Dulcinea in the Factory: Myths, Morals, Men and Women in Colombia's Industrial Experiment, 1905–60* (Durham, NC: Duke University Press, 2000), chap. 4. Of course, women also amply participated in most of the events and processes described in this narrative; it should not be assumed that all gender-indeterminate references—to strikes, riots, protests, layoffs, migrations, and the like—concern only men. That inference would only be justified with respect to the armed forces, (Catholic) clerics, and most elite politicians.

226 Snodgrass, *Deference and Defiance in Monterrey*, 161–62.

227 Assuming, of course, that male workers could be substituted by female; in several major sectors—such as mining, metallurgy, and the railways—this was not feasible, at least in the eyes of the companies; see Klubock, *Contested Communities*, 44–45. On wage differentials, which could be very large, see Monteón, *Chile and the Great Depression*, 176.

228 Wolfe, *Working Women, Working Men*, 57–58, describes the policy of the male textile union leadership, who "led" a largely female workforce. In the big Mon-

terrey brewery, even the company *sindicato blanco* excluded women workers—who were numerous—from union posts; Snodgrass, *Deference and Defiance in Monterrey*, 208. Wolfe, *Working Women, Working Men*, 73, 80.

229 According to Teresa Valdés and Indira Palacios, *Participation and Leadership in Latin America and the Caribbean: Gender Indicators* (Santiago: CEPAL, 1999), 28, only three countries introduced a form of female suffrage during the 1930s: Uruguay and Brazil in 1932, Cuba in 1934; this contrasts with six countries in the 1940s and a further eight in the 1950s. (This chronology may be open to debate, in part because of the different forms of female suffrage introduced in different countries.) In Mexico, President Cárdenas (1934–40) promised women the vote, but the "revolutionary family," of which he was paterfamilias, declined to implement the promise, for fear that women would support the Catholic opposition. This was not an entirely groundless fear. We should note that, in Chile, women "tended to favor Conservative candidates" in the 1935 (municipal) elections; Pavilack, *Mining for the Nation*, 77.

230 However, I would agree with the Colliers that the Depression, though "extremely important" in conditioning state-labor relations, was but one among several key conjunctures in a much longer process; the (so-called) "incorporation period sometimes came earlier . . . and sometimes came later"; in short, "there was no regular pattern"—a conclusion that perhaps comes easier to a historian than to a political scientist? See Ruth Berins Collier and David Collier, *Shaping the Political Arena: Critical Junctures, The Labor Movement, and Regime Dynamics in Latin America* (Princeton, NJ: Princeton University Press, 1991), 769

231 On the decline of Anarchism in Brazil, see French, *Brazilian Workers' ABC*, 37–38, 60–61; and Wolfe, *Working Women, Working Men*, 34, 38, 67–68, which shows how Anarchist influence persisted in São Paulo—for example, among the printers—when it had succumbed in the federal capital, Rio. In more general accounts of Latin American labor movements, the eclipse of Anarchism is often an *argumentum ex silentio*: that is, the Anarchists tend to drop out of sight soon after the First World War, and by the 1930s they have often become invisible. However, that disappearing act is rarely explained; often, it seems to be teleologically taken for granted.

232 As Drinot, *Allure of Labor*, 73–74, points out, Anarchism was highly literate—it made a splash in the press—but its social roots were somewhat shallow; it often depended on small groups of enlightened urban artisans (rather than a mass rural or industrial proletariat); it was cosmopolitan and even antinationalist; and, above all, it had great difficulty resisting the pragmatic appeal of reformist administrations (even authoritarian ones like Leguía's).

233 Even in Mexico, where the revolution had brought a real measure of social reform and popular empowerment, including worker-peasant collaboration (occasionally under the aegis of the Communist Party), the ethnic and sectoral barriers remained, and the decision of the Cárdenas government to separate

worker and peasant organizations (roughly, the CTM and CNC) ensured that this separation would be institutionalized within the official party; see Ashby, *Organized Labor*, 80, 90.

234 Economic nationalism, of course, also favored domestic producers at the expense of domestic consumers: no less rational (from the point of view of producers' lobbies) but somewhat less respectable.

235 See chap. 7 of this volume; and, regarding anti-Semitism in Argentina, Brazil, and Chile, see Sandra McGee Deutsch, *Las Derechas: The Extreme Right in Argentina, Brazil and Chile, 1890–1939* (Stanford, CA: Stanford University Press, 1999), 167–68, 227–31, 275–76. Mexico, too, saw a spike in anti-Semitism in the 1930s; Alicia Gojman de Backal, *Camisas, escudos y desfiles militares: Los Dorados y el antisemitismo en México (1934–1940)* (Mexico: FCE, 2000).

236 Alan Knight, *U.S.-Mexican Relations, 1910–1940: An Interpretation* (San Diego: Center for U.S.-Mexican Studies, 1987), 67–69.

237 Knight, "Politics of the Expropriation," 104–5.

238 Mexico's Sinarquista movement, which boomed during the later 1930s, adopted a Catholic-integralist stance (which included a measure of anti-Semitism), distanced itself from Nazism, and warmly supported Franco. While a product of the 1930s, it was not particularly a product of the Depression: its growth coincided with economic recovery, not slump; it reacted to global political (not economic) events, above all the Spanish Civil War; and it represented the continuation by other means of the mass Cristero insurrection of the 1920s. See Pablo Serrano Alvarez, *La batalla del espíritu: El movimiento sinarquista en el Bajío (1932–1951)* (2 vols.; Mexico: Consejo Nacional para la Cultura y las Artes, 1992).

239 Collier and Sater, *History of Chile*, 233–34; Juan Luis Ossa, "El Nacismo en Chile: Auge y caída de una ilusión mesiánica," in *XX. Historia del siglo veinte chileno*, 131–84; Deutsch, *Las Derechas*, chap.11.

240 Particularly with regard to the labor movement and the largely Indian peasantry; see Klein, *Parties and Political Change*, 337–38. I am making the comparison with the paradigmatic cases of Italy and Germany, where Fascism destroyed both liberal democracy and left-wing parties and unions; the MNR played no such negative role and, indeed, increasingly embodied both democratic and leftist tendencies within its own broad ranks. Again, comparisons with Eastern Europe (where Fascism sometimes assumed a more popular, less reactionary guise) may be pertinent.

241 R. G. Williams, *States and Social Evolution*, 236, makes the same point regarding Central America, stressing the "amazing diversity of economic and political structures," hence the need to look for "local causes" of change, rather than attributing change to "world system forces."

242 For the Mexican case, see Friedrich Schuler, *Mexico between Hitler and Roosevelt: Mexican Foreign Relations in the Age of Lázaro Cárdenas, 1934–40* (Albuquerque: University of New Mexico Press, 1998). To posit a purely speculative

counterfactual, had Jacobo Arbenz attempted his socioeconomic project in the 1930s rather than the 1950s, Guatemala might well have avoided U.S. intervention and domestic counterrevolution.

243 Drake, *Between Tyranny and Anarchy*, 164. See also Ian Roxborough, "Unity and Diversity in Latin American History," *Journal of Latin American Studies* 16, no. 1 (1984): 8, which identifies (and criticizes) a "modal pattern" (i.e., standard interpretation) of Latin American politico-economic development, in which the 1930s sees the start of a thirty-year stage of "Bonapartist" state forms and "populist" political movements.

244 I have elsewhere critiqued the use of "populism" as a fundamental organizing concept; Alan Knight, "Populism and Neo-populism in Latin America (especially Mexico)," *Journal of Latin American Studies* 30, no. 2 (1998): 223–48.

245 Alain Rouquié, *Amérique latine: Introduction à l'extrême occident* (Paris: Seuil, 1987).

246 Daniel James, *Doña María's Story: Life History, Memory and Political Identity* (Durham, NC: Duke University Press, 2000), 37–41.

247 Mary Kay Vaughan, *Cultural Politics in Revolution: Teachers, Peasants and Schools in Mexico, 1930–40* (Tucson: University of Arizona Press, 1997).

248 W. H. Auden, "September 1 1939," in *Poetry of the Thirties*, ed. Robin Skelton (Harmondsworth, UK: Penguin, 1964), 280; Richard Overy, *The Morbid Age: Britain and the Crisis of Civilization, 1919–39* (London: Penguin, 2010), 360. Although the latter book focuses on Britain, it seems to claim, if only in its title, that a similar malaise infected all "civilization" (which, I would hope, includes Latin America).

249 Quoted by Randolp Starn, "Historians and 'Crisis,'" *Past and Present* 52, no. 1 (1971): 6.

MARCELO BUCHELI (PhD Stanford University) is an associate professor of business administration and history at the University of Illinois at Urbana-Champaign. He has published the book *Bananas and Business: The United Fruit Company in Colombia, 1899–2000* (2005) and several articles on the oil and banana industries in Latin America in scholarly journals and edited collections.

CARLOS CONTRERAS is a historian and professor in the Economics Department of the Pontificia Universidad Católica del Perú and a member of the Instituto de Estudios Peruanos. He obtained his PhD at the Colegio de México, with a dissertation on the making of the Peruvian economy in the late nineteenth and early twentieth centuries, to be published shortly. He has previously researched the history of mining and the evolution of the Peruvian economy following the period of independence. He is the author of *Mineros y campesinos en los Andes* (1988), *El aprendizaje del capitalismo* (2004), and (with Marcos Cueto) *Historia del Perú contemporáneo* (latest edition 2007).

PAULO DRINOT is senior lecturer in Latin American history at the Institute of the Americas, University College London. He is the author of *The Allure of Labor: Workers, Race, and the Making of the Peruvian State* (Duke University Press, 2011) and of several articles and book chapters on various aspects of Peruvian history, editor of *Che's Travels: The Making of a Revolutionary in 1950s Latin America* (Duke University Press, 2010), and coeditor of *Mas allá de la dominación y la resistencia: Estudios de historia peruana, siglos XVI–XX* (2005).

JEFFREY L. GOULD is the James H. Rudy Professor of History at Indiana University. From 1995 to 2008, he was director of the Center for Latin American and Caribbean Studies. His most recent book is *To Rise in Darkness: Revolution, Repression, and Memory in El Salvador, 1920–32* (coauthored with Aldo Lauria, Duke University Press, 2008). Previous books include *To Lead as Equals: Rural Protest and Political Consciousness in Chinandega, Nicaragua, 1912–1979* (1990); *El Mito de Nicaragua Mestiza y la Resistencia Indígena* (1997); and *To Die in This Way: Nicaraguan*

Indian Communities and the Myth of Mestizaje, 1880–1965 (Duke University Press, 1998). He is coauthor of *The Twentieth Century: A Retrospective* (2002). He is also coeditor of *Memorias de Mestizaje: La política cultural en América Central desde 1900*. The latter book derived from an NEH collaborative project that he codirected with Charles Hale and Darío Euraque. Gould codirected and coproduced *Scars of Memory: El Salvador, 1932* (2003), a documentary film (Award of Merit, LASA). He has completed another documentary film, titled *La Palabra en el Bosque*, which deals with Christian Base Communities in Morazán, El Salvador, during the 1970s (also with Carlos Henríquez Consalvi). In 2002, he was awarded a John Simon Guggenheim Fellowship.

ROY HORA is full professor at the Universidad Nacional de Quilmes, Argentina, and a researcher at CONICET. He received his PhD in modern history from the University of Oxford (1998). He is the author of *The Landowners of the Argentine Pampas: A Social and Political History, 1860–1945* (2001), *Los estancieros contra el Estado: La Liga Agraria y los orígenes del ruralismo político en Argentina* (2009), and *Historia económica de la Argentina en el siglo XIX* (2010).

ALAN KNIGHT is professor of the history of Latin America at the University of Oxford. His chief interest is twentieth-century Latin American history, with a focus on Mexico, agrarian society, state building, and revolutions. He is the author of *The Mexican Revolution* (2 vols., 1986); *US-Mexican Relations, 1910–40* (1987); the chapter on Mexico, 1930–1946, in *The Cambridge History of Latin America* (vol. 7, 1990); and two volumes of a three-volume general history of Mexico, *Mexico: From the Beginning to the Conquest*, and *Mexico: The Colonial Era* (2002). He has written several articles dealing with aspects of twentieth-century Mexico (state building, popular movements, education and culture, current politics) and coedited *The Mexican Petroleum Industry in the 20th Century* (1992). He is completing the third volume of the general history (*Mexico since Independence*) and researching a sociopolitical study of Mexico in the 1930s. He previously taught at the University of Essex and the University of Texas at Austin, where he held the C. B. Smith Chair, and in 1986 was a visiting fellow at the Center for U.S.-Mexican Studies at the University of California, San Diego.

GILLIAN MCGILLIVRAY is an associate professor at Glendon College (York University) in Toronto, Canada. McGillivray's commitment to comparative studies and microhistory, combined with her gravitation toward early twentieth-century developments—war, boom, and bust at the global level and nationalism, populism, and revolution at the local level—motivated her book *Blazing Cane: Sugar Communities, Class, and State Formation in Cuba, 1868–1958* (Duke University Press, 2009) and her new research project on "Sugar and Power in the Brazilian Countryside, 1928–1963." *Blazing Cane* won a Choice Outstanding Academic Title award in 2010 and the Georgetown University Glassman Award for Best Dissertation in the Humanities in 2003.

LUIS FELIPE SÁENZ received a BS and MA in economics at Universidad de los Andes (Bogotá, Colombia). He worked as a research fellow at the Inter-American Development Bank (Washington, DC) and is currently working toward his PhD in economics at the University of Illinois at Urbana-Champaign.

ANGELA VERGARA is an associate professor of history at California State University, Los Angeles. She obtained her PhD at the University of California San Diego (2002), and she is the author of *Copper Workers, International Business, and Domestic Politics in Cold War Chile* (2008) and coeditor of *Company Towns in the Americas*. She has researched, presented, and published on a wide range of topics, such as labor relations, public health, paternalism and welfare capitalism, social movements, rural cooperatives, and labor internationalism. Her chapter in this volume is part of a larger project on the social and labor history of the Great Depression in Chile and the long-term impact of unemployment on working people's political identity.

JOEL WOLFE is a professor of Latin American history at the University of Massachusetts Amherst. He is the author of *Autos and Progress: The Brazilian Search for Modernity* (2010) and *Working Women, Working Men: São Paulo and the Rise of Brazil's Industrial Working Class, 1900–1955* (Duke University Press, 1993). He is at present writing a book tentatively titled *The Global Twenties: Trade and Society in the Western Hemisphere in the 1920s.*

DOUG YARRINGTON is an associate professor of history at Colorado State University. He is the author of *A Coffee Frontier: Land, Society and Politics in Duaca, Venezuela, 1830–1936* (1997), as well as articles in *Hispanic American Historical Review, Journal of Latin American Studies, Latin American Research Review,* and *The Americas.* He is currently writing a book on corruption, anticorruption, and state formation in Venezuela between 1908 and 1948.

mining in, 83; oil industry in, 93;
peasants in, 307–308; populism in, 81,
84–85, 93, 95; repression of labor, 83;
strikes in, 83, 85, 306, 308; wages in,
85; women in, 336–337; workers in,
10–11, 81–84, 93, 95–97, 336
Brazilian Constitution of 1934, 324
British Foreign Office, 241
Buenos Aires, 28–29, 34, 43, 47, 302,
305–306
Bulmer-Thomas, Victor, 3, 17, 19, 189–
190, 204, 209, 236, 280, 284, 292,
314–315, 317, 322, 326, 330

Cacao, 162, 278, 285
Caja Agraria (Colombia), 141
Caja de Depósitos y Consignaciones
(Peru), 116
Caja de Seguro Obrero (Chile), 61, 77
Calama, 55
Caldera Rodríguez, Rafael, 173–174,
176, 179, 181, 186
Callao, 110
Calles, Plutarco Elías, 215, 217–218,
221–223, 225–226, 228, 230–231, 237–
238, 240–241, 293–294, 303, 306
Camacho, Avila, 229
Camagüey, 254
Camarero, Hernán, 46, 49–50
Canada, 3, 26
Cananea, 216
Canudos, 89, 99
Capitalist Welfare, 248–249, 269, 271
Carabineros, 76
Carabobo, 168
Caracas, 164, 169–170, 173, 175, 177,
179, 182
Cárdenas, Lázaro, 5–6, 14, 94, 191, 218,
225–232, 240, 242, 246, 268, 277, 288–
289, 293, 296, 298, 300, 304, 334, 337
Cardenismo, 213, 294, 311, 329. See also
Cárdenas, Lázaro
CaribSyndicate, 148

Carranza, Venustiano, 222
Carrera Rebellion of 1837, 201
Carta de Lavoro of 1927, 120
Cartagena Oil Refining Company, 146
Casa de Limpieza, 66
Castilla, Ramón, 122
Castillo Libertador, 164, 169
Castro, Cipriano, 167
Castro, Fidel, 294
Catamarca, 28
Catholic Action (Venezuela), 173–174
Catholic Church, 25, 298, 301; in Argen-
tina, 31, 35; in Chile, 54, 64–65, 78; in
El Salvador, 197; in Mexico, 218, 294,
337; in Venezuela, 171–174, 180
Catholic Youth (Venezuela), 173
Cattle, 162
Cayaltí, 107–108
Central America, 6, 7, 102, 142, 157, 165,
188–189, 195, 217, 279, 284, 293–294,
296, 298, 304, 319, 322, 326–327, 332,
334–335; banana industry in, 285, 295;
coffee industry in, 319, 282, 295, 303;
exports in, 13, 188–190; import substitution industrialization in, 189;
Indians in, 13, 188, 190–192, 207–208,
285; industrialization in, 189; infrastructure, 190; liberalism in, 191; military in, 188, 190, 291; peasants in, 282;
wages in, 189; workers in, 189–191;
race in, 13, 188, 190–192, 207–208
Central Bank, 302, 317; in Chile, 67; in
Colombia, 134, 138, 141; in Mexico,
215, 222, 224, 239, 241; in Peru, 11,
103, 117; in Venezuela, 182
Central General de Trabajadores del
Perú (CGTP), 112
Central Railway (Peru), 110
CEPAL, 5, 298
Cerro de Pasco, 107, 110, 125
Chachapoyas, 127, 307
Chaco War, 1, 16, 288, 290, 299, 324,
327, 331

Chamorro, Emiliano, 208
Chaparra, 249, 263–266, 273
Chaparra Light and Power Company, 264
Chapultepec Conference, 302
Chávez, Hugo, 13, 181
Chayanov, Alexander, 284
Chihuahua, 243
Chile, 1, 3, 6–7, 17, 21, 26, 94, 100, 106, 154, 168, 172, 278, 280, 283, 285, 286, 288, 291–297, 303, 307–308, 310–311, 320, 326, 332, 334, 338; anarchism in, 65, 69; Catholic Church in, 54, 64–65, 78; Communist Party of, 61, 66, 69, 80; copper industry in, 55, 69–70, 74, 278, 281; *enganche* system in, 54–55, 57, 74–76; exports of, 17, 51–52, 219, 221, 238, 278–279, 281; fascism in, 78, 310; gold industry in, 59–60, 321; industrialization in, 73–74, 285, 298; import substitution industrialization in, 73; labor laws in, 10, 55–56, 68–72, 74–76, 79, 304; labor unions in, 10, 53, 70–72, 76, 78–79; middle classes in, 74; migration in, 52, 54–58, 76, 281, 334; military in, 55, 71, 308; mining in, 51–53, 55, 58, 60, 69–71, 74, 76, 305, 334; monetary policy of, 67; nitrate industry in, 7, 10, 51, 54–55, 75–77, 285, 295, 334; political instability in, 52, 306; populism in, 10, 52–53; Radical Party of, 73, 79; repression of labor, 69, 71–72; social and political consequences of unemployment in, 60–62; Socialist Party of, 73–74, 79; social welfare, 7, 10, 62–68, 77; social welfare and social control, 64–67; unemployment in, 10, 56–58, 76–77, 305; unemployment and public works, 58–60; women in, 74, 337; workers in, 10, 55–56, 68–72, 74, 76–77, 80, 306, 334
Chilla, 59

Chillán, 285
Chimaltenango, 207
China, 4, 233, 279, 321
Christian Democratic Party (Chile), 78
Chuquicamata, 55, 69
Civil War of 1895, 104
Civil War of 1932, 90, 82
Coca-Cola, 254
Cocaine, 104
Coffee, 12, 13, 48, 82, 84–90, 96, 104, 130–135, 137–142, 150–151, 162, 164–165, 188–191, 193–194, 198, 201–202, 204, 219, 220, 279, 281–284, 286, 295–296, 303, 306, 318–319
Coffee Valorization, 84, 88–90
Cold War, 99, 230, 300
Colgate-Palmolive, 230
Collective action (theory), 130, 133, 138, 140, 143, 153
Colombia, 1, 165, 166, 168, 280–281, 283, 288–289, 292–293, 295, 296, 304, 307, 309, 311, 319, 331, 333; agrarian reform in, 244; banana industry in, 1, 113–114, 130–135, 142–145, 150–151, 153, 156–157, 235, 321; coffee industry in, 12, 130–142, 150–151, 219, 282, 303, 318; export sector in, 130–136, 138–150, 279; import substitution industrialization in, 129, 133, 138; industrialization in, 134, 136–137, 150; Keynesianism in, 296; labor unions in, 134, 149; military in, 144, 149, 152; oil industry in, 12, 130–135, 145–151, 153, 303, 332; peasants in, 285, 306–307; populism in, 129–130, 132, 144–145, 149, 151–153; repression in, 145, 149; strikes in, 145, 149; workers in, 145, 149
Colombia-Peru War. *See* Leticia War
Colonialism, 3–4
Comintern, 166–167, 170, 174, 250, 269
Comisión Distribuidora (Peru), 115–116
Comités Pro-Auxilio de Cesantes, 64–65, 67

Cuba (*continued*)
   Trotskyism in, 248, 260–261, 264,
   266; wages in, 249, 256, 259, 263–266;
   women in, 14, 259, 267–268, 273, 308,
   337; workers in, 246–251, 254–264,
   267–270, 273; xenophobia in, 305,
   309
Cuba Company, 248
Cuban American Sugar Company, 248–
   249, 264, 266
Cuban American Treaty of 1903, 254
Cuban Commercial Association, 252
Cuban Communist Party (PCC), 166,
   264, 304
Cuban Constitution of 1940, 325
Cuban Sugar Stabilization Institute
   (ICAE), 270
Cuba–United States Reciprocity Treaty,
   282
Cuisnahuat, 198
Curepto, 51
Cutín, 57, 59
Cuzco, 108, 110

Da Cunha, Euclides, 99
Da Fonseca, Deodoro, 88
Daniels, Josephus, 242
Década Infame, 23–25, 37, 43–44, 311
De Céspedes, Carlos Manuel, 256, 258
Deindianization, 188, 190
De la Huerta, Adolfo, 238
Delicias, 249, 263–266, 273
De Mares, Roberto, 146–147
Democrats (USA), 4
Departamento Nacional del Trabajo
   (DNT) (Argentina), 37, 38
Department of Agriculture (Cuba), 265
Department of State, 131
Dependency theory, 125
Devaluation, 26, 84, 140, 165, 189
Development Bank (Peru), 103
Díaz, Porfirio, 216, 235. *See also* Porfi-
   riato

Díaz Alejandro, Carlos F., 102, 114, 289,
   298, 312, 323, 327–328
Dominican Republic, 219, 236, 303, 305,
   309, 326, 328
Dominicans (religious order), 211
Duarte, Eva, 29

Echeverría, Luis, 231
ECLA, 5, 19, 129
Ecuador, 278, 285–286, 289, 290, 304,
   317, 320, 322, 332, 303
Egypt, 321
El Salvador, 200–201, 204, 206–207, 209,
   211, 291, 294–296, 321, 326; agrarian
   reform in, 195; coffee industry in,
   194–196, 282, 306, 309; communists
   in, 196–197, 206; exports in, 188–189,
   279, 285; import substitution industrialization, 286; Indians in, 13, 191–198,
   206–207; labor unions in, 194–196;
   land reform in, 195; military in, 13,
   196–198, 206–207, 292; peasants in,
   193; political instability in, 196; race
   in, 13, 191–198, 206–207; religious
   tensions in, 195; repression in, 193,
   196–197; social unrest in, 191, 193,
   202, 306; strikes in, 194; wages in, 189;
   workers in, 193–196, 207, 209, 284
El Teniente, 334
Estado Novo, 83–85, 87, 93, 97, 290,
   297, 304, 308, 334
Europe, 1–2, 29–30, 34–35, 48, 90, 297,
   300, 312, 320–321, 331, 338
Exchange controls, 26
Exchange rate, 140, 141, 165, 183
Export-led growth, 5, 103, 298–299,
   301, 305
Export protectionism, 12, 130–133, 137,
   150
Exports: of Argentina, 22, 26–27, 219,
   279; of Brazil, 82, 84, 88–90, 219, 279,
   333, 337; of Central America, 13, 188–
   190; of Chile, 51–52, 219, 221, 238,

278–279, 281; of Colombia, 130–136, 138–150, 279; of Cuba, 17, 246–247, 270; of El Salvador, 188–189, 279, 285; of Guatemala, 188–189; of Mexico, 216, 219–221, 234–235, 279; of Nicaragua, 188–189, 279; of Peru, 102–104, 107, 113–114, 121, 279, 298–299; of Venezuela, 161, 164–165

Expropriation. *See* Nationalism: economic

ExxonMobil, 153

Falange (Spain), 177

Falange Nacional (Chile), 78

Fascism, 8, 16, 39, 72, 79, 169, 176, 229, 260, 269, 309, 310, 338; in Brazil, 310; in Chile, 78; in Cuba, 260; in Guatemala, 206; in Peru, 112, 115; in Venezuela, 177

February Program (Venezuela), 170, 174, 180

Federación Nacional de Cafeteros de Colombia (FNCC), 131, 133–134, 139–142

Federación Obrera de Alimentación, 40

Federación Obrera de Chile (FOCH), 55

Federación Obrera Nacional de la Construcción (FONC), 40–41

Federal Labour Code, 230 (Mexico)

Federal Labour Law, 228

Federal Reserve, 233

Federation of Havana Workers (FOH), 260–264

Federation of Venezuelan Students (FEV), 164, 170, 173, 178–179

Fiat money, 117

First Coffee Congress (1920), 139

First International Meeting of Mild Coffee Producers, 139

First World War, 33, 36, 54, 75, 117, 129, 134, 139, 217, 246, 250, 252, 254, 278, 281, 285, 287, 298, 300, 337

Força Pública Paulista, 86

Fordism, 93, 271

Ford Motor Co., 230, 254

Foreign Debt, 17, 75, 84, 105, 114, 182, 215–217, 223, 234, 238–239, 248, 281–282, 317, 328

France, 174, 223, 231, 311

Franciscans, 211

Franco, Francisco, 177, 269, 310, 338

Frei Montalva, Eduardo, 174

Frente Nacional (Colombia), 152

Freyre, Gilberto, 277

Fujimori, Alberto, 118

Furtado, Celso, 18–19, 98, 278, 314, 318, 328

Gaitán, Jorge Eliécer, 145, 152

Galavís, Félix, 172

Garrido Canabal, Tómas, 157

Geisel, Ernesto, 95

General Motors, 230

General Union of Workers (Venezuela), 176

Germani, Gino, 33

Germany, 16, 104, 176, 260, 280, 283, 289, 300, 310, 315, 319, 338

Gil Robles, José María, 174

Goiás, 92

Gold, 59, 60, 104, 114, 281, 321

Gold Standard, 114, 117, 134, 138, 140, 221–222, 239, 281, 295–296, 317, 328

Gómez, Juan Vicente, 12, 160–174, 176, 178–180, 182, 288, 294, 308, 322

Gómez, Laureano, 148

González Casanova, Pablo, 2

Good Neighbor Policy, 259, 311

Gracias, 192

Grau San Martín, Ramón, 14, 258–260, 261, 263–266, 269–270

Great Britain, 26, 29, 104, 105, 128, 147–148, 190, 229–231, 280, 282–283, 296, 305, 312, 315, 319, 339

Great Depression: interpretations of, 276–278

Greece, 289

Grove, Marmaduke, 73
Guano, 106
Guárico, 168
Guatemala, 200, 206–208, 211, 291, 295, 296, 299, 301, 306, 318, 326, 334, 339; agrarian reform in, 207; agricultural sector in, 201; coffee industry in, 201–202, 204, 282; Communist Party of, 203–204; exports in, 188–189; Indians in, 13, 191–194, 201–207; infrastructure in, 190; labor unions in, 203–204; land reform in, 207; middle classes in, 205; migration in, 205; military in, 13, 202–203, 205; peasants in, 204–205; populism in, 205, 212, 291, 326; race in, 13, 191–194, 201–207; repression in, 203–204, 207; revolts in, 203–205, 207; strikes in, 203; wages in, 189; workers in, 194, 201–204, 207
Guerrero, 241
Guiteras, Antonio, 260, 263–266
Gunder Frank, Andre, 18–19
Guomindang, 233

Haiti, 8, 236, 281, 317, 328, 334
Hale, Charles, 209, 212
Hall, Stuart, 21
Harlem Renaissance, 246
Havana, 247, 251, 254, 256–257
Haya de la Torre, Víctor Raúl, 103, 112
Henequén, 220
Hernández Martínez, Maximiliano, 197–198, 207, 292
Hirschman, Albert O., 321, 323, 329
Hitler, Adolf, 260, 311
Hobsbawm, Eric, 1, 15
Honduras, 179, 188, 192–193, 201–202, 208–209, 289, 291, 295, 304, 317
Hong Kong, 4
Hoover, Herbert, 218, 262
Houston, 252
Huachipato, 74
Huntington, Samuel, 292, 327

Ibañez del Campo, Carlos, 1, 52, 55, 64, 67, 69, 76, 78–79, 291–292, 294
Import substitution industrialization (ISI), 5, 15, 19, 285–287, 302, 323; in Argentina, 26, 48; in Central America, 189; in Chile, 73; in Colombia, 129, 133, 138; in Cuba, 247, 254, 286; in El Salvador, 286; in Mexico, 220–221, 229, 232; in Nicaragua, 286; in Peru, 102, 118, 286–287, 298, 332
Inconfidência Mineira, 87, 92, 98
India, 3, 18, 279
Indigenismo, 188, 191, 200, 204, 206–207, 209, 246
Indigo, 201
Indohispanismo, 199
Industrialization: in Argentina, 23, 26, 37, 285, 297–298; in Brazil, 11, 85–88, 90–92, 285, 298; in Central America, 189; in Chile, 73–74, 285, 298; in Colombia, 134, 136–137, 150; in Cuba, 254; in Mexico, 13, 216, 220–221, 227–230, 237, 242–243, 277, 285, 298; in Peru, 104; textiles, 8, 88–89, 104, 110, 217, 220, 228, 242–243; in Venezuela, 165
Ingenio San Antonio, 199
Integralists, 310
International division of labor, 278
International Labor Conference, 211
International Petroleum Company (IPC), 110
International Telephone & Telegraph, 230
Intibucá, 192, 202
Iquique, 51, 55–56
Italy, 115, 169, 176, 231, 310, 338
Izalco, 193, 195–197

Jacobinism, 307, 335
Jamaica, 8
Japan, 4, 128, 300, 331
Java, 254

Jayaque, 195
Jinotega, 192, 208
Jones, Maldwyn, 4
Juayúa, 195, 197
Junín, 108, 110
Junta Pro-Desocupados de Lima (Peru), 110, 115
Justo, Agustín P., 38, 318

Kemmerer Mission. *See* Kemmerer, Edwin
Kemmerer, Edwin, 110, 114–115, 117
Keynes, John Maynard, 16, 239
Keynesianism, 2, 4, 239, 300; in Brazil, 86, 225; in Colombia, 296; in Mexico, 13–14, 239, 223–225, 296
Krugman, Paul, 18
Kubitschek, Juscelino, 93, 95

Labor Code of 1931 (Mexico), 307
Labor Code of 1933 (Chile), 78–79
Labor Department (Chile), 55–56, 58–59, 60, 62, 67, 70–71, 79
Labor Ministry (Cuba), 246, 259, 261, 263–264, 267
Labor unions: in Argentina, 10, 23, 24–25, 34–42, 44–45, 304–305; in Brazil, 10–11, 81–84, 101, 304, 333, 336; in Chile, 10, 53, 70–72, 78–79; in Colombia, 134, 149; in Cuba, 248, 255, 260–264, 266, 268–269, 304; in El Salvador, 194–196; in Guatemala, 203–204; in Mexico, 215–217, 227–230, 242–244, 306, 308; in Nicaragua, 199; in Peru, 105, 110, 112, 116, 307; in Venezuela, 168, 175–176, 179, 187. *See also* Workers
Laissez-faire, 88, 95, 99, 129–130, 133, 252, 297, 300–301
La Laguna, 226–228, 241, 333, 335
La Libertad (El Salvador), 192–194, 198, 210
Lambayeque, 107

Land reform. *See* Agrarian reform
Lara, 168
Lara Law, 174, 178
La Revolución en Marcha, 306
La Rioja, 28
La Rotunda Prison, 164, 169
Latin American Wars of Independence, 327
Lead, 104, 107, 114
League of National Defense, 178
League of Nations, 209
Leguía, Augusto B., 103, 105–108, 111, 115, 121, 295, 298, 301, 303, 335, 337
Leite, Aureliano, 98
Leo XIII, 124
Leticia War, 1, 113–114, 142, 288, 331
Lewis, Arthur W., 315
Ley de Conscripción Vial (Peru), 107, 124
Ley de Fuga, 248
Liberal Party (Colombia), 12, 130, 132–134, 142, 144–145, 148–149, 151–152, 292, 304
Liberal Revolution, 201
Liberals (Guatemala), 202, 206
Liberating Revolution, 331
Lima, 108–110, 115–116, 125, 127
Lleras Restrepo, Carlos, 296
Lombardo Toledano, Vicente, 242, 306, 327
López Contreras, Eleazar, 12, 160–161, 167–175, 178–180
López Pumarejo, Alfonso, 142, 145, 292, 304, 306
Los Angeles, 59, 69
Los Toldos, 29

Mabay, 261
Maceo, Antonio, 251
Machado, Absalón, 138
Machado, Cuba, 306
Machado, Gerardo, 14, 247–249, 253–258, 261, 269, 292–293, 306

Machado, Gustavo, 166–167
Madero, Francisco, 217
Madrid, 222
Magallanes, 57, 70
Magdalena (Colombia), 12, 142–145
Malinowski, Bronislaw, 240
Managua, 321
Manchuria, 4
Mann Act, 238
Manufactura de Cobre (MADECO), 74
Manufactura de Metales (MADEMSA), 74
Maquito, 50
Maracaibo, 168
Martí, Farabundo, 294
Martí, José, 251
Massacre of 1932, 193, 196–197, 206, 294, 335
Matagalpa, 198, 200–202, 208
Mato Grosso, 92
Mato Grosso do Sul, 92
Medellín, 134, 150, 308
Medina Angarita, Isaías, 179
Mendieta, Carlos, 263, 266–267
Mendoza, 16
Mestizaje, 190–194, 197–202, 205, 246
Mexican Constitution of 1917, 120, 225
Mexican Light and Power Company, 234
Mexican Revolution, 147, 167, 216–218, 221, 223, 228, 225, 229–232, 245, 313; evaluations of, 213–215, 277, 288–289, 301–302, 303–304, 331
Mexico, 5–8, 26, 94, 100–101, 147, 154, 157–158, 166, 168, 172, 177, 191, 200, 202, 205, 233–235, 238, 246, 268–269, 277, 280, 283, 284, 287–289, 293–296, 299, 303–304, 306, 309, 311, 323, 330, 332, 334, 338; agrarian reform in, 14, 216–217, 221–222, 225–228, 231–232, 241, 244, 302–303, 307; agricultural sector of, 13, 220, 226, 237, 240–241; Catholic Church in, 218, 294, 337; Communist Party of, 218, 229, 231, 234, 335, 337; economic nationalism in, 14, 221,225, 229–231; exports in, 216, 219–221, 234–235, 279; fiscal policy in, 221–222; foreign direct investment in, 216; import substitution industrialization in, 220–221, 229, 232; industrialization in, 13, 216, 220–221, 227–230, 237, 242–243, 277, 285, 298; Keynesianism in, 13–14, 239, 223–225, 296; labor reform in, 221, 225, 227–229, 231–232, 304; labor unions in, 215–217, 227–230, 242–244, 306, 308; migration in, 13, 219–221, 226, 236–237, 241, 305; military in, 215–217, 235, 239, 289; mining in, 216, 217, 219–220, 228, 230, 236, 243, 303; monetary policy in, 221–224; oil industry in, 14, 216–217, 219, 224, 228–231, 234, 236, 243, 288, 303–304, 310, 324; peasants in, 216–217, 221, 224–225, 228, 237, 244, 307, 337–338; populism in, 216, 224, 227, 231–232, 240; relations of the United States with, 13, 216–217, 219–221, 226, 230, 234–235, 238, 244; silver mining in, 219–221, 236, 281; strikes in, 228, 242, 308; textile industry in, 217, 220, 228, 242–243; unemployment in, 13, 212, 220; women in, 308, 337; workers, 217, 219–221, 224, 227–230, 236, 242–244, 333; xenophobia in, 309–310
Mexico City, 234
Miami, 252
Michoacán, 224, 241
Middle classes, 5, 10, 18, 20, 214; in Argentina, 10, 24–25, 29–34, 39, 42–46, 318; in Brazil, 94; in Chile, 74; in Cuba, 248, 253, 256–258, 270; in Guatemala, 205; in Mexico, 228; in Peru, 103, 106, 108–109, 112, 121, 123, 307, 335; in Venezuela, 173
Migration, 305; in Argentina, 10, 28–30, 35, 43, 305; in Brazil, 305; in Chile, 52,

54–58, 76, 281, 334; in Cuba, 251–253; in Guatemala, 205; in Mexico, 13, 219–221, 226, 236–237, 241, 305; in Peru, 107–108, 116

Military, 290, 292, 297, 298–299, 301, 325, 327, 336; in Argentina, 25, 288, 291, 295, 323–326; in Brazil, 81–83, 88–89, 91, 93, 95–97, 99, 327–328; in Central America, 188, 190, 291; in Chile, 55, 71, 308; in Colombia, 144, 149, 152; in Cuba, 247–248, 250, 256, 258, 260, 266, 268–269, 292; in El Salvador, 13, 196–198, 206–207, 292; in Guatemala, 13, 202–203, 205; in Mexico, 215–217, 235, 239, 289; in Nicaragua, 13; in Peru, 11, 103, 106–107, 112–113, 124, 292, 295; in Venezuela, 161–164, 167–169, 171–172, 176, 179, 181

Military coups, 14, 22, 44, 93, 100–101, 102, 103, 107, 167, 196, 256, 268–269, 288–291, 295, 324–325, 336

Military dictatorship, 1, 6, 13, 38, 93, 95–96, 103, 112, 152, 161–162, 168, 178, 180, 188, 190, 197, 203, 205–206, 247, 255–259, 268–270, 292

Minas Gerais, 11, 81, 87, 90–93, 96

Miners, 60, 69–70, 107, 109, 116, 295, 305, 333. *See also* Workers

Mining: in Brazil, 87; in Chile, 51–53, 55, 58, 60, 69–71, 74, 76, 305, 334; in Mexico, 216, 217, 219–220, 228, 230, 236, 243, 303; in Peru, 11, 103–105, 107, 109–110, 112, 114, 116–117, 122, 125, 281, 334, 336

Mining Bank (Peru), 117

Ministerio de Fomento (Ministry of Development) (Peru), 105

Ministry of Education: in Brazil, 87; in Venezuela, 172

Ministry of Finance (Mexico), 222

Ministry of Interior Relations (Venezuela), 163

Ministry of Labor (Brazil), 83–85, 333

Ministry of Social Welfare (Chile), 51

Miskito, 199

Momostenango, 204

Monetarists, 1

Montalvo, José Antonio, 148

Montero, Juan Antonio, 67

Monterrey, 287, 302, 308, 337

Montes de Oca-Lamont Agreement, 222

Morelos, 216, 240

Morones, 306, 333

Morones, Luis, 218, 240

Morrow, Dwight, 217

Mossadegh, Mohammad, 244

Movimiento Nacionalista Revolucionario (MNR), 310, 327

Multinational Corporations, 129, 131, 234, 142–151

Murmis, Miguel, 28, 45

Mussolini, Benito, 115

Nahuatl, 192–194, 197, 210

Nahuizalco, 193, 195, 197, 210

National Cane Farmers Association, 259

National Coffee Council (CNC), 84–86, 338

National Congress of Cuban Workers (CNOC), 260–264

National Democratic Party (PDN), 178–179

National Guard (Nicaragua), 200, 291

Nationalism, 3–4, 16, 25, 29, 87, 116, 129, 166, 190, 199, 216, 246–247, 250–251, 259, 276–277, 283, 302, 309–310; cultural, 253–254; economic, 14, 130, 148–148, 151, 157, 207, 221, 224–225, 229–231, 234, 236, 244, 246, 253–254, 270, 288, 294, 302–304, 306, 309–310, 324, 332, 338

Nationalists (Spain), 176–177

Nationalization. *See* Nationalism: economic

Nationalization of Labor (Cuba), 260

National Labor Bureau, 304
National Labor Codes, 304
National Labor Office (Venezuela), 174
National Motors Company (FNM), 91
National Petroleum Council, 93
National Railways (Mexico), 230
National Recovery Act, 259
National Republican Union (UNR), 170, 175
National Socialism, 177, 338, 177
National Steel Company (CSN), 91
National Student Union (UNE), 173–174, 177–179
National Sugar Export Corporation, 270
National Sugar Institute, 246
National Tourist Commission, 252
National Traffic Code, 92
National Union of Sugar Industry Workers (SNOIA), 255, 261–263, 266
Nebaj, 205
Negritos, 107
Neopopulism, 231
New Deal, 3–4, 18, 115, 169, 246, 258
New York, 252
Nicaragua, 190, 201, 205–206, 208, 227, 277, 284, 291, 295, 304, 317, 321, 328; coffee industry in, 198, 286; exports in, 188–189, 279; import substitution industrialization in, 286; Indians in, 13, 192–194, 198–202, 206–207; labor unions in, 199; military in, 13; peasants in, 277, 312–313; populism in, 291, 326; race in, 13, 192–194, 198–202, 206–207; strikes in, 199, 211; United States intervention in, 199–200, 326; wages in, 189; workers in, 199
Nitrates, 7, 10, 51, 54–55, 75–77, 195, 285

Oaxaca, 224
Obama, Barack, 4, 18
Obregón, Álvaro, 217, 228

Obrerismo, 191
Oficina de Colocaciones. *See* Servicio de Colocaciones
Oil, 12, 14, 74, 93, 104, 108, 110, 116, 130–135, 145–151, 153, 160, 162–163, 165, 168, 170, 179, 216–217, 219, 221, 224, 228, 230–231, 234, 236, 243, 246, 277, 279, 281, 288, 303–304, 310, 317, 322, 324, 332
Olaya Herrera, Enrique, 142, 144–145, 149
Old Republic, 81, 88, 96, 99
Olson, Mancur, 133
Organized labor. *See* Labor unions
Oriente (Cuba), 249
Ortiz Rubio, Pascual, 217–218, 221–222, 225, 237–238, 241
Otero Silva, Miguel, 164, 166
Ouro Preto, 87

Pact of Punto Fijo, 161
Paipote, 74
Palacios, Alfredo, 27
Panama, 134, 146–147, 322, 326
Pani, Alberto J., 13, 222–223, 237–240
Paper currency, 103, 117, 222–224, 239
Pará, 92
Paraguay, 1, 287–289, 295, 331
Paraná, 89
Pardo y Lavalle, Manuel, 122
Partido Civil (Peru), 123
Partido Revolucionario Institucional (PRI), 301
Partido Social Democrático (PSD), 94
Partido Trabalhista Brasileiro (PTB), 94
Patria Nueva, 105, 115, 123
Patzicía, 207
Pearson and Son, 147
Peasants, 18, 244, 284–285, 303, 306, 307–308, 320, 326–327; in Central America, 282, 304; in Colombia, 138, 285, 306–307, 332; in Cuba, 252, 292; in El Salvador, 193; in Guatemala,

204–205; in Mexico, 216–217, 221, 224–225, 228, 237, 244, 337–338; in Nicaragua, 277, 312–313; in Peru, 105–106, 111, 124–126, 320; in Venezuela, 168, 175–176

Pedro II, 94

Peixoto, Floriano, 88

Pellegrini, Carlos, 328

PEMEX, 94, 230, 332

Pérez Soto, Vincencio, 172

Perón, Juan Domingo, 5, 22–23, 25, 34, 47, 212, 240, 305, 318. *See also* Peronism

Peronism, 10, 23–24, 32, 45, 291, 297, 311–312, 318, 325–326. *See also* Perón, Juan Domingo

Peru, 1, 6–8, 11–12, 167–168, 201, 221, 295, 301, 303, 306, 320, 331; agricultural sector in, 104–105, 107, 109–110, 114, 117, 125–126, 282, 332; anarchism in, 337; Communist Party of, 11, 102–103, 111–112, 124; demographic changes, 109; exports in, 102–104, 107, 113–114, 121, 279, 298–299; import substitution industrialization, 102, 118, 286–287, 298, 332; indigenous people, 105, 111–112, 121–122, 124, 126; industrialization in, 104; labor laws, 116, 118, 120; labor unions in, 105, 110, 112, 116, 307; middle classes, 103, 106, 108–109, 112, 121, 123, 307, 335; migration in, 107–108, 116; military in, 11, 103, 106–107, 112–113, 124, 292, 295; mining in, 11, 103–105, 107, 109–110, 112, 114, 116–117, 122, 125, 281, 334, 336; peasants in, 105–106, 111, 124–126, 320; political instability in, 106–107, 112, 307; race in, 8, 20, 116–117, 119–122; regulation of the social, 103, 104, 118–121; repression, 105–106, 113; social legislation and race in, 8, 20–21, 121–122, 307; social welfare in, 7, 11, 103, 115–

121; strikes in, 112, 126; taxation in, 115; unemployment in, 109–111, 115; wages in, 110–111; women in, 112, 126; workers in, 11, 103, 106–112, 116, 118, 121, 123–124, 126

Peruvian Constitution of 1920, 120–121

Peruvian Constitution of 1933, 120–121, 128

Peruvian Corporation, 128

Pessoa, Epitácio, 90

Peter, José, 40, 50

Petrobras, 93, 95

Philippines, 247

Picón Salas, Mariano, 175

Piérola, Nicolás de, 122

Pinedo, Federico, 298

Pisco, 320, 336

Plan of Barranquilla, 166–167

Plan Pinedo, 297

Platt Amendment, 259, 266

Political instability: in Argentina, 22, 308; in Chile, 52, 306; in Cuba, 254–258, 261–266; in El Salvador, 196; in Peru, 106–107, 112, 307; in Venezuela, 161, 164, 168, 170

Ponce, Federico, 206–207

Popular Front, 74, 250, 276, 309

Popular Front (Chile), 52–53, 73–74, 79, 94, 283, 293, 307, 310, 320

Popular Front (Cuba), 268–269

Popular Front (Spain), 173

Populism, 5, 10, 19, 74, 94, 278, 290–292, 311, 330, 339; in Brazil, 81, 84–85, 93, 95; in Chile, 10, 52–53; in Colombia; 129–130, 132, 144–145, 149, 151–153; in Cuba, 250, 264, 268–269; in Guatemala, 205, 212, 291, 326; in Mexico, 216, 224, 227, 231–232, 240; in Nicaragua, 291, 326; in Venezuela, 168, 181

Porfiriato, 105, 216. *See also* Díaz, Porfirio

Portes Gil, Emilio, 217

Salamanca, Daniel, 288
Salt March, 18
Salvador, 98
Samanez Ocampo, David, 112, 115, 117
San Felipe, 58
San Julián, 196
San Marcos (Guatemala), 205
San Marcos University, 123
San Salvador, 197, 306
Sánchez Cerro, Luis Miguel, 103, 107, 112–114, 118, 120, 288, 290
Sandino, Augusto César, 166, 199–201, 277, 294, 312, 320
Santa Catarina, 89
Santa Clara, 255
Santa Lucía, 262
Santa Marta, 321, 332
Santiago de Chile, 51, 52, 56, 63, 65, 66, 67, 69, 302, 306
Santiago del Estero, 28
Santo Domingo de Gúzman, 192, 197
Santos Discépolo, Enrique, 313
Sanz, Víctor, 177
São Paulo, 11, 81–92, 95–96, 286, 302, 305, 308, 333, 337
São Paulo Republican Party, 88
Schumpeter, Joseph, 323
Sección de Asuntos Indígenas (Peru), 105
Sección del Trabajo (Peru), 105
Second Industrial Revolution, 283
Second War for Independence (Cuba), 248, 250–251, 273
Second World War, 1–3, 25, 38, 83–84, 91, 94, 114–115, 224, 245, 271, 299, 313
Segovias, 277
Senior, Ana, 175
Servicio de Colocaciones, 54, 58
Shanghai, 4
Siles Zuazo, Hernán, 290
Silver, 104, 219, 221, 281
Simpson, Eyler, 226, 237, 241

Sinarquistas, 310, 338
Sindicatos. *See* Labor unions
Six Year Plan (Mexico), 231, 297
Slavery, 90
Smoot-Hawley Tariff, 3, 14, 217, 235, 247, 262, 282, 312, 323
Social assistance. *See* Social welfare
Social Catholicism, 106, 104
Social Darwinism, 246, 252
Socialist Party (Chile), 73–74, 80
Socialist Republic of 1932 (Chile), 52, 67, 73, 283, 293, 308
Social protection. *See* Social welfare
Social Security Act (U.S.), 7, 9
Social welfare, 7–8, 10, 11, 51, 53–59, 62–68, 72, 103, 115–121, 170, 271, 300, 331
Sociedad de Productores de Ciénaga y Santa Marta (SPCSM), 144
Sociedades de Color, 254
Sociedad Nacional de Agricultura (Chile), 307
Socorro Rojo Internacional, 195–196
Somoza, Anastasio, 199–200, 208, 211–212, 227, 291, 294, 298, 311, 326
Sonoran Dynasty, 230
Sonsonate, 193–194
Sonzacate, 192
South American Gulf Company, 149
Southeast Asia, 3, 18
Southern Cone, 1, 291–293, 305–306, 309
Soviets, 261
Soviet Union, 115, 176–177, 233, 254, 261–262, 306, 309
Spain, 173–178, 222–223, 259, 289, 327. *See also* Spanish Civil War
Spanish Civil War, 12, 161, 173–178, 268, 338
Spanish Republicanism, 250
Stalin, Joseph, 115, 231, 248, 311
Standard Fruit, 332

238; relations with Cuba, 14, 221, 247, 250–254, 256, 258–260, 262, 264–266, 268–270; relations with Mexico of, 216–217, 219–221, 226, 230, 234–235, 238, 244

University Student Directorate (DEU), 248, 258–259

Uriburu, José F., 1, 22, 38, 44

Urrutia-Thompson Treaty, 147–148

Uruguay, 168, 224, 238, 291–295, 303, 305, 332, 337

Valle del Cauca, 306

Valpa, 65

Valparaíso, 51, 52, 56

Vargas, Getúlio, 5–6, 10, 81–99, 227, 240, 277, 290, 298, 300, 306, 308, 327, 310–311, 329, 333

Vatican. *See* Catholic Church

Vegas, Carlos, 69

Velasco Alvarado, Juan, 103

Velasco Ibarra, José María, 290

Velásquez, Fidel, 242

Venezuela, 276, 281, 288, 294–295, 299, 301, 308, 322; agrarian reform in, 166, 176; agricultural export sector, 160, 162, 164; Catholic Church in, 171–174, 180; coffee industry in, 12, 162, 164–165, 282, 318; communism in, 13, 153, 158, 164, 166–167, 171–180; conservatives in, 161, 170–178, 180; corruption in, 162–164, 169; exports in, 161, 164–165; fascism in, 177; import substitution industrialization, 286; industrialization in, 165; labor legislation in, 175–176; labor unions in, 168, 175–176, 179, 187; military in, 161–164, 167–169, 171–172, 176, 179, 181; oil industry in, 12, 160, 162–163, 165, 168, 170, 179, 277, 279, 281, 303, 322; peasants in, 168, 175–176; political instability in, 161, 164, 168, 170;

populism in, 168, 181; repression in, 163–164, 170, 168; strikes in, 174–175, 179; women in, 175, 182; workers in, 166, 168, 175–176, 179, 187

Venezuelan Confederation of Teachers (FVM), 172

Venezuelan Organization (ORVE), 170–176, 178–179

Venezuelan Revolutionary Party (PRV), 166

Veracruz, 228, 241

Verdeja Act, 254

Villalba, Jóvito, 164, 170

Volta Redonda, 91–92, 95

Wages, 278; in Argentina, 37–38; in Brazil, 85; in Central America, 189; in Cuba, 249, 256, 259, 263–266; in El Salvador, 189; in Guatemala, 189; in Nicaragua, 189; in Peru, 110–111

Wall Street Crash, 114, 214–215, 218, 233, 247, 291

War of the Pacific, 54, 104, 106

Welfare state, 2

Welles, Sumner, 256, 257–258, 264, 269, 332

Wheat, 217, 278, 281–282, 315

Women, 7–8, 336; in Argentina, 30–32; in Brazil, 336–337; in Chile, 74, 337; in Cuba, 14, 259, 267–268, 273, 308, 337; in Mexico, 308, 337; in Peru, 112, 126; in Venezuela, 175, 182

Women's Cultural Association (ACF), 175

Wool, 104, 125

Workers, 7, 18; in Argentina, 10, 23, 24–25, 34–42, 44–45, 318; in Brazil, 10–11, 81–84, 93, 95–97, 336; in Central America, 189, 191; in Chile, 10, 55–56, 68–72, 76–77, 80, 306, 334; in Colombia, 145, 149; in Cuba, 246–251, 254–264, 267–270, 273; in

Made in United States
Orlando, FL
19 January 2023

28822690R00221